THE HEART OF TIME

Moral Agency in Twentieth-Century Chinese Fiction

Harvard East Asian Monographs 274

THE HEART OF TIME

Moral Agency in Twentieth-Century Chinese Fiction

Sabina Knight

Published by the Harvard University Asia Center
Distributed by Harvard University Press
Cambridge (Massachusetts) and London, 2006

Printed in the United States of America

The Harvard University Asia Center publishes a monograph series and, in coordination with the Fairbank Center for East Asian Research, the Korea Institute, the Reischauer Institute of Japanese Studies, and other faculties and institutes, administers research projects designed to further scholarly understanding of China, Japan, Vietnam, Korea, and other Asian countries. The Center also sponsors projects addressing multidisciplinary and regional issues in Asia.

Library of Congress Cataloging-in-Publication Data

Knight, Sabina, 1966–
The heart of time: Moral agency in twentieth-century Chinese fiction / Sabina Knight.
p. cm. — (Harvard East Asian monographs ; 274)
Includes bibliographical references and index.
ISBN-13: 978-0-674-02267-6 (hbk. : alk. paper)
ISBN-10: 0-674-02267-X (hbk. : alk. paper)
1. Chinese fiction—20th century—History and criticism. 2. Ethics in literature. I. Title. II. Series.
PL2443.K64 2006
895.1'350938--dc22

2006015383

Index by David Prout

Designed and typeset by Pinnacle Design, New York City

♾ Printed on acid-free paper

Last figure below indicates year of this printing
16 15 14 13 12 11 10 09 08 07 06

For my parents

Acknowledgments

Were it not for my teacher, Joseph S. M. Lau, I would never have written on Chinese literature. I owe him a great debt for having faith in me when I had none, and for the rigorous training by which he sought to make good of his protégée. Deepest thanks also go to my other mentors at the University of Wisconsin-Madison, especially to Mary N. Layoun and Robert Joe Cutter. I am also grateful to other teachers who took extra pains to help me in my development: Arthur G. T. Chen, Cheng Tsai-fa, and Clara Sun of the University of Wisconsin-Madison, Cyril Birch and Samuel H. N. Cheung of the University of California at Berkeley, and Chang Chien and Ho Chi-Peng of National Taiwan University.

Jeffrey Kinkley and Jon Kowallis deserve special mention for taking pains to help me far beyond the call of any duty. For guidance and conversation, I also thank colleagues from my year as an An Wang fellow at Harvard's Fairbank Center for East Asian Research, especially Lydia Sing-chen Chiang, Eileen Chow, Paul Cohen, Merle Goldman, Patrick Hanan, Wilt Idema, Felicity Lufkin, Elizabeth Perry, Robert Ross, John Schrecker, Hue-Tam Ho Tai, and Zhong Xueping. Special thanks also go to the Fairbank Center staff, especially Wen-Hao Tien, Stefanie van Pelt, and Richard Foster.

My understanding of Chinese literature was enriched during a year's study at the Graduate Institute of Chinese Literature at National Taiwan University made possible by a Fulbright scholarship through the Institute for International Exchange. In addition to my teachers, classmates, and friends in Taipei, I extend thanks to Peng Hsiao-yan of the Academia

Sinica and the staffs of the Foundation for Scholarly Exchange and the Center for Chinese Studies at the National Central Library. I also wish to thank the University of Wisconsin for two graduate fellowships and four undergraduate scholarships, and the University of California at Berkeley for three years of fellowship for graduate study. I also thank Smith College for ongoing research support and Sharon Domier for help in the library. I also extend deepest gratitude to colleagues at Smith who have offered intellectual and moral support: Tom Rohlich, Thalia Pandiri, Ernie Alleva, Margaret Bruzelius, Rick Fantasia, Peter Gregory, Maki Hubbard, Elizabeth Hopkins, Ann Jones, Joel Kaminsky, Roger Kaufman, Reyes Lazaro, Dana Leibsohn, Grant Xiaoguang Li, Bill Oram, Victoria Poletto, Paula Varsano, Sujane Wu, and Ling Zhao.

David S. Weberman deserves special thanks, not only for his understanding during the years in which I drafted the first version of this work, but also for his ongoing questions, criticisms, and loyalty. For conversation and comments, I also thank Rob Campany, Megan Ferry, Edward Friedman, Howard Goldblatt, Richard Hardack, Michel Hockx, Nicole Huang, Pierre Keller, Charles Laughlin, Christopher Lupke, Julia K. Murray, Steve and Natalie Riep, Kidder Smith, Richard J. Smith, Peter Staudenmaier, David Der-wei Wang, Ellen Widmer, Steve Yao, and Zhang Xudong. Other friends who offered kindness and support include Charlie Bertsch, Zelman Bokser, Cynthia Harrison, Junko Imamura, Judith Miller, Michael Puett, Mark Stambovsky, Steve Thiebaud and Yang Meifen. For painstakingly copy editing and proofreading the final version, I thank Wilson Wei Hsin Chao.

The anonymous readers, and especially one seemingly tireless one, offered assistance as generous as I could have hoped for. I also owe a debt to Katherine Lawn and David Prout for patient and persistent editorial assistance.

I owe my greatest debt to my family, particularly my parents. My interest in freedom and philosophy was greatly encouraged by my mother, Vicky Bay Knight, my step-father, Samuel A. Richmond, and my father, Richard V. Knight. Vicky Knight also edited and gave patient encouragement. For faith, stalwartness, and the deepest solidarity, I thank Marc W. Steinberg. Finally, I thank my students from Berkeley, Madison, and Smith College. Their enthusiasm and questions kept me mindful of the larger conversation in which scholarship is but one part.

I also wish to thank journals and publishers who graciously granted permission to reprint material from earlier publications. Passages in Chapters 2, 4, and 6 appeared in an essay entitled "Gendered Fate" in *The Magnitude of Ming: Essays on Command, Allotment, and Fate in Chinese Culture,* ed. Christopher Lupke (Copyright © 2005 University of Hawaii Press). Major portions of Chapter 3 were published under the title "Agency Beyond Subjectivity: The Unredeemed Project of May Fourth Fiction" in the *Journal of Modern Literature in Chinese* 1.2 (1998). A version of passages in Chapter 6 was published under the title "Scar Literature and the Memory of Trauma" from *The Columbia Companion to Modern East Asian Literature,* edited by Joshua Mostow et al. (Copyright © 2003 Columbia University Press. Reprinted with permission of the publisher). Sections of Chapter 7 were published under the title "Decadence, Revolution and Self-Determination in Su Tong's Fiction" in *Modern Chinese Literature* 10 (1998). Major portions of Chapter 8 appeared in two journal articles both published by Taylor and Francis. Some sections appeared under the title "Capitalist and Enlightenment Values in 1990s Chinese Fiction: The Case of Yu Hua's *Blood Seller*" in *Textual Practice* 16.3 (2002). Other sections appeared under the title "Shanghai Cosmopolitan: Class, Gender and Cultural Citizenship in Weihui's *Shanghai Babe*," *Journal of Contemporary China* 12.37 (2003). For permission to republish this material, I thank Taylor and Francis: http://www.tandf.co.uk.

S.K.

Contents

THE HEART OF TIME

Moral Agency in Twentieth-Century Chinese Fiction

Introduction

不知命，無以爲君子也。
Not understanding fate, there is no means by which to act as a noble one.

—*Analects* 20.3

知德者鮮矣！
How rare are those who understand moral power!

—*Analects* 15.4, translated by Simon Leys

AGENCY AND CONSTRAINT

To believe in moral agency is to believe that human beings enjoy at least a measure of decisive influence on the ethical impact of their actions. Maintaining that at least some events are not ruled by iron necessity is a prerequisite for the notion of responsibility and the possibility of a future open to human determination. One reason for reading fiction is for the hope it offers that history, economics, character, upbringing, and other material and social forces, powerful as they are, do not determine everything—they do not determine who we are, what we do, or the kind of world we make.

If we view narrative as falling along a spectrum that ranges between impossible poles of absolute fatalism and unqualified freedom, why do narratives that restrain the purview of moral agency dominate certain literatures or periods? Why, in the case of China, do successive movements to create a modern emancipatory literature stage stern challenges to human agency? What explains the contrast between the moral complications in many twentieth-century works and the rich sense of moral decision present in many classical works? More broadly, if the stories a culture tells itself can foster or impede the capacity for dissent, what are the political implications of fiction that tends to repress expansive notions of human freedom?

This book examines how fictional narratives reinforce or contest deterministic paradigms, a tension that appears to me to dominate twentieth-century Chinese fiction. How does Chinese fiction express the desire for freedom as well as fears of attendant responsibilities and abuses? How does it represent struggles for and against freedom? How do the texts allow for or deny the possibility of freedom and agency? Since moral responsibility depends on some, however limited, notion of human agency, I highlight works that allow for an open sense of time that may be at the heart of a sense, real or supposed, of free will. Through analyses of discourses of agency and fatalism and of the ethical import of narrative structures, and through an example from traditional fiction (Part I), I explore how representations of distinct determinisms and moral responsibility changed over the twentieth century (Parts II and III). To bring out what is distinctive in the treatment of dilemmas of human agency in Chinese fiction, I underscore how these changes were linked to the representation of time and to enduring commitments to human-heartedness and social justice. Although, story for story, Chinese fiction may contain some of the most disconsolate pages in the twentieth century's long literature of disenchantment, it also bespeaks a passion for freedom and moral responsibility.

In studying moral agency, I do not deny or minimize the powerful effects that culture, economic and political systems, social roles, and historical situation have upon human action. Instead, I suggest that the power of these constraints only makes more compelling the inquiry into how societies reproduce them and what possibilities exist to change them. Since the beneficiaries of power and privilege often maintain control by limiting understandings of the possible, fictional works and their interpretation can play an important role in broadening moral imagination and the possibilities for change.

WHY FOCUS ON MORAL EXPERIENCE?

A major theme of modern literature, the human confrontation with freedom, has been especially momentous for China in the twentieth century. In important ways, perplexity over the promise of freedom and the failures of that promise sustain an ongoing conflict between the claims of modernity and the tenacity of past traditions. Although scholars have long regarded this conflict as one of the dominant themes of twentieth-century Chinese literature, underlying questions about freedom and agency have been little studied.

I first read Chinese fiction because I was interested in human experience. I went to it out of a love of literature and a conviction that Chinese literature is as vital a part of human civilization as any other national literature. In this regard, I wanted to learn what witness Chinese fiction would bear to the violence that successive wars and political struggles have inflicted on those living within China's borders. I also speculated that the extreme nature of China's recent history would have left marks more apparent and more readable than considerations of responsibility which were developed in protected enclaves of relative safety. Having no idea how difficult it would be to read these marks, I hoped to learn from them something about human responsibility. I did not approach Chinese fiction with predetermined ideas about how this responsibility should look, although I did believe it might lie in moments of choice and habits of action.

What I found often disheartened me. In a phrase, a profound demoralization pervades a large portion of these twentieth-century Chinese stories and novels. Although many works present sustained attention to subjective introspection, the way individual consciousness is drawn often consolidates the individual's alienation from the possibility of meaningful agency and seems to reaffirm the power of fate or circumstance. Whether these texts suggest that the hidden agent of history is the hand of fate, traditional cultural norms and imperatives, the juggernaut of capitalism and imperialism, or the inevitable transformation of society preached by Marxist–Leninist–Mao Zedong thought, they frame their representations of responsible choice and action within stark limitations.

My concern with moral experience increased as I considered why many Western readers do not like Chinese literature better than they currently seem to. Does what some call its "gloomy and depressing" nature stem from the force much modern Chinese fiction accords to determining factors? Since the will of Alfred Nobel (1833–1896) sought to support a "most outstanding work of an idealistic tendency,"[1] Chinese fiction's engagement with deterministic paradigms may in part explain why the Nobel Prize committee overlooked Chinese writers until the 2000 award to the exile Gao Xingjian 高行健. (This selection hardly silenced debate

1. Sohlman, *The Legacy*, 137, quoted in Larson and Kraus, "China's Writers," 145.

on the subject since many strenuously objected to his selection.)[2] As colleagues told me of persistent obstacles they faced in seeking to market modern Chinese literature in the United States, I wondered what it meant when editors at *The New Yorker*, for example, rejected Chinese stories because they simply were not "good" enough or did not have "appeal."[3]

In considering why other national literatures may be more popular, I returned to general questions about why people read and love stories. What characteristics of modern Chinese literature might run counter to these expectations? I concluded that this literature offers more limited representations of ethical agency and moral decision. Whereas characteristic themes of our century—alienation, nihilism, and apocalypse—certainly inform the stories, many Western readers find the works remote from their own experience. Yet the same readers engage readily with Chekhov's landowners or Gordimer's South Africans. To readers schooled in Western literatures that tend to privilege individual agency, these characters may feel more familiar in that they seem better able to affect the course of their fictional lives. After a dose of "trauma" literature, be it about the Holocaust or the Cultural Revolution, many Western readers want stories that portray a world in which human actions make a difference, and such readers may perceive a "gloomy fatalism" in literature that frames moral agency within less familiar strictures.

Of course, issues of agency and determinism mark a great deal of modern Western literature as well, but in the West they do not monopolize a century of literary imagination to the extent that they do in China. At first, many of these fictional worlds appeared so closed to me that I wondered whether asking about responsibility was a legitimate pursuit. Was I reading in the wrong way? To talk about moral agency, does one not need to consider the very real constraints placed on freedom of action in addition to the philosophical problem of internal freedom? How much room do authors have to present moral agency in narratives confronting events such as the Japanese invasion (1931–1945) or the Cultural Revolution (1966–1976)? Might the trouble lie in my limited sample of texts? Might my readings of Western media and scholarship have further beclouded my Western eyes? Or might it simply be unfair to ask these questions of fiction? Perhaps it is parochial or Eurocentric to seek in fiction the sense that

2. See Lovell, "Gao Xingjian." For a positive appraisal of Gao's work, see Knight, Review of *The Other Shore*.

3. Telephone conversation with Howard Goldblatt, June 11, 1995.

characters can be ethical subjects in their own history. My reading of poststructuralist arguments about the constructed nature of the humanist subject exacerbated my reservations. Yet if agency is a construct, an absence of agency is no less a construct. Much everyday experience engenders a sense of agency that must be *unmade* before people will relinquish it.

I thus take as a challenge the prevalence, variety, and power of stories limiting agency in Chinese literature. That an entire century of a national literature appears to provide so little room for moral agency struck me as an issue calling to be addressed, especially given the rapid historical and epistemological changes in China's recent history. What testimony does this fiction offer regarding the terrible predicaments of victimization and responsibility that accompany such upheavals? I acknowledge that posing such questions raises problems. I may anger people who would blame my ignorance or foreignness. To their objections I have two responses: First, I cannot read Chinese fiction without asking these questions. Second, sustained analysis of representations of moral agency in Chinese fiction offers not only ways to appreciate this literature better but also new insights for understanding dilemmas of agency in terms of both philosophical approaches and narrative practices.

TERMS, CATEGORIES, AND LARGER STAKES

A Westerner easily perceives questions of moral agency as founded in realizations or limitations of individual freedom. Using perspectives in Confucian thought, one might focus instead on *ren* 仁, human-heartedness and moral responsibility. It was for this reason that whereas I commenced with notions of fate and free will, a closer appreciation of the material led me to focus on time and moral agency.

Since traditional and modern Chinese terms for "will" and "fate" differ from Western categories, I should say a word here about discourse. Given the dissension among thinkers within national traditions, I argue against assuming that the most significant conceptual boundaries split East and West. Thus, just as scholars of Greek philosophy discuss contested concepts such as "free will" by examining clusters of related terms,[4] I investigate several conceptions of agency and fatalism in traditional and modern Chinese texts. How does the Confucian appreciation of the complexity of the human heart-mind (*xin* 心) and the need for courage born of a sense of moral rightness (*haoran zhi qi* 浩然之氣,

4. Kahn, "Discovering the Will."

"flood-like *qi*") complement fatalistic conceptions of Heaven's will (*tianming* 天命)? How fatalistic were conceptions of will (*ming* 命) in the first place?[5] I side with scholars who interpret the dominant Confucian tradition as not only allowing for human agency but also encouraging self-cultivation for the purpose of exercising greater moral responsibility. Drawing on Confucian ethics in my readings of literary works, I seek to further the recent work of feminist philosophers who dispute the notion of an autonomous subject, which grounds most strands of liberalism, in favor of viewing subjects as radically embedded in our dependencies.[6]

I begin in Chapter 1 by defining agency and determinism and distinguishing the notion of agency from the notion of subjectivity more commonly treated by scholars of Chinese literature. In calling attention to agency and exploring its place in twentieth-century Chinese fiction, I do not mean to belittle the first line of inquiry into subjectivity and its various aspects. My point is simply that investigations of subjectivity encompass only some aspects of modernity and modern consciousness and only some of the questions that modern literature can pose. Modernity may depend on a rise of individual consciousness, yet equally crucial is the possibility that reason, empathy, and will can advance human freedom and well-being.

In suggesting why challenging determinism is vital to an appreciation of what defines modernity, what its legacy is to become, and Chinese fiction's unique contribution to these concerns, Chapter 1 also emphasizes the commitment to human betterment in modern Chinese literary thought and its earlier roots in Confucian thought. Although often distorted and repudiated by twentieth-century thinkers, Confucian thought offers important resources for modern reformers. Hence this study seeks to support the emancipatory potential of the project of modernity and at the same time to humanize that project by drawing on resources from traditional and modern Chinese writings.

ETHICS AND NARRATIVE

The second half of Chapter 1 turns to the ethical import of narrative structures. Specifically, my emphasis on how accounts of moral experience are linked to portrayals of time insists on the complex and situated

5. For notions of fate in traditional Chinese thought, see Santangelo, "Destiny and Retribution."

6. Kittay, *Love's Labor*; Nussbaum, "The Future"; and Harrington, *Care and Equality*.

nature of much ethical reasoning. Rather than consider moral values as abstract principles among which individuals pick and choose, I approach changes in moral beliefs and practices as intricately bound up with conceptions of time and inferences about causality that depend on narrative representations.

Can authors or critics underscore human agency yet remain sensitive to the enormity of historical events and constraints facing the people of China? This question led me to look at recent scholarly work on Holocaust fiction. Some scholars hold experiences such as the Holocaust to be "unnarratable" since our historical knowledge and retrospective judgments cast an aura of inevitability that diminishes the importance of choices the victims or survivors held to be meaningful.[7] In order to reject historical inevitability and recognize the legitimacy of reflecting on alternative possibilities, I draw on Gary Saul Morson's concept "sideshadowing." Whereas foreshadowing arranges narrative so as to suggest later developments and increase structural and thematic unity, sideshadowing names narrative elements that convey an open sense of temporality and contingency to challenge the determinism inherent in any completed narrative design.[8] Sideshadowing may present two or more plot lines, provide alternative endings, allow different interpretations to inhere in a work, or suggest alternative scenarios through characters' reflections, checked impulses, or different perspectives. By projecting to the "side" the shadow of alternatives, unfulfilled or unrealized possibilities, sideshadowing also challenges the sense-making authority of retrospective judgments that Michael André Bernstein terms "backshadowing." This scholarship on narrative recalls Henri Bergson's (1859–1941) insight that only a sense of duration and possibility allows for the process of human deliberation that is necessary for a coherent notion of freedom and ethics.

TWENTIETH-CENTURY CHINESE FICTION

In Parts II and III, I identify distinct forms of determinism and narratives of moral responsibility that dispute such determinisms within major trends and in specific works from late-Qing (1895–1911) novels by

7. See the discussion in Bernstein, *Foregone Conclusions,* especially in 10–17, 42–46.

8. Morson, *Narrative and Freedom*, 6.

Wu Woyao 吳沃堯 and Liu E 劉鶚 to the new realism and the roots-seeking and experimental fiction of the 1980s and 1990s. I depart from the premise that determinism functions as a veiled dominant ideology in many of these works, but I privilege works that challenge deterministic paradigms. Using the notion of sideshadowing, I argue for reading the conventional canon of modern Chinese literature for the insights its works offer into considerations of moral agency.

Although late-Qing and May Fourth works clearly register a perception of change and an awareness of lost foundations that characterize a shift to a modern consciousness, I question whether these works challenge fatalism so much as substitute new forms of determinism. Although vis-à-vis classical Chinese literature much modern Chinese fiction gives increased attention to individual subjectivity and consciousness, these works debilitate more often than strengthen the possibility for moral agency. In many, the painfulness of the characters' visions alienates them from the larger world, and concern for the victims of an inhuman society often turns into an exaltation of the sensitive observer's own spiritual distress.

Although recognizing that the attenuation of agency is rooted partly in discourse and thematic content, Chapters 2 and 3 also highlight the role of narrative structures that cast a pall of determinism over their fictional world. In May Fourth works, the characters' emotional distance is often compounded by a sense of temporal distance. In the brevity of the short stories and the retrospective nature of the epistolary novels and diaries, some of these works show but modest interest in time. Some even convey a sense that time does not exist insofar as they portray an individual's revelations about the way things are rather than a concern for the way they are becoming.

A rising concern for representing time, context, and social relations comes out in the trend from the late 1920s and 1930s that I call "social fiction" and address in Chapter 4. Since social fiction concerns itself with relations, and relations take place over time, this mode generally requires longer treatments. Beginning in the late 1920s, more lengthy stories appear and the novel reemerges as a major genre. Many of these works grapple with the temporal dimension of selfhood in a more concrete way than the circumscribed musings of the early May Fourth works. The characters are no longer condemned by some kind of logic built into the universe. Yet the room opened for human determination is often precluded by teleological conceptions of economic and political history.

Part III looks at the changing representations of moral agency and determinism in mainland fiction during the second half of the twentieth century. In examining Mao-era works in Chapter 5, I explore the tension between voluntarism and determinism to emphasize a narrative complexity that has been scarcely addressed. These works presumably seek to construct a logic based on the inevitable transformation toward a classless society. Yet this logic often breaks down as many works portray not the Communist utopia but the path to it, including individuals' moral struggles journeying along that path. I argue that stories written in response to Mao's directives raise fundamental questions about the nature of moral choice in the context of political imperatives. What should be the role of autonomous decision vis-à-vis the Party line? What should individuals do when service to the revolution means hurting their families? Frequently, fiction offers answers more ambiguous than those commanded.

Engagement in or conscious disengagement from questions about historical destiny, moral responsibility, and political, social, and economic freedom structure much of the post-Mao fiction discussed in Chapters 6 through 8. Whereas the "scar" literature and subsequent new realist works make bolstering humanist values and moral agency a central thematic preoccupation, a refusal of historical agency marks much of the "search-for-roots" fiction and avant-garde experimentalism.[9] Chapter 6 presents humanist works as seeking to recover human agency while acknowledging the undeniable weight of the recent traumatic past. Against critics who classify these works as of primarily historical or sociological interest, I view them as momentous interventions into ethical and literary debates concerning the interpersonal nature of moral experience and selfhood.

Chapter 7 turns to the troubled representation of agency in avant-garde, metafictional works that challenge dominant realist models. Taken as a whole, these works voice the confusion that occurs when a discourse of liberation, in this case Maoism and for some Deng-era modernization as well, becomes the enemy. Whereas many of these works challenge the determinism that may accompany naturalistic realism, the detached spectatorship that results usually presents at best a negative freedom (freedom

9. "Scar" literature refers to post-Mao works testifying to the traumas of the Cultural Revolution. See Knight, "Scar Literature"; and Chapter 6. "Search-for-roots" works privilege depictions of China's cultural and aesthetic traditions. See Chapter 7.

from a totalitarian past or oppressive social norms) rather than a positive freedom to engage in meaningful pursuits. I also explore ways in which experiments with sideshadowing sometimes give strength to and sometimes undermine ethical conceptions, as in some works by Mo Yan 莫言 and Su Tong 蘇童. By considering ways in which sideshadowing can create fictional worlds that preclude moral agency, this chapter also probes the line between modernism and postmodernism. Whereas critical modernism uses experimentation in the hope of revising and humanizing the project of modernity and its legacies, postmodernism rejects Enlightenment ideals altogether as corrupt at their foundations. By departing from the realism promoted during the Mao era but ultimately denying agency, many of these avant-garde works may defuse potential political dissent conveniently for the Party regime. It may be for this reason that the censors mostly overlook depictions of decadence and extreme violence while keeping a closer eye on more humanist works.

In the last chapter, I turn to fictional works from the 1990s to examine ideological effects of their bold presentations of individual freedom within the changing ethical landscape of China's market transition. Do such works render heroic the predatory nature of capitalist society, the pursuit of commodities, consumption, and leisure, or do they represent a troubled but enduring commitment to Confucian values of human-heartedness, compassion, and moderation and Enlightenment values of secularism, social justice, and equality? I bring out the political disenchantment that results when authors show market capitalism as delivering only the material promises of modernity, and I suggest that their characters' struggles for moral identities directly dispute the relativity of values and abstractions contrived by market ideology.

I want to acknowledge and address here a serious limitation of my dialogue with a past entity that I call "modern Chinese fiction." For the purposes of this work, I limit the discussion to fiction written in Mandarin on the Chinese mainland. For the most part, moreover, I analyze works of the traditional, politicized canon of modern Chinese fiction, a canon that represents only a fraction of what was written, particularly during the Republican period. Fiction written in other dialects, in Taiwan, and in the diaspora would offer further insights into the problems I confront. From my readings of fiction from Taiwan, I surmise that fatalism and determinism remain central themes, but the narratives generally present more fundamental challenges to their power than mainland ones, a conclusion, if proven to be valid, that would give further weight to a link between determinism and the specific political predicaments of Chinese writers on the mainland.

METHODOLOGY

I approach literary works not as isolated monuments but as part of a cultural history. Although an intellectual history of moral agency in China exceeds the scope of this book, I nonetheless interpret stories and novels in the context of such a history. For this reason I adopt a mainly chronological presentation. By reading narratives of moral responsibility in their historical phases and in relation to other works in the tradition, I seek to address both the extent to which ethical understandings are socially conditioned and the specific significance of individual treatments.

I also venture to relate Chinese fiction to broader questions about social, political, and economic change. Without exaggerating literature's place in the scale of human concerns or the ability of literary scholars to calculate political effects, I address this complex set of moral issues in the hope that attending to the particularities of stories and novels can deepen understandings of questions treated in more abstract terms in other disciplines. Unlike social science models that necessarily limit the number of relevant factors, fiction can expose the messiness of lived experience. It can also consider for what purposes and in whose interests agency is, can be, or should be exercised.

My interpretations illuminate conceptions of moral responsibility in particular texts to spotlight Chinese fiction's distinctive contribution to treatments of dilemmas of human agency. Much of this work thus focuses on close readings of representative primary texts. I draw on secondary sources to better situate the works in their cultural and historical contexts, yet I subordinate such research to a conversation among the primary works. This attention to specific discourse and values may help students and scholars of other national literatures and in other disciplines. Even more, I hope to bring out these works' continuing significance to present debates about agency and moral responsibility.

To address moral agency as I do raises larger questions about when and how literature can help readers understand life. It is probable that most of these questions are unanswerable, yet it is worth articulating my working hypotheses. First, I start from the premise that fictional stories offer a window to intimate psychological habits that may be expressions of larger political-historical trends. Second, I speculate on how stories and storytelling practices may affect transitions in moral beliefs, conceptions of social and historical processes, and rationales for life choices and the conduct of daily life. Without claiming any certainty about the relationship between literature and belief, I hold that readers may be susceptible to learning values from literature, both through confronting explicit themes and subject matter and by adopting habits of viewing the world conveyed in narrative. In this way, literature not only reflects but also reinforces and may even shape the ethical values and knowledge practices of a cultural community.

In holding that fiction can offer valuable lessons in the staging of responsibility, I do not claim that literature tells the full story. Literature tells part of the story without pretending to do more. For this reason many overlook literature, but therein lies its power and its freedom.

PART I

Agency, Modernity, and Narrative

I

Moral Agency and Narrative Storytelling

> This is how the battle lines appear to me: The individual confronts two opponents simultaneously. One enemy is fate and circumstances. The other is one's self. The opposing self often becomes one with the battling self, yet just as often turns traitor and conspires with fate.
>
> —Wang Anyi, 王安憶

This chapter introduces the problem of moral agency and makes a case for its central importance to the study of twentieth-century Chinese fiction. In clarifying what I mean by terms such as "agency" and "determinism," I consider these values within the contexts of different histories, East and West. In the first section, I distinguish between two key aspects of Western modernity and the Enlightenment: (1) subjectivity, or the realm of (self-)consciousness including a capacity for critical reasoning, and (2) agency, or acting on the world outside consciousness in a way that furthers one's values and purposes. This distinction is refined in the chapters that follow, through analyses of fictional narratives. In the second section, I offer an overview of concepts of moral agency and determinism in traditional Chinese thought and sketch how approaches to these concerns shifted as Chinese writers grappled with ideas of modernity and literary techniques that emphasized individual subjectivity.

To explore how Chinese novels and stories reinforce distinct positions on the spectrum between fatalism and freedom, I examine several aspects of narrative, including discourse, voice, structure, and figures of speech. Section 3 addresses questions of narrative structure and function to frame a method of literary analysis for the rest of the book. To ground this discussion of narrative's relation to moral agency, the fourth section offers an example of narrative openness in traditional Chinese fiction.

1.1 Agency, Moral Responsibility, and Determinism

In Western thought, agency refers to both freedom to make choices and freedom to act on one's choices. Considering agency means facing both the philosophical problem of internal freedom and the practical problem of external freedom. Since the rise of science in the seventeenth century and many philosophers' ensuing conviction that all natural events, including all human actions, occur according to natural laws, skepticism regarding both forms of freedom has prevailed.[1] Even many people who experience and take seriously a capacity for choice and responsibility in their own lives nonetheless proclaim themselves intellectually committed to some form of determinism.

Simply put, determinism is the doctrine that laws of cause and effect make every event the inevitable result of previous events or conditions. Some forms of determinism hold that if something is true about the future then it is also already true in the present, thereby nullifying the chance for the introduction of anything genuinely new. Such determinism is closely related to fatalism, namely, the view that the future is fixed, although not by physical forces as much as by some other inevitable force, principle, or destiny.

To refer to the possibility that people can decide events in the world in a way richer, that is, more independent and creative, than simply as conduits in a causal chain, one can use the term "agency." I choose this term because it can accommodate either individual or collective power and avoids some of the problems, discussed below, associated with the category of the subject or the individual. The term "agent" denotes someone who acts or has the power and authority to act and connotes a force or substance that causes some change.

To believe in human agency is to believe that despite limitations imposed by physical, social, psychological, and cultural forces, human beings enjoy at least a measure of decisive influence. Some thinkers argue that human agency is compatible with determinism because of the theo-

1. The locus classicus for viewing Newtonian mechanics as deterministic is French mathematician and astronomer Pierre Simon de Laplace's famous 1820 introduction, translated as follows: "We ought then to regard the present state of the universe as the effect of its anterior state and as the cause of the one which is to follow. Given for one instant an intelligence which could comprehend all the forces by which nature is animated . . . for it, nothing would be uncertain and the future, as the past, would be present to its eyes" (*Théorie analytique*, 4).

retical possibility that an agent could have done otherwise although actually determined to do as he did.[2] Whereas such a "compatibilist" position holds that freedom and determinism can coexist, a strong defense of human agency requires that one dispute determinism. One can take seriously the power of many determining forces but still maintain that at least some events are not ruled by an iron necessity.

Human creativity and compassionate influence depend on the possibility of an open universe in which agency is possible. Since to be responsible means to respond or to be answerable, conditions meaningful only if agents have some power over their choices and actions, such freedom is indispensable to taking seriously the notion of responsibility, value orientations, and, ultimately, the possibility of leading a mindful and meaningful life. Having and perceiving alternatives is fundamental to moral appraisal. Moreover, moral appraisal, based in reflective self-evaluation, grounds the ability to form "higher-order volitions" that some hold to be essential to the concept of a person.[3] Such self-determination depends on the ability to decide one's life without undue constraint, an ideal of existential philosophy wherein people are not limited or determined by innate fixed natures but bring their natures into being by force of their own choices.[4]

It is important to acknowledge that modern notions of agency have their origins in Enlightenment thought centered on the belief that human beings can determine their own fate. Though hardly forming a coherent movement, these philosophical discussions in seventeenth- and eighteenth-century Europe and America expressed the desire of people who considered themselves *les modernes* to set their own agendas, based on reason, rather than accepting those of another age, church dogma, revelation, or other traditions. Committed to rationalism and a set of interconnected values including faith in progress and empirical science, liberty, equality, autonomy, and tolerance, Enlightenment thinkers were dedicated to a this-worldly conception of the good, based in "nature," and were suspicious of any faith in supernatural or unnatural forces that

---

2. For the compatibilist position, see Ayer, "Freedom and Necessity"; Foot, "Free Will as Involving Determinism"; and Dennett, *Elbow Room.*

3. Having a higher-order volition means that a person not only desires to act or not act in a certain way, but that he "wants this desire to X to be the desire that moves him effectively to act" (Frankfurt, "Freedom of the Will," 85).

4. See Jean-Paul Sartre (1905–1980), *L'être et le néant* and *L'existentialisme est un humanisme.*

might diminish human agency and responsibility. Challenging determinism was thus essential to "the project of modernity" and the creation of a modern era that German philosopher Jürgen Habermas (b. 1929) characterizes as "the epoch that lives for the future, that opens itself up to the novelty of the future."[5]

Modern Western notions of agency and connected values have been fervently contested over the past 300 years. On one hand, commitments to individual reason have been used to legitimate institutions of representative democracy, based on the notion of "one person, one vote," that some credit with bolstering self-determination, liberty, and equality. On the other hand, in promoting the formation of individual subjects and citizens, such systems may rest on a foundation of absolutism and universalism insufficiently attentive to historically entrenched differences of race, gender, and disability. Along these lines, critics of the Enlightenment argue that reason, or at least the "instrumental reason" privileged in capitalist societies, necessarily involves using nature, things, other people, and eventually even oneself as tools for ultimate goals and that such rationality relies on a "logic" of domination and oppression that can easily lead to mass destruction.[6]

In this light, a word should be said about the positive value I attach to the term "agency." Of course, when it is a "power over" things or people, power can lead to domination, but agency seeks to name a simple "power to," a capacity for actions that need not be coercive. Having power is an essential condition for moral responsibility, but humane exercises of power depend on communication, and communication may entail viewing moral agency as fundamentally interpersonal rather than subjective.[7]

Thus, bearing in mind that terms like "reason," "power," and "agency" need to be constantly reviewed, I nonetheless put these notions at the center of my investigations and assessments of literary texts. Not only are the ways narratives allow for an open sense of time and agency crucial to their aesthetic workings and effects, as will be discussed in Section 3, but the extent to which literary texts confer upon or withhold from their

5. Habermas, *Philosophical Discourse*, 5.

6. A key work that develops this argument is Horkheimer and Adorno, *Dialektik der Aufklärung*.

7. Some theorists even argue that the exercise of one will over another without communication is not an act of power at all, but an act of force or violence. This distinction is made in works by Arendt, Habermas, Foucault, and Giddens; see Ball, "Power," 552; Arendt, *On Violence*; and Giddens, *The Constitution of Society*, 14, 257.

characters moral agency also has important philosophical implications and even political significance. To exercise agency, one must distinguish between limitations one places on oneself, limitations imposed by others, and limitations that result from structures in the culture at large. Fatalistic discourses and narrative structures mask these distinctions and thus make it harder to think clearly about both internalized and external oppression.

1.2 The Gap between Subjectivity and Agency

In Western literature, increasing focus on subjectivity stemmed in part from growing skepticism about the optimism of the Enlightenment concerning human agency. Misgivings over the direction of human endeavors worsened as the industrial revolution, urban centralization, improved means of communication and transportation, and the theories of Karl Marx (1818–1883) and Sigmund Freud (1856–1939) left the world's inhabitants confronted with unprecedented alienation, dislocation, and anxiety. In the late nineteenth and early twentieth centuries cultural responses coalesced in the movement named modernism.

Faced with an external world that seemed increasingly unknowable, uncontrollable, and barbaric, modernist writers turned their attention to the inner world as something that seemed more comprehensible and more human. With Charles Baudelaire's (1821–1867) portrayals of decadence and dandyism, skepticism about epic representations led to increased attention to individual subjectivity, to an obligation to look inward, and to language in order to explore, repossess, and transform the world. This inward turn was motivated in part by the belief that a capacity for reflection brings a kind of freedom. Yet while self-consciousness and reflection are necessary for freedom, awareness of inner subjective states does not in and of itself yield the power of autonomy. To the contrary, the increasingly sensitive interiority of modern consciousness is often accompanied by a profound sense of alienation and disempowerment.

There are at least three important ways that considerations of agency differ from questions of subjectivity more commonly addressed by scholars of literature. First, attention only to subjectivity (i.e., the capacity for and activity of conscious reflection and self-reflection) may locate the foundations of will and consciousness in individuals and their thought processes without attributing to them any measure of real autonomy.

The influence of Freud's theories of how unconscious forces drive individual behavior has exacerbated this tendency. Because a classical notion of autonomy supposes that people can be transparent to themselves, many thinkers invoke Freud's theories, in a way possibly quite different from what he intended, to undermine autonomy. Focusing on inner consciousness can mean confronting difficult problems of choice, but it does not guarantee that such choice be conceived of as free. To the contrary, an obsessive focus on inner consciousness may even hinder an agent's ability to respond to external criteria and to act in the world.

Second, there is a sense in which the very notion of "subjectivity" works against a notion of freedom. The term "subject," especially in the political sense of being a nation's subject, can refer to one who is subjected to forms of compulsion,[8] and such subjection may be all the more insidious when it is not to an identifiable political body or to social institutions but to systems of belief. Ideology, according to the French thinker Louis Althusser (1918–1990), works by interpellating or hailing individuals as subjects. For the moment that people identify with the subject position created by a given ideology, they are already trapped in and fixed by its specific formulations of reality.[9] Some linguistic relativists even claim that the individual subject is only "a language effect," by which they mean that language and other impersonal forces mediate experience in a way so fundamental as to exclude autonomous human agency. Although it is fair to say that individuals are "interpellated" in subject positions, both linguistically and ideologically, there may also be ways in which they can exercise some limited free agency from those positions. Insufficient attention to the capacity for free action can easily lead to manipulation since when people accept a given formulation as fixed they abnegate responsibility to challenge that formulation, whether its locus of power resides in other people, institutions, or larger belief systems.

There is one last, rather obvious difference between subjectivity and agency. Subjectivity is almost by definition a rather solitary enterprise. It may even magnify a subject's isolation, as Huck Gutman explains:

> In order for a man or woman to be constituted as a subject, he or she must first be divided from the totality of the world, or the totality of the social body. . . . Although the first reward of constituting oneself as a subject is a feeling of

8. A full account of this idea can be found in Balibar, "Citizen Subject."

9. See Althusser, *Lenin and Philosophy and Other Essays,* 170–77.

centrality and well-being, an inevitable consequence of that construction, which depends upon division, is isolation.[10]

No matter how developed, individuals' activities of reflection and self-reflection cannot by themselves reconcile an alienated subject with his or her world. For any measure of reconciliation requires acting in the world and establishing relations to other subjects. It is also in such relations, established through actions, that moral responsibility has its point of entry. Since Chinese traditions have long attended to the role of natural forces, social circumstances, and human relations in the cultivation of ethical agency, these traditions offer valuable insights for curbing what some see as an overemphasis on individual liberty and subjectivity in much Enlightenment thought.

2. CHINESE THEORIES OF CAUSATION AND MORAL RESPONSIBILITY

> 天命不常
> The mandate of Heaven is not immutable.
>
> —*Shi jing* 詩經 (Classic of poetry)

In this section, I introduce influential Chinese concepts articulating concerns about agency and determinism and then consider how the pursuit of modernity altered intellectual and literary treatments of these concerns in China. The section begins with a brief discussion of terminology in cross-cultural study. I then contend that the notion of fate or destiny (*ming* 命) in classical Confucian thought amounts to an exalted sense of duty. Next, I briefly consider sources of determinism in Daoist and Buddhist traditions. This discussion seeks to underscore that, though often neglected and even denigrated by modern reformers, all three traditions have important resources for thinking about agency and the exercise of moral responsibility. Finally, I make a case for the centrality of moral agency and offer four hypotheses about the distinction between subjectivity and agency in twentieth-century Chinese fiction.

2.1 *Terminology in Cross-Cultural Inquiry*

The fact that traditional and modern Chinese vocabulary words for terms such as "will," "intention," "fate," and "freedom" differ from Western ones suggests differing underlying conceptions of these issues. Awareness

10. Gutman, "Rousseau's *Confessions*," 107, 109.

of these differences often results in a focus on language, translation, and the incommensurability of key terms.[11] But one should not assume that the greatest conceptual divides fall between East and West. Since these issues of translation arise repeatedly throughout this book, I begin here by making three points about terminology. First, the incommensurability of terms and categories offers an important asset for thinking about ethical issues. Recognizing differences encourages scholars across cultures to embrace or at least consider all points of view.

Second, important concepts are always contested, even within a relatively bounded intellectual inheritance.[12] The influences of these inheritances are especially complex in this case because Chinese discussions of such notions, at least since the middle of the nineteenth century, have largely turned around readings of Western thinkers.[13] At the same time, acknowledging such influences should not imply that transformations labeled by terms such as "agency" or "modernity" are culturally or politically neutral. In a scheme of unequal modernity, globalization has meant the spread of specific liberal values of the Western Enlightenment: rationality, faith in progress, liberty, equality, autonomy, tolerance, and so on. It is also a modernity in many ways infected by a corruption of those same ideals, a topic touched on above and addressed in Chapter 8. Yet if twentieth-century Chinese fiction offers one avenue to consider recent controversies over what defines modernity and what its legacy is to become, then much may be lost and little, if anything, gained from treating the problem of moral agency as somehow essentially different in modern China.

Hence, third, rather than focus on the equivalence or incommensurability of translations of individual terms, I approach various notions of will and determinism in classical and modern Chinese by examining clusters of related terms. This method is used by scholars who discuss the concept of the will or free will in Aristotle (384–322 B.C.E.) and other early philosophers such as Epicurus (341?–270 B.C.E.) and

11. Lydia Liu, *Translingual Practice.*

12. Just as freedom for Kant is different from freedom for Hegel, Confucius's 孔子 concept of love is different from that of Mozi 墨子.

13. The term "free will" (*ziyou yizhi* 自由意志), for example, entered into China only near the end of the nineteenth century. Without belittling the complications involved in the translation and translatability of such terms, through the close readings that follow this study addresses the meaningfulness of this notion in the Chinese context. Cf. Liu, *Translingual Practice*, 17.

Epictetus (55?–135? C.E.).[14] Some potential sources of fatalism in Chinese traditions include the concept of Heaven's will (*tianming* 天命), especially as understood in some interpretations of Confucian thought, the chain of causes and consequences (*yinguo* 因果), and traditional schemes of retribution (*bao* 報 or *baoying* 報應) derived from Buddhist thought.

2.2 *Confucian Duty: The Heart of Time*

By the early Zhou dynasty (1027–256 B.C.E.), and possibly even earlier, the term "fate" (*ming* 命) was used to refer to the mandate that nature's Heaven (*tian* 天) gave to the ruling house. At once a purposive force beyond human control and a kind of moral imperative, this mandate had to be fulfilled by the empire. In the *Lunyu* 論語 (Analects), the master Confucius 孔子 (551–479 B.C.E.) advises standing in awe of Heaven's *ming*, a term that he and many later Confucians use for the totality of existing forces and conditions in the universe.

Considerable debate surrounds the question of how classical Confucian conceptions of fate relate to possibilities for human agency. In order to explain fate's relation to human affairs, the fourth-century philosopher Mencius 孟子 extended the concept of Heaven's will from empires to people: "Whatever is done without man's doing it is from Heaven; whatever happens without man's causing it is fate."[15] Such lines have been used by critics of Confucian culture to condemn what they interpret as the fatalism of the Confucian notion of fate.[16] In his argument "Fei ming" 非命 (Against fate), the philosopher Mozi 墨子 (470–391 B.C.E.) blamed Confucians for the way their belief in a predetermined fate caused resignation and laziness in people.[17] Even if resignation is too strong a characterization, Confucian notions of fate can certainly promote attitudes

14. Such as Voelke, *L'idée de volonté*; Kenny, *Aristotle's Theory of the Will*; and Dihle, *The Theory of Will*.

15. *Mengzi* 5A/6; The translation is by Patrick Hanan, *The Sea of Regret*, 193.

16. For an example from a recent critic, see Liu Zaifu, "Zhongguo chuantong wenhua dui ren de sheji." Although Liu acknowledges the importance of creative initiative, his article is largely a lament about the debilitating effects of the ritual order and what he calls the master-slave disposition inherited from traditional Chinese thought.

17. Against the resignation he saw in Confucian thought, Mozi proposed an active practice of universal love. Later Mohists sought to provide a rational basis for Mozi's utilitarianism based upon logical (and causal) necessity (*bi* 必).

close to Greek stoicism. The short span of human life and the apparently futile effects of human actions can make ideas of Heaven's will a consolation promising meaning, order, and harmony.

Eschewing notions of a static fate, other scholars of Chinese philosophy interpret classical Confucian texts as invoking fate in a way that entails a dynamic interaction between human and natural agency. Such scholars see the accusation of fatalism as based on a misinterpretation of the Confucian sense of fate. T'ang Chün-yi 唐君毅 (1909–1978) argues that the notion of predetermination stemmed from popular religious thought,[18] and Fung Yu-lan 馮友蘭 (1895–1990) asserts that, although fate named processes beyond human control, "there are other things that remain within man's power to control if he will exert himself."[19] For insofar as Confucians follow many ancient Chinese schools in viewing humans as an integral part of nature, fate is not an external destiny but a name for the mutual influence and response between Heaven and human beings. For classical Confucians, the unity of nature and humanity (*tian ren he yi* 天人合一) means that many forces stem from Heaven but manifest in people through their living relations with others. Thus, in addition to standing in awe of Heaven's will, a superior person would also actively devote him- or herself to Heaven's will, and it is in order to cultivate such devotion that Confucians teach human-heartedness (*ren* 仁), duty-consciousness (or righteousness, *yi* 義), ritual propriety (*li* 禮), wisdom (*zhi* 智), loyalty (*zhong* 忠), reciprocity (*shu* 恕), and filial piety (*xiao* 孝).

For many Confucian thinkers, human nature lies in the possibility of transforming the outer world. In this way, Confucius's "knowing fate" (*zhi ming* 知命) can be understood, in the words of T'ang Chün-yi, as "an exalted sense of duty" (215). For Fung Yu-lan, the point behind knowing fate is that "only after man has done everything he can himself, therefore, should he accept with calm and resignation what comes thereafter as inevitable" (53). Heaven's will and human virtue share a common root, and the utmost exertion of human effort and ethical self-cultivation is required even before Heaven confers its mandate. Recognizing fate (*ren ming* 認命) places one "at the starting point of something to be done, rather than a terminal point of something already accomplished" (T'ang

18. T'ang, "The T'ien Ming," 205. Further references to this article are given in parentheses.

19. Fung, *A Short History*, 53. Further references to this work are given in parentheses.

201). Such recognition entails a deep appreciation of change over time and a profound humility as embodied in the master Confucius who, according to *Analects* 9.4, abstained from four attitudes: he was without preconceived conclusions, without inevitability, without stubbornness, and without egoism.

This unassuming perspective grants the power of external determining forces, but it also allows for an open sense of time and thus a chance for meaningful human action and development. In the *Mencius*, the Confucian notion of knowing fate is extended to a responsibility to establish fate (*li ming* 立命), a charge that clearly implies human agency. Fate refers to Heaven's command, a natural order that includes each individual's lot and predetermined lifespan, and human nature (*xing* 性) connotes endowed qualities. Yet whether the four sprouts of human-heartedness, righteousness, ritual propriety, and wisdom evolve or wither depends on a person's moral self-cultivation. In the Mencian tradition, the inability to bear the suffering of others grounds a person's humanity, and this conception of human-heartedness entails that time be dynamic enough to open opportunities for response to suffering. Compassion for others also grounds a culture's humanity, as in the emphasis on the ruler's duty to nourish and care for the people voiced in the *Mencius* and the *Zuo zhuan* 左傳 (The Zuo commentary).

At the same time, Confucians took so seriously the weight of circumstances that they saw how difficult it would be to change things. For classical Confucians, when circumstances prevent a person from realizing the moral way (*dao* 道) in the world, one's duty becomes to accept and stand in awe of fate. Yet rather than conveying an act of resignation, this acceptance amounts to an act of loyal devotion to moral action. A superior person refrains from acting unjustly out of the wise belief that unjust means could never realize the *dao* (T'ang 214).

2.3 Sources of Agency and Determinism in Daoism and Chinese Buddhism

This section presents deterministic discourses in Daoism and Chinese Buddhism as well as resources these traditions offer for conceiving of human agency. Of course, many twentieth-century critics have repudiated the supposed fatalism of these traditions. For example, in his article "Zhongguo chuantong wenhua dui ren de sheji" 中國傳統文化對人

的設計 (Traditional Chinese culture's designs on humanity; 1988), Liu Zaifu 劉再復 criticizes the Confucian ritual order for suppressing subjectivity and the self through coercive external norms, and he criticizes Daoist and Chan Buddhist philosophies for teaching people to calm their emotions and will.[20] Noting that Daoism and Chan Buddhism view the self, will, and desire as the roots of human suffering, Liu nonetheless warns against relinquishing attachments through practices such as Laozi's 老子 "muddying one's heart" (*hun qi xin* 渾其心), Zhuangzi's 莊子 "losing the self" (*wu sang wo* 吾喪我), and Chan Buddhism's "nirvana" (*niepan* 涅槃) and "sudden enlightenment" (*dunwu* 頓悟): "The essential spirit behind these ways of detachment is to implore people to exterminate subjectivity, abandon the self, and abide in the 'transformation of things.'"[21]

Yet although the concept of fate figures prominently in Daoist and other Chinese philosophical and religious traditions, these schools of thought are not unambiguously fatalistic. For early Daoists, the term fate (*ming*) indicated the spontaneous agency of the celestial Way (*Dao* 道). One of a cluster of terms Daoists used to articulate understandings of the world and its spontaneous natural processes (*ziran* 自然), fate and other notions of destiny refer not to an original cause but to an appreciation of the continuous movement of the times (*shi* 時) and circumstances (*shi* 勢). Since fate both determines necessity (*budeyi* 不得以) and allows for a spontaneous freedom of noncoercive participation (*wuwei* 無爲), Zhuangzi and Laozi discuss "returning to fate" (*gui ming* 歸命 or *fu ming* 復命), and other early texts mention "resting in fate" (*an ming* 安命), but Daoists also refer to the transmission of responsibility (*cheng fu* 承負) in a way that implies a type of retribution similar to Buddhist notions of karma. Whereas lines such as the *Daodejing*'s 道德經 famous *tian di bu ren* 天地不仁 ("Heaven and earth are not human-hearted")[22] imply nature's indifference to human ends, a paradox arises between such indifference and Daoist notions of resonance (*ganying* 感應). Resonance here refers to processes of stimulus and response wherein the *Dao* incites an impetus and both Heaven and the Sage respond naturally, spontaneously, and without personal will.[23]

---

20. Liu Zaifu, "Zhongguo chuantong wenhua," 383.

21. Liu Zaifu, "Zhongguo chuantong wenhua," 382.

22. Yu Peilin, ed., *Laozi duben,* chap. 5, 24.

23. Robinet, *Taoism*, 198.

Sources of fatalism can also be found in Buddhist thought. First, there is the chain of acts and their effects most well-known by the term "karma" and expressed in Chinese by a cluster of terms, including the notion of karmic destiny (*suming* 宿命), the chain of causality based on causes and consequences, traditional schemes of retribution for previous behavior, and the idea of human responsibility realized through response or resonance (*ganying* 感應). Second, there is an appreciation of the arranged contextual conditions (*yuan* 緣 or *yuanfen* 緣份) that bring people together.

These overlapping concepts of agency and fatalism may explain why so much syncretism emerged among Confucian, Daoist, Buddhist, and other beliefs. For example, the notion of retribution has deep roots in Buddhist notions of karma, but Paolo Santangelo traces what he calls the "retributive tradition" of Chinese thought back to the ancient *Yi jing* 易經 (Classic of changes) and the *Shu jing* 書經 (Classic of documents).[24] In viewing Chinese theories of retribution as interrelated, Santangelo recalls the range of ways that retribution might relate to notions of destiny. As diffused by Buddhism and incorporated in popular religion, theories of retribution often insist that it is possible to favorably influence the course of destiny by meritorious acts. For this reason, moral works (*shanshu* 善書) encourage good acts and defend against a fatalistic and passive conception of destiny. Similarly, Chinese divination arts (*shushu* 數術) may assume a predetermined destiny and the influence of the accumulated deeds of one's ancestors, but they also allow humans to make strategic decisions about important life events.

What this discussion makes clear is that notions of agency in Chinese religious and philosophical traditions often differ radically from the sort of autonomous rationality promoted by Western Enlightenment thought. In Neo-Confucianism as well, the ethical-moral subject posited by the notion of intuitive knowledge (*liangzhi* 良知) is somewhat distinct from cognitive subjectivity or individual autonomy. "The determined and human-hearted man," writes T'ang Chün-yi, "does not feel that his purpose and his human-heartedness are possessions of his own; they are rooted, rather, in Heaven. . . . His task of self-examination and realization of his purpose . . . is absolutely identical with the entire situation sent to him by Heaven" (215). Given the range of meanings for terms such as fate, one must attend to such cultural

24. For a thorough discussion, see Santangelo, "Destiny and Retribution."

categories' own frames of reference to perceive their influence on modern Chinese fiction.[25]

2.4 *Chinese Modernity*

Moral agency, one of the guiding ideas of Western modernity, is almost a missing term in the scholarly treatment of modern Chinese fiction. To be sure, a contemporary Western reader might perceive a foreclosure of the possibility for moral agency and thus a sense of demoralization in Chinese fiction. Yet the same stories may be interpreted differently by readers familiar with traditional Chinese approaches to dilemmas of ethical agency. In Parts II and III, I confront the pervasive issues of agency and determinism in twentieth-century Chinese fiction. Here I only touch upon some of the main theses that will guide that discussion—namely, how the project of modernity altered the intellectual landscape in China and why it makes sense to discuss China's modern fiction in light of the distinction between subjectivity and agency.

It would hardly be oversimplifying to view the pursuit of modernity as a dominant project in twentieth-century China. Since the late nineteenth century, discussions of Enlightenment notions have largely turned around selected readings and interpretations of Western thinkers.[26] Of course, related notions of enlightenment can be found far back in Chinese traditions, particularly in Buddhist texts and practices and in Neo-Confucian scholarship,[27] but from the late Qing period, and especially in the New Culture movement (1915–1925) that informed the May Fourth political movement of 1919, leading thinkers critiqued Confucian traditions in an explicit project to reorient historical and cultural consciousness toward ideas of individualism, dynamism, and progressive teleology. Pressed by urgent concern about China's threatened sovereignty and consequent need for nation building and modernization, many intellectuals turned to Enlightenment ideals in the hope that Western values would enable China to catch up to the West in industrial and military power.[28]

---

25. Recent interdisciplinary scholarship has offered more extensive background about concepts of fate and their expression in different periods and genres. See the essays in Lupke, ed., *Magnitude.*

26. Xiong Yuezhi, *Xixue dongjian.*

27. See, for example, de Bary, "Neo-Confucian Cultivation."

28. Schwartz, *In Search of Wealth and Power*, 18–19.

Although it is important to keep in mind the heterogeneity of ideas associated with the New Culture movement and the limitations of Western terminology in the Chinese context, many participants and subsequent scholars have likened the May Fourth movement to the European Enlightenment.[29] From the overthrow of the Qing dynasty to the Communist revolution, and from Deng Xiaoping's Four Modernizations to the present market transition, Chinese intellectuals have expressly sought to break with the past and to achieve freedoms and amenities promised by the project of modernity and its trope of Enlightenment, or, as historian John Fitzgerald more precisely calls the Chinese counterpart, "awakening":

> The earliest of China's modern awakenings were awakenings to selfhood and individuality in relation to a rational and material universe. . . . The awakening of this universal self was soon displaced by the awakening of a distinctly Chinese self that preferred to commune with its nation. Defining the particularity of this nation invited reflection, in turn, on the ideal form of a state charged with the responsibility of awakening the people as "self-conscious" citizens. And a determination to "awaken the people" prompted those first awakened (*xian juezhe*) to develop organizations, technologies, and procedures for awakening the people to citizenship and nationhood.[30]

Writers' explicit pursuit of modernity was articulated in calls for a literary revolution, and the development of literary modernity was intimately connected to an accelerated confrontation with historical modernity based on Enlightenment ideals and with modernist aesthetic reactions to that project.[31] China's historical situation and unrelenting succession of traumatic upheavals led to a desire for modernity, both in order to strengthen China vis-à-vis the West and as an antidote to bureaucratization and paralysis of individual will, ills perceived as stemming from China's own traditions. The degree of writers' attraction to Enlightenment

---

29. See Schwarcz, *The Chinese Enlightenment;* and Fitzgerald, *Awakening China.* For a substantial, subtle discussion of the heterogeneous nature of the May Fourth movement and literature's subordination to political agendas, see Denton, "General Introduction."

30. Fitzgerald, *Awakening China*, 6.

31. Western literature has influenced Chinese writers on a large scale since the late Qing dynasty, when translators such as Zhou Guisheng (1873–1936) and Lin Shu (Lin Qinnan, 1852–1924) rendered countless Western works into Chinese. Information on these early translators can be found in Luo He, "Wan Qing xiaoshuo zhuanji." For a discussion of the influx of Western theories in the early Republican period, see McDougall, *The Introduction of Western Literary Theories*; and Ng, *The Russian Hero.*

ideals of science, progress, and freedom causes Kirk Denton to characterize Western and Chinese literary experiences in the twentieth century as "fundamentally different":

> As members of a semicolonized nation confronted with the palpable threat of the West, Chinese intellectuals were attracted to the values of Western historical modernity. But the slowness of historical modernity's arrival and the obsession among Chinese with bringing it about in order to restore to China its lost cultural grandeur precluded the emergence of an antagonistic literary modernity. . . . The obsessive priority placed on historical modernity caused literature to be used to promote that modernity, to aid in the process of nation building and revolution.[32]

Given the priority Chinese intellectuals placed on the ideals behind modernity and their use of literature to promote those ideals, it is all the more critical to explore the considerable attention modern Chinese writers accorded to dilemmas of agency and determinism.

2.5 Subjectivity and Agency in Modern Chinese Fiction

Key differences between Enlightenment notions of agency and the framing of dilemmas of agency and constraint in Chinese fiction have received little scholarly attention. This paucity of such discussions may be due in part to the success with which modern Chinese authors assimilated Western notions of subjectivity. It is not surprising that the turn toward interiority that marked European modernism was even more pronounced in China. In China, this inward turn was given further impetus by the widespread sense of humiliation and defeat in the face of foreign aggression and the fervent desire to catch up to the achievements of the First World. Authors deliberately sought to depict subjectivity and individual consciousness out of a conviction that focusing on those concepts could make Chinese writing modern and ultimately modernize the consciousness of the people.

In a seminal paper on modern Chinese literature, Jaroslav Průšek identifies the rise of subjectivism and individualism as indicative of "the emancipation of the individual from feudal traditions": "The modern revolution in China is thus, first and foremost, in the sphere of ideas, a revolution of the individual and of individualism in opposition to traditional dogmas. In this context, we can then realize the immense importance of

32. Denton, "General Introduction," 59.

subjectivistic and individualistic tendencies in modern Chinese thought and art."[33] The traditions to which Průšek refers include what he characterizes as the Buddhist teaching of karma that diminishes the importance of the individual in favor of viewing life as "a chain of cause and effect," the Confucian privileging of duties to family and society above individual interests, and the Daoist yearning to overcome the self and merge with the universe.[34] As suggested in the previous section, scholars continue to debate the extent to which these traditions of thought promote or deny human agency, yet Průšek aptly generalizes the modern reformers' relationship to their heritage in this way.

In opposition to these purportedly deterministic worldviews, by 1917 many writers expressly sought to create a literature that would embody the revolutionary principle that people can be the architects of their own fortunes. Given their goal, how is it that much of this fiction expresses a sense of helplessness? Could it be that this literature that sought to be new and modern brought about a radical attenuation of agency clearly at odds with its stated intentions? Though readers who perceive a pervasive helplessness in the characters may be tempted to assent to this idea, I propose that although modern Chinese writers frame issues of agency within limiting conditions, they nonetheless privilege moral responsibility as a central theme. For although these writers embrace Western Enlightenment notions, traditional Chinese teachings, the bases of their earlier educations, continue to influence and shape their fictional worlds. Hence, I do not see modern Chinese fiction as diminishing the sense of open-endedness present in many classical works. Instead, I contend that the integrity of this tradition persisted in narrative structures but became less obvious as modern writers made a fetish of inner experience in ways that may seem to flatten out the world portrayed into a fixed, block universe.[35]

Before moving on to more specifically literary factors, I should make explicit four philosophical reasons why the obsession with interiority and with ways of responding emotionally to the world has often worked against a sense of human agency or active engagement in Chinese fiction. First, if subjectivity becomes primarily spectatorial, as it does in much of

33. Průšek, "Subjectivism and Individualism," 2.

34. Průšek, "Subjectivism and Individualism," 1–2.

35. The term "block universe" comes from the philosopher William James's treatment of determinism.

this fiction, it may become a filter through which to perceive different possibilities without providing any basis for preferring one to another. Whereas the perception of options is crucial to freedom and moral choice, without some conception of what values and commitments one wants to pursue, such freedom is at best extremely circumscribed. It may be no more than a freedom of arbitrary choice. Although this choice may be free of external coercion or deterministic influences, it is not the choice of a deliberately self-determining person.

Second, in this light, it is not the general notion of agency that is missing but notions of how one's subjectivity might inform one's agency. For, of course, these modern Chinese works do depict agency—the characters are doing things, but as mere spectators of their interiority they do not seem to be empowered to make choices in individual terms. As in many texts of European modernism, illustrations of subjectivity in Chinese fiction—largely limited to descriptions of individual consciousness and introspection—often make it seem as if consciousness stops short of the possibility of affecting anything outside of itself.

Third, the absence of support for new ways of viewing the self leaves many of the characters caught in a kind of double vision. On the one hand, they experience the heightened interiority of an individual with a unique subjective vision; on the other, they still experience the world in terms of prescribed social roles. Whether these are traditional roles dictated by the Confucian relations, those required of the "new socialist man," or those of a successful entrepreneur, the characters seem to have few means and little faith in their ability to change these roles.

Of course, many people may experience a similar double vision much of the time—a vision split between the way we interpret the world as knowers and spectators and the way we understand ourselves as agents capable of acting freely. The experience of this tension between inner reflection and outward engagement offers a rich source of material for literature. It may also suggest why many people come to literature and why, for some readers, depictions of subjectivity alone are not enough. Thus, fourth, the notion of subjectivity may enable certain modes of reflection, but it can also lead people to conceive of themselves as predetermined entities rather than as agents with some power to create themselves and their world through their choices and actions. Yet the degree to which subjects' orientations circumscribe free agency depends on circumstances and contexts. It is one province of fiction to show these circumstances and contexts and, in so doing, to represent human actions as making a difference as well as to question for what and for whom.

3. SIDESHADOWING AND NARRATIVE OPENNESS

Fictional representations of agency stand or fall by virtue of the ordering of time that normally interprets experience. On one hand, narrative strategies for presenting time in fiction may reinforce fatalistic conceptions that frame current social arrangements as natural and inevitable. On the other hand, by making these temporal conceptions tangible, fictional narratives can challenge unwarranted assumptions that may unnecessarily limit conceptions of freedom. Against the determinism inherent in any finished story and reinforced by many techniques of foreshadowing, narrative elements of "sideshadowing" point to contingency and an open sense of time. I draw on sideshadowing as a theoretical framework to explore the role of narrative in moral reflection. Rather than viewing moral values as abstract principles among which individuals choose, this emphasis on narrative techniques insists on the situated nature and complexity of the task of forming moral judgments. Attention to sideshadowing helps illuminate conceptions of time, inferences about causality, and their influence on moral ideas.

In parallel projects, Gary Saul Morson and Michael André Bernstein explore how narrative structures can either reinforce or contest deterministic paradigms for thinking about time.[36] Holding that "some of the greatest discoveries of world thought have taken place first, and sometimes exclusively, in the visualization of artistic *form*" (Morson 87), Morson and Bernstein develop formal criteria to discuss representations of time. Their projects focus on Morson's notion of sideshadowing and its contrast with Bernstein's notion of "backshadowing." To reject historical inevitability and legitimize reflection on alternative possibilities, Morson, a scholar of Russian literature, has introduced the concept of sideshadowing to name "both an open sense of temporality and a set of devices used to convey that sense" (6). Since present actions matter only if life is an open process, not if the future is already given, sideshadowing fosters a

36. In their acknowledgments, Bernstein and Morson explain that their works began as a single project for a two-part book. As their sections became "too long and too disparate in their focuses" for a single book, the authors continued to read and discuss their work together. See Bernstein, *Foregone Conclusions*, xi–xii; and Morson, *Narrative and Freedom*, xi–xii. References to these two works appear in parentheses for the rest of this chapter.

coherent sense of human freedom and a meaningful sense of responsibility. By contrast, Bernstein's backshadowing names a structure resulting in a closed conception of time that may disable creativity, freedom, and a sense of responsibility.

Sideshadowing and backshadowing are new names for techniques that authors have long used. In this section, I explain the theory of sideshadowing through an explication of foreshadowing, backshadowing, and sideshadowing and then draw attention to the resonance between these terms and those of traditional Chinese commentary. This discussion prepares the ground for the last section's consideration of sideshadowing in a traditional Chinese tale and for the rest of this book's investigation of moral agency in Chinese fiction of the twentieth century.

3.1 Real Time versus Narrative Time

Time may be viewed as an open branching of alternatives, as "the inevitable enactment of a timeless pattern," or as basically determined but with certain crucial moments of choice (Morson 19). Unfortunately, conventions of narrative unity and readers' training to seek significance in fiction make it difficult to represent even the possibility of open time (Morson 158–59). By imposing beginnings and endings and reducing the disorder of multiple wills, impulses, and purposes to neat patterns, narrative structures falsify the nature of time as an ongoing process (Morson 38). One symptom of this denaturing of time's unpredictable contingencies is the way narratives often present events as if they "unfolded" along an inevitable path (Morson 243). Such metaphors for time's processes often become so ingrained that readers lose sight of their metaphorical nature and import meanings without considering their implications.

Morson's concern with sideshadowing emerges out of concern that dominant genres and their "chronotopes" frequently force readers' reflections on time into deterministic paradigms as they forget that "real time is an ongoing process without anything resembling literary closure" (Morson 8). In articulating his concern, Morson responds to Mikhail Bakhtin's (1895–1975) analyses of what he terms the "chronotopes" (narrative manifestations of time and space) of different genres and how they present varied fields of possibilities, different senses of historical process, of human identity and development, and of the relation between biographical and historical time.[37] For example, Greek romances imply a single line, adventure novels often entail a sudden metamorphosis, and realist novels often allow for indeterminacy. The frequent failure to recognize the sway of temporal conceptions is driven home by Michael Holquist's use of the term "chronotopic unconscious" to underscore the influence of "a set of unspoken assumptions about the coordinates of our experience."[38]

Bernstein similarly cautions that many people compose narratives, both historical and personal, according to epistemological principles long ago rejected (124). The way narratives can edit out multiplicity is especially suspect in historical accounts that "transform contingency into necessity" in order to reduce endless ramifications into a linear narrative (Morson 157). How might fiction writers counter an overdeveloped tendency to present history or contemporary social processes in aesthetic terms? How might fictional narratives present an open sense of time to suggest that the past does not determine the future? How can historical fiction resolve the contradictions inherent in representing unprecedented, unimaginable events with literary conventions reinforcing notions of inevitability? How can writers write fiction set in the past as if "blind to the future"?[39] To address these questions, I turn to the notions of foreshadowing, sideshadowing and backshadowing.

3.2 Foreshadowing

Many teachers and dictionaries of literary terms introduce foreshadowing by praising its virtues for achieving artistic unity:

> [Foreshadowing is] the technique of arranging events and information in a narrative in such a way that later events are prepared for or shadowed forth beforehand. A well-constructed novel, for instance, will suggest at the very beginning what the outcome may be; the end is contained in the beginning and this gives structural and thematic unity.[40]

Such a definition does not address how foreshadowing conflicts with the commonsense, asymmetrical notion of directed time in which the past

37. See the discussion in Morson, 106–10. On the chronotope, see Holquist, *Dialogism*, 109–15.

38. Holquist, *Dialogism*, 141–42.

39. Michael Ignatieff's wish for historians, discussed in Bernstein, 16.

40. Cuddon, *Dictionary of Literary Terms*, 276.

leaves its traces on subsequent times but the future does not project signs backward. In foreshadowing, the power of future events to send signs backward entails that the future must already exist. In this way, foreshadowing implies a closed universe and a fatalistic conception. Since the author privileges his own design over the representation of the characters' lived experience, such foreshadowing utterly precludes the possibility of options. Choices become illusory. The logic of foreshadowing, Bernstein writes, "must always value the present, not for itself, but as the harbinger of an already determined future" (2).

To distinguish the belief in advance indicators or in some kind of backward causation from a future pulling events forward, Morson points out that foreshadowing involves an instance only the reader can detect, not the characters. If the characters could detect these moments they would be omens, or registers of otherwise unnoticed causes (Morson 62–63).

A less heavy-handed version of foreshadowing might present such omens as warnings but refuse to fall into fatalism or causal determinism by accepting that a merely potential event can also cast a shadow backward and that "even possibilities, if they are likely enough to occur, may have a substantiality of their own" (Morson 70). Such openness already implies a kind of sideshadowing. An even more subtle kind of foreshadowing is one the reader detects only upon rereading.

3.3 Backshadowing

Whereas the outcome of events is necessarily decided in a finished novel and suspense is ultimately illusory, reading fiction depends on an implicit convention whereby readers pretend that what they do not yet know remains undetermined (Morson 175). Backshadowing, where a later historical event known to the author and reader casts a shadow over the events of a text, prevents even the possibility of such indeterminism. As Morson explains, "An event remote in time is weighted with so many subsequent events that it seems impossible to imagine that it, too, had alternatives" (183).

Because knowledge of subsequent events distorts any memory or reading of past times, Morson defines backshadowing as "foreshadowing after the fact" (234). Here the "gestalt" effects of memory "reprocess the messiness of reality" by eliminating what, "in light of later experiences, turned out to be irrelevant, purely contingent, or unproductive" (178, 184). Turning the past into a well-plotted story, backshadowing erases lines of development that might have led elsewhere (236, 247). Such backshadowing often relies on a kind of "vortex time" that attracts everything, "every stray thought or chance event," to its center and makes everything conspire, with ever-increasing momentum, to produce a crisis (Morson 163–65). In this way, historical novels and stories risk attributing a spurious sense of inevitability to those events that happen to have come to pass.[41] Excessive backshadowing may even lead some readers to forget that lived history, no matter how terrible, is not an already narrated genre such as tragedy (Bernstein 11).

Bernstein makes explicit some of the assumptions implicit in viewing events as inevitable. First, by bringing later events into a representation or understanding of earlier ones, backshadowing often involves conflating different times or even adding a third time from beyond the events that presumes an authority to judge earlier events.[42] "Such writing is in its deepest nature atemporal, linking everything together into a permanently deferred but everywhere implied total vision" (Bernstein 114–15). Second, the shared familiarity with the outcome of events may lead the writer and reader to pass unfair judgment on the characters' projects and predictions based on a hierarchy of significance possible only in light of subsequent events.[43] A stance of superiority marks the backshadowing observer who often assumes that the past contained legible signs of the future and therefore judges the characters "*as though they too should have known what was to come*" (Bernstein 16). If a reader is sensitive to this temptation to backshadow, it is less likely that a known outcome will minimize the characters' very real concerns and choices.

3.4 Sideshadowing

In exploring how some authors overcome the determinism inherent in any completed narrative design, Morson considers the technique of *sideshadowing* to be the best solution for restoring the freedom, contingency,

41. The temptation to backshadow is stronger yet in nonfictional historical narratives, especially when historians fail to see their middle position in time and conceive of the present as somehow "posthistorical" and their contemporaries as able to comprehend history in its totality. See Bernstein, 38; and Morson, 255.

42. See Bernstein's discussion of Aharon Appelfeld's *Badenheim 1939*, 64–65.

43. Against the temptation to blame characters for failing to confront imminent catastrophe, Bernstein reminds us that "to focus on one's private family ties, love affairs, careers, or artistic longings, is completely unobjectionable by normal, quotidian standards" (68).

and openness of the lived experience of time (41). Restoring "the possibility of possibility," sideshadowing "projects—from the 'side'—the shadow of an alternative present" (Morson 11). Attention to the unfulfilled or unrealized possibilities of the past challenges the sense-making authority of retrospective judgments and adds to the categories of actualities and impossibilities "a *middle realm* of real possibilities that could have happened even if they did not" (Morson 6). By introducing a dialogue between possibilities, sideshadowing allows for polyphonic works in which "plot loses its inevitability" and aesthetic design yields to open-endedness (Morson 98–99).

By allowing the reader to see what might have been, sideshadowing changes her view of what is. By retaining the complexity of alternatives, it encourages recognition of the still latent potential of unrealized moments, intentions, or possibilities. "Counterlives count," writes Bernstein, "because they are a constituent element of the lives we have" (8), and he particularly values sideshadowing for the challenge it presents to ideologies that encourage apocalyptic tendencies. Against an "ideology of the extreme" (91) that privileges extreme limits of human experience as the true test of our humanity, Bernstein argues that only "a prosaics of sideshadowing" (89) can do justice to the richness of ordinary life.[44]

Sideshadowing may be played out along a spectrum, from strong to weak. It is usually heavy-handed when an author presents two or more plot lines with equal force or provides alternative endings or an appendix of lost variants. The four accounts of Tu Xiaoying 屠小英 near the end of Mo Yan's *Shisan bu* 十三步 (Thirteen steps; 1989) discussed in Chapter 7 offer an example. A strong instance of sideshadowing may involve a sea of rumor presenting many possibilities. Morson discusses Dostoevsky's *The Possessed*, but a good Chinese example can be found in Ge Fei's 格非 first published story, "Zhuiyi Wuyou xiansheng" 追憶烏攸先生 (Remembering Mr. Wuyou; 1986). In Ge's story, a police investigation into the strange deaths of Mr. Wuyou and the student Apricot makes increasingly elusive the goal of uncovering a single account.

44. Bernstein centers his own project on showing the validity of sideshadowing for the extreme case of the Shoah where the desire to make sense of the cataclysm and "com[e] to terms with the pain by enfolding it within some larger pattern of signification" often leads to a deceptively natural and therefore particularly manipulative form of backshadowing (13).

More subtle forms of sideshadowing may occur when characters' reflections or checked impulses suggest other possible choices. Morson discusses how Anna Karenina's memories "offer the image of *other possibilities*, other sources of meaning that she has experienced but not brought to mind" (79). Many of the humanist works discussed in Chapter 6 employ sideshadowing as they recount the characters' reflections on other paths their lives might have taken. The temptation to speculate about how one might have lived differently is forcefully brought out, for example, in Shen Rong's 諶容 satirical "Jianqu shisui" 減去十歲 (Ten years deducted; 1986). In this story, rumor of a Party directive to make everyone ten years younger inspires the characters to imagine how they would remake their lives and brings out their disappointments in the socialist system, their deep-rooted jealousies, their discontent with their marriages, and, most of all, their regrets for the time "stolen" by the Cultural Revolution.

When characters, or even a single character, at the same or different times, have distinct beliefs, perspectives, frames of reference, or sources of knowledge, their various believed worlds or partial interpretations may also constitute sideshadows. Finally, another type of sideshadowing results from the interplay of interpretations within a literary work and the critical interpretations surrounding that work.[45] As the complexity of the literary work opens but also constrains possible interpretations, it also warns us "that our view of the actual world may be as imperfect as that of fictional characters."[46]

3.5 Open Time and Human Freedom

Falling between the impossible limits of absolute fatalism and unqualified freedom, fictional narratives can present later points in time as if already determined or as if open to multiple possibilities such that genuine ethical decisions must be risked. As Morson writes, "Properly conceived, *time is the form of plurality*; and freedom can exist only if time is so understood" (96). It is this conviction about the link between an open sense of time and freedom that motivates Bernstein and Morson to promote sideshadowing as a "fundamentally democratic and pluralistic [principle]" (Bernstein 37).

45. This idea relates to Hans Georg Gadamer's theory that hermeneutic understanding is not just reproductive but productive. See Gadamer, *Wahrheit und Methode*, 280.
46. Eco, *Limits*, 74.

Respecting the radical integrity of the present time, sideshadowing as Morson and Bernstein conceive it allows an "aperture" through which to view events "free of foreshadowing, closure and final signification" (Morson 171). In opposition to a bipolar model of temporality that would treat time as if it had but two significant moments, beginning and end, sideshadowing "attribute[s] causal effectiveness to countless intervening moments" (Morson 237). In so doing, sideshadowing admits contingency, chance, and human choices in a way that privileges "eventness," Mikhail Bakhtin's concept that an act depends on the unrepeatable particularities of its occurrence and yet exceeds those circumstances in a directed motion of choice that produces something genuinely new.[47] Similarly, because ambivalence may plague people's intentions, it is important not to reduce the field of possibility to a line predetermined by prior intention (Morson 144–45). Whereas moral thinking perforce attends to the linear sequence of events, it must also address an "evolving concatenation of wishes, desires, and possibilities" (Morson 141).

Sideshadows of unexpected stories also upset presumptions of order and restore a radical instability to the world. Sideshadowing reinforces the humility required to acknowledge that things do not merely seem arbitrary or ambiguous but may well be so. Such a scruple is important because a failure to realize that things could be otherwise can lead to the belief that the social order is naturally ordained and unavoidable. Sideshadowing emphasizes that the order of the world is not natural, but rather that it is socially shaped and therefore both contingent and open to reform. On a personal level, when one recognizes that characters', and by extension people's, personalities and motives usually contain sideshadows, one opens up a dialogue that encourages an appreciation of oneself or others not as finished entities but as agents capable of choices that may change previous self-definitions (Morson 89, 92).

3.6 The Pluralism of Sideshadowing

Since many people, including scholars in a variety of academic disciplines, use stories to organize accounts of social processes, it is important to understand how narratives not only depend on and embody but also influence human purposes. Whereas both common sense and rational-

47. According to Bakhtin, the most exhaustive narrative could never recapture the surplus that "turns what is given [*dan*] into what is truly created [*sozdan*]" (Morson 23).

choice theory take for granted adherence to logical reasoning, causal assumptions that frame such reasoning are sometimes grounded on little more than familiar stories or common metaphors. Awareness of the role of storytelling in the manufacture of knowledge has risen as both humanists and social scientists have shifted analytic paradigms away from the study of general physical, logical, or historical laws toward a focus on narrative as an organizing concept. In response to this shift, some social scientists warn that story-like structures often mislead people about the role of institutional and economic structures in determining social processes. Sociologist Charles Tilly, for example, calls attention to the way stories can distort explanations about social processes. "Most social processes," writes Tilly, "involve cause-and-effect relations that are indirect, incremental, interactive, unintended, collective, and/or mediated by the nonhuman environment."[48]

Sideshadowing offers a way to respond to such concerns. For one of sideshadowing's lessons is that things can have meaning as much because of their contemporary relations as because of their origins in the past or their significance for the future. Too much emphasis on antecedents and consequences may blind one to other meaningful elements and structures. Sideshadowing honors the importance of contemporary relations as well as sequential or purposive relations.

This emphasis on nonsequential structure recalls Andrew Plaks's discussion of technique in traditional Chinese fiction:

> As in other branches of Chinese aesthetics, the significant function of parallelism in fiction composition lies neither in achieving mechanical balance and rhythm nor even in prescribing a precise relation of similarity and difference . . . but rather in the attempt of the artist to set up the coordinates of his world along each of a number of axes of time, space, and various perceptual and abstract correlatives.[49]

A writer's effort to set up such complementary coordinates and contrastive analogies, Plaks explains, aims at "a certain dualistic vision . . . a vision within which the aesthetic impulse toward mutual implication or cyclical alternation of apparent 'opposites' outweighs the surface impression of dialectical opposition" (101).

Whereas a focus on contemporaneous relations might de-emphasize their historical nature, sideshadowing fosters appreciation for overlooked

48. Tilly, "The Trouble with Stories," 265.
49. Plaks, "Terminology," 101.

historical influences. By underscoring that an actual event carries possible events "as a sort of recessive gene invisible to the eye but capable of affecting future generations of events" (Morson 120), sideshadowing's richer picture recovers otherwise invisible directions and significance. A worldview attentive to sideshadows may also be consoling insofar as it suggests that actions may retain significance although invisible to later times. As Bernstein writes, "Each present, and each separate life, has its own distinct value that later events cannot wholly take away" (41). Though imaginative investments in the future constitute part of one's sense of the present (Bernstein 29), sideshadowing encourages recognition that people make choices based on factors other than consequences and the probability of success. Acknowledging the validity of sideshadowing, Bernstein explains, "means learning to value the contingencies and multiple paths leading from each concrete moment of lived experience, and recognizing the importance of those moments not for their place in an already determined larger pattern but as significant in their own right" (70–71).

By enriching any one perspective through a dialogue with alternatives, sideshadowing emphasizes that much knowledge is only partial and thus helps to guard against a single version of events. In this light, Morson takes pains to underscore that the heart of his theory is not relativism but pluralism (273). Similarly, Bernstein distances himself from radical relativism and emphasizes that sideshadowing demands and enables a sense of moral responsibility: "To stress the claims of sideshadowing and counterlives, far from undermining the authority of the concrete instance, is its most radical guarantor precisely because it insists on the primacy of human freedom" (7). In this way, sideshadowing's pluralism offers an alternative to the dialogue between dogmatism and skepticism. Whereas the dogmatist insists that there is one and only one truth, the skeptic holds that because there is not a single truth or because such a truth cannot be known, there is no truth at all. By acknowledging that the truth may be pluralistic, sensitivity to sideshadows offers a way to reject the determinist's singular world without falling into the skeptic's cynical relativism.[50] Sideshadowing suggests a world with "a certain pluralism," one in which "the fit between the parts and whole is not perfect."[51]

50. These ideas stem from a reading of the pluralist William James, although rather than using the terms dogmatism and skepticism, James uses rationalism and empiricism. See James, *Pragmatism*, esp. lecture 4, "The One and The Many," 127–62.

51. See the discussion of James's "The Dilemma of Determinism" in Morson, 82–86.

3.7 "Shadowing" in Traditional Chinese Commentary

The terms "foreshadowing," "backshadowing," and "sideshadowing" are especially useful for the study of Chinese fiction insofar as these terms have counterparts in traditional Chinese fictional commentary. The "how to read" (*dufa* 讀法) essays in commentary editions frequently use the term "shadow" (*yingzi* 影子) to refer to narrative reflection. With foreshadowing I bracket together terms such as "hidden brushstrokes" (*fubi* 伏筆), "advanced insertion" (*daocha fa* 倒插法), and "cross-reflection" (*zhaoying* 照應, *yingzhao* 映照, and *yingshe* 映射). Related to backshadowing are the terms for "backward reflection" (*fanji fa* 反激法, *fanchen* 反襯, and *fan ying* 反映).[52]

I associate explicit notions of sideshadowing with terms for describing "analogous but different" narrative patterns, such as "mutual reflection" (*duizhao* 對照), "contrastive reflection" (*fanzhao* 反照), and "reflection between opposites" (*zhengfan xiangdui* 正反相對). With more subtle forms of sideshadowing, I associate terms such as "lining" or "padding" that are used to describe elements that "flesh out" other incidents (*peichen* 陪襯, *chentie* 襯貼, and *chenying* 襯映). Analogies also exist between sideshadowing and terms used to analyze asides, digressions, and passages that shift focus from center stage to the wings (*chuancha* 穿插 and *pangwen* 旁文, literally "side writing").[53]

The existence of this rich terminology suggests that commentators were highly attuned to fine nuances in the array of representations of temporal relations in traditional Chinese fiction. The variety of techniques employed to represent time in traditional fiction and the intricate matrix of terms used to describe these representations attest to the importance of time and change in traditional Chinese thought. As Andrew Plaks explains, traditional Chinese fiction writers strove to evoke "a rhythm of recurrence as the essential ground for the representation of reality." Yet this conception invoked no simple idea of an eternal recurrence of the same, for, as Plaks stresses, "the recognition of difference within identity was just as important to them as its contrary."[54]

As with much literary criticism, judgments of craft in traditional Chinese fictional commentary were frequently steeped in ethical criteria. As David Rolston has shown, a strong argument can be made that

52. Plaks, "Terminology," 75–123, esp. 95–105, 110.

53. Plaks, "Terminology," 110.

54. Plaks, "Terminology," 100.

discussions of narrative structure and literary achievement were usually presented for the purpose of offering readers moral guidance. Namely, traditional commentary instructed readers in how to read novels so as to avoid being corrupted by dangerous texts ambivalent in their presentation of Confucian moral virtues such as loyalty, filial piety, and self-containment.[55] The perception that certain texts might be perilous in their resistance to the commentator's Confucian rationalizations can be seen in commentators' wariness of texts that present too much narrative openness. Although some contemporary critics hold greater openness to be systematically better than more closed fictional worlds,[56] if a story becomes too open-ended, it can cease to engage questions of agency in a meaningful way. As a nineteenth-century commentary on the *Jing hua yuan* 鏡花緣 (Flowers in the mirror; 1828) explains: "If it is too 'loose' [*kuan* 寬], then it easily loses its sense of direction, if it is too 'tight' [*jin* 緊], then it easily becomes forced. To avoid excessive adherence [to fixed patterns] and excessive departure from them is the mark of the master [writer]."[57] It is for this reason that it is so helpful to think about a spectrum of narrative openness between absolute fatalism and unqualified freedom.

4. THE LIMITS OF FATALISM IN EARLY CHINESE NARRATIVE

To demonstrate sideshadowing's power to bolster perceptions of moral agency, this section offers an example of narrative openness from traditional Chinese fiction. As it does their twentieth-century counterparts, resignation to destiny often blinds characters in classical works from seeing fatalistic logics as artifices of human composition.[58] Yet even as traditional narratives ostensibly profess the overriding role of fate, the use of sideshadowing in these works often suggests alternative paths or ironic perspectives that subtly honor the role of human decision.

55. Rolston, *Traditional Chinese Fiction.*

56. For an example of a scholar who underscores the value of inconsistencies and incompatibilities as "impetus toward the searching out of [ethical] consensus," see Handwerk, *Irony and Ethics*, 4.

57. *Jinghua yuan*, chapter commentary, p. 1/7b, quoted and translated in Plaks, "Terminology," 103.

58. These ideas were inspired by my reading of Sangren, "Dialectics of Alienation."

In recognizing the human construction of both fatalism and the moral way, many early texts suggest that one limit to fatalism is narrative writing itself. From the Han dynasty (206 B.C.E.–220 C.E.) onward, the use of narrative to support a specific Confucian moral system led to a widespread didactic mandate called by Zhou Dunyi 周敦頤 (1017–1073) *wenyi zai dao* 文以載道 (writing should convey the way). Yet the *dao* that writers were to transmit was neither static nor given but a way of correct moral engagement always in a process of dynamic becoming. As Confucian conceptions of Heaven's will need not imply fatalism, the fatalism of much traditional Chinese fiction was a limited fatalism. Lifespan, wealth, and position depended on Heaven's will, but humans still had the freedom to be moral.[59] Furthermore, at least by the writing of the *Mencius* in the fourth century B.C.E., many texts express a deep appreciation of the complexity of the human heart-mind as something not completely fated. Mencius and his followers emphasized the need for courage born of a sense of moral rightness—called *haoran zhi qi* 浩然之氣, the "flood-like *qi*"—that bears many similarities to modern notions of agency. Emphasis on the development of the human heart complemented appeals to Heaven's will and posited the ability to choose moral ends in a way that presupposed a freedom to make the choice.

Moreover, in much traditional Chinese fiction, though the characters suffer sadness or tragedy, their lot is ultimately resolved at some higher level of harmony. In this way, many tales convey the message that the universe is fundamentally ordered and essentially benign. In casting sideshadows toward messy departures from ideal patterns, these texts take seriously the seeming chaos of human experience. Yet they present apparent chaos as deviations or fluctuations within a pattern that contains these disturbances and allows them to settle. People given to excess may disrupt the social order, but the narrative frames these disruptions within a world ultimately subject to laws of destiny (*ming*), retribution, or cause and effect. As these forces run their course, the traditional narrator functions, in the words of Cyril Birch, as a "technician-demonstrator" who reinforces dominant norms, "norms marked by common humanity, the distrust of any kind of excess, of evil or even of good."[60] Although these normative beliefs offer consolation, their reiteration could discourage reflection on alternative frameworks. Yet I propose that the rich side-

59. D. C. Lau, *Mencius*, xxi.

60. Birch, "Change and Continuity," 386.

shadowing in much traditional fiction inspires such reflections despite the narrator's ostensible endorsement of dominant Confucian norms.

The Open-Endedness of Traditional Fiction: A Tang Tale

To recall in more detail the open-ended sense of moral decision in much traditional fiction, I turn to a Tang dynasty (618–907) *chuanqi* 傳奇 (tale of the marvelous) written by the poet Yuan Zhen 元稹 (779–831). Perhaps the most celebrated Chinese love tale, "Yingying zhuan" 鶯鶯傳 (The story of Yingying; 804), describes a young scholar's seduction and abandonment of a young woman named Cui Yingying. The story can be divided into three parts: An opening frame tells of Scholar Zhang's scrupulous temperance, his protection of Yingying's family, and the initial meeting between Zhang and Yingying. A middle segment describes Zhang's impatient seduction, Yingying's initial rebuff, and their subsequent love affair. A final section recounts Zhang's departure for the capital, the trauma Yingying suffers, and Zhang's rationalization of his desertion. Zhang's ultimate defense depends in part on his hypothesis about the inevitable workings of fate (*ming* 命): "If those destined by Heaven to be exquisite beings do not destroy themselves, then they will inevitably bring harm upon others. . . . My virtue is not sufficient to overcome such bewitching evil; thus I have repressed my feelings."

The implication here is twofold. First, Zhang's appeal to inevitability denies his responsibility for his behavior. His claim that he is simply not up to resisting his own impulses reinforces this abdication of responsibility. It is as if his weakness were determined from outside and therefore not his fault. Second, Zhang implies that Yingying's extraordinary beauty means that she is not entirely human and thus not fully deserving of moral concern. (The term translated as "bewitching evil," *yaonie* 妖孽, was commonly used during this period to demonize beautiful women.) Yet while the narrator ostensibly endorses Zhang's decision to sacrifice Yingying in order to privilege conventional Confucian obligations, the stirring portrayal of Yingying in the story betrays a commitment to the value of love and loyalty that disputes Zhang's definition of virtue.[61] The tale renders this portrayal not only through the narrator's account but also through sideshadowing this account with Yingying's self-portrayal

61. Stephen Owen calls attention to the importance of the values of the Tang love story in his discussion in *Anthology of Chinese Literature*, 540.

through her letters and poems. The inclusion of these writings undercuts the story's superficial sanction of Zhang's fatalistic rationalizations.

Moreover, although the characters *ming* and *bi* 必 both invoke the power of fate and inevitability (the word *ming* appears nine times, *bi* three times), many other elements in the story underscore the role of human decision. For example, the narrator implies a definite element of choice by noting Zhang's friends' initial alarm at his behavior—an alarm that implies disapproval—and then explaining, "Yet Zhang's will was already decided." The implication of moral responsibility becomes stronger yet in Yingying's eloquent letter, the sending of which can be read as an attempt to control her destiny. Toward the beginning of the letter, Yingying invokes the notion of fate as if to interrogate the concept and thus emphasize its denial in what follows: "The path to progress in studies is firmly in convenience and not being disturbed. Yet I resent that this distant and lowly person [that I am] will forever by [your social role] be cast aside. But fate is like this. What more is there to say?" Yingying's alleged resignation here is quickly belied by the moral allegations she puts forth in the remainder of her long letter. The letter clearly charges that Zhang could have acted otherwise, at least in offering her his love, and the implicit accusations further compel the reader to weigh Zhang's actions.

What gives "The Story of Yingying" its power is this presence of moral decision. It is the force of this moral dilemma that makes the tale so memorable and worthy of its numerous later adaptations. As evidence of the plausibility of an alternative ending, some of these retellings show Zhang marrying Yingying instead of rejecting her. The most famous of these adaptations, of course, is Wang Shifu's 王實甫 (fl. thirteenth century) masterpiece of Yuan dynasty (1271–1368) *zaju* 雜劇 drama, *Xixiangji* 西廂記 (Story of the Western Wing).

"The Story of Yingying" is just one example of the rich open-endedness of much classical fiction. Yet perceptive treatments of the dialectic of freedom and determinism by scholars of classical Chinese literature also suggest that, despite frequent mentions of the role played by Heaven's will, particularly in narrators' comments, many works of premodern fiction do not preclude the possibility that characters can challenge fate.[62]

62. In a book-length work, *Yizhi yu mingyun*, Yue Hengjun offers a perceptive discussion contrasting expressions of will in *chuanqi* with the prominence of fate in Sung dynasty (960–1279) *huaben* 話本 stories. In his discussion of the sixteenth-century novel *San guo zhi yanyi* 三國志演義 (Romance of the Three Kingdoms), Andrew Plaks attributes the novel's grandeur and futility to the tension between human struggle and determinism.

Instead, the use of sideshadowing in these works creates an open sense of possibility within which characters can assume genuine moral agency and become morally responsible for those processes that thought and actions can influence. In this way, works of premodern Chinese fiction offer a rich array of reflections on fatalism and its limits. The rest of this book explores the legacy of this tradition in Chinese fiction of the twentieth century. Since the representation of the weight of historical conditions and beliefs in both old and new determinisms could be read as foreclosing open-endedness, attention to sideshadows becomes key to interpreting moral agency in this light.

See Plaks, *Four Masterworks*, chap. 5, esp. 455, 490–95. Similarly, in discussing *Sui Yangdi yanshi* 隋煬帝豔史 (The merry adventures of Emperor Yang of the Sui; 1631), Robert Hegel brings out the conflict between fatalistic worldviews appealing to divine retribution and those insisting on freedom and personal responsibility. See Hegel, *The Novel in Seventeenth-Century China*, 106–11, here 111.

PART II

The Wages of Freedom in Modern Chinese Fiction

2

Predicaments of Modernity in Late-Qing Novels, 1895–1911

> But the voice of foresight does not come to shatter China's desolation. This being so, is there nothing for us but reflection, simply nothing but reflection?
>
> —Lu Xun 魯迅, translated by Shu-ying Tsau and Donald Holoch

The problem of human freedom and the forces that limit or are thought to limit it emerges as a major theme in the novels of the last decade and a half of the Qing dynasty. Furthermore, in these novels we begin to see specifically modern approaches to problems of freedom and agency. By depicting present times and expressing indignation about existing social conditions, they amount to a plea for the amelioration of those bad circumstances. In satirizing superstition and hypocrisy, they express new skepticism about ruling institutions and traditional conceptual schemes. This skepticism persists even as the novels champion these schemes or illustrate the difficulty of escaping traditional paradigms. By portraying the often debilitating effects of a knowledge that destroys faith in traditional prescriptions, they convey the individual's crushing sense of disorientation and insignificance in the face of an ever larger and less hospitable world. By focusing on the emotional turmoil of their characters, the novels suggest that an individual's unique circumstances and perspective could help communicate the nature of social relationships.

To what extent do these texts still subscribe to a worldview that posits an underlying order to these social relationships and ascribes the reality of that order to traditional concepts and metaphysical laws? To address this question, I begin by discussing changes in late-Qing ideas about fiction and their underlying assumptions about human agency. I then consider the much more ambiguous treatment of these issues in the novels themselves. Many of the themes intended to promote freedom were presented within a deterministic framework. Formal features, discussed below, allowed room for human maneuver but very often simultaneously ceded such great weight to chance or larger historical forces that they undermined the meaningfulness of human action. Linguistic changes similarly cut both ways, particularly the use of the vernacular, which made for significantly longer works and a great deal more grammatical repetition.[1]

Although a thorough investigation of these crucial developments exceeds the scope of this work, to ignore them would compromise my treatment of the following period.[2] What follows is thus a preliminary exploration of the representation of agency in late-Qing novels. I end the section with longer treatments of Wu Woyao's 吳沃堯 (Wu Jianren 吳趼人, 1866–1910) innovative novel *Hen hai* 恨海 (Sea of regret; 1906) and Liu E's 劉鶚 (1857–1909) influential novel *Lao Can youji* 老殘遊記 (The travels of Lao Can; 1904–1907).

1. THEORIES OF FICTION AS A MEANS OF EFFECTING POLITICAL CHANGE

The last decade and a half of the Qing dynasty witnessed a fundamental shift toward a more specialized conception of literature,[3] a veritable explosion of fiction writing, and a number of innovations in composition.[4] These developments were part of a larger movement to rejuvenate

1. For a systematic presentation of the linguistic changes, see Gunn, *Rewriting Chinese*.
2. Although Chinese scholars such as A Ying and Zhou Zuoren were writing in the 1930s about the late Qing as an important transitional period, some Western scholarship, perhaps due to an overemphasis on the influence of foreign literature, has exaggerated the radical discontinuity of May Fourth fiction from earlier Chinese works and has downplayed the influence of indigenous developments. As a corrective to this view, much scholarship since the late 1970s argues for viewing late-Qing writers as forerunners to the new literature movement of the May Fourth period. For the earlier Chinese views, see A Ying, *Wan Qing xiaoshuo shi* (1937), and Zhou Zuoren, *Zhongguo xin wenxue de yuanliu* (1932). Recent Western works include Dolezelová-Velingerová, *The Chinese Novel*; Huters, "From Writing to Literature"; and David Wang, *Fin-de-Siècle Splendor*.
3. For the importance of late-Qing theories of literature, including the rise of the current concept of *wenxue* 文學 (literature) and accompanying changes in the demands placed on literature, see Huters, "A New Way of Writing." Huters discusses five intellectual groupings in the late-Qing period to show their links to earlier nineteenth-century theories and their crucial legacy for theories of the May Fourth era.
4. According to A Ying, over 1,000 volumes of fiction were produced during the late-Qing period. A third of these were original works; two-thirds were translations of foreign works. See A Ying, *Wan Qing xiaoshuo shi*, 1, 180.

Chinese society and culture born out of fears that China had become a civilization in decline, unable to defend itself against either internal strife or an increasingly threatening outside world. Already shaken by humiliation at the hands of Western imperialists earlier in the century, Chinese intellectuals saw China's defeat in the 1894–1895 Sino-Japanese War over Korea[5] as further evidence of the urgent need to strengthen China and actively defend its position as a major civilization.[6] Attributing Japan's power to the Meiji court's (1868–1912) conscious promotion of Western learning and modernization, Chinese intellectuals began to consider more seriously the possible value of Western ideas and cultural practices. As a result, China's encounter with imperialism engendered both a political crisis and a deep existential crisis regarding traditional orientational orders.[7]

In response to this crisis, Chinese intellectuals were forced to grapple with Western notions of unilinear time, historical progress, and human volition that departed radically from traditional schemes based on a cyclical cosmology.[8] Particularly influential were the translations and writings of Yan Fu 嚴復 (1853–1921), who introduced works by Thomas Huxley, Herbert Spencer, Adam Smith, John Stuart Mill, Montesquieu, and other thinkers from the Western liberal tradition.[9] Yan Fu's commentaries promoted liberal values such as freedom, equality, and democracy as

5. The humiliating Treaty of Shimonoseki (1895) gave Japan control of Taiwan and the Pescadores as well as trade access to seven ports in China.

6. I use the term "civilization" here instead of the term "nation" in light of the argument that theories of Chinese nationalism tend to obscure the concern for more universal themes expressed by at least some of the late-Qing thinkers. See, for example, Price, *Russia and the Roots of Chinese Revolution*, 9–28.

7. For a detailed discussion of the late-Qing "crisis of consciousness" or "crisis of orientational order," see Hao Chang, *Chinese Intellectuals in Crisis*. Hao's study documents how contact with Western ideas influenced four specific thinkers and their reinterpretations of issues internal to Chinese philosophical traditions.

8. For the rise of an historical consciousness based on a unilinear concept of time, see Sun, "Chinese Intellectuals' Notion of 'Epoch' (*Shidai*)," and Leo Lee, "In Search of Modernity."

9. Yan Fu published his *On Evolution*, a translation with commentary of Huxley's *Evolution and Ethics* (1893), in 1898. His translation of Smith's *The Wealth of Nations*, Mill's *On Liberty*, and Mill's *System of Logic* appeared in 1901, 1903, and 1904, respectively. Yan's rendering of Spencer's *Study of Sociology* appeared in 1903. His translation of Montesquieu's *L'esprit des lois* appeared from 1904 to 1909. See Chow Tse-tsung, *The May Fourth Movement*, 294.

means toward the liberation of human energy and dynamism that he saw as necessary to increase China's power.[10]

Translations of Western and Japanese fiction reinforced the rising interest in freedom and voluntarism. Lin Shu's 林紓 (1852–1924) renderings into exquisite literary Chinese of more than a hundred works of foreign literature popularized the individual focus of Western literature, a preference for which Lin Shu made plain in his theoretical writings.[11] Whereas his selection of novels by writers such as Rider Haggard, Conan Doyle, and Walter Scott promoted a new emphasis on individual vitality and heroism, his many translations of novels by Dickens, Balzac, and Tolstoy inspired admiration for the Western novel's interest in social reform and the ethical significance of the commonplace.[12]

Whereas late-Qing thinkers were divided, often in their own minds as well as among themselves, between loyalty to Confucian ideals of social harmony and their attraction to Western values such as individual freedom, most of them reluctantly subscribed to a heightened faith in the power of fiction to impart such values. This increased regard for fiction, together with unprecedented expectations about its power to promote social and political reform, announced a fundamental shift to more optimistic attitudes regarding the purview of human control.[13] Believing that fiction had helped modernize Western countries and Japan, thinkers such as Yan Fu and Xia Zengyou 夏曾佑 (1863–1924) argued that fiction

---

10. See Schwartz, *In Search of Wealth and Power*, esp. chap. 12, 237–47.

11. For example, Lin Shu admires the novels of Dickens and makes the following disparaging comment on Shi Nai'an's *Shui hu zhuan* (The water margin; dates contested, ca. fourteenth century): "the characters pour out onto the scene like a pack of coyotes, no longer distinguishable from one another." See Lin, "*Kuairou yusheng hsu* qian bian xu," 85.

12. For further discussion of the influence of Lin Shu's theoretical writings in winning greater attention, status, and readership for fiction, see Huters, "A New Way of Writing," 252–53. For Lin Shu's thought, see Leo Lee, *The Romantic Generation*, 44–56; and McDougall, *The Introduction of Western Literary Theories*, 9.

13. Of course, there is a long Chinese tradition of emphasizing the didactic function of writing. This emphasis was reinforced in the Sung dynasty when prominent Neo-Confucians promoted the notion that "writing should convey the way." The saying comes from Zhou Dunyi (1017–1073), and the concept was championed by Zhu Xi (1130–1200). See James Liu, *Chinese Theories of Literature,* 114; and Huters, "A New Way of Writing," 260–61.

could be a means of enlightening people and changing the fate of the nation.[14]

To bring out some of the specific assumptions underlying such attitudes, I turn briefly to expressions of these new ambitions for fiction. A sample of statements made by the influential poet and essayist Liang Qichao 梁啓超 (1873–1929) demonstrates the influence he attributed to fiction despite his disdain for the traditionally denigrated genre. Recognizing that it would be better to guide than attempt to stem people's natural inclinations to read fiction, Liang in 1898 explained why his journal planned to publish a series of Western political novels: "Indeed, political novels should be given the highest credit for being instrumental in the steady progress made in the political sphere in America, England, Germany, France, Austria, Italy, and Japan."[15] In a later article (1902), Liang opened with similarly dramatic pronouncements about the power of fiction:

> If one intends to renovate the people of a nation, one must first renovate its fiction. Therefore, to renovate morality, one must renovate fiction; to renovate religion, one must renovate fiction; to renovate politics, one must renovate fiction; to renovate social customs, one must renovate fiction; to renovate learning and arts, one must renovate fiction; and to renovate even the human mind and remold its character, one must renovate fiction.[16]

To invest such great faith in fiction entailed a number of new assumptions: First, this passage presupposes that the human mind and character are malleable from the outside. Second, it presumes that literary culture could be primary in the solution of social and political problems. Third, it assumes that writers might consciously and unproblematically control the ideological effects of their works. Fourth, Liang's imperative to extend

---

14. See Tsau, "The Rise of 'New Fiction.'" A Ying identifies the first article to explain the value of fiction as Yan Fu and Xia Zengyou's "Benguan fuyin shuobu yuanqi" (Announcing our policy to print a supplementary fiction section), *Guowen bao*, October 16 and November 18, 1897. A Ying, *Wan Qing xiaoshuo shi*, 2.

15. Liang, "Yi yin zhengzhi xiaoshuo xu," 303; trans. Cheng, 73.

16. Liang, "Lun xiaoshuo yu qunzhi zhi guanxi," 303; trans. Cheng, 74. Liang goes on to present the powers of fiction and discuss its hitherto corrupting influence before calling for a "revolution in fiction" to reform the people. He identifies fiction's four powers as (1) thurification: the way fiction's influence permeates outward like incense, (2) immersion: the way fiction's influence endures in proportion to a work's length, (3) stimulation: the immediate evocation of strong feelings, and (4) elevation: the way literature enables readers to enter a state of self-transformation.

the reach of fiction's influence calls upon writers to address a public much larger than their peer group of the educated elite. Finally, and related to the previous point, is the extent to which taking responsibility for others may have enfeebled traditional notions linking writing to self-cultivation.[17]

The desire on the part of the educated elite to address a larger public accounts in part for their turn to the novel, a genre that could use the more accessible vernacular language and whose episodic structure was popular with a wide readership.[18] Material reasons also account for the novel's increasing popularity. The rise of the modern press and the publication of serials facilitated the circulation of longer works and created a potential for regular income that made writing a viable profession.[19] As literature became a commodity, a separation occurred between the cultural and political elites, a phenomenon common in and possibly even constitutive of modern culture.[20] The abolition of the imperial examination in 1905 further severed the two spheres and forced the literati into a more independent position. Not only did some writers decline official appointments, but many intellectuals openly opposed the Manchu regime, the bureaucracy and corruption of the governing institutions, the system of arranged marriages, and other hallowed traditions.[21] Writers' desire to reform society, expose corruption, castigate the compradores, condemn superstition, and confront the oppression of women led many to turn to the novel as the most appropriate literary genre to convey these concerns.[22]

---

17. Here I am extending an argument made in Huters, "A New Way of Writing," 263.
18. The vernacular language, although more accessible than the literary language known as *wenyan* 文言, was still quite different from the colloquial. For a discussion of the relation between fiction's dominance in modern Chinese letters and the development of the northern vernacular *baihua* 白話 as the "national language," see Dolezelová-Velingerová, "The Origins of Modern Chinese Literature."
19. In 1902, Liang Qichao started the magazine *Xin xiaoshuo* (New fiction), the first publication devoted exclusively to fiction and analyses of fiction. Other magazines followed. See Tsau, "The Rise," 23–24.
20. See the discussion of the "alienation" of members of the cultural elite in LaCapra, *History and Criticism*, 74. In an extreme example of the new commercial use of literature, Wu Woyao wrote one novel, *The Return of the Soul* (not extant), to advertise a drug. See Lu Xun, *A Brief History*, 358.
21. According to Lu Xun, the writer Li Baojia declined an official government appointment and was highly respected for having done so. See Lu Xun, *A Brief History*, 353.
22. Arguing against Hu Shi, who attributes the upsurge in novel writing primarily to the

2. THEMATIC, DISCURSIVE, AND FORMAL CHARACTERISTICS

Many of the features that make the novel an opportune instrument for expressing social concerns are closely related to the representation of human agency. The novel can present characters in a detailed social context over an extended period. It can also explore more fully than other genres the causes or deliberations influencing characters' actions and the repercussions of their actions. In these ways, the novel can both express the extent to which society and history determine the conditions and development of any story and also present the outcomes, both positive and negative, of struggles for freedom within these constraints. To write a novel is to assert the importance of time and social relations to human experience.

Such concerns are evident in the late-Qing writers' prolific production of "social novels" (*shehui xiaoshuo* 社會小說), including the genre Lu Xun later named "novels of denunciation" (*qianze xiaoshuo* 譴責小說) to underscore their exposure of political amoralism.[23] Novels such as Li Boyuan's 李伯元 (Li Baojia, 1867–1906) *Guanchang xianxing ji* 官場現形記 (Record of the operations of official circles; 1901–1906) and Wu Woyao's *Ershinian mudu zhi guai xianzhuang* 二十年目睹之怪現狀 (The strange situation witnessed over the last twenty years; 1903–1909) present panoramic visions of late-Qing society that underscore the characters' subjection to both social conventions and larger historical and metaphysical forces. As Henry Zhao has pointed out, Li Boyuan's novel underscores the predetermination of the characters' behaviors through plays on names that turn the characters into stereotypes. A character who avoids his responsibilities is named Tao Ziyao, which sounds like "The Escapee." One who sells out his friends is called Diao Maipeng, "The Betrayer." Another is named Jia Xiaozi, a moniker that sounds like "Fake Filial Piety."[24]

---

influence of traditional novels such as *Rulin waishi* (The scholars; first half of the seventeenth century), A Ying links the choice of this genre to the complicated nature of the material late-Qing writers wished to convey. See A Ying, *Wan Qing xiaoshou shi*, 5.

23. Whereas the influence of foreign works, especially the novels of Dickens, is evident in these novels, they also reflect the influence of traditional fiction, particularly Wu Jingzi's *The Scholars*. See Lu Xun, *A Brief History*, 354.

24. Henry Zhao discusses these and other examples in *The Uneasy Narrator*, 82–83.

Set in contemporary times, these social novels register a distinctly modern anxiety about the pressure and threat of new intellectual, political, and economic forces. Rather than depict one local area as in much traditional fiction, most of these works shift the setting among different regions, including large cosmopolitan cities and foreign countries. For example, in his roman à clef *Nie hai hua* 孽海花 (Flower in the sea of sin; 1907), Zeng Pu 曾樸 (1872–1935) thematizes the influx of foreign ideas by sending the official Jin Wenqing 金雯青 (Jin Jun) and his concubine Fu Caiyun 傅彩雲 on a grand tour of Berlin and St. Petersburg, where they meet German royalty and Russian nihilists. Written by a "Lover of Freedom" (*ai ziyou zhe* 愛自由者) and recorded by his friend the "Sick Man of East Asia" (*dongya bingfu* 東亞病夫), *Flower* documents the currency of foreign ideas in China and the linguistic positioning of East Asia as one part of a larger world.[25] Such features underline an acute consciousness of the historical moment, including the paramount threat of colonialism and imperialism.

The possibilities for human intervention in the face of these historical forces appear all the more feeble given the great proportion of the narratives devoted to descriptions of setting, social distinctions, and everyday practices. In their inclusiveness, the social novels taken together offer a kind of encyclopedia of late-Qing society. Although focusing on official corruption, they present characters from many different social spheres and levels: government and military officials, their minions, and their wives and concubines, as well as merchants, writers, entertainers, prostitutes, and foreigners. The main theme is usually these characters' venal pursuit of wealth and position, but copious nonessential details present innumerable background problems and social issues. Although these details create a reality effect lending an aura of authenticity to the fictional world, the thickness of their presentation marginalizes the possibility of meaningful human influence. The result in many of the social novels is well summarized by one scholar in his discussion of Li Baojia's *Record of the Operations of Official Circles*: the primary characters seem little more than "creatures of plot," and the secondary characters mere "aspects of setting."[26]

25. The "Sick Man of East Asia" may well be a takeoff of the "Sick Man of Europe," an epithet Europeans used for the Ottoman Empire. From at least the time of the Berlin Conference (1884–1885), English and French cartoons depicted Ottoman officials as sick men with big stomachs.

26. Holoch, "A Novel of Setting: *The Bureaucrats*," 81.

The first vernacular novel to use first-person narration, *Strange Situation*, is particularly significant for the way Wu Woyao creates a spectatorial locus of observation without engendering a sense of agency.[27] An ardent reformist, Wu hoped that his writing would warn young people about the contemporary decline of society and revive traditional morality. To this end he creates a naive observer, the narrator-protagonist "Nine Lives" (*Jiu si yi sheng* 九死一生), who provides an eyewitness account of the sordid practices of late-Qing society. Whereas traditional novels presented the "strange" as supernatural, Wu uses the technique of defamiliarization to alert readers to how strange, and objectionable, everyday conditions and conventions have become.[28] An abundance of concrete detail makes convincing the protagonist's disillusionment with external society, but it leaves little room for either emotional reaction or moral intervention, particularly regarding events in his personal life such as his father's death and his uncle's betrayal.[29]

In its disorienting capaciousness, *Strange Situation* seems to be a text committed to expressing a lack of coherence.[30] Even more than Nine

---

27. The first 45 chapters of Wu's novel were serialized in Liang Qichao's *Xin xiaoshuo* from 1903 to 1905. From 1906 to 1910, subsequent book editions added new chapters for a total of 108 chapters. See Dolezelová-Velingerová, "Typology of Plot Structures," 42, 56, n. 26.

28. The notion of defamiliarization (*ostranenie*, literally "making strange") comes from the Russian formalist Viktor Shklovsky; see "Iskusstvo kak priëm," esp. 13–22. In "Narrative Modes in Late Qing Novels," Dolezelová-Velingerová points out the notion's usefulness for discussing Wu's novel (69) and then distinguishes the technique from earlier ones: "Unlike the 'strange' (*qi*) of traditional fiction designating something abnormal which everybody could see but no one could explain, the strange or abnormal in Wu Woyao's novel is an invisible, unperceptible property of 'normal' things, events and characters and is unveiled as such by an 'alien' narrator." She continues: "In this I see the modernity of *Strange Events*, foretelling Lu Xun's *Diary of a Madman*" (70).

29. See Dolezelová-Velingerová, "Narrative Modes," 57–75, esp. 71.

30. Where I see a lack of coherence, Dolezelová-Velingerová proposes that the novel possesses a deep structure organized around a unifying theme that she names a "progress to knowledge" ("Typology of Plot Structures," 48). Working within the structuralist tradition, she and the other contributors to her volume assume that one can find a formula or underlying structure that orders a novel's elements. Although positing such a structure conveniently supports a unified interpretation despite the late-Qing novel's episodic nature, this unifying theme of cognitive ascension seems doubtful in light of the novel's pessimistic temper, not to mention the conditions of its composition and publication. Insofar as it makes sense to emphasize Nine Lives's gradual awakening

Lives's disappointed expectations, the sheer quantity of information willfully obstructs the possibility of making sense of moral action, loyalty, piety, or the other Confucian virtues with which the young protagonist begins. Protracted moralizing compensates to some extent by appealing to positive values of what appears negative, but the force of these pronouncements is undercut by the fact that the characters seldom do anything but talk. The incongruity between the moral pronouncements and the events presented makes the former sound more like self-conscious and perhaps ironically nostalgic citations of formulas from earlier works.

The use of delayed presentation and time inversion further reinforces a distinctly modern anxiety about the world's lack of order. [31] Furthermore, although appeal to traditional cosmology may offer some consolation, it does little to render moral reasoning meaningful. In a world too incomprehensible for moral action, the only morally upright characters are passive victims. This predicament becomes endemic in later works as characters increasingly discover that their social surroundings not only do not incarnate their values—whether traditional or modern—but seemingly thwart their own attempts to enact such values.

Thus, more than offering a convincing plea for reform, the critical satire in these novels may express resignation over a seemingly irreversible decline of society. The intention may have been to call for vigilance and action against official corruption or Western aggression, but the detached mockery and sensationalism in these works bespeak an aesthetic of passive disillusionment. This aesthetic may reflect the influence of Western novels of the period, but it should be stressed that the Chinese novels' depiction of the world as confused is quite different from the antagonistic denial of bourgeois notions about humankind's control of its fate that dominates aesthetic modernity in the West.[32] Instead of antagonism, the resignation in these novels probably corresponds to a pessimistic current

---

and disillusionment, Dolezelová-Velingerová characterizes his experience better when she calls it a "shattering cognitive process" ("Narrative Modes," 69).

31. Dolezelová-Velingerová points out that the technique of "time inversion" was common in traditional Chinese mystery-story and storyteller genres, but rare in traditional novels. See "Typology of Plot Structures," 46–47. For a discussion of time inversion in Wu Woyao's *Jiuming qiyuan* (The strange case of nine murders), see Fong, "Time in *Nine Murders*."

32. For a succinct account of the West's "two modernities"—one a modernity of capitalistic progress, the other a hostile aesthetic reaction—see Calinescu, *Five Faces of Modernity*, 41–46.

in late-Qing Confucianism.[33] Allegorical representations of this decline include the sinking boat in the opening chapter of *The Travels of Lao Can* and the "Island of Enslaved Happiness" in the first chapter of Zeng Pu's *Flower in a Sea of Sin.*[34]

The profound pessimism and discouragement expressed in these novels is all the more glaring when juxtaposed against the theorists' Pollyannaish confidence regarding fiction's power to effect positive change. Although the increased energy invested in writing and reading novels attentive to social issues answered the theorists' optimistic calls for a fiction that would support the goals of the reform movement, actual writing practices were, not surprisingly, much more intractable. This discord between theoretical program and creative response reminds us that the new authorial freedom, albeit liberating in theory, could be fairly disconcerting on the ground.

Even writers who expressly enlisted the novel to serve the cause of reform could hardly control the effects of the unruly genre. Their purpose in exposing corruption may have been to inspire a return to traditional values such as filial piety, human-heartedness, and moderation (*zhongyong* 中庸), but it was no easy matter to harness the indignation expressed and to control readers' reactions. Instead of convincing readers of the necessity of traditional values, these novels may well have contributed to the radical contestation and even rejection of such values during the iconoclastic May Fourth movement.

Significantly, many writers of the May Fourth period scorned and rejected the late-Qing novels.[35] Their determination to distance themselves from the late-Qing reform program stemmed from both a commitment to a more revolutionary agenda and a desire to acclaim the radical nature of their own literary and linguistic innovations. Yet the

---

33. See Metzger, *Escape from Predicament*, esp. 158–60.

34. Yang Xianyi details the first novel's allegorical parallels to China as follows: "The boat in danger of being wrecked is China, the four men at the helm being the four ministers of war, the six old masts standing for the six old departments of war and two new masts for the two newly created departments. The length of the boat was two hundred and forty feet, symbolising the twenty-four provinces of China." He adds: "China in the past had relied upon experience and precedent in guiding the ship of state, but such methods would not serve in times of crisis, and the gift of a compass to the pilot symbolises the scientific spirit of the West which would enable statesmen to set a definite course and take effective steps to follow it." See Yang, "On 'The Travels of Lao Can,'" 82–83.

35. An exception is Hu Shi, who speaks well of Wu Woyao, Li Baojia, and Liu E, in his "Wenxue gailiang chuyi," 127.

May Fourth writers may also have scorned the late-Qing novels out of a reluctance, conscious or not, to endorse these novels' promotion of traditional worldviews that the later writers believed implicitly denied the possibility of human intervention and change. In particular, these novels' thematic and formal elements often rendered stronger and more absolute the fatalism that comprised only one level of discourse in traditional fiction. Here I will mention briefly the thematic determinism of one particularly popular novel and then discuss how formal elements worked to reinforce deterministic paradigms in late-Qing novels.

Zeng Pu's novel *Flower in the Sea of Sin*, unusual for its revolutionary aspirations, displays an acute tension between a narrative discourse that contests fatalism and a narrative structure that enacts a cycle of retribution. The narrator's opposition to fatalism emerges in his description of the Island of Enslaved Happiness: "Here was a nation that worshipped power and fawned upon foreigners, and that received from the traditions of the past a foolish belief in fate and the operation of karma" (1/138).[36] In case the reader might have missed it, Zeng Pu drives home the relevance of this allegory to China, writing that after the island sinks into the Sea of Sin, the Lover of Freedom seeks to investigate what happened, and a beautiful woman asks him, "What place is not the Island of Enslaved Happiness?" (3).

Yet, wittingly or unwittingly, Zeng Pu reinforces the "foolish belief in fate and the operation of karma" by constructing a narrative in which the principle of retribution decides the events of the novel: Jin Wenqing's spiritual debt to Liang Xinyan 梁新燕, a former lover who hanged herself when he reneged on his promise to marry her, determines both his attraction for Fu Caiyun and the outcome of their romance. From Fu Caiyun's entry in chapter 7, Jin's observation of the red birthmark on her neck makes him speculate about her connection to his former lover.

In this and other late-Qing novels, formal elements reinforce deterministic themes. Not surprisingly, since formal experimentation often takes time to create the desired effects in the novel and its reception, innovations that might have facilitated the representation of agency often worked to foreclose it.[37] Comparing the more traditional long novels of

---

36. In this paragraph, the first number in the parentheses refers to Zeng, *Nie hai hua*. Where a second number appears, it refers to the translation by de Crespigny and Liu, "Tseng P'u: A Flower in a Sinful Sea."

37. Although they often followed tradition, novelists of the late-Qing period also intro-

the period with the more experimental, shorter works sheds light on the complex effects of innovation in both forms.

The episodic structure of the late-Qing novels offers recurrent opportunities for sideshadowing innovative action, but the proliferation of sideshadows often makes it so difficult to foresee the consequences of action that the exercise of moral agency becomes tenuous. Most of the social novels were written in the form of traditional *zhanghui xiaoshuo* 章回小說 (novels in chapters) in which authors use suspense to link successive chapters but otherwise only loosely integrate the events.[38] Insofar as this use of suspense depends on an open universe, or at least one that is not wholly predictable, like most traditional Chinese fiction these novels avoid the kind of unitary plot trajectory that produces a sense of inevitability in many nineteenth-century novels in the West. However, in the late-Qing novels, the anecdotes become so diffuse as to create the impression that anything might happen next. The sequence of events becomes so unpredictable and the cast of characters so vast that they severely compromise the possibility of rational human agency. For agency to be meaningful, there must be limits on the workings of chance and at least some possibility of predictable causal relations.

3. PLOT, DISCOURSE, AND RESIGNATION IN *SEA OF REGRET*

The introduction of shorter works whose unitary plot structure could focus on the emotions and actions of fewer characters diminished the sense of an ungraspable and arbitrary universe, but the way it did so often shut down the kind of openness achieved in the longer novels. One particularly representative example is Wu Woyao's novel *Sea of Regret*, the story of two couples whose arranged marriages fall through after Bohe 伯和, the husband-to-be of the first couple, dies from his opium addiction, and his brother's bride-to-be turns to prostitution.[39] Whereas some scholars see the novel as the story of how social forces crush the

---

duced formal innovations. For a study of formal innovations from 1902 through 1927, see Chen Pingyuan, *Zhongguo xiaoshuo xushi moshi de zhuanbian*.

38. Some scholars translate this term as "linked-chapter novels" to capture the way the beginning of each new chapter answers the suspense-producing ending of the preceding one. The rhetoric of the chapter beginnings and endings often suggests that the narrator is a storyteller addressing an audience rather than a novelist writing for solitary readers.

39. Unlike many late-Qing novels, *Sea of Regret* appeared as a book, not serialized in a magazine.

individual, I propose that Wu leaves open the question of whether it is the larger social context that destroys the characters or rather their own inability or unwillingness to change.[40] This tension arises chiefly because sustained attention to the thoughts of Bohe's fiancée Dihua 棣華 in the end simply makes more absolute her allegiance to the rules of propriety and her inability to entertain alternatives to a tragedy that is largely self-inflicted.

It should be mentioned that Dihua does take certain steps to influence events. First, she writes a note to a doctor describing her mother's symptoms (26).[41] Second, after Bohe is separated from Dihua and her mother, Dihua writes notices to post along the docks and roads to inform Bohe of their whereabouts (42). In drawing attention to the usefulness of educating women to write, these two incidents support the classical Confucian and Enlightenment notion that self-cultivation can enhance human agency. Later, Dihua goes to extraordinary measures to nurse the dying Bohe (70–73), although the stamina she exhibits could suggest either a heroic force of will or an irrational compulsion. Yet despite the initiative she takes at these moments, Dihua remains stubbornly blind to other opportunities to shape her life. The novel sows the seeds of Dihua's fatalism in her upbringing and her parents' discourse when early on her mother tries to comfort her with the idea that "everything that happens is foreordained" (33/145). Dihua's father, for the most part much less acquiescent than his wife or daughter, also at one point attributes Bohe's tragedy to his daughter's fate (68/192).

Although Dihua's parents help inculcate her fatalistic resignation, Dihua is even more ready than her parents to attribute her sorrows to fate. Whereas her father ends his account of Bohe's dissolute lifestyle and opium addiction with an expression of anger toward Bohe—"Doesn't it make your blood boil?" (63/184)—Dihua counters that Bohe's demise has "been brought about because of your daughter's bitter fate,"[42] and she

40. See Dolezelová-Velingerová, "Typology of Plot Structures," 52. Although never developing the idea, Michael Egan touches on the dialectic of freedom and determinism at the end of his essay "Characterization in *Sea of Woe*": "In a very modern way, freedom and causality are extremely important in *Sea of Woe*" (175).

41. Where one page number is given, it refers to the edition published in Wang Xiaolian et al., *Wan Qing xiaoshuo daxi*. Where two numbers are given, the second refers to Hanan's translation, *The Sea of Regret*.

42. I have emended Hanan's translation here to bring out the original, which reads *ming ku suo zhi* 命苦所致.

urges her father not to damage his health by being angry (63/185). Dihua appeals to the notion of predestination several more times in the novel, even quoting nearly verbatim her mother's earlier words that "everything that happens is foreordained" (68/192–93) and directly quoting from *Mencius*: "Whatever is done without man's doing it is from Heaven; whatever happens without man causing it is fate" (69/193). Dihua comments on the last quotation: "All we can do is resign ourselves to our lot [*an ming* 安命], not harbor resentment against others" (69/193).

Dihua's conception of fate does not, however, keep her from blaming herself for events over which she clearly has little control. First, although the novel casts a sideshadow on Dihua's excessive adherence to rules of behavior when she speculates that she might have been more comfortable in Bohe's presence had her family not moved away from his family early on (10), she later blames herself for expressing her uneasiness and thereby bringing about their separation (66/188–89). Second, after Dihua's mother dies, Dihua briefly questions the reliability of the traditional ritual by which she attempted to save her mother, then chooses to blame herself instead: "Perhaps her failure to cure her mother with a morsel of her own flesh showed that the ancients were lying, she thought. But how could lies have been passed down over so many years without anyone seeing through them? No doubt the ancients weren't lying at all; it was her own heart that wasn't sincere enough" (59/179).

Over and over, Dihua blames herself for events (31/129, 63/185, 66/188–89, 67/190) but invokes the role of fate to forgive those she loves, most notably her father and Bohe. Dihua blames her lack of sincerity (59/179, 67/190), her own personal fate (63/185), her excessive concern over what others might think (66/190), and her limited powers of expression (67/190). But when her father wants to assume the blame for accepting Bohe's parents' marriage proposal, Dihua counters that everything is foreordained and that "all we can do is let matters take their course" (*zhi you ting qi ziran bale* 只有聽其自然罷了; 68/193).

Accounts of Bohe's thoughts, although less sustained, show a similar refusal to resist a self-imposed tragedy. Bohe's early search for his lost companions demonstrates confidence in his ability to influence events as unlikely as finding his fiancée amid the chaos of the Boxer Uprising and the allied invasion. But when it comes to his opium addiction, he exclaims that he will never be able to give up the drug: "Even if *my* father were alive again, I couldn't give it up—it's my life [*xingming* 性命]!"

(67/190). The narrator's emphasis on the possibility of an alternative outcome throws a sideshadow on the plot and underscores Bohe's role in determining his life: "Now, wouldn't it have been wonderful if he had changed his ways, given up his opium habit, and married his fiancée?" (65/187–88).

An unstated question arises that the reader cannot help but ask: Wouldn't it be wonderful if Dihua could change her ways? But Dihua does not deign to consider alternatives to courses of action that lead to her suffering. Even once Bohe makes clear how little he cares about her, Dihua persists in her abject devotion to him. After he dies, she shaves her head and insists on becoming a nun, refusing to consider the options her father offers.[43] Significantly, Dihua sees her self-demeaning sacrifice to nurse Bohe on his deathbed and her decision to become a nun as fulfillments of fate rather than as commitments she has chosen. Yet her appeals to fate also allow the novel to problematize the concept and draw attention to the unrealized possibility that Dihua might have avoided her self-defeating trajectory.

The novel's narrative structure reinforces the thematic determinism. Although only briefly sketched, the story of Bohe's younger brother, Zhong'ai 仲藹, and his fiancée, Juanjuan 娟娟, sideshadows the story of Dihua and Bohe, reversing the genders insofar as it is the woman, Juanjuan, who abandons the man, by falling into prostitution, and the man, Zhong'ai, who renounces the world rather than find another partner. The mirror nature of the two couples' stories not only makes *Sea of Regret* a heavily plotted novel, but it also makes the plotline seem more natural and inevitable.

In light of this naturalizing effect, how do appeals to destiny reinforce the unequal range of choices allowed to men and women? For it seems reasonable to assume that Juanjuan has far less choice in becoming a prostitute than Bohe does in becoming addicted to opium. Furthermore, since Wu Woyao calls his work a "novel of sentiment" (*xie qing xiaoshuo* 寫情小說), the question arises as to how the perception of fate structures emotional responses and fixes emotional patterns.[44] For example,

43. For a modern reader, the characters' resignation to circumstance is all the more bewildering insofar as they actually surmount many external obstacles in a rather unlikely way.

44. Dolezelová-Velingerová suggests that Wu's sentimental fiction may have prepared the way both for the popular "Mandarin Ducks and Butterflies" fiction of the following decade and for the psychological emphasis of the May Fourth stories.

the presentation of Dihua, the female character disappointed in love, differs markedly from that of Zhong'ai, the male character disappointed in love. Upon discovering that his fiancée Juanjuan has become a prostitute, Zhong'ai's reaction to his loss differs markedly from Dihua's resignation to fate. Zhong'ai makes a similar decision to withdraw from the world, but his act of going to the mountains (*ru shan* 入山) is clearly a matter of choice. Having attended to his parents' funerals, his last worldly act is to give away his inheritance to needy friends and relatives (78/205). It is worth underscoring that the novel's women characters speak much more fatalistically than the men. Fate applies to Dihua, her mother, and the helpless Juanjuan, whereas Bohe, Zhong'ai, and Dihua's father all enjoy a considerable measure of choice. At the same time, and in part because of her privileged social status, Dihua exercises more choice than many of the later female characters of modern Chinese fiction.

4. *THE TRAVELS OF LAO CAN* BY LIU E

Most often praised as a masterpiece of style and language, Liu E's 劉鶚 novel *The Travels of Lao Can* is also a deeply philosophical work.[45] I discuss Liu's novel at some length for its presentation of considered late-Qing views on freedom and determinism that derive from traditional Chinese philosophical teachings. On one level, the novel embodies the qualities and possibilities of a life limited by the workings of greater impersonal forces. Paradoxically, it is also a novel about self-assertion, full of sideshadows that emphasize the characters' liberty to pursue their chosen values.

The life of the novel stems above all from Lao Can's freedom, particularly his refusal to accept a fixed position. This sense of freedom underlies and enlivens the highly praised detailed descriptions of natural scenes and cultural settings. For the wonders that Liu E depicts are more than pretty pictures; they embody the great force (太極 *taiji*) of the universe, a universe in which humankind can live in harmony, provided people follow a path of public-spirited disinterestedness (公 *gong*). In this vein, Lao Can promotes naturalness and spontaneity, such as when he blames a patient's throat disorder on her repression of her feelings (25/34) and

45. Although passages from Liu's novel became a staple of schoolbooks because of the beauty of the style and scenic description, the selections often safely avoid the philosophical and political questions posed by the novel. For instance, one of the most common excerpts is the idyllic description of the Wang sisters singing in chapter 2.

encourages the abused young prostitute Cuihuan 翠環 to cry out her misery (144/148).[46] Yet Lao Can also demonstrates confidence in modest human endeavor. As Leo Lee writes, "Despite the sad fate of his country, which he bemoans, he does not feel totally superfluous. The expression of self in the novel is, on balance, more positive than negative. Through his travels Lau Ts'an [Lao Can] has performed a variety of useful functions."[47]

Lao Can refuses society's imperatives and thus embraces moral agency when he declines to become an official, settling his accounts in haste to flee entanglements rather than staying to help the governor (chaps. 3–4). He exercises agency when he cures the sick (chap. 3), advises on flood control (chap. 3), recommends a plan to deter bandits and a friend to carry it out (chap. 7), rescues innocent victims from despotic officials (chap. 17), and saves young Cuihuan from her miserable life as a prostitute (chaps. 14 and 17). In promising to rescue Cuihuan and reunite her with her brother, Lao Can utters a promise that presupposes his own faith in his ability to fulfill it: "You don't need to cry. I guarantee that you two, brother and sister, shan't ever be separated" (155/159).[48]

Ironically, Lao Can's power to keep his word is illustrated in a moment that simultaneously stresses the limitations of circumstance and social norms; when Lao Can can see no other way to save Cuihuan, his friend Renrui 人瑞 tricks Lao Can into marrying Cuihuan as his concubine (chap. 17). The role of fate is conveyed by the couplets hung on the wall in the inner room into which Renrui drags Lao Can and Cuihuan:

> May all lovers under the sky achieve the marriage state;
> These things are fixed in heaven: do not miss your mate [*yinyuan* 姻緣]. (190/194)

The term *yinyuan*, literally the happy fate that brings marriages, conveys a connotation of fortuitous predestination, but Lao Can feels hoodwinked. When he asks Renrui why he had to trick him, Renrui articulates one of the novel's messages about the range and limitations of human action: "I was thinking of Cuihuan's good. If you're going to help somebody, you must help them thoroughly. . . . In this world things have to be done

46. The first number in the parentheses refers to Liu E, *Laocan youji*. The second number refers to Harold Shadick's translation, *The Travels of Lao Ts'an*.

47. Leo Lee, "The Solitary Traveler," 286.

48. I follow Shadick's translation here except that I translate *baoguan* 包管 as "guarantee."

in this way" (191/195). Furthermore, in its accounts of the murders of innocent people and its representations of torture (particularly chap. 16), the novel invokes classic examples of the extreme force of external coercion and the deprivation of human freedom.

Lao Can's active engagement is nonetheless possible because his attitude toward human affairs is not one of resignation. A studied humility drives his withdrawal from public life, one based upon a rebellious recognition of the limitations of human power and intention. He knows better than to assume a power for which he could not be responsible. He also knows better than all those characters in the novel who attempt to serve principles only to corrupt them. A political innocent, Lao Can does not condescend to get his hands dirty:

> I admit that shaking a string of bells [working as an itinerant healer] contributes little to the world, but then does it contribute anything to be an official? . . .
>
> . . . The really bad thing is when men of ability want to be officials. After all, isn't this Excellency Yü a man of ability? But just because he is overanxious to be an official, or rather hankers after being a great official, he acts as he does, wounding heaven and damaging all principles of justice. . . . If he were to go about like me, shaking a string of bells and curing disease, people would not want him to treat serious disorders; and in treating minor troubles he couldn't kill anybody. (64/69–70)

Lao Can's skepticism concerning grand ambitions is important here. For his refusal to join the system of officialdom is rooted less in high-mindedness than in a lack of faith in his ability or, more pertinent, in anyone's ability to carry out good intentions. For Lao Can, even the noblest motives are not sufficient to generate just and honorable outcomes. The obvious example is the governor who unwittingly becomes the "tool of bandits" (chaps. 4–5). Where past works had criticized corrupt officials, Liu E criticizes those who do evil out of intransigence, even if it is intransigence devoted to ideals of justice. He deplores personal ambition of all kinds not because fame is transient, or because power necessarily corrupts, but because on a theoretical level he denies a reliable connection between acts and their consequences.

Yet neither does Lao Can believe that the world is ruled by chance. To the contrary, a sense of predestination and divine coincidence emerges both in the philosophy espoused by Lao Can, Yellow Dragon 黃龍子, and other characters and in Lao Can's meeting up with old friends in far-flung places. These events create a sense of fecundity, but one decidedly beyond the ken of human control. In addition to empirical observations demonstrating the impotence of human intention, the denial of agency derives primarily from a cosmology of cycles, most clearly expressed in the conversation between Yellow Dragon and Shen Ziping 申子平 in chapter 11:

> "His [the August One's] real name is 'Force Supreme [*shili zun zhe* 勢力尊者],' Yellow Dragon answered. "Even Shang Ti [*Shangdi* 上帝] cannot disobey the authority of Force. . . . For this reason frost and snow, cold and wind are allowed to appear and use all their strength to kill off the surplus life. Then High Heaven is allowed to come and show his love for life again. . . . The whole process of creating and killing is the activity of 'Force Supreme.'" (116–17/121)

The length that Liu E devotes to the exposition of this view (especially in chaps. 9 and 11) suggests sympathy for a traditional organicist cosmology that some might deem mechanistic.[49]

Yet whereas some of the philosophical passages might appear to commit the text to a deterministic position, the novel as a whole avoids any sense of rigidity. Moreover, the fact that Liu chose the form of a novel to deliver his message and felt obliged to philosophize explicitly within it belies the notion of nonintervention espoused within the work. Gratuitous as his desultory wanderings may appear, Lao Can's travels are hardly aimless, as the discussion above of his good deeds should demonstrate. The very "whodunit" question implicit in the detective-type episodes also promises to reveal both a criminal agent and the agency of Lao Can or other characters in uncovering the evil.

It is thus no easy matter to decide to what extent Liu E expects his readers to believe in the great force and his taxonomy of the universe. The reader could easily understand the principle to mean that natural forces determine all human actions. Yet such a reading would compromise the Confucian model of human responsibility the novel supports in having Lao Can follow his heart's promptings to act rather than endure the suffering of others. Lao Can's indignation about public servants' abuses of power also requires conviction about ideals of human responsibility. If people could rely on the great force to rectify all contradictions, why take seriously Lao Can's exhortations to pursue selflessness and the common

49. Simply put, "organicism" is the belief that society or the world is analogous to a biological organism, a living body with connected parts. Scholars often describe traditional notions of yin-yang cosmology and the theory of the Five Agents as stemming from an organicist worldview.

good? The novel's cosmology sideshadows and perhaps even runs counter to its ethical purposes.

Some of the novel's secondary characters also take seriously the power of natural forces while at the same time stressing the power of ethical conduct and the role of education in its cultivation. The young maiden Yugu 璵姑, for example, both makes explicit reference to the great force (117/122) and comments on the importance of public-spiritedness (*gong* 公): "Their [the Confucian, Daoist, and Buddhist teachings'] similarity consists in encouraging man to be good, leading man to be disinterested. If all men were disinterested, the Empire would have peace. If all men scheme for private advantage, then the Empire is in chaos" (94/98). In case any doubt might linger about the primacy of Confucian morality, Yugu adds that "only Confucianism is thoroughly disinterested" (94/98). Similarly, although in the passage quoted above he argues for the omnipotence of Force Supreme, Yellow Dragon also concedes that human altruism or selfishness may have some limited influence: "Those who consider the common good are of one heart in loving other men and therefore breathe out warmth. Those who teach private interest are of one mind in hating other men, and they breathe out coldness" (121/126).

Yet other passages might suggest that a deterministic cosmology trumps the role of human decision. For example, when Lao Can does help, the novel attributes his intervention to fate, as in the fateful way his friend Renrui tricks him into fulfilling his promise to save Cuihuan. Does this episode diminish Lao Can's agency? If it does, perhaps whatever agency he loses does not disappear but rather is transferred to Renrui, with whose good intentions Lao Can is completely in agreement. The Daoist hermit Green Dragon 青龍子 also chooses to view fate as calling him when he agrees to provide the antidote to the "Thousand Days' Sleep" poison afflicting thirteen innocent victims. Although he had moved on to more remote mountain areas because too many pilgrims were coming to see him, Green Dragon responds willingly when Lao Can finds him in order to procure the antidote: "It is fated [*you yuan* 有緣] that I should help" (225/228).

The novel seems to regard the exercise of responsibility for others as the rightful fulfillment of a person's empathic nature, yet, even as such, responsible action usually entails a limitation of a person's freedom. Furthermore, one might conclude that Liu E believes that one should favor the common good over selfish pursuits not because it is right to privilege the good for its own sake but because people are inextricably caught up in the larger natural order. The novel repeatedly appeals to this order, and the consoling function of these appeals supports Milena Doleželová-Velingerová's characterization of the novel as "an apologia for the status quo."[50] In *The Travels of Lao Can*, human agency is allowed, but only as a discontinuous force. The characters may briefly escape from larger determining forces, but their actions at these moments have only short-term consequences. Liu E presents little possibility for a larger constructive freedom. Freedom is at best piecemeal and limited in force. Yet by remaining attentive to small emerging possibilities, characters such as Lao Can are able to intervene in morally significant ways.

In this light, it is not surprising that the novel's comments on revolutionaries express a clear antipathy toward radical measures and fixed programs. Aside from what for the time was a progressive treatment of women, ultimately the novel conveys a "reformist" ideology. It urges against revolution in favor of a return to tradition and its teachings, as when Yellow Dragon begins his discourse on southern revolutionaries: "If you claim to believe in revolution you don't need to submit to the control of justice, national law, or social custom" (120/124–25). A little later he elaborates:

> The revolutionaries use disbelief in spirits. . . . If you say there are no spirits, . . . then you don't need to respect your ancestors: this is the prime source of revolution in the family. If you say there are no spirits, then there is no retribution from Hell, or punishment from Heaven, and you can act in any way, defying Heaven's laws. . . . In short, . . . all morality will be twisted and destroyed by them. (121/126–27)

Since Yellow Dragon's argument against revolution seems to imply that morality can come only from spirits, divine retribution, or Heaven's laws, one could counter that there might be other foundations for morality and justice. Yet part of the novel's argument may be that in the absence of viable alternatives, it is hubris to struggle for change. It was this type of assumption that the next generation of writers could not accept.

50. Doleželová-Velingerová, *The Chinese Novel*, 12.

3

The Prison of Self-Consciousness in May Fourth Fiction

> We want to seek the crucial point of self-consciousness, but we have lost our way in a fog of pessimism.
>
> —Li Dazhao 李大釗, translated by Maurice Meisner

Whereas the "literary revolution" which was announced in theoretical writings in 1917 and pursued in much of the literature of the following decades continued many processes of innovation already begun in the late-Qing novels and texts written earlier, it also marked linguistic, formal, and philosophical changes that may warrant its characterization as a monumental rupture.[1] Whereas many of the late-Qing novelists sought to use fiction to shore up traditional values, the writers associated with the New Culture movement sought to transform the very basis of those values.[2] Disappointed by the failed reform movement of 1898, resentful over the betrayal of the Republic founded in 1912, and humiliated by Japan's delivery of its "Twenty-One Demands" in January 1915, many intellectuals were by this date convinced that China's survival depended on a radical break from traditional ways of thinking.[3] Hoping to usher in nothing less than a revolution in consciousness, they wrote to analyze the "national character," expose the inhumanity of their society, and demystify hallowed traditional codes that they blamed for cruel practices and for their country's defenselessness in the face of foreign aggression.

---

1. For the long-range development of subjective elements, see Zhou Zuoren, *Zhongguo xin wenxue de yuanliu*; Průšek, "Subjectivism and Individualism"; and the essays in Hegel and Hessney, *Expressions of Self.*

2. For the New Culture movement's attack on tradition, see Chow Tse-tsung, *The May Fourth Movement*, esp. 289–313.

3. In May 1915, Yuan Shikai's government capitulated to most of the Twenty-One Demands in exchange for Japan's support for Yuan's plan to end the Republic and proclaim himself emperor of a new dynasty.

Some of these intellectuals turned to writing fiction as part of a larger project to contest a repressive order, itself a reaction to a sense of national crisis. Many of these writers were deeply concerned about the relationship between consciousness and language, and fiction afforded considerable freedom to experiment with new forms, styles, and even grammatical and rhetorical patterns.[4] Stories and novels could also focus on the tragic waste of human life that these writers insisted was unnecessary. For tragedy was not new in Chinese literature. What was new was the refusal to confer a meaning or significance on tragedy through an appeal to some kind of ultimate pattern. Refusing the consolation of a worldview based on providential cycles or the "will of Heaven," these writers viewed inhuman practices as the consequence of backward beliefs and institutions that could be challenged and changed.

What emerges in this fiction is the idea that the principal limitations on human freedom are those that people create or adopt for themselves, or, in more harrowing cases, those that some people force upon others. At the same time, in their explicit discourse, their themes, and their silences, many of these works underscore the difficulties of escaping the hold of long-standing values and practices. Disputing traditional beliefs created an urgent hunger for new moral and conceptual frameworks. Rejection of traditional roles, ritual, and taboos forced characters to face the nature of their own compulsions. A commitment to sincerity and truth led to an aporia about how to ground these values.

Rather than dwell in the darkness of uncertainty—a purgatory arguably necessary for the possibility of ethical choice—many writers chose instead to assume the moral high ground: The fastest route to "truth" was often a cynical defeatism. Tragedy seeming preferable to absurdity, the difficulty of finding positive alternatives to the callous practices of their society led many writers to equate optimism with naïveté and pessimism with truth.[5] For, as the writers themselves were acutely aware, turning inward to effect outward change, pursuing realism with the goal of changing reality, and using elite culture to challenge the injustice of social hierarchies posed fundamental challenges and contradictions.

---

4. On formal changes in writing, see Gunn, *Rewriting Chinese.*

5. As William Lyell writes of Lu Xun, "Ever concerned lest easy optimism sooth his readers into the same lethargy from which he sought to rouse them, Lu Xun remained rigorously pessimistic in his writings." See Lyell, *Lu Xun*, xxiv.

To bring out these contradictions and their singular painfulness, this chapter confronts the dual effect of the attention to subjectivity that characterizes the fiction of this period. For while the extreme self-consciousness of this writing is important insofar as it underscores the freedom to reexamine the world, take an independent stand, and make one's understanding public, it does not guarantee that the characters may take charge of their fate. To the contrary, although most of these writers began with compelling themes, confronting their society's oppressive practices and their own participation and responsibility therein, many focused increasingly on the plight of the intellectual protagonist trapped in his own consciousness. This self-obsession did not preclude the presentation of social evils, but it did discourage questions about what reflective and compassionate people might do to redress them. As a result, many of these works seem, implicitly or explicitly, to adopt deterministic paradigms that deny possibilities for freedom, agency, and responsibility.

This chapter addresses the denial of agency in May Fourth fiction by focusing on five concerns. First, I situate the fictional developments within the context of intellectual debates concerning the link between individual consciousness and national salvation. Second, I confront how the focus on introspection reinforced perceptions of alienation and devastating imprisonment in one's individual consciousness. Third, I analyze what I call "spectatorial consciousness" to discern how confining characters to observation disabled their chances for participation. Fourth, I examine how disillusionment often led to a pessimistic fatalism and the moral implications of such fatalism for the possibility of respecting the experiences of the characters. Finally, I discuss the characteristics of the Creationist school, a kind of romanticism gone wrong, as the extreme end of May Fourth–era works tending toward solipsism.

1. INDIVIDUAL CONSCIOUSNESS AND NATIONAL SALVATION

As discussed in Chapter 1, writers' deliberate intention to depict subjectivity and individual consciousness was based in large part on the conviction that such a focus could modernize both Chinese writing and the consciousness of the people. These tasks were made urgent by the perception that China risked becoming a vanquished nation (*wang guo* 亡國) and so was in desperate need of spiritual renewal to "save the nation" (*jiu guo* 救

國).[6] Lu Xun 魯迅 (Zhou Shuren 周樹人; 1881–1936) makes explicit the connection between increased individual consciousness and national strength in his essay "Wenhua pianzhi lun" 文化偏至論 (Extremities in cultural development; 1907):

> If we want to establish a plan for the present, we must examine the past and prepare for the future, discard the material and elevate the spirit, rely on the individual and exclude the mass. When the individual is exalted to develop his full capacity, then the country will be strengthened and will arise.[7]

Although few people had read the still relatively unknown Lu Xun at the time of this essay, the debate on the notion of the individual and its link to national reform reached a larger audience with the rise of journals such as *Dongfang zazhi* 東方雜誌 (Eastern miscellany), *Xin qingnian* 新青年 (New youth), originally called *Qingnian zazhi* 青年雜誌 (Youth magazine), and *Xin chao* 新潮 (New tide).[8] To analyze the shifting discourse of individualism from the mid-1910s to the early 1920s, Lydia Liu begins with Du Yaquan's 杜亞泉 "Geren zhi gaige" 個人之改格 (Reforming the individual; 1914).[9] This article is particularly significant, Liu notes, because it advanced a positive conception of individualism that (1) departed from Liang Qichao's denigration of the concept, which Liang saw as inimical to the nation-state and the people's collective liberty, and (2) was still ostensibly compatible with both Confucian and socialist thought. Liu then examines ways in which the New Culture movement writers redefined the concept of individualism to make it a weapon against traditional Chinese culture.

In her analysis, Liu stresses the degree to which the discourse of individualism was complicit with nationalism. To articulate the utility of the

---

6. Before the twentieth century, the term *wang guo* was used to refer to the collapse of a dynasty, but writers such as Li Dazhao used it to refer to the conquest and collapse of the Chinese nation. See Meisner, *Li Dazhao*, 19.

7. *Fen*, in Lu Xun, *Lu Xun quanji*, 1: 38–54, here 41. The translation that appears here was modified from those in Leo Lee, "Genesis of a Writer," 181; and Mills, "Lu Xun: Literature and Revolution," 194.

8. *Eastern Miscellany* was founded in 1904. Chen Duxiu and his colleagues began publishing *Youth Magazine* in September 1915 and renamed the journal *New Youth* in September of the following year. During the period in which *Youth Magazine* was founded, Chen was dean of humanities at Beijing University. *New Tide* was founded in January 1919 by students at Beijing University.

9. Discussed in Lydia Liu, *Translingual Practice*, 87–89. When he wrote "Reforming the Individual," Du Yaquan had been, since 1911, the editor-in-chief of *Eastern Miscellany*.

notion of the individual for the project of nation building, she quotes Chow Tse-tsung's related point: "While the disintegration of the old ethics probably emancipated the individual somewhat from the bond with his family and clan, it also cleared the way for placing the individual in bondage to state, party, or other social and economic organizations."[10] Discussing Hu Shi's 胡適 (1891–1962) subordination of the *xiaowo* 小我 (small self) to the *dawo* 大我 (greater self), Liu restates her thesis: "His position was a logical expression of the theory of modernity, which did not seek so much to liberate individuals as to constitute them as citizens of the nation-state and members of modern society."[11]

As Liu's argument suggests, it is crucial to recognize that a focus on the individual and attention to values such as individual rights can function as alibis for the deployment of power. However, this characterization of the theory of modernity as seeking to constitute individuals as citizens elides the sincere aspirations and efforts of intellectuals committed to working for a range of other values promised by the idea of modernity. Whereas it is important to acknowledge the potential for repression in certain categories central to the project of modernity—the notion of individual consciousness among them—it is also vital to remember their significance for ethical reflection and responsibility.

To demonstrate the primacy of such ethical and emancipatory concerns to the leaders of the New Culture movement, even in their explicit appeals to patriotism, I turn to an early debate about "self-consciousness" (*zi jue* 自覺) between Chen Duxiu 陳獨秀 (1879–1942) and Li Dazhao 李大釗 (1889–1927), thinkers who would together found the Chinese Communist Party in 1921.[12] Forasmuch as these writers were concerned about the nation's political survival, their debate suggests that they sought, first and foremost, to enlighten people about the oppressive nature of existing social conditions and the need to change them.

In "Aiguo yu zijuexin" 愛國與自覺心 (Patriotism and self-consciousness; April 1915), Chen linked patriotism to emotion and irrational action while he extolled self-consciousness as a state of mind based on

10. Chow Tse-tsung, "The Anti-Confucian Movement," 312, quoted in Lydia Liu, *Translingual Practice,* 91.

11. Lydia Liu, *Translingual Practice,* 95. Liu is discussing Hu Shi's article "Buxiu" (Immortality; 1919). A leading spokesman of Chinese liberalism, Hu Shi held important academic and political positions, including the presidency of Beijing University and the ambassadorship to the United States.

12. See the discussion in Meisner, *Li Dazhao,* 21–26.

knowledge and reasoning about particular problems. Chen believed patriotism was beneficial to Westerners, who viewed the state as promoting the people's rights and welfare, but harmful in the Chinese context where it led to enslavement and ritualized relationships of dependency. To make patriotism a positive force, Chen argued, the Chinese needed to develop self-consciousness.

For Li Dazhao, self-consciousness meant not just gaining knowledge about specific problems but actively working to transform one's political and social surroundings.[13] In "Yanshixin yu zijuexin" 厭世心與自覺心 (Pessimism and self-consciousness; August 1915), Li argued that the barrier to self-consciousness was not patriotism but pessimism, which he gently suggested might be fostered by "misunderstandings" of Chen's article. Thus, Li's insistence on activist patriotism:

> The meaning of self-consciousness lies in the spirit of changing the nation and in seeking to make the country lovable and loving it. We ought not to stop thinking about our country and refuse to love it because the country has deficiencies. . . . A country is a creation of men, the individual exists within the universe and within the vastness of the universe the individual is his own master.[14]

This expression of voluntarism, that is, the belief in the primacy of the will, is highly significant here, but it must be read carefully, since Li goes on to appeal to the "theory of free will."[15] Disturbed by the pessimism of traditional cultural heroes who retreated from society, Li wanted increased self-consciousness to lead people to participate in collective projects. As Maurice Meisner explains, "He took 'free will' to mean not freedom of individual action but the duty and ability of self-conscious men to change the conditions under which they live."[16]

Articles that appeared in the months and years following the exchange between Chen and Li frequently stressed this ethical and social dimension of national salvation. To this end, many writers repudiated tradition and placed great emphasis on the development of both self-conscious-

---

13. Meisner, *Li Dazhao*, 25.

14. Li Dazhao, *Li Dazhao xuanji*, 30, quoted in Meisner, *Li Dazhao*, 22–23. At the time of this essay, Li Dazhao was a librarian at Beijing University.

15. Li's interest in free will was inspired by his reading of Henri Bergson, to whose *L'évolution créatrice* (Creative evolution; 1907) Li refers on page 31 of the article under discussion. See Meisner, *Li Dazhao*, 23.

16. Meisner, *Li Dazhao*, 24.

ness and agency.[17] They blamed Confucian ritual and social morality for promoting a slave mentality and contrasted Oriental familism, traditionalism, and antilegalism with Western individuality, respect for law, and interest in the present.[18] Subsequent articles continued to grapple with notions of autonomy, passivity, education, "national character," and the effects of the traditional family system.[19]

Repudiating traditional beliefs, many writers turned to Western ideas, familiarizing themselves in a few years with the intellectual developments of over a century. The unresolved tensions inherent in the concepts and theories to which they turned made this assimilation doubly difficult. Freedom for Bergson, to whom Li Dazhao referred in his 1915 essay and whom Feng Youlan 馮友蘭 presented to the readers of the journal *New Tide* in 1921, was not the same as freedom for Kant or the neo-Kantian Paulson, to whose work the philosopher Yang Changji 楊昌濟 introduced his student Mao Zedong 毛澤東 in 1917.[20] As in other contexts, however, the semantic range of the notion of freedom augmented rather than diminished the promise it held forth. Many articles relied on this promise to articulate a dialectic of progress whereby a young China could be reborn from a declining civilization.[21] Faith that human agency could effect change was also implicit in the pervasive use of the term "new" in articles of the period.[22]

17. For example, in "Jinggao qingnian" (Call to youth; September 1915), Chen Duxiu called for the rejection of traditional "virtues," which he identified as servility, apathy, conservatism, isolationism, formalism, and mysticism, in favor of self-consciousness, independence, vitality, progressivism, cosmopolitanism, utilitarianism, and a scientific outlook.

18. See especially Chen Duxiu, "Dong xi minzu genben sixiang zhi chayi." For articles expressing similar positions, see Li Yizhi, "Rensheng weiyi zhi mudi"; Chen Duxiu, "Yijiuyiliu nian," and "Wuren zuihou zhi juewu"; and Yi Baisha, "Kongzi pingyi."

19. See Gao Yihan, "Yijiuyiqi nian sixiang zhi geming"; Guang Sheng, "Zhongguo guomin xing ji qi ruodian"; Cai Yuanpei, "Yi meiyu dai zongjiao shuo"; Fu Sinian, "Rensheng wenti faduan"; and Gu Jiegang, "Duiyu jiu jiating de ganxiang."

20. Feng Youlan, "Bogesen de zhexue fangfa." For the influence of Bergson's *L'évolution créatrice* on Li Dazhao, see Meisner, *Li Dazhao*, 21–25. For Paulson's work's influence on Mao's voluntarism, see Wakeman, *History and Will*, 201–6.

21. See especially Li Dazhao's influential article "Qingchun" (Spring; 1916), discussed in Meisner, *Li Dazhao*, 26–27. See also Gao Yihan's 1916 "Zizhi yu ziyou."

22. Several scholars have commented on the prevalence of the term "new." See Leo Lee, "In Search of Modernity," 111; and Rey Chow, "Rereading Mandarin Ducks and Butterflies," 72.

The paramount mission to create a more humane society also marked calls to reform literature, from Hu Shi's 胡適 tentative "Wenxue gailiang chuyi" 文學改良芻議 (Modest suggestions for a reform of literature; January 1917) and Chen Duxiu's strident "Wenxue geming lun" 文學革命論 (On literary revolution; February 1917) to Zhou Zuoren's 周作人 "Ren de wenxue" 人的文學 (Humane literature; December 1918) and Fu Sinian's 傅斯年 "Zhongguo wenyi jie zhi binggen" 中國文藝界之病根 (The source of the disease in China's literary circles; February 1919). Hu Shi presented eight proposals, including imperatives not to imitate the ancients, not to "moan without an illness," not to use allusions in a way reflecting "self-deception and a deception of others," and not to write parallel prose texts that "constrict people's freedom."[23] Opposing classical literature as aristocratic and full of "mountains and forests," meaning "escapist," Chen Duxiu called for a literature of political significance that would be "living and realist."[24] Referring to Tolstoy, Hardy, and Ibsen, Zhou Zuoren underscored the importance of individual emancipation and advocated the description of life based on a morality of love, wisdom, trust, and courage that would denounce inhuman practices and attacks on the individual.[25] Fu Sinian and his generation contested the "inert emotional passivity" of classical literature.[26]

These debates, hitherto confined largely to intellectual circles, took on new significance after May 4, 1919. On this day over 3,000 students protested the government's plan to accept the partial suspension of China's sovereignty stipulated in the Treaty of Versailles.[27] This and ensuing dem-

23. Hu Shi, "Wenxue gailiang chuyi."

24. Chen Duxiu, "Wenxue geming lun."

25. Zhou Zuoren, "Ren de wenxue."

26. Fu Sinian, "Zhongguo wenyi jie zhi binggen," 345, discussed in Schwarcz, *The Chinese Enlightenment*, 82.

27. The Treaty of Versailles transferred to Japan rights in Shandong province that China had under duress leased to Germany in 1898. The Chinese people had hoped that the Versailles Peace Conference would restore these rights to China and overturn the humiliating Sino-Japanese Treaty of May 25, 1915. These hopes were dashed by news reports on May 1, 1919, concerning secret agreements that imperiled China's sovereignty: First, in February 1917, Great Britain, France, and Italy had signed pledges to support Japan's claims in Shandong. Second, in September 1918, Duan Qirui's warlord government had secretly negotiated a loan from Japan to construct railroads and "gladly" agreed to seven points demanded by Japan in a secret exchange of notes. After the initial student demonstration, popular boycotts ensued in several cities, and the government backed down and declined to sign the treaty on June 28. The success of these protests encouraged the young

onstrations linked nationalism with cultural self-scrutiny and freedom from imperialism with the repudiation of feudal traditions. Although the immediate enemy was imperialism, and the immediate crisis was the Republic's degeneration into warlordism (1915–1928), the students blamed Chinese traditions for China's feeble response and chanted "Down with the Confucian family shop" (*dadao Kongjiadian* 打倒孔家店). Subsequent mass demonstrations, street speeches, and the larger May Fourth political movement popularized the use of the vernacular and promoted ideas advanced in journals such as *New Youth*.[28]

It is significant that May Fourth quickly became the dominant symbol for the longer New Culture movement. The affinity between the students' commitments and the ideas of the *New Youth* writers, many of whom were the students' teachers at Beijing University, can be seen in a manifesto published in the first issue of the student magazine *New Tide* in January 1919, just four months before the demonstrations:

> Most people in China today do not live what may be called a truly human life. They are fettered by destructive customs and rules of propriety that destroy individual integrity. We cannot help but be anguished and try to redress this injustice. Therefore, we call on all students in China to forsake the old examination system mentality and to adopt modern scientific thought. We must rid ourselves of arbitrary credulity and adopt the spirit of objective doubt. We must stand on the side of the future rather than the present [social system]. We must forge a temperament that might overcome society rather than be overcome by it.[29]

The decade between 1919 and the Japanese invasion of Manchuria in 1931 saw passionate literary activity devoted to doubting and scrutiny. Reviews published strident debates and trenchant new fictional works, almost all of which were written in the vernacular (*baihua* 白話) rather than the classical language (*guwen* 古文). With the founding of the Wenxue yanjiu hui 文學研究會 (Association for literary studies) in 1921, many writers proclaimed their commitment to humanitarian writing concerned with social problems and "Art for life's sake" (*wei rensheng*

---

intellectuals in their critique of Chinese culture. See Chow Tse-tsung, *The May Fourth Movement*, esp. 84–94, 166–67.

28. The first article to refer to May Fourth as a "movement" appeared within three weeks of the incident. Luo Jialun (writing under the pseudonym Yi 毅 [Resolute]), "Wusi yundong de jingshen," discussed in Schwarcz, *The Chinese Enlightenment*, 22.

29. "Xin chao fakan zhiqu shu," 2, quoted in Schwarcz, *The Chinese Enlightenment*, 2–3.

er yishu 爲人生而藝術).[30] In the same year, Chinese students in Japan founded the Chuangzao she 創造社 (Creation society), professing allegiance to European romanticism and the idea of *l'art pour l'art* (*wei yishu er yishu* 爲藝術而藝術).[31]

This latter position did not exclude nationalist preoccupations. Even for the Creationists, the need for self-expression was rooted in social responsibility and the "obsession with China" that pervades modern Chinese fiction.[32] If some writers increasingly focused on individual development as self-fulfillment, this shift was intimately connected with their mission to create a more humane society and, in turn, a stronger country.[33] To note a canonical example from China's first book of modern short stories, here is what the narrator-protagonist in Yu Dafu's 郁達夫 (1896–1945) famous story "Chenlun" 沉淪 (Sinking; 1921) writes in his diary: "Why did I come to Japan? . . . Is it any wonder that the Japanese treat you with contempt? China, O my China! Why don't you grow rich and strong? I cannot bear your shame in silence any longer."[34] Yet the reader must ask, for all his indignation, does the protagonist of Yu's story do anything at all for China? He writes in his diary. He reads the romantic poems of Wordsworth, the lyric poems of Heine and the eighteenth-century Chinese poet Huang Zhongze 黃仲則 (Huang Jingren 黃景仁). He engages in voyeurism and masturbation, tortures himself with guilt, and ultimately takes his own life. Do these activities help his country?

---

30. See "Wenxue yanjiu hui jianzhang." Prominent writers in the Association for Literary Studies included Shen Yanbing (Mao Dun), Ye Shengtao, Wang Tongzhao, Zhou Zuoren, Xu Dishan, and Zheng Zhenduo.

31. Prominent members of the Creation Society included Guo Moruo, Yu Dafu, Cheng Fangwu, Tian Han, and Zhang Ziping.

32. Scholarship on modern Chinese literature has been sensitive to writers' "obsession with China" ever since 1971 when C. T. Hsia formed his seminal thesis: "What distinguishes this 'modern' phase of Chinese literature alike from the traditional and Communist phases is rather its burden of moral contemplation: its obsessive concern with China as a nation afflicted with a spiritual disease and therefore unable to strengthen itself or change its set ways of inhumanity" ("Obsession with China," 533–34). Fredric Jameson argued a similar point in 1986 when he suggested that Third-World texts should be read as "national allegory" because these cultures do not have the public/private distinction that purportedly makes literature an independent realm in the West. See Jameson, "Third-World Literature," 69.

33. One of the most prominent creationists, Yu Dafu stressed writers' social responsibility in his "Wenxue gaishuo," esp. 79–83, discussed in Ng, *The Russian Hero*, 95.

34. Yu Dafu, "Sinking," 48.

Writers' lofty ambitions for fiction, ambitions that assumed a high degree of human agency, make all the more salient the short shrift so many works of the May Fourth period give to the possibility of human freedom. Why do these stories present a vision of life so unremittingly pessimistic? Do the disenchantment and defeatism of these works leave much room for choice and initiative? Why is there so little place for love, honor, or courage? How is it that for all its national allegory and political concerns, this writing seems confined to an aesthetic sphere isolated from the larger world? If such questions can be answered in a univocal manner, it might be because many of these texts project a logic that profoundly constricts human agency.

How should readers interpret this constriction of agency? Do these texts ask readers to accept severe limits on agency or does their presentation merely call attention to its limitations? If the latter, might the point be to lead readers to recognize its importance? Might failures to realize moral choice suggest that the formulation of such choices needs to be rethought? The focus on subjectivity was part of an effort to reexamine such questions. To consider the consequences of this intense concern with subjectivity, I turn to the ways these texts handle the dialectic of agency and determinism.

2. INTROSPECTION AND ALIENATION

The desire to focus on individual consciousness led to an explosion of new approaches to fiction writing. Writers adopted a wider variety of narrative modes and forms, including the modern short story.[35] Whereas traditional fiction generally portrayed a vast fictional world full of human adventure and great impersonal forces, these modern stories focused on concrete details of individual experience. The use of more explicit grammatical subjects and more obvious grammatical relations located perception and agency in individual characters and diminished the sense that their actions were determined by a pattern larger than that of simply their own lives.[36] At the same time, any resulting possibilities for agency were

35. May Fourth works continued to use the objective or rhetorical third-person and the subjective first-person modes widely used in late-Qing novels, but they added the third-person subjective and, occasionally, even the first-person objective and rhetorical modes. See Dolezelová-Velingerová, "Narrative Modes."

36. As Cyril Birch writes, "The old feeling of order disrupted and restored is gone: order

undercut by the rise of formal features and lexical elements that emphasized disjunction, unpredictability, and uncertainty.[37]

The refusal of an ultimate order was essential to the writers' very modern project of opposing tradition, its norms, and the conditions it takes for granted. Hence instead of creating the obvious enemies, easy solutions, and sense of resolution found in much traditional fiction, including some late-Qing novels, many modern stories offered a minimal sketch of a single character's subjective apprehension of reality. The focus on individual consciousness carried a tacit acknowledgment of the relativism and prejudice that mark any given perception.

The judgment that the world lacks a firm foundation is central to the experience of modernity, and the decision to turn inward is one way the modern writer can cope in an incomprehensible external world. In this way, the introspection and impressionism of these stories creates a distinct modernist aesthetic.[38] Gone is the pretense of constructing a fictional world capable of bestowing meaning; many of these early stories concern precisely the breakdown of such meaning, its possibility, and even its desirability. Yet a question remains: Did skepticism about traditional answers and the breakdown of faith in ultimate patterns create greater openings for human agency or further obstruct its realization?

If traditional fiction recounted heroic or supernatural tales to please or entertain, the new fiction submitted a confession, a painful truth designed to enlighten or chasten the reader.[39] Not surprisingly, the overdetermined notion of truth pledged by the confessional nature of this writing often turned out to be deceptive or unattainable. It was easier to break down received knowledge and put the lie to the pretensions of convention than to offer alternative models or new directions about where to turn. To portray the world in a more honest way, writers thus sought more to

itself is gone, the world is in chaos, any kind of happy ending unthinkable." See Birch, "Change and Continuity," 391.

37. For a careful analysis of stylistic developments, see Gunn, *Rewriting Chinese*, 10–13, 28–30, 95–108, and the relevant examples in the appendix.

38. Jenner stresses the importance of this aspect in "Is a Modern Chinese Literature Possible?": "A literature belonging fully to the modern world is a literature informed, or at least influenced, by the unprecedented and unending intellectual upheavals of the last century and more, as a result of which no knowledge can be regarded as absolute or permanent. . . . It is an awareness of the implications of change that counts, the sense of the abyss where earlier thinkers had seen firm ground" (195).

39. For the confessional nature of modern Chinese literature, see Leo Lee, *The Romantic Generation*, 58–123.

destroy old illusions than to depict a new truth. Perhaps for this reason, in many of these stories, some truer or more genuine event, experience, or revelation disrupts the narrative of everyday reality and the routine of everyday convention. Often connected with the human body (i.e., forces of hunger, violence, disease, sexual desire, and death), the "agent of demystification," as Marston Anderson names it, "resists orderly absorption into the world of fiction, and its irruption signifies the destabilizing presence of chaos, chance, and the arbitrary."[40] In so doing, it also casts doubt on the idea of an ultimate pattern.

To further this goal of exposing the lies of their society, many writers turned to realism.[41] Originally translated as *xieshi zhuyi* 寫實主義, "the doctrine of writing about reality," realism to these writers centered on the belief that a detailed examination of society would expose the distance between appearance and reality that they saw as buttressing repressive feudal traditions. To them it was axiomatic that people in positions of privilege would hide the workings of power and use false appearances to obscure the oppressive forces that waste human life.[42] As Gao Yuan 高元 wrote, "Secrets arise from the stealthy pursuit of self-interest."[43] This notion of a truth discoverable beneath the lies of tradition emerges in the founding work of modern Chinese fiction, Lu Xun's 1918 story "Kuangren riji" 狂人日記 (Diary of a madman):

Everything requires careful consideration if one is to understand it. In ancient times, as I recollect, people often ate human beings, but I am rather hazy about it. I tried to look this up, but my history has no chronology, and scrawled all over each page are the words: "Virtue and Morality." Since I could not sleep anyway,

40. Anderson, *The Limits of Realism*, 17.

41. In his discussion of the spirited polemics that surrounded writers' advocacy of the term "realism," Anderson suggests that it was the term's protean quality that made it so useful. See Anderson, *The Limits of Realism*, 6–7.

42. In his 1919 defense of the new poetry, Yu Pingbo leveled a direct indictment of his society's reluctance to accept the new literature's exposure of harrowing conditions: "If you want to understand why Chinese society refuses to accept new poetry, you must first understand the unseen side of Chinese social life. . . . It is miserable, dark. . . . So those who guide elite culture would prefer poetry to be cosmetic. They sanction love poems, vague descriptions of natural beauty. . . . They would prefer not to make public our society's many-layered domestic shame. . . . Because we insist on writing about all of that, they naturally hate us" (Yu, "Shehui shang duiyu xin shi de gezhong xinli guan," quoted in Schwarcz, *The Chinese Enlightenment*, 83).

43. Gao Yuan, "Fei mimi zhuyi," 667.

I read intently half the night, until I began to see words between the lines, the whole book being filled with the two words—"Eat People." (1: 281/10)[44]

Lu Xun depicts here the excruciating difficulty of living with the kind of insight that the madman briefly achieves. Conscious reflection and self-reflection may enable one to achieve a truer view of social reality, but, very often, this heightened awareness leads to alienation rather than to any increase of moral or personal autonomy. A crisis of consciousness emerges as characters awaken from their illusions not to truth but to a disorienting aporia. Lu's madman suffers a particularly acute case, but this affliction soon becomes endemic among the protagonists in May Fourth stories. It reaches a paroxysm in the works of the Creationists discussed at the end of this chapter. In these works, particularly those of Yu Dafu, the characters' insights and experiences often leave them suspended in complete moral abeyance. Seeing only what is wrong with the world, these characters fail to find any person, goal, or ideal to which to commit themselves.

Lu's first story is an extreme example of the debilitating paralysis that can result when heightened awareness isolates an individual as an enlightened but lonely spectator. The madman's paranoid ranting expresses Lu's incisive critique of Chinese culture, but it falls on deaf ears as the madman becomes increasingly estranged from other people:

Then I realized part of their cunning. They would never be willing to change their stand, and their plans were all laid; they had stigmatized me as a madman. . . .

. . . I had to speak to those people:

"You should change, change from the bottom of your hearts!" I said. "You must know that in future there will be no place for man-eaters in the world.

"If you don't change, you may all be eaten by each other. . . ."

Old Chen drove everybody away. My brother had disappeared. Old Chen advised me to go back to my room. (1: 289/17)

In pointing out how attention to subjectivity can lead to disaffection, I should emphasize that the authors themselves were acutely aware of this danger. In the second line of "Sinking," for example, Yu Dafu's narrator explicitly links his protagonist's alienation with his intense self-consciousness: "His emotional precocity had placed him at constant odds

44. "Diary of a Madman" first appeared in *Xin qingnian* 4.5 (May 1918). In this and subsequent references to Lu Xun's stories, the first term in the parentheses refers to the volume and page numbers in *Lu Xun quanji*. The second number refers to the location in the translation by Yang Hsien-yi and Gladys Yang, *Selected Stories*.

with his fellow men, and inevitably the wall separating . . . them had gradually grown thicker and thicker."[45] Lu Xun's narrators and characters also comment expressly on the separation between people. For example, the significance of Lu's "Gu xiang" 故鄉 (My old home; 1921) lies in the chilling realization made by the first-person narrator when he finds himself unable to speak to his childhood friend Runtu: "I felt a shiver run through me; for I knew then what a lamentably thick wall had grown up between us" (1: 353/60). Although the last lines of the story hint of a more hopeful attitude, they cannot eclipse the dejection expressed just a few lines earlier: "I only felt that all round me was an invisible high wall, cutting me off from my fellows, . . ." (1: 356–57/63). Such metaphors of isolation admit no sideshadows of possibilities for greater communication or compassion, and they are common in the works of other May Fourth writers as well, particularly Ye Shaojun 葉紹鈞 (Ye Shengtao 葉聖陶; 1894–1988) and Wang Tongzhao 王統照 (1897–1957).[46]

If the focus of these modern short stories is the estrangement of people from one another, it also problematizes the perception of a continuous self. The crowning example of subjective rationalizations resulting in a divided self, disabled for meaningful action, is Lu Xun's "Ah Q zhengzhuan" 阿Q正傳 (The true story of Ah Q; 1921) with the title character's "method of spiritual victory," seen in the following two quotations:

> In less than ten seconds, however, Ah Q would walk away also satisfied that he had won, thinking that he was the "foremost self-belittler" and after subtracting "self-belittler" what remained was "foremost." (1: 366–67/72)

> But presently he changed defeat into victory. Raising his right hand he slapped his own face hard twice, so that it tingled with pain. After this slapping his heart felt lighter for it seemed as if the one who had given the slap was himself, the one slapped some other self, and soon it was just as if he had beaten someone

---

45. Yu Dafu, "Sinking," 44.

46. As if to highlight the theme of estrangement, Ye Shaojun titled his first collection of stories *Gemo* 隔膜 (Barriers; 1922). Composed of stories published between 1919 and 1921, *Barriers* was the second published collection of modern Chinese short stories, and it exercised considerable influence. The stories depict oppression and alienation, especially as regards women, resulting from rapid social changes. Wang Tongzhao's early collection *Chunyu zhi ye* 春雨之夜 (Night of Spring Rain; 1924) also contains several inner monologues in which characters reflect on the difficulty of realizing love between people. See especially "Chensi" 沉思 (Deep thoughts), "Bianhen" 鞭痕 (Whip scars), and "Yiyin" 遺音 (Last tiding).

else—in spite of the fact that his face was still tingling. He lay down satisfied that he had gained the victory. (1: 368/74)

Stories such as "Diary of a Madman" and "The True Story of Ah Q" also modeled how a conspicuous narrator could make readers duly skeptical about the events recounted and could prevent them from identifying with a story's characters. Written in classical Chinese by a first-person narrator, the preface of "Diary of a Madman" constructs a frame that forcibly distances the reader from the events and colors any reading of the story. For before the reader even becomes acquainted with the madman's predicament, the narrator informs us that the diarist has since "recovered" and taken up an official post. The source of this information is the diarist's brother, whose account the reader has no immediate reason to doubt. The narrator then informs us that he has recorded several excerpts from the confused diary to provide to medical doctors. This casual comment downplays the significance of the narrator's omission of other parts of the diary, omissions that may have distorted the madman's message. This editing and its announced purpose also make the madman an object of research rather than the subject of his own story. Finally, we learn that the diarist himself suggested the title "A Diary of a Madman," implying a disavowal of his earlier insights.

By the end of the story, the reader's sympathy for the madman may render suspect the initial account concerning his "recovery." Furthermore, the ellipsis that follows the haunting last line, the imperative "Save the children," leaves open the story's ending. The diarist's physical absence makes it possible, though unlikely, that the diarist's brother or someone else did eat or otherwise harm the suffering madman. Of course, the more likely interpretation is that the ellipsis simply indicates an omission of further entries. Yet in this reading as well the punctuation draws attention to the diary's truncation. The dilemmas posed by the story are not resolved in the preface but are left up to the reader, calling on her to imagine what the diarist might have gone on to do in order to save the children, or how he might have come to terms with his renunciation of that goal.[47]

---

47. Theodore Huters calls attention to the precarious position in which the story leaves the reader and its implications for the possibility of moral choice: "The reader is confronted with only two alternatives to the madman's plight: continued total alienation from society or caving in to social pressure, both of which are manifestly unacceptable given the reality the story portrays. The paradoxical process of investing our sympathies in the writer of the diary, even after having been given an objective overview of the writer's

In part, Lu Xun's stories unsettle the reader by voicing the extreme discomfort of his narrators. In the preface of "The True Story of Ah Q," the narrator begins by expressing his reluctance to write an account of Ah Q and recounting how he postponed the task for two years in which the intention kept returning "like a ghost in [my] thoughts" (1: 359). He then enumerates four difficulties he encountered in writing his account, difficulties of choosing an appropriate title and contending with Ah Q's unknown surname, ancestry, and origin. This digression not only postpones the tale but also reveals the narrator's obtrusive need to distance himself from Ah Q. He even ostentatiously insists on their nonidentity: "[Might I call it] an autobiography? But I'm certainly not Ah Q!" (1: 359). The narrator goes on to create Ah Q, possibly the most tortured character in modern Chinese letters. Yet as the dual demons of external and internal persecution plague Ah Q, the narrator seems just as tortured, perhaps even more so, since his demons are left unexplored.

The intense subjectivity in Lu Xun's stories has a hermetic, suffocating quality. The madman and Ah Q are painfully self-conscious, perhaps as one can only be when losing one's mind. But the protagonists of Lu's later stories are hardly less ill at ease in their self-conscious roles as observers. From the madman and Ah Q to the narrators of "Zhufu" 祝福 (Benediction; 1924) and "Shangshi" 傷逝 (Regret for the past; 1925), these characters seem above all concerned with their projections of how others see them. I term this sort of subjectivity "spectatorial" to refer to the passive or even static state of a spectator and to distinguish it from the more dynamic predicament of a moral agent. Such unrelenting and debilitating self-consciousness plagues many of the May Fourth characters, from the narrator-protagonists in the first modern stories by Lu Xun and Yu Dafu to characters such as Ding Ling's 丁玲 (1904–1986) Sophie in "Shafei nüshi de riji" 莎菲女士的日記 (Diary of Miss Sophie; 1928) and beyond.

3. SPECTATORIAL CONSCIOUSNESS

At least three types of spectatorial consciousness can be identified in early May Fourth stories. All three diminish the sense of human agency. First, there is the spectral presence of the conspicuous narrator who tells many

final compromise, mirrors the agonizing reality of the choices for social action—or even the possibilities for significant choice—in the early May Fourth years" ("Blossoms in the Snow," 61–62).

of the stories. This non-omniscient narrator speaks in a way very different from that of earlier storytellers. A kind of disembodied reflector, this modern raconteur is usually at a loss as to how to tell the story, for he is, as Birch writes, "analyzing a world from whose power structure he feels himself to be alienated."[48]

Early examples of this type of spectatorial consciousness appear in Lu Xun's "Yao" 藥 (Medicine; 1919) and "The True Story of Ah Q." In "Medicine," the indirect use of description leaves the reader guessing about what is happening. She must piece together the story about the executed revolutionary out of clues given from the shifting perspectives of Old Shuan 老栓, Little Shuan 小栓, and Uncle Kang 康大叔 in the first three sections of the story and the two mothers in the final scene.[49] In "Ah Q," the staging of the public spectacle of punishment establishes an uneasy tension between the perspective of the third-person narrator and that of the victim. A significant consequence of this obtrusive, but disempowered narrator is that he is no longer an innocent storyteller—if indeed a narrator ever was or could be—but a kind of voyeuristic onlooker.

Significantly, the alienation conveyed by the narrators also positions the reader as an outsider. No longer a member of the audience merely listening to the story, the reader becomes an onlooker implicated and interrogated by its questions. In the penultimate line of "Medicine," the dead revolutionary's gray-haired mother mutters, "What does it mean?" (1: 310/33), and the reader is left with this question. In other stories, the questions are more strident. For example, in Yu Dafu's "Bodian" 薄奠 (A humble sacrifice; 1924), when the protagonist angrily demands what the passers-by want to see, the reader cannot but hear the question as addressed to her as well: "Pigs and dogs! Beasts! What are you looking at? My friend, this pitiful rickshaw puller, was driven to his death for you. What more [is there for] you to look at?"[50]

A second kind of spectatorship arises when the narrator appears on the scene as a character in the story but has virtually no possibility of affecting the outcome of the narrative. A hypnotic mood emerges in these

48. Birch, "Change and Continuity," 403.

49. In "Lu Xun's 'Medicine,'" Dolezelová-Velingerová analyzes the story's narrative technique in terms of "information manipulation" (222). One might ask whether the notion of "manipulation" ascribes a power to the author or narrator that Lu is humbly trying to relinquish.

50. Yu Dafu, *Yu Dafu wenji*, 1: 299.

stories, as psychic and external elements combine to create an ambiguous spectacle in which the observer cannot hope to participate. For example, in Lu Xun's "Yi jian xiao shi" 一件小事 (An incident; 1920), a rickshaw puller stops to help a woman he has hit, refusing to go on as his customer the narrator would have him do. The narrator's contemplation of the rickshaw puller as a policeman leads the man away underscores the moral wasteland the narrator finds within himself: "Indeed, the further he walked the larger he loomed, until I had to look up to him. At the same time he seemed gradually to be exerting a pressure on me, which threatened to overpower the small self under my fur-lined gown" (1: 323/43).

The narrator of Lu Xun's "Benediction" similarly struggles with moral discomfort in his passive recounting of the story of Xianglin's wife 祥林嫂. He begins the story by describing their meeting and his awkward equivocations in response to her questions regarding the existence of an afterlife. The following evening he learns of her death and reflects back as "fragments of her life, seen or heard before, now combined to form a whole" (2: 146/131).

The tragedy in the composition of this whole is that a set of man-made superstitions has needlessly driven Xianglin's wife insane. For the story inflicts Xianglin's wife with a misfortune unrelated to her own decisions. Furthermore, although life is unkind to Xianglin's wife, the immediate agent of cruelty is her society. To be sure, the wolves' brutal killing of Xianglin's wife's young son could only leave her bereaved, but the story casts sideshadows that show that she recovers the will within herself to find small pleasures thereafter. She wants nothing more than to tell her story and perform meaningful work. But the scholar's family views her as a "bad moral influence" and refuses to let her help prepare the New Year's sacrifice. Although her second marriage was forced by her in-laws, the villagers condemn her for having remarried and frighten her with stories about how after death the devil will cut her in half to appease her two husbands. Xianglin's wife does what she can to avoid this punishment: she saves up her wages and exchanges them for twelve silver dollars to buy a threshold at a temple. But such acts do not redeem her in the villagers' eyes. Their lack of compassion shows that Xianglin's wife errs in projecting mercilessness on the natural world of the unknown. It is the villagers who have caused her misery.

The human production of this fate is denied in part through the narrator's efforts to control Xianglin's wife's grief by making it an object of his story. One may read the story as the narrator's attempt to substantiate the quotation in his uncle's study that he notices near the beginning: "By understanding reason we achieve tranquility of mind" (2: 140/126). Yet the narrator's uneasiness betrays the silent pathos of the story: the nature of grief exceeds words. The repetition of Xianglin's wife's sorrowful tale cannot communicate the depth of her grief, and it cannot make the villagers care for her. The events can be communicated in words, but her wailing signals something more inchoate. The human connection for which she longs would call for sympathy, something none of the villagers is willing to sustain.

Furthermore, Xianglin's wife's ability to grieve points up the narrator's inability to do so, his lack of sympathy, and his failure to communicate authentically. In addition, the narrator has no one else with whom he can talk. As he listens to the sounds of the New Year festivities at the end of the story, he is very much alone. He proclaims his tranquility of mind, but in a way that is ultimately unconvincing: "The doubt which had preyed on me from dawn to early night was swept clean away by the atmosphere of celebration" (2: 162/143).

A third kind of spectatorial consciousness emerges when a character regards his or her actions as the scripted actions of a performer rather than as genuine risks taken by an autonomous agent. Chinese critics have long analyzed May Fourth works in terms of the dichotomy between *lijiao* 禮教 (the Confucian or feudal ethical code) and individualism. To deepen these analyses, a further distinction can be drawn between actions that essentially enact rules and norms—whether traditional or "modern"—and actions grounded in autonomously chosen commitments.

Most important, the heightened subjectivity in these works creates a self-consciousness that tortures the characters with a moral burden that often remains exclusively reflective. In some cases, there is an absence of moral consciousness altogether, or at least a willful refusal to recognize its prodding, as in Lu Xun's "Regret for the Past," discussed in a moment. In other cases, particularly in the first modern novels, a high level of moral consciousness emerges, but little sense of agency accompanies it. Debilitating guilt, depression, and suicide often result, as in Zhang Ziping's 張資平 (1893–1947) early novel *Chongjiqi huashi* 沖積期化石 (Fossils in alluvial deposits; 1922). Whether these works use first-person narration, as does Zhang, or third-person narration with interior monologue, as does Wang Tongzhao in depicting the fatalistic Li Tiangen 李天根 in *Yi ye* 一葉 (A leaf; 1922), they give the sense that the characters view themselves as if standing helplessly outside. They recognize their positions as individual agents and pangs of conscience plague them, but they have scant means to deploy this conscience in action. Although the characters perform actions, and these actions have effects, they remain spectators of both their interiority and their outward behavior. The extensive use of flashbacks in these novels contributes to this attenuation of agency insofar as these flashbacks backshadow a focus on an irremediable past at the expense of sideshadowing possibilities in an open present.

Because they situate the subject as a spectator, these works generally privilege the representation of an alienated consciousness over the casting of sideshadows that might fully engage dilemmas of moral agency. Often it is a consciousness that has utterly relinquished to the objective world power it might otherwise assume as its own, as can be seen in the readiness to embrace suffering exhibited by many of the characters in the early stories of Lu Yin 廬隱 (1889–1934) and Xu Dishan 許地山 (1893–1994). As an illustration, consider Lu Xun's "Regret for the Past," a story thematically very similar to "The Story of Yingying" discussed in Chapter 1. Like Scholar Zhang in the earlier tale, the protagonist of "Regret for the Past" recounts how he abandoned his lover, in this case telling her that he no longer loves her and thus driving her to leave. Yet when Juansheng 涓生 explains that "fate [*ming yun* 命運] had decided she should die knowing the truth I had told her—die unloved!" (2: 301/213), he appeals to fate as if he had done nothing. Whereas Scholar Zhang was caught in a moral struggle between conflicting obligations, the narrator-protagonist in "Regret for the Past" appears to have simply lost interest. This story, though told in the first person, diminishes any sense of human agency and moral responsibility that can be found therein. The narrator's rationalizations of his shabby action ring not only false but solipsistic and contrived, and the story's power relies on the ironic rift between the implied author's views and those of the protagonist. Juansheng's appeals to fate also underpin his discourse about the power of truth as something beyond human control. As Lydia Liu has argued, by insisting on allegiance to truth, Juansheng sets up a false dichotomy between truth and love that obscures the extent to which the meaning of and possibilities for individual freedom differ for men and women and thus disguises his self-centered desire to escape his ties to his lover.[51] Whereas "Yingying"

51. See Lydia Liu, *Translingual Practice*, 165–71.

sideshadows Zhang's account with Yingying's self-portrayal through her letters and poems, "Regret" allows Juansheng's lover no such voice.

Like "Regret for the Past," many of Lu Xun's stories leave the characters frozen in moral dilemmas with little hope of resolution. The token epiphany with which Lu sometimes ends these stories offers a metafictional gesture of consolation, but it may startle more than console, as in the ending of "Benediction" discussed above. Too honest to conceal the gap between perception and agency, Lu may have wanted these endings to force readers to perceive the meagerness of what the narrator's individual perception and efforts at understanding could offer in light of the irreducible, cruel realities he depicted.[52]

Lu Xun understood that ironic gestures rarely fully substitute for moral conviction, and so a sense of futility marks many of these stories. As mentioned in Chapter 1, one result of a subjectivity limited primarily to a capacity for observation is that the subject may come to conceive of consciousness as a kind of filter for perception rather than as a center of choice. Even when a character perceives the possibility of choice—of different interpretations or different courses of action—he or she is bereft of any basis for ranking them, rendering action arbitrary or meaningless.

4. DISILLUSIONMENT AND DETERMINISM

The pervasive theme of the futility of life or purposeful human action may result in part from some writers' desire to demonstrate their own maturity. In many of the May Fourth stories, characters publicize their disillusionment as an antidote for youthful ideals, although one can also read such statements as excuses for their abandonment. In Lu Xun's "Zai jiulou shang" 在酒樓上 (In the wine shop; 1924), for example, the narrator listens to his bygone friend Lu Weifu 呂緯甫 tell of his disillusionment:

> Yes, I still remember the time . . . how all day long we used to discuss methods of revolutionizing China until we even came to blows. But now I am like this, willing to let things slide and to compromise. Sometimes I think: "If my old

52. This point relates to Theodore Huters's insight that Lu Xun's use of the first-person mode may have been part of an effort to highlight the narrator's own moral responsibility and thereby to prevent readers from misconstruing his stories in ways that critics subsequently did. See Huters, "Blossoms," 72–74.

friends were to see me now, probably they would no longer acknowledge me as a friend." But this is what I am like now. (2: 170/149)

In place of his revolutionary aspirations, Lu Weifu seems to have resigned himself to a fatalism evident in his retelling of an account of the young Ah Shun's 阿順 death:

"If her man was really not as good as Chang Keng, that would be truly frightful! . . . Obviously he must really have been a good man, and everything Chang Keng said was false. It was only a pity Ah Shun believed such a rascally liar, and died for nothing. But we can't blame anyone else: this was Ah Shun's fate" [literally: Ah Shun simply did not have this lot of good fortune]. (2: 175/153)

Although growing disillusionment was certainly genuine and heartfelt in a writer such as Lu Xun, it may have become contagious, secondhand, and even programmatic among younger May Fourth writers. A kind of wiser-than-thou attitude underlies many of these expressions of disillusionment. Rather than admit that some things are beyond their understanding and then seek to identify what they can do within those limits, many characters throw up their hands and bemoan the cruelty of the world, all the while congratulating themselves for seeing its true colors.

What I find disheartening about the meekness and resignation that mark these narratives is that there often creeps in a note of disdain toward the characters. Sometimes it is as if the authors themselves have grown impatient with the characters' resignation. In several cases, impatience and disrespect toward the characters seem to emerge and grow in the course of an author's career. The works of Ye Shaojun illustrate such a shift in attitude.

Whereas most of Ye's early stories expressing his disapproval of society end sadly, they in no way disparage the value of the characters' sincere efforts to avoid their tragic ends. For example, in his early story "Zhe ye shi yi ge ren" 這也是一個人 (This is also a person; 1919), later retitled "Yi sheng" 一生 (A life), a young woman runs away from her oppressive, arranged marriage and manages for a brief time to choose a more humane life.[53] Even if, in the end, she can control her destiny no more than might a cow, the story highlights her bravery. She does all she can, and the fact that others force her to resume her former role as an animal to be bought and sold does not belittle the judiciousness of her efforts. She fails

53. "Zhe ye shi yi ge ren" was first published in *Xin chao* 1.3 (1919). Ye changed the title to "Yi sheng" for his 1922 collection *Gemo*.

to free herself from her obligations to her husband's family not because of any fault of her own, nor because she attempted the impossible, but because in order to succeed she must depend on the cooperation and support of others. That she comes close to securing this support, which her employer initially extends until his wife dissuades him from accepting the attendant risks, underscores the reasonableness of her endeavor. Since nothing forecloses the sideshadowed possibility that her employer might have chosen differently, the story leaves open the possibility that in the future such people might find courage.

In marked contrast to the empathy Ye evokes in his early stories, in his novel *Ni Huanzhi* 倪煥之 (Ni Huanzhi; 1928) and later stories, he seems to condemn the servility of his characters. This scorn toward the characters strikes me as unjust in the context of the increasingly deterministic framework in which he sets them. For as Ye matured as a writer, he subscribed to a kind of social determinism, and in many of his works he depicts a ruthless world in which sustained courage would require such superhuman hopefulness as to represent a kind of lunacy. Yet because his attention to social forces does not eclipse his intense concern for depicting characters' individual decisions, the impression remains that the characters bear responsibility for their sad lots. Like many other authors, Ye seems to grow angry at the characters at the same time that he renders them incapable of more responsible action. The result is often a refusal of dignity.[54]

The fact that some authors may have identified with their characters does not mean that they were without condescension. One can be condescending toward oneself, for such is the stuff of shame. Shame may even be a likely consequence of extreme self-consciousness when introspection fails to yield some corresponding measure of moral autonomy.

Writers' desires to renew the national character provide a second reason that the new focus on uncovering the depths of inner consciousness may have led to a preoccupation with feelings of shame. Any program committed to making people more fully human, such as the New

---

54. The early stories of Xu Dishan are a notable exception to the trend of authors' implying that their characters bear responsibility for their fates despite the social determinism stressed in the works. Xu's stories are among the most fatalistic of the May Fourth works, but Xu seems to approve of rather than condemn his characters' resignation, which usually accords with a religious worldview, either Buddhist or Christian. See Xu, *Zhui wang laozhu*.

Culture movement, is likely to breed pride and hence its shadow of shame. As theoretical writings proclaimed the goal of making people more human, fiction writing expressed shame about not being sufficiently human. Such an obsessive focus on shame can be traced back to Lu Xun's "Diary of a Madman": "When those who eat men compare themselves with those who do not, how ashamed they must be. Probably much more ashamed than the reptiles are before monkeys" (1: 288/15).

The notion of evolution implied by the reference to reptiles and monkeys in this passage has significant implications for a reading of the potential for human agency. On one hand, it implies a responsibility to be better than beasts.[55] On the other hand, belief in evolution can also bolster a deterministic view in which China's predicament could be attributed to natural causes rather than being the moral responsibility of its intellectuals.

Consciousness of evolution raises the crucial question about whether the characters evolve. For fictional characters can act in at least four ways: (1) they can remain static representatives of social types; (2) they can change in ways causally determined by internal factors, such changes having been programmed by their character type or psychology; (3) they can change in ways causally determined by external factors; or (4) they can change, at least in part, as a result of their own decisions and, potentially, so as to further their own commitments and projects.

Many of the early May Fourth stories seem to contain some element of choice, even when that choice is misbegotten. Personal choice sometimes plays a role even when a heightened subjectivity leads characters to conceive of themselves as predetermined entities and not as agents capable of choosing their values and actions. For example, in Lu Xun's 1925 story "Guduzhe" 孤獨者 (The loner), the narrator explicitly comments on how reading fiction about inner psychology can lead people to adopt stock romantic postures: "As a result, probably, of reading 'Sinking,' they constantly referred to themselves as 'the young unfortunate' or 'the outcast'; and sprawling on big chairs like lazy and arrogant crabs, they would sigh, smoke and frown all at the same time" (126/180). In the original Chinese, this passage conveys a double entendre that is lost in the English. The English translation reads that they "referred to themselves

55. The notion that humans are distinct from and superior to animals has a long history in Chinese thought, dating back at least to the *Li ji* 禮記 (Record of ritual): "If a person is without ritual, although one can speak, is not one's heart that of a beast?" (1A.3a).

as the 'young unfortunate,'" but the Chinese *zi ming wei* 自命爲 has a second meaning of "fated themselves to be": "They fated themselves to be 'the young unfortunate' or 'the outcast.'" Reading psychological fiction may have led them to limit themselves to fixed, passive identities.

Though it may be overreading the text, this second interpretation points to the gap between writers' goals concerning the effects of their works and their actual effects. Works by writers such as Lu Xun and Ye Shaojun usually imply that although characters may be shaped by outside forces, they are not determined by them. At the same time, these writers often drew characters as symbols of general types, and a type is by definition determined. The resultant determinism was reinforced by these writers' reluctance to demonstrate positive outcomes. Perhaps they believed that to paint a positive picture would be dishonest, but, taking these works as a whole, a certain bad faith marks the way they set up and then condemn their characters.

As a result, despite certain fine renderings of experience, an almost programmatic gloom marks these works. To call attention to suffering and expose social injustice without offering a way to escape leads to the "iron-house problem" Lu Xun articulated in the preface (1922) to his first collection of short stories, *Nahan* 吶喊 (Battlecries; 1923):

> Imagine an iron house without windows, absolutely indestructible, with many people fast asleep inside who will soon die of suffocation. But you know since they will die in their sleep, they will not feel the pain of death. Now if you cry aloud to wake a few of the lighter sleepers, making these unfortunate few suffer the agony of irrevocable death, do you think you are doing them a good turn? (1: 274/5)

The pain of these conflicts may account for the speed with which many intellectuals turned from calls for an active, creative, and even antagonistic self toward the representation of social forces that limit the possibilities for freedom.[56] After the early stories, the next wave of fic-

---

56. This formulation was inspired by Kirk Denton's discussion of Hu Shi's early retreat: "In his 1918 essay 'Ibsenism,' Hu favored the radical individualism exemplified by the egoistic characters in Ibsen's plays: the individual as an antagonist to society, one who will lead society out of its darkness by offering an enlightened example. . . . In his 'The Anti-Individualist New Life' (1920), . . . Hu retreated from that earlier radicalism to focus on the external social factors that shape and give meaning to the life of the individual. The latter position posits a far more passive self that changes only with the outer material world" ("General Introduction," 44–45).

tion writing went in two main directions. The first direction placed great stress on individual subjectivity, severing the individual from the larger environment. The second brought out social factors and the way they call the individual's behavior into question. Here I briefly discuss the first direction, the delving into subjectivity; the rise of social fiction will be the subject of Chapter 4.

5. A ROMANTICISM GONE SOUR

Heavily influenced by European romanticism and the Japanese I-novel (*watakushi-shōsetsu* 私小説), writers in the Creation Society exerted perhaps as great an influence as the more humanitarian writers affiliated with the Association for Literary Studies.[57] To separate and compare the influence of the two schools is moreover misleading given their considerable interaction, an example of which is Lu Xun's reference to Yu's "Sinking" discussed above. Nonetheless, speaking in broad terms, the works of the Creationists were distinctive because they wrestled with existential questions primarily through explorations of individual subjectivity, whereas the humanitarian writers usually situated self-searching more fully in the context of the subject's social relations with other people. Writers such as Lu Xun, Ye Shaojun, and Mao Dun 茅盾 (1896–1981) depicted intellectual protagonists caught between public commitments to better society and private self-searching; the Creationists often constructed the second as an insurmountable barrier to the first.

Průšek suggests that the motivation for the Creation writers' inward turn lay not in an effort to extol the exceptional individual but in an effort to express the common predicament of the individual crushed by society, traditional mores, and "family despotism":

> In a society in which the main task was the fight against the remnants of feudalism it was necessary to show what a person looks like in reality and what his

---

57. According to Patrick Hanan, the first "I-novel" in Chinese was probably *Qin hai shi* 禽海石 (Stones in the sea; 1906). Yet as Hanan points out, this novel was a rather obscure work, however undeservedly so. See Hanan, "Introduction," in *The Sea of Regret*, 10. More scholarly attention could be paid to the influence of early Japanese autobiographical works such as Shimazaki Tōson's 島崎藤村 *Hakai* 破戒 (The broken vow; 1906) and Tayama Katai's 田山花袋 *Futon* 蒲團 (The futon; 1907), both of which were highly influential at a time when many Chinese writers were studying in Japan. For the Japanese works read and translated, see Cheng Ching-mao, "The Impact of Japanese Literary Trends."

inner life is, what his desires, needs and feelings are, in order to break the false morality and untrue stereotyped assertions about man and his feelings that were repeated in feudal works of ethics and literature.[58]

Focus on subjectivity was essential to show the nature of these compulsions. Without knowledge of this context, however, the reader may ask why the writers have their characters engage in this form of self-analysis. For introspection and self-analysis not balanced by attempts at communication or action often end in a dreary complacency or outright suicidal despair. Since most of their characters stop well short of exploring how a more developed sense of self could lead to ethical agency, the Creationists' stories seem to suggest that masochistic self-exposure might be enough. Such solipsism, the belief that only one's own self is knowable, is especially prominent in works exalting the alienated individual.

For example, in the collections *Chenlun* (Sinking; 1921) and *Hanhui ji* 寒灰集 (Cold ashes; 1927), Yu Dafu often conveys a romanticized surging of inner impulses, but the source of these impulses is left unclear, as is the question of whether they may affect individuals in any way more positive than simply overwhelming them in a sea of emotions. The attention to the self and to the dark power of sexuality allows brave reflection on topics perhaps more easily repressed, but the endless ruminations on the protagonists' failures and shortcomings, intense feelings of shame, and the involuntary nature of masturbatory compulsions create a morbid complacency.

Such despair and its introspective focus derived in part from Yu's and other Creation writers' interest in European literary movements. These writers were particularly taken with romanticism, symbolism, and the decadents, but their theoretical writings also mention Bergson and Freud. In light of these multiple sources of inspiration, it is worth asking why the Creation writers accorded such a central place to expressions of futility.

The question is particularly pertinent given that most of the Creationists spent years studying in Japan, and, like Yu's protagonist quoted earlier, they were acutely distressed by China's lack of prestige and their sense of inferiority vis-à-vis the Japanese. In the context of these concerns, despondency is a strange response. Yet the futility and shame in other May Fourth works reaches a paroxysm in the "superfluous man" (*duoyu de ren* 多餘的人) of the Creationists. Yu's protagonist in "Lingyuzhe" 零餘者 (The superfluous man; 1927) articulates the feeling of futility that

58. Průšek, "Introduction to *Studies*," 71.

haunts most of Yu's protagonists: "I am a superfluous man and nothing more. I am entirely useless to mankind and society. A superfluous man! A useless man! Superfluous! Superfluous. . . ."[59]

Yu's fellow Creationist Guo Moruo 郭沫若 (1892–1978) also focuses on the shame of being Chinese in his early works, especially in "Xinglu nan" 行路難 (Hardships of wandering), the second part of his collection *Ganlan* 橄欖 (Olives; 1926), and in his short epistolary novel *Luo ye* 落葉 (Fallen leaf; 1926). In *Fallen Leaf*, Guo presents a series of 41 letters from a young Japanese nurse, Kikuko 菊子, to the Chinese student she loves, Hong Shiwu 洪師武. The tragedy of the novella lies in the fact that although the characters exercise agency, their actions cannot accomplish their goals because they are ignorant of crucial facts about their situation. Kikuko never learns why Hong rejected her, but the futility of her suffering is conveyed in the novel's preface: the narrator explains that Hong needlessly ran away because he falsely believed he had syphilis. Privileged with this information before reading Kikuko's letters, the reader can still choose to read the novella as a story of impossible love, but the backshadowing of the would-be lovers' senseless separation renders the despair and introspection of the letters pathetic. The influence of Goethe's *Die Leiden des jungen Werthers* (The sorrows of young Werther; 1774), which Guo translated in 1921,[60] is evident, but the novella may strike readers as a somewhat maudlin variation.

The moral dilemmas posed by solipsism come to the fore with the rise of explicitly autobiographical modern novels with sustained inner monologues such as Yu Dafu's *Miyang* 迷羊 (Lost sheep; 1928) and Guo Moruo's *Wo de younian* 我的幼年 (Years of my youth; 1929). These novels furthered the May Fourth project of differentiating experience as lived through the senses and emotions from experience as grasped by the mind and in discourse.[61] Still, although the extended first-person monologues

59. Yu, *Yu Dafu wenji,* 3.88. The translation is by Mau-sang Ng, *The Russian Hero,* 100. The use of the English word "superfluous" in the original suggests the influence of foreign literature in shaping the construction of the alienated individual in May Fourth fiction. In an extended study, Ng argues that the origins of the divided intellectual protagonist lie in the superfluous man of nineteenth-century Russian literature; see Ng, *The Russian Hero.*

60. Guo's translation, *Shaonian Weite de fannao* 少年維特的煩腦, was immensely popular and apparently provoked a wave of suicides. For the novel's influence on May Fourth writers and its place in their writings, see Leo Lee, *The Romantic Generation,* 283–86.

61. In his preface in the reprinted edition, entitled *Wo de tongnian* 我的童年 (My

create a lyrical, subjective effect, some of the subject matter grows tiresome. Yu's narrator-protagonist, Wang Jiecheng 王介成, for example, details at great length his suffering from a nervous disorder, his physical self-scrutiny in the mirror (73–74), his concentration on his actress girlfriend's clothes and cosmetics (109, 129), his worries that his sexual overexcitement may be depleting his strength (130), his fears of abandonment (131), and his feelings of inadequacy next to his girlfriend's increasingly healthy body (132). After she leaves him, he recounts his search for her, but here too the action is secondary to his feelings that he can't go on living without her (153) and his declarations about his "bleeding heart" (156). Though the novel excels in its lyricism, the seriousness with which such first-person narrators take their inner selves and expect the reader to take them suggests a certain lack of perspective or proportion. As Theodore Huters writes, "Mere subjective impulse was often taken as a profound statement about external reality."[62]

For this reason, whereas Leo Lee makes an important point in characterizing these writers as "the Romantic generation of modern Chinese writers," it may help to remember that this wave of Chinese romanticism was from the outset a romanticism gone sour. Perhaps it was romantic yearnings that generated disappointment and dejection, but it is the dejection that lingers. The unhappy characters are terribly guilt ridden and anxious for redemption through love or private matters, but they demonstrate little interest in the larger projects or social concerns that mark the early May Fourth works.

What is nonetheless important about these characters' guilt and their attempts to expiate it is the implication that the characters assume some measure of responsibility for having created their situation. The persistent sense of responsibility in these works supports Huters's argument that the young romantic writers may have been as influenced by Neo-Confucianism as by European literature.[63] At the same time, the element of accountability implicit in confession is often limited to backshadows

childhood years), Guo denies any intention to follow the confessional writings of Augustine, Rousseau, Goethe, or Tolstoy and writes that he wanted to show how "this type of society produced this type of man"; see Guo, *Wo de tongnian*, 2. Yet although his novel offers insights into the social forces that surrounded him, the narrator is clearly most interested in his own precocious literary and sexual development.

62. Huters, "Blossoms," 55.

63. Huters, "Blossoms," 50.

of regret over the missed opportunities of the past. Such regret falls short of an assumption of responsibility for the future. Like more communal forms of nostalgia, an introspection focused on the past very often refuses the future. It was a need to work more pragmatically for the future that led to the rise of social fiction.

4

Social Fiction: Must Context Entail Determinism?

> Men make their own history, but they do not make it just as they please; they do not make it under circumstances chosen by themselves, but under circumstances directly encountered, given and transmitted from the past. The tradition of all the dead generations weighs like a nightmare on the brain of the living.
>
> —Karl Marx

Two decades after late-Qing thinkers extolled literature's power to reform people's consciousness and a decade after the May Fourth iconoclasts called for a literary revolution, by the late 1920s modern consciousness had found firmer roots and fiction writing devoted to its pursuit was becoming less awkwardly self-conscious. Since "modern consciousness" here refers to an awareness of a breakdown of traditional ideological foundations, to ascribe "roots" to such a perception of change may seem paradoxical. Yet awakenings are seldom as spontaneous as is sometimes thought, either for individuals or for social groups. They often occur in stages, the order of which may vary in different contexts. The early May Fourth works seemed to yell: "Stop! We cannot accept our society's inhumanity as a matter of course." The social fiction written from the late 1920s into the early 1940s answered this injunction with a more patient proposal: "Let us examine this course."

I refer to the dominant trend during this period as "social fiction" because of authors' rising concern to represent society and social relations. This attention to the social world departed from the more limited focus on individual awakening in early May Fourth works. Of course, depictions of individual consciousness continued, but less often as the dominant focus. Instead, writers created broader treatments of social conditions, economic and historical forces, and, increasingly, class relations and consciousness. The first stage of critical realism, focusing on minute portrayals of individual perception, gradually yielded to writers' efforts to measure their world in a naturalistic vein.

This shift altered the nature of fiction writing in two significant ways. First, the social fiction testified to a growing concern for context. These writers were not turning away from the urgent question "What am I to do?" that haunts the early May Fourth stories. They were tackling that question with an appreciation of its difficulty. Namely, the increasing scope of these literary works suggests a new willingness to place ethical questions within a concrete social framework. Such frameworks almost invariably contain limitations, but it is precisely the appraisal of these limitations and the courage to find and grasp moments of choice within them that mark ethical action and distinguish it from abstract reasoning and reflection. For, as ethicist Alasdair MacIntyre writes, "I can only answer the question of 'What am I to do?' if I can answer the prior question 'Of what story or stories do I find myself a part?'"[1]

The second development in this period is a heightened concern for time. To identify the stories of which one is a part, one must approach, ascertain, and live these narratives all in medias res. In order for moral agency to have a place, an author must depict context as dynamic rather than as an already written story or one unfolding according to a set script. Although many everyday reflections assume a concept of time as an ongoing duration in which space exists for the creation of new possibilities, it is not easy to present such a conception in fiction. As writers craft works to have structure, unity, and closure, they may wittingly or unwittingly oversimplify the presentation of time to achieve these goals. Thus increased attention to context may as easily diminish as increase the scope for human agency.

In this chapter, I explore the rise of social fiction and its concern with time and context, and I discern the development of two opposing tendencies: Some works of social fiction use sideshadowing to transcend the solipsistic fatalism of earlier works and depict the temporal and social dimension of experience necessary for choice and the exercise of agency. Other works suggest that possibilities for human freedom are often shut down by distinctly "modern" determinisms founded on belief in the decisive power of economic structures or teleological conceptions of time and history.

---

1. MacIntyre, *After Virtue*, 216.

1. THE RISE OF SOCIAL FICTION

As discussed in Chapter 3, the early May Fourth works clearly registered a perception of change and an awareness of lost foundations that characterize a shift to a modern consciousness. Because many writers viewed a reappraisal or even a rejection of traditional ideological foundations as indispensable for the betterment of their society and the strengthening of their country, they deliberately crafted their works with formal and thematic elements to mark their departure from past traditions. Having assumed a mission to change people's consciousness and cure the nation's spirit, writers designed their stories to jolt readers from their uncritical acceptance of customs and conventions. The immediacy of their message makes these works honest and trenchant, if strident and frequently spasmodic. Yet the pain of their vision plagues the early May Fourth protagonists with such weariness and emotional numbness that, like an invisible veil, these afflictions seem to separate them from the larger world.

The early May Fourth characters' emotional distance from the events upon which they reflect is compounded by a sense of temporal distance. For, in the brevity of the short stories and the retrospective nature of the epistolary novels and diaries, many of these works show but modest interest in time. Similarly, in these works' pronounced desire to critique falsehood and expose their inhuman society, they pay less attention to that society's historical situation and ongoing evolution. By portraying an individual's revelations about the way things are rather than a concern for the way they are becoming, such works downplay the sense of time. Many protagonists bemoan the lack of opportunity to change their oppressive circumstances, but the weight of their vision exhausts and incapacitates them, forestalling action.[2] The present upon which they reflect seems set and inescapable.

The combination of emotional and temporal distance often disables the possibility for agency in these works. An aura of fatalism results whereby destiny seems to have predetermined the events and the characters' efforts to avoid their fate are often revealed to be instruments of that fate. More precisely, since these works prioritize the reflection on experience over

2. Regarding the hopelessness of intervention, consider Leo Lee's comment on Yu Dafu's "Ganshang de xinglü" (Sentimental journey; 1929), "Yü Ta-fu's [Yu Dafu's] traveler is no longer a free spirit like Lao Ts'an [Can], but a frustrated, bitter, and harassed man who is at a loss to cope with the complexities of modern life." See Lee, "The Solitary Traveler," 292.

the unfolding of experience, individuals seem to view themselves as having *already* become the instruments of fate. Since the characters feel too helpless to act, introspection takes on a compensatory importance. If one cannot change the world, one can at least record one's objections and the pain of one's predicament. Faced with chaos and barbarity, the characters seek refuge, meaning, and honesty in critical self-reflection.

Whereas writers had already for several years written theoretical works skeptical about the wisdom of privileging a focus on individual consciousness,[3] the May Thirtieth movement of 1925 (*Wusa yundong* 五卅運動) and subsequent history drove home the urgent need to portray social and historical circumstances. By recalling these historic events and viewing writers' increasing attention to context as a reaction to them, one can avoid misinterpreting the rise of social realism as predetermined by some natural progression of literary genres.[4] Appreciating its political urgency also helps to defend social realism from the charge that it represented a retreat from the modernism of many early May Fourth works.[5]

The rise of social fiction followed on the heels of a series of violent events. In the May Thirtieth Incident of 1925, police in the employ of the British fired on demonstrators protesting the death of a Chinese worker in a Japanese-owned factory in Shanghai, igniting anti-imperialist strikes and boycotts throughout China. As depicted in Hu Yepin's 胡也頻 (1905–31) novel on the incident, *Guangming zai women de mianqian* 光明在我們的面前 (The light is before us; 1930), intense feelings of national humiliation led activists to work at once for national revolution, awakened the consciousness of even the less-engaged writers, and led to a sudden surge in Chinese Communist Party membership.[6] The increasing influence of those advocating a thoroughgoing social revolution in turn alarmed Chiang Kai-shek's 蔣介石 financial backers and prompted

---

3. For a discussion of the negative image of individualism as bourgeois ideology and an obstacle to socialism, see Lydia Liu, *Translingual Practice*, 88, 96–99.

4. The fact that many writers read, translated, and modeled their fiction on works of Western realism and naturalism should not mislead one into thinking that the rise of these genres occurred according to a sequence of stages analogous to developments in European literature. Such reflections may, moreover, instill skepticism about the way literary historians posit such lines of development in the first place.

5. On the "modernism" of Lu Xun's writings, see Sabin, "Lu Xun."

6. CCP membership rose from around 1,000 at the beginning of 1925 to around 20,000 by the middle of 1926. On the rise of Communism in China, see Dirlik, *The Origins of Chinese Communism*.

Chiang's bloody purge of the Communists in 1927.[7] This sudden rupture of the first United Front (1923–1927) began a decade of political division and social disruption that did not stem the outpouring of literary works but did transform the nature of debate.[8] Even many of the most ardent Creationists turned away from individualism, pessimism, and their call for "art for art's sake" to advocate and write "revolutionary literature" (*geming wenxue* 革命文學).[9]

In works written after 1927, the overriding sense of shock and stasis of the early May Fourth works gives way to more warm-blooded characters who face at least the possibility for meaningful action. Making subjectivism and individualism the primary foci became at best a luxury the country could ill afford. At worst such foci seemed a remnant of the Confucian concern with self-cultivation or a Daoist passivity that many intellectuals since the New Culture movement were seeking to contest as barriers to progress. Self-examination may be an essential step toward responsible action, but confining one's quest for freedom to inner reflections seemed similar to Ah Q's method of spiritual victory. In this limited sense, the two camps of May Fourth writers had embraced the same Weltanschauung. Both those writing "art for art's sake" and those writing "art for life's sake" seemed to be writing "art for self's sake." As a result, expressions of concern for the victims of an inhuman society often turned into an exaltation of the sensitive observer's own spiritual distress. In the late 1920s, the Nationalists' war on the Communists gave new urgency to the examination of social institutions and political commitments.

---

7. Chiang's coup began the White Terror (*baise kongbu*) and precipitated the Chinese Communist Party's independent leadership of a revolutionary war. In addition to ending cooperation between the Communists and the Nationalists, the coup also briefly divided the Nationalist Party itself into a left wing based in Wuhan and Chiang's forces in Shanghai.

8. While the production of literature continued apace during this period, the Nationalists assassinated several important writers for their political activities. The most famous executions occurred on February 7, 1931, when the Nationalists machine-gunned to death Hu Yepin, Rou Shi, three other writers, and eighteen other revolutionaries. See Wong, *Politics and Literature*, 100.

9. Although an increasingly activist orientation is evident in articles published throughout the 1920s, the notion of revolutionary literature was given its classic theoretical formulation by Cheng Fangwu in early 1928. See Cheng, "Cong wenxue geming dao geming wenxue." For earlier calls for engaged literature, see Gálik, *The Genesis*, esp. chaps. 5, 6, and 9.

Formal changes corresponded to this epistemological shift. Since social fiction depicts relations, and relations take place over time, this mode generally required longer treatments. Beginning in the late 1920s, more of the longer stories were written and the novel reemerged as a major genre. Although these novels are still often situated in a fatalistic worldview, their narratives grapple with the temporal dimension of selfhood in a more concrete way than did the circumscribed musings of the early May Fourth works.

These works still establish the protagonists' sensitivity, horror, and objections, but they also confront the perils of actual engagement. Many late 1920s novels center on this problem of political engagement: Mao Dun's 茅盾 (1896–1981) trilogy *Shi* 蝕 (Eclipse; 1927–1928), Ye Shengtao's *Ni Huanzhi*, Hong Lingfei's 洪靈非 (1903–1933) *Liuwang* 流亡 (Exile; 1928), Ba Jin's 巴金 (1904–2005) *Miewang* 滅亡 (Destruction; 1929), and Rou Shi's 柔石 (1901–1931) *Eryue* 二月 (February; 1929). With their characters' desperate desire to embrace grand visions and causes, these works testify to people's need for hope and action. In each of these novels, however, an intense subjectivism yields both a utopian vision of the possibilities of human action and, as characters discover the difficulty of such action, a deep pessimism. These characters yearn to join a larger struggle to improve society, but political engagement leads to irreconcilable individual conflicts, often involving a break with family or the rupture of a romance.

The fatalism explicit in these early modern novels is remarkable, and it is occasionally so extreme as to question the feasibility of political programs as a solution. Consider, for example, Jing's 靜 resignation to fate in *Huanmie* 幻滅 (Disillusion), the first part of Mao Dun's *Eclipse*:

> She wasn't willing to think about the past, and she didn't dare think of the future. Human beings are but the playthings of fate. Who could escape the sowing of fate? Who could say that today's plans based on one's own wishes would not be lightly but completely overturned by fate's poisonous hand tomorrow? The blows of her past experiences were so harsh that Jing no longer dared have confidence, no longer dared have hope. Now she [could] only live mechanically. She had already decided to return home after leaving the hospital. [Her] future affairs would simply be in accordance with fate's control. (1: 51–52)[10]

10. Page numbers refer to Mao Dun, *Mao Dun quanji*. Translations are my own.

Does an author need to paint such a desperate and fatalistic character for a revolutionary call to become meaningful? Perhaps such expressions show the extent to which Mao Dun consciously struggled to shore up faith in human will, perhaps even his own faith, at a time when fatalism was a widespread and tempting way to adjust psychologically in the face of China's dire predicament.

Mao Dun contrasts voluntarism and fatalism countless times in his early novels, and often with seemingly little attempt to transform political sermon into fiction. In *Disillusion*, a doctor first challenges Jing's fatalism: "How can you superstitiously believe in fate? . . . Those of us who have been baptized by science should no longer be superstitious" (1: 53). Jing's discouragement about the limits of her abilities is then rebutted by a friend as he urges her to accompany them to Wuhan to do revolutionary work: "As for the problem of individual ability, not everyone is a hero of indomitable spirit. Reforming society is not something one or two heroes can achieve. The age of heroes has already passed. Now it's the age when people of common sense and above are joining forces to create history" (1: 57). As Jing wavers between pessimism and the attraction of new ideals, these two voices war inside her head, but the voice of voluntarism wins out in her conscious deliberations:[11] "Fate is no more than the vain self-comfort of the defeated, no more than the explaining away of ridicule by the cowardly. People's future can only be determined by their own will and hard work" (1: 58). Yet Mao Dun resists an easy dismissal of fate, and his narrator slips fate back into the equation at the end of the chapter. As Jing leaves Shanghai for Wuhan, the narrator's description is that "following the assignment of fate, she left to seek her new life. Although there was decidedly no trace of the word 'fate' in Miss Jing's mind" (1: 60).

After the Japanese invasion of Manchuria in 1931, the threat of territorial dismemberment further propelled writers to create a revolutionary literature. To citizens of a country risking annihilation, it may seem that nothing is worse than paralysis. Some writers thus sought to move beyond fatalism by turning to the analysis of socioeconomic conditions. Suggesting that "Symphony of Fate" would make a fitting title for Mao's early works *Eclipse*, *Hong* 虹 (Rainbow; 1929), and *Lu* 路 (Road; 1931), Mau-sang Ng divides Mao Dun's work into two phases along these lines: whereas Mao's early heroes are crushed by "an inescapable iron Fate,"

11. This reading was inspired by the one in Ng, *The Russian Hero*, 142–43.

those of his fiction from 1932 on are crushed by "the macro-economic and market forces prevailing at the time."[12] Ng identifies an important shift here, and one that characterizes much of the fiction written in the early 1930s. In works by writers such as Rou Shi, Lao She 老舍 (1889–1966), Zhang Tianyi 張天翼 (1906–1985), and Wu Zuxiang 吳組湘 (1908–1994), the characters may be crushed by prevailing conditions created by men, but they are not condemned by some logic inherent in the universe. Revolutionaries concern themselves with economic and political institutions because they maintain faith that, although it is no easy matter, these institutions can be changed in a way that a mystical fate cannot.

2. SOCIAL FICTION AS DISTINCT FROM SOCIALIST REALISM

Greater emphasis on human determination had, however, to be reconciled with explanations of historical developments put forth by political theories to which many writers increasingly subscribed. A tension arose between depictions of individual problems and actions in the context of specific historical circumstances and an epic and sometimes schematic vision of historical developments. However, writers' initial interest in explanatory schemes based on class clearly was neither an abandonment of critical thought nor a mistrust of individual agency in favor of later conceptions of collective power.

To project the totalitarian policies and utopian visions that would soon dominate literary production back on these authors and their works would be anachronistic. First, even if many influential critics were advocating revolutionary literature and several, most notably Qian Xingcun 錢杏邨 (1900–1977), had around 1928 turned to the notion of proletarian realism (*puluo xianshizhuyi* 普羅現實主義) that had gained currency in the Soviet Union and Japan, no clear consensus then existed on the aesthetic requirements of revolutionary literature. In part because debates on such issues were so intense, writers felt a need to establish the Zuoyi zuojia lianmeng 左翼作家聯盟 (League of left-wing writers) in 1930.[13] Founded primarily as an attempt to reconcile

---

12. Ng, *The Russian Hero*, 140, 141.

13. For more on the League of Left-Wing Writers, see Wong, *Politics and Literature*, esp. 87–144.

different camps, the league institutionalized ongoing efforts to establish the kind of united front called for at the Communist Party's Sixth Congress in 1928. Yet vigorous debate continued as leftist theorists called on writers to pursue a variety of imported means for writing fiction that could serve political aims: Qian Xingcun attacked Lu Xun, Ye Shaojun, and even Mao Dun for writing "bourgeois realism" and called for an "active realism" or "activist realism" (*dong de xianshizhuyi* 動的現實主義). Qian invoked the term *dong* 動 (active or dynamic) as a corrective to the *jing* 靜 (passive) qualities he attributed to these writers.[14] Other theorists focused on the need to write for the masses, as in Qu Qiubai's 瞿秋白 arguments for "popular proletarian art and literature" (*puluo dazhong wenyi* 普羅大眾文藝), which, significantly, were grounded partly in his reservations about the determinism of naturalistic writings.[15] It was also in the early 1930s that theorists introduced the Soviet notion of "socialist realism" (*shehuizhuyi xianshizhuyi* 社會主義現實主義).[16]

Second, it is important not to conflate what theorists called for in the name of revolutionary literature and what writers actually wrote at this time. Although writers such as Jiang Guangci 蔣光慈 (1901–1931) and Hu Yepin responded to the call for proletarian fiction in the late 1920s, many works from the late 1920s to at least the mid-1930s belong to a mode of social realism closer to Western naturalism.[17] These works were much more complicated than what theorists were calling for, even in cases in which critic and creative writer were the same person.[18] At the very least, there was a time lag between the theorizing about an activist, proletarian literature and important literary works embody-

---

14. See Qian Xingcun, "Zhongguo xinxing wenxue zhong de jige juti de wenti," 930–31. See also Qian, "Siqu le de A Q shidai." For a discussion of these changing concepts of realism, see Anderson, *The Limits of Realism*, 48–56.

15. Qu Qiubai, "Dazhong wenyi de wenti." See the discussion in Pickowicz, "Qu Qiubai's Critique."

16. The term "socialist realism" was introduced in 1933 by Zhou Yang, who later became the chair of the Writers Union and Mao's vice-minister of culture. See Zhou, "Guanyu 'shehuizhuyi de xianshizhuyi yu geming de langmanzhuyi.'"

17. Though Mao Dun would later argue for the value of realism by distinguishing it from naturalism, a mode he held to embody the dangers of mechanism, determinism, and pessimism, many of his stories and novels could be seen as examples of naturalism. See Mao Dun, "Ziranzhuyi," discussed in Anderson, *The Limits of Realism*, 42–43.

18. Mao Dun and Yu Dafu, both mentioned below, are two examples of writer-critics whose fictional works transcend their theorizing at this time.

ing such an episteme. The theoretical works are perhaps best read as a window into what writers thought and the concerns that preoccupied them rather than as a representation of what they did in their fictional works.

Whereas many works of the 1930s could illustrate a Marxian analysis of Chinese society and of the limitations of individual action within such a society, there is a third reason why it would be wrong to view this social fiction as the first stage in a progression toward the socialist realism and revolutionary romanticism of the Mao era. Simply put, the authors of this period had no idea what Communism would bring to China. Their efforts to demonstrate the need for social transformation were a response to horrific conditions of the time and were carried out in complete ignorance of the directions in which Communism and leftist literary policy would lead. Although the two periods and literary modes are related, to posit a causal connection between them would be to oversimplify.

It is vital to examine the social fiction of this period as distinct from that of later leftist writings because many works contain humanitarian impulses that could have led in other directions. In considering why Mao Zedong wanted to prescribe ideological parameters for fiction and how these were taken up in the writing of revolutionary romanticism, it is important to look at the constructions of agency in the altogether different mode of social realism that preceded it, including these constructions' limitations and the needs they left unanswered.

Did the new attention to social relations successfully challenge fatalism or simply result in the substitution of a new form of determinism for earlier ones? This complicated question casts new light on scholarship that has read these works primarily as social documents (and often dismissed them as such), diagnosed a heightened burden of representationalism,[19] analyzed the changing discourse of individualism, or bemoaned the ideological fetters of literature committed to a leftist agenda. In what follows, I discuss the implications of these developments for the possibility of moral agency by focusing on the use of sideshadowing in the handling of time.

---

19. In exploring rising concerns about "representationalism," Huters proposes that writers felt guilty about "creating something out of nothing." See Huters, "Ideologies of Realism," 162.

3. EXPERIENCE IN TIME

Although a sociological conception of character led authors to focus on the social conditions that shape and define individuals, many of these works of social fiction create small but significant openings for self-determination. Rather than standing on the sidelines as perspicacious observers, these characters find themselves thrust into the midst of a story that demands their participation. Even when the characters fail to act to create the brighter future of which they dream, these works turn the question of engagement from a bemoaning expression of pain into a true question, that is, one that allows for the possibility of answers. Whereas the May Fourth focus on individual psychology and perception continues in works of social fiction, these works increasingly depict a developing context that could presumably be influenced by the characters' actions. Though the openings for agency remain meager, they still permit the characters to live in a new way.

What make participation possible in these works are sideshadowing techniques that create a sense that the time in which their plots occur is truly ongoing. Most important, these techniques involve switching from a retrospective vision to the creation of a sense of an ongoing present. Fewer narratorial intrusions make these works more objective insofar as they portray a material world of events, actions, and relations in the process of developing rather than the psychological or emotional reactions of a narrator contemplating a world already made.[20] By balancing introspection with more outward action, these works perforce limit the radical questioning present in the earlier May Fourth fiction. Gone are many of the distancing effects that established a critical detachment in the May Fourth works. As a result, works of social fiction express an equally trenchant criticism, but they do so more by showing than by telling. Furthermore, they restore priority to the issue of what people make of their reflections. In particular, their use of sideshadowing respects the

20. It was also at this time that writers departed from an earlier concept of realism they named *xieshi zhuyi*, "the doctrine of writing about reality," the term mentioned in Chapter 3. Faithful to this idea, earlier works stressed the distance between reality and appearance, but it was as if reality were timeless. The term writers later adopted to name realism, *xianshi zhuyi* 現實主義, "doctrine of contemporary reality," could be interpreted as emphasizing either the idea of reflection, the notion of the present, or both. Although Leo Lee interprets it in a different way, he draws attention to this shift in his "Afterword," 364, 366.

characters' lived experience of time by allowing them to dream and to make genuine efforts before conveying to the reader their often dismal ends. Such structures are fundamentally different from those in which the characters' struggles must inevitably lead to failure.

The sheer size of some of the fictional works written in the 1930s attests to writers' pains to present complex networks of personal and historical relations. The first editions of Mao Dun's *Ziye* 子夜 (Midnight; 1933) and Ba Jin's *Jia* 家 (Family; 1933) were 576 and 497 pages respectively, and *Family* was but one volume of Ba's second voluminous trilogy. From the vicissitudes of industrialists' power plays, to the intricate pressures within family households, to the shifting mentalities of rural communities, these works reflect a rapidly changing modern world. Yet in terms of structure they recall the vast novels of the Ming and Qing dynasties. As with the traditional novels, it is precisely the elements of loose structure for which these works have been faulted that are integral to their success in presenting time as ongoing duration.

With their episodic structures, these works create a sense of the irreducibly dynamic and messy terms from which most moral reasoning must begin. That they do not tie up all the loose ends or reconcile different sideshadows demonstrates the extent to which possibilities may exceed actualities. The repetitions in Ba's *Family*, for example, reinforce the experience of time's passage as a closing of possibilities. Thus, when Juehui's 覺慧 inaction leads, somewhat heavy-handedly, to two deaths, the novel underscores how people affect the world even when they do not consciously reflect upon the consequences of their actions or of the lack thereof. A similar argument can be made in reading Li Jieren's 李劼人 1936–1937 historical trilogy *Sishui weilan* 死水微瀾 (Ripples on dead water), *Baofengyu qian* 暴風雨前 (Before the storm), and *Dabo* 大波 (Great wave), a work of over 1,400 pages in all. One could fault Li's trilogy for an overabundance of detail or an excessive number of secondary characters, but their inclusion situates the developing initiative of the protagonist Deng Yaogu 鄧么姑 within a naturalistic perspective without which her success in improving her lot might seem like a fairy tale.

Many critics have insisted on these works' value as historical documents. Yet the inclusion of prosaic detail and historical breadth not only records history but also allows writers to explore the epistemological implications of setting human experience within the context of larger social and historical dynamics. Whereas most of these works stress how painful societal transitions were imposed on individual and often helpless victims, in presenting these larger forces they also sought to establish some basis for moral reasoning within them. Their acknowledgment of the power of external dynamics was a step toward imagining what people could do within those constraints. Some of these works draw external forces so powerfully that, like earlier works, they may seem to expose free action as a childish illusion, but on the whole a great deal of uncertainty remains as to the part played by human agency.

4. FREE WILL IN FORBIDDING WORLDS

Many of the stories of the early 1930s offer particularly sophisticated presentations of the possibilities of agency within the narrow limits of severe conditions and harsh times. One interpretation of the subject matter of these stories is that they illustrate chances to exercise agency under extreme duress. Countless works of this period focus on the lives of women, particularly servant girls, young wives, or prostitutes, who suffer poverty and the degrading and abusive treatment of brutish husbands or mean-spirited mothers-in-law.[21] These works do not stop at the presentation of indignity, however. They usually depict women who make every possible effort to influence the course of their lives in the tiny ways possible for them.

Rou Shi's "Wei nuli de muqin" 爲奴隸的母親 (Slave mother; 1930), for example, tells the story of a woman who is systematically deprived of almost all possibility for self-determination but who nonetheless struggles to reconcile her responsibilities to her different children. After a few vivid strokes draw a picture of her family's extreme poverty and her husband's moral and physical decline, the first line of dialogue announces her husband's ominous plan: "[Let's] try to figure out a solution using your body." "[Using] my body?" she replies in disbelief (285).[22] Without even consulting her, he has agreed to rent her for three to five years to an older, well-to-do couple who want her to produce a son for them.

The woman pleads with her husband to consider the welfare of their four-year-old son, but his insensitivity is already all too familiar to her.

21. A sustained investigation of stories concerning the lives of women might begin with earlier stories by Ye Shaojun, such as "A life" discussed in Chapter 3, and then treat stories by Wang Luyan such as "Wuding xia" (Under the roof; 1933) and "Lima" (Servant Li; 1936).

22. Rou Shi, "Wei nuli du muqin," 285. Translations here are my own.

In a flashback, she recalls how he callously thrust their newborn daughter into a pail of boiling water a year earlier. The contrast is savage: the family's straightened circumstances have condemned this woman to witness the murder of her daughter and then, within the year, to be sold in a cash transaction to produce another baby. She barely voices resistance to her husband, but she does ask aloud how she can abandon her young son, thereby blaming herself. The slave mother's complete lack of power and importance is further underscored when her neighbor demands a reward for having arranged the rental and by the way this woman rushes the slave mother's parting with her son because the sedan-bearers want to make it home for lunch.

The taut tempo and pathos of the story relax somewhat when the slave mother reaches her new home. The *xiucai* 秀才 (a degree-holder in the county level of the imperial examination) is a refined and gentle man who treats her kindly, and even his first wife makes a show of magnanimity toward the new arrival. The depiction of the older woman's character development over the course of the slave mother's stay is particularly well crafted. After the slave mother becomes pregnant and bears a son, the old woman becomes jealous and suspicious and treats her more and more like a servant. She objects to the special treatment the slave mother receives by saying that she must have been like a "street bitch" (294) during her other pregnancies, while all the while rubbing the string of beads that symbolize her pious adherence to a sect of Pure Land Buddhism.

Although the slave mother feels stung by the old woman's comments and never stops worrying about her little son left behind, she cannot help but feel grateful for the comfort of her new surroundings. The new baby restores her to life, and she even asserts herself by proposing a name for him. She suggests calling him Qiubao 秋寶 (Autumn Treasure) and gives as a reason his autumn birth. The elderly *xiucai* highly approves since the baby has arrived in the autumn of his life. But for the slave mother the name recalls her first baby, Chunbao 春寶 (Spring Treasure), and in this naming she connects the two lives that her rental to the new family has so terribly sundered. The recollection of her first baby at this moment marks a turning point in the story since the delivery of a son means that her days in the new household are now numbered.

The narrative then describes Qiubao's constant attachment to his mother, whom he is taught to call "Shenshen" 嬸嬸 (Auntie), his indifference toward his father, and his outright dislike for his "mother," the *xiucai*'s wife. Out of love for his son, the *xiucai* suggests to his wife that they buy the slave mother outright. This suggestion casts the story's most significant sideshadow as the *xiucai* continues to harbor such intentions despite his wife's objections. The slave mother also considers the possibility of staying on and thus finds herself contemplating the terrible choice of parting definitively with one or the other of her two sons. In a rare fantasy, she imagines controlling the course of her life for the first time. She reasons that since her poor husband's illness is bound to kill him within a few years, if she were to stay with the well-to-do family, she might be able to arrange for Chunbao to join her.

This brief interlude of relative ease allows for a sideshadowing of multiple possibilities that is foreclosed when the realities of the slave mother's other life intervene. As the *xiucai* schemes about how at least to rent the slave mother for another term, she commits an act to help her first son that turns the *xiucai* against her. When her impoverished husband comes to tell her of their son's serious illness, she gives him a blue jade ring to buy medicine. Her disloyalty in giving away this ring, her reward from the *xiucai* for bearing Qiubao, injures the old man's pride. He wishes that she would forget her other husband and child and devote all of her love to him and their son. But it does not occur to the slave mother to feign love for him, just as she does not consider how she jeopardizes her chances for remaining in the materially comfortable household when she gives away the heirloom.

There follows the slave mother's painful separation from her second son and the pitiful scene, conveyed in a mere two sentences, in which a servant ostensibly comes to console her but actually supervises her packing to make sure that she does not steal anything. The slave mother is then sent back, on foot, to her former household. Upon her return, her husband does not even speak to her until he orders her to make dinner. Her discovery that they have only a tiny bit of rice reveals that the family is no better off than before her rental, and Chunbao is a coarse, stunted child, scarcely bigger than he was three years earlier.

What this story shows is that people are not reducible to the roles they inhabit. Despite her powerlessness, the slave mother does not relinquish her dignity, her sanity, or her efforts to do what little she can for her sons. Although one cannot avoid many of one's roles, such as being sold as a concubine, there may be some latitude in how one takes up one's role. Poverty and an inhuman social structure set the terms of the slave mother's choices, but her moral decisions are not ultimately determined by fate, her class, or even her environment. The story's sideshadows make it conceivable that she could have decided differently, or at least that another woman of her class and position might well have decided differently.

The openings for agency may be prohibitively slim, but once one admits a sliver of liberty, one admits the principle of the matter. The overwhelming place of coercion in such stories makes the small measure of freedom more salient. Freedom is most dear when it must be won, earned, or fought for. Its value increases in proportion to its scarcity. Furthermore, if individuals can face coercive structures and find the courage to resist their rules, they exercise a creativity that also defines them as subjects. Like the slave mother, many of the characters in the stories and novels of the early and mid-1930s are memorable precisely because they resist being reduced to their assigned roles. Lao She's Xiangzi 祥子, Mao Dun's Wu Sunfu 吳蓀甫, and Li Jieren's Deng Yaogu 鄧么姑 live as do few characters of the previous or subsequent fiction because they commit acts that cannot be explained simply in terms of their positions.

For example, in Lao She's *Luotuo Xiangzi* 駱駝祥子 (Camel Xiangzi; 1936–1937), Xiangzi may represent a whole class of rickshaw drivers, but his ideals, his resilient spirit, his struggle, and even his demise are all too individualized to make him a typical representative of a class. In terms of literary structure, the failure of Xiangzi's dreams is foreshadowed when he meets the old impoverished rickshaw puller and learns that he too once owned his own rickshaw. In continuing to carry on what C. T. Hsia calls his "Sisyphean struggle for decency," however, Xiangzi must certainly be said to exercise agency.[23] The fact that his actions do not lead to success does nothing to undo their freely willed character.

Of course, one could argue that Xiangzi's demise is a result of evil actions that his straitened circumstances force him to take, but the novel's power derives from its depiction of sideshadows that make these turns moments of real decision. It is precisely because the reader has come to view Xiangzi as a responsible actor that she recoils when he takes away business from older rickshaw drivers or betrays the union organizer to the police for the monetary reward. Furthermore, to blame his demise on his own moral failings would be to read the novel as an illustration of karmic retribution or a Christian teaching on punishment for sin. Given

23. Hsia, *A History of Modern Chinese Fiction*, 184.

Lao She's politics, however, a more likely interpretation is that he sought to drive home the futility of individual effort in order to announce the need for *collective* action.[24]

Were Lao She to show human action to be meaningless by creating a type who is crushed by fate, his novel would not succeed as it does.[25] Lao's novel succeeds both as a work of art and in making a case for the limitations of individual action because he depicts a man who, despite cruel oppression, manipulation, and his own weaknesses, nonetheless exercises moral agency in a world that offers him just enough hope to keep him engaged in a nearly impossible struggle. It is because moral agency is possible, yet the agency of a single individual insufficient, that the argument for collective action can be made.

5. FATE'S HOLD ON THE DISPOSSESSED OF TIME

Lao She's "Yueyar" 月牙兒 (Moon crescent; 1935) also tackles the difficult problem of allowing a character a measure of agency when her circumstances seem to deprive her of any power.[26] Written a year earlier than *Camel Xiangzi*, "Moon Crescent" presents a young woman's account of her attempts to maintain a sense of agency even as she is forced into prostitution to survive. As she is coerced by economic necessity, seasoned by experience, and criminalized and jailed by a hostile legal system, the young woman's belief in fate (*ming* 命) plays an important role in helping her make sense of her conversion from a relatively competent, independent girl into a prostitute and criminal. The story's attention to the protagonist's perceptions of the moon also illustrates the extent to which the exercise of agency depends on a sense of time as open rather than as fated or cyclical.

The story begins by building up the wages of poverty. As a child, the girl is horrified to realize that her mother works as a prostitute, yet she loves her and attributes her actions to their need for food. She reasons that hunger has reduced them to desperate slaves and first expresses what will become her philosophy of life, "A hungry stomach is the truth that

24. As C. T. Hsia writes, "Lao Shê has apparently come to the conclusion that, in a sick society, it requires some form of collective action to improve the lot of the proletariat, and that any member of that class, in trying to better himself by his own effort, merely hastens his own ruin." See Hsia, *History*, 185.

25. For a careful interpretation of the novel, see Bady, "*Le pousse-pousse*."

26. Page numbers refer to Lao She, "Yueyar," and all translations are my own.

matters most" (125): "My mother and I, we were like two dogs without anyone to care for them. For the sake of our mouths, we had to suffer every kind of hardship. It was as if our bodies had nothing else, just mouths. For these mouths, we had to sell everything else" (115).

As the protagonist matures, however, she grows cynical, particularly about the lot of women. What makes so compelling her despair at turning to prostitution is that she first recounts periods in which she tries to better her life, such as when the kindly school director allows her to live and work at the school, and when she first begins work as a hostess. Until circumstances leave her no other option, these sideshadows demonstrate her refusal to give up trying to live in another way, at times even in a moral way. For example, when the wife of the man supporting her begs her to leave him, she agrees out of sympathy for the woman. Another sideshadow is cast when she refuses to receive clients as the restaurant's "Number One" hostess does and therefore loses her job. Both decisions are complicated because the narrator has no other way to support herself and realizes that she may be giving up a bad situation for an even less savory one. Yet she continues to struggle: "I wasn't willing to take that road just yet, but I knew that it was waiting for me just around the corner" (122).

The numerous references to the moon, including the story's title, are indicative of how the protagonist's sense of time reinforces her fatalism regarding her life. Because the moon waxes and wanes in a cycle, it offers the bereft girl a stable reference point: "Again it had been a long time since I saw the moon crescent. I didn't dare look at it, although I wanted to. . . . The slight breeze seemed to make that little bit of light blow into my heart, making me recollect the past and making heavier my present tragic sorrow" (116–17). Significantly, this point of reference does not help the protagonist develop a sense of time as dynamic or as a framework in which she might be able to achieve personal progress. Instead, she views her descent into prostitution as the inevitable completion of a cycle. This outlook becomes particularly clear toward the end of the story, after her mother reappears. Remembering that her mother had turned to prostitution to provide for her when she was young, the narrator accepts her responsibility to support her mother as a fatality. She attributes their predicament to the fulfillment of a cycle of mutual obligation, concluding that "women's profession is hereditary; it's specialized!" (128).

The story's power derives from the conflict between (1) the protagonist's cynical conviction that her fate is sealed because she is a woman in a society that leaves women little option and (2) her desperate attempts to put off her decline and nurture some measure of self-control even as she loses her youth, her health, and her freedom. As she relinquishes her self-respect and her sense of capacity or agency, the narrator-protagonist's appeals to fate increase, and she stresses several times the extent to which she sees her fate as a gendered one: "An 'if-all-else-fails' (*wan bu de yi* 萬不得已) always awaits us women. At best I could make it wait a few more days. I could grind my teeth, I could feel anger in my heart. But a woman's fate does not lie in her own hands" (123).

What is women's fate in this story? First, the protagonist's appeals to fate suggest that her gender is *the* major causal factor in her inability to achieve any semblance of economic power or self-determination, even the leisure to look at the moon. Second, part of fate here seems to be the notion that men naturally have a right of sexual access to women and that women must negotiate some way to survive by means of sexual relations. Simply being a woman condemns one to some form of prostitution. "However, if [she] truly cannot earn food to eat, a woman must recognize that she's a woman; [she] must sell her flesh!" (124). As the story progresses, the protagonist's grasp on sanity increasingly depends on her cynical appraisal of the cruel nature of transactions between men and women. Quickly realizing that she would starve if she continued to play with men in a "romantic" struggle for food, she decides to conduct straightforward business and details how she insists on her prices for different acts.

After she has been virtually annihilated as an agent, when she does regain a modicum of agency, it is at a remove from her own interests and self-preservation. She wants to believe that she exercises some degree of control, even if that agency may be explained at best in terms of a survival instinct and at worst in terms of vengeance: "Someone at the door again, looking for me. Fine. I'll serve him, I'll do my best to give him my disease. I don't feel that this is unfair to people. It simply isn't my fault. . . . You must have money to be able to live. Satisfy your hunger first, then think about the rest of it" (128).

With the words "I'll do my best" (*wo jin li de* 我盡力地), the question arises as to whether the narrator's decision to transmit her sickness stems completely from physical desperation, or whether it might also betray her psychological need to grasp a shred of power. A similar tension marks the narrator's reactions to her mother's practice of robbing the men who visit her. Her mother's behavior worries her, but she marvels at the immunity they enjoy as the men do not dare return to make a fuss.

The last sections of the story literally deprive the narrator of her freedom, for she is placed in a reeducation center and then in prison. The brevity and rapidity of the narration of these events suggest the narrator's loss of control. She views the reeducation center as a cheap way to take advantage of women since the center's best results consist in having turned a dozen or so women into wives for men who paid the two-*yuan* processing fee. She thus refuses to be reeducated, noting that she already knows how to clean, cook, and sew: if she could have found work using those skills, she would not have been doing that "bitter business" in the first place (132). Her recalcitrance, including her act of spitting in the face of a high official, angers the authorities and they throw her in jail, where she writes: "Inside a jail is a great place. It firmly convinces you that humanity can never improve. Even in my dreams I never saw such a sordid thing. . . . [But] the world really does not have anything much better" (132). Then she notes seeing her old friend, the moon crescent. As she reflects on how long it has been since the last time she saw it, the reader's recognition that her last few months of "freedom" had permitted her not even this simple leisure helps to explain the protagonist's readiness to come to terms with her imprisonment. These lines also bring the story back to its opening section and cast new meaning on its comment that the moon awakens her memory: "It wakes up my memory as a night wind blows to pieces a flower that wishes to sleep" (107).

This return to the opening image alerts the reader to the opening's foreshadowing of the narrator's fate. This foreshadowing arranges the narrative so as to increase structural and thematic unity, yet in so doing it reinforces the determinism inherent in any completed narrative design. The final invocation of the moon also highlights the story's sustained attention to the narrator's consciousness of time and suggests the extent to which the exercise of agency depends on a coherent and meaningful sense of time's passing. For example, near the beginning of the story, the narrator explains how her hunger and powerlessness deprived her of a sense of time when she was a little girl: "I could only concern myself with the present. I had no future, and I didn't dare think about it seriously.

When eating someone's food, I knew that it was morning or evening, otherwise I simply didn't think of time. Without hope, time does not exist" (116).

6. MODERN CONSCIOUSNESS: TOWARD FREEDOM OR DETERMINISM?

A sense of alienation still pervades works such as "Yueyar," but this form of alienation is fundamentally different from that plaguing the narrators of works from the late 1910s and 1920s. In the earlier works, a scrupulous but restricted focus on individual subjectivity and moral alienation fatally estranges the characters from the external world. In the social fiction, the point of demonstrating the effects of social and economic alienation was to place the blame on existing political and social systems. These stories and novels thus resist presenting their characters as fatally alienated: they are contingently alienated, that is, alienated as a result of contingent social or economic conditions. In documenting contingent reasons for the characters' sad ends, these works begin to depart from the fatalism in the critical realism of the late 1910s and 1920s.

The difficulty of replacing that fatalism with a meaningful portrayal of moral agency, however, is suggested by the slip into new forms of determinism that accompanied the development of social fiction. For far from guaranteeing a space of freedom, situating oneself within a story can pose distinct risks to independent thinking and may close off the perceived space for creative action. Just as radical undecidability may be more paralyzing than liberating, efforts to create a context can construct either a richly open possible world or a set stage ruled by a single linear script.

Attention to context introduces depth and intricacy to the presentation of a story, but it can also lead to the conscious or unconscious adoption of constructions of meaning that may deny the complexity of any lived situation. If the conception of context is limited to or unduly dominated by an explanation based on a single factor, such as economics, class, or imperialism, then it may do little more than replace mystical fatalism with a narrow economic or political determinism. If it fails to consider a sufficient number of factors, the simplicity of such determinism may render the new conception almost equally mystical.

I want nonetheless to distinguish clearly between the fatalism of the early May Fourth works and the determinism of the social fiction. For whereas in many instances the latter writings continue to thwart a positive conception of freedom, they do so in ways that indicate a subtle shift in worldview, particularly in their conceptions of time. The early works had struggled against a resigned fatalism based on certain traditional ideas about destiny, but the world they created—often confined to the products of a fetishized introspection—laid little foundation for the exercise of agency. In rejecting introspection as a sufficient means for exercising agency and by integrating specific historical determinants, works of social fiction sought to confront the possibilities and limitations for action beyond reflection. However, whereas they continued to contest the shackles of superstition and its fatalism, broadly speaking, these works placed greater emphasis on deterministic paradigms grounded in a directional view of time and history.

These paradigms often restricted the room for human agency in a way different from but hardly less severe than more fatalistic principles. In contrast to the cyclical view of time in many works of classical fiction, this directional view of history already evident in the late-Qing works consolidated by the late 1920s. This view of time brought new possibilities but also limitations for the representation of agency. Shifting from a cyclical to a linear conception of time may confer more faith in the power of human endeavor. Yet linear conceptions also allow a vision of apocalypse, since depictions of decadence and decline are no longer tempered by the expectation that the pendulum will eventually swing back. The tragic endings of so many works since the late Qing express new struggles with visions of doom.

One work devoted to representing the inescapable effects of changing economic conditions is "Chuncan" 春蠶 (Spring silkworms; 1932), the first part of Mao Dun's trilogy on rural conditions. In this story, Mao presents superstition and fatalism such that these forces accrue no power of their own. At the same time, he illustrates how the peasants' reliance on superstition blinds them to the rapid changes in the sericulture economy on which they depend. In this way, the depiction of their superstitious practices emphasizes the peasants' utter lack of preparation for understanding, let alone for succeeding within, this economic landscape. For example, Old Tong Bao 老通寶 finds it easier to worry that his grandfather's murder of a longhair Taiping revolutionary may have destined his family to financial hardship, or that it was unlucky to use paper with writing on it to cushion the silkworms, than to examine his resistance to raising the more marketable "foreign" silkworms. Likewise, the family finds it easier to plant garlic and watch its sprouts as an omen of their harvest's success than to open their eyes to the fact that the silk factories are not opening their doors that year.

Yet though the family clings to such superstitious beliefs, these concerns press less heavily on their minds than do the weight of their debt and the pressure from their creditors. The story makes thirteen mentions of the family's debt, borrowing, and creditors in its short 26 pages. Their superstition is neither right nor wrong; it is simply beside the point. What destroys the family is that the silk factories will not open to buy their cocoons. In this way, like much of the social fiction, this story reflects a new and arguably quite "modern" determinism. Yet it must be asked if "determinism" is the right term here, for a structural analysis claiming that economics determines outcomes need not entail that those structures be impervious to human agency. Structures of economic inequality may deny agency to individuals caught within them, but they leave open the possibility that groups of people might collectively challenge them.

"Spring Silkworms" shows the tendency for individual actors to experience economic predicaments in terms of a determinism that reinforces apocalyptic interpretations. At the story's close, the peasant family is left bankrupt and ruined. They are deeper in debt than ever, and they have lost their mortgaged grove of mulberry trees. In discussing Mao Dun's stories, Hsia thus poses a crucial problem:

> But they, too, fail to transcend the perplexing problem with which proletarian fiction is saddled: how to explore the enormity of oppression and destitution without reducing human beings into mere pawns of callous fortune. The social evil depicted in proletarian fiction is usually of such weight and magnitude that the characters caught under it cannot possibly counteract it in any human manner; hence no tragedy.[27]

Hsia perceptively identifies the danger that fiction depicting social forces may disable the possibility for a dimension of human agency. But the dimension denied, the intervention possible for an individual or a small group, is not the only dimension of human agency. The problem is not an absence of tragedy, but the lack of room for agency or hope as conceived in a narrowly individualistic, humanist perspective. Works such as "Spring Silkworms" paint a picture unremittingly pessimistic only if the

27. Hsia, *History*, 162.

reader confines her consideration to the characters' individual outcomes. If the story is read as a depiction of a predicament that illuminates larger social issues and historical inequalities, then the story does constitute a tragedy. This is not because nature operates blindly, but because creditors and industrialists observe no moral rules. To take seriously problems of inequality, literature may have to attend to larger economic structures that supersede but never eliminate the experience of individual courage or tragic flaws.[28]

Mao Dun's lengthy novel *Midnight* can also be read as presenting an apocalyptic vision. The novel depicts the ruin of the Shanghai industrialist Wu Sunfu, and Marxist scholars often interpret the novel as illustrating what Mao Zedong would call the unfeasibility of the capitalist system in semi-feudal, semi-colonial China. Moreover, the sympathetic portrayal of Wu may suggest that he stands for the Chinese nation in the position of oppressed proletariat vis-à-vis imperialist powers. Perhaps to emphasize that Wu's failure stems not from his own character or actions but from the workings of a system at the mercy of foreign competition, throughout most of the novel Wu remains shut in his study waiting for news he cannot control: news of his provincial enterprises, of the workers striking at his factory, and of the stock market.[29]

One of the most heavily plotted novels in this era of Chinese literature, *Midnight* contains many instances of carefully crafted foreshadowing. As Birch has discussed, the opening chapter "prefigures future plots and subplots," and this is just one of the ways that foreshadowing operates in the novel.[30] Another example is Mao's choice of the character *tao* 韜 for the last character of the name of Wu's chief adversary, Zhao Botao 趙伯韜. Since *tao* carries the meaning of the sheath or case for a bow, suggesting the hiding and concealing of weapons and the duplicitous art of war, the name suggests that this character lies low and conceals his true features.

What gives the novel its force is the detailed psychological portrayal of Wu and his tenacious conviction that he can still influence the outcome of events. Until the end, Wu manages to maintain a hope that his destiny

28. Moreover, traditional tragedy is not the only genre for great literature, and it is not one necessarily conducive to depictions of moral agency. Since in tragedy a character's greatness is also the source of his ultimate downfall, tragedy entails a kind of character determinism.

29. Sun's foil, the industrialist Zhou Zhongwei, is similarly trapped in his residence (chap. 16). See Birch's reading of this episode in "Change and Continuity."

30. Birch, "Change and Continuity," 392.

might go either way. Over the course of the lengthy novel, Wu's reflections cast sideshadows that create suspense even as numerous elements of the novel's construction foreclose the kind of open future to which Wu clings. At the same time, though some readers interpret the title to imply that the novel depicts the depth of night yet suggests a coming dawn, such a novel presents little support for an optimistic appraisal of China's future.

The seeming insolubility of China's contemporary material and historical conditions pushed many writers to adopt politically motivated explanations of history. Many factors, from a belief in materialism to a desire for verisimilitude, credibility, or persuasiveness may have led these writers to base their settings on historical observation. Given their allegiance to particular forms of political analysis, it is important to examine why writers may have been dissatisfied with the philosophical implications of the naturalistic works of the 1920s and 1930s.

7. FROM NATURALISM TO TELEOLOGICAL REALISM

The charge that naturalistic works often result in a rigid determinism is familiar, and one that Chinese writers took to heart from their first discussions of the genre. From the early 1920s, writers debated the virtues and pitfalls of naturalism in their theoretical works. Some, such as Mao Dun, expressed reservations about the fatalism or mechanism of naturalism, but they nonetheless promoted it as an important avenue for reflection.[31] Other writers wrote strident attacks against the genre. Yu Dafu, for example, decried naturalism as a hindrance to self-expression: "Naturalism caught on for a while, since it seemed capable of capturing the totality of things. Its fatalism and lack of initiative, however, made it impossible for writers to freely express their individualism."[32] A decade later, however, Yu himself forayed into a realist, almost naturalistic genre of fiction representing specific historical events with his *Ta shi yige ruo nuzi* 她是一個弱女子 (She is a weak woman; 1932).

Because naturalistic works seek to analyze society by investigating natural and material causes, adherence to naturalism can imply an uncritical faith in scientism, that is, the theory that methods of investigation used in the natural sciences should be applied to other fields of inquiry. As the

31. See Mao Dun, "Ziranzhuyi."

32. Yu Dafu, "Wenxue shang de jieji douzheng," 265.

writers saw, faith in science, even when it includes the belief that science holds the key to a brighter future, can also lead to a resignation regarding the limits of human potential in the face of natural, economic, or political forces.

Another problem with scientism lies in a possible underlying assumption that human experience and social and historical forces are causally necessitated and thus are preset, at least insofar as they are seen as developing along a single linear path. Of course, the belief that phenomena are susceptible to objective inquiry does not imply that they are fixed, but an overzealous desire to present the truth, that is, a simple, predictable, and not overly complicated truth, may lead thinkers to conflate determinism and the possibility of objective knowledge. Literature that focuses on recording evidence of how things are may neglect to show ways in which the future remains open and subject to human intervention. Such literature may discourage people from taking responsibility for their future. Specifically, by focusing on detailed description, naturalistic realism may reinforce present social arrangements rather than suggest how people might act to change them. It was for this reason that even an ardent materialist such as Qu Qiubai challenged the determinism of naturalistic writings.[33]

Does attention to context automatically lead to acceptance of deterministic paradigms? Must portrayal of specific historical determinants entail a kind of scientism that leads to the belief that human powers are paltry relative to the strength of economic forces? The social fiction of the 1930s grappled with the challenge to depict human decision within given historical contexts. The promise of these works suggests that this challenge is not insurmountable. To the contrary, the most probing of these novels and stories reckon with context but cast sideshadows that leave open at least some minimal space for moral decision. They underscore the real force of structural determinants and yet present moments in which human decisions can matter.

In the following decades, works of socialist realism and revolutionary romanticism would treat many of the same problems and themes as the social fiction, but these treatments would be ruled by an optimistic perspective stemming from a utopian faith in the inevitable revolutionary transformation of society. Written to illustrate such political ideals, these works would usually assume a teleological conception of human

33. Qu Qiubai, "Dazhong wenyi de wenti."

experience. By teleological, I mean the idea that natural phenomena can be explained through appeal to an ultimate pattern, design, or purpose.

Furthermore, perhaps because authors were striving for principles of unity and selection, some of these works reduced the world to overly obvious dichotomies. As with the early social novels treating the problem of political engagement, many of these works set up simplistic oppositions between the characters' emotional lives and their sense of duty to the revolution. The either/or nature of this dichotomy between duty and love is evident in works such as Xiao Jun's 蕭軍 (1907–1988) *Bayue de xiangcun* 八月的鄉村 (Village in August; 1935). In such works, characters become symbols of the conflict between antagonistic interests. Convincing characterization may have already been compromised in works of social fiction such as Ba Jin's *Family*, in which the characters serve to illustrate generational conflicts between forces of conservatism and those committed to a modern spirit. Yet early works of socialist realism further compromised on characterization as efforts to draw characters representing social classes often led authors to turn their characters into moral propositions.

In the next chapter, I explore works of socialist realism from the 1950s through the mid-1970s and their failure to avoid an overly schematic and hence deterministic utopianism. Whereas I seek to show that these works are not as simple or univocal as has been presumed, they did represent a retreat from the quest of the earlier social fiction. For the conclusion to be drawn from this examination of social fiction is that context, although introducing social and historical determinants, need not exclude, but can sometimes thrust to the forefront, moments of moral decision.

PART III

Moral Responsibility in Fiction from the People's Republic

5

Moral Decision in Mao-Era Fiction

> Freedom is the knowing of necessity and the transformation of the objective world. Only on the basis of knowing necessity can there be free activities for people.
>
> —Mao Zedong

Since the founding of the People's Republic of China, human agency has had effects of such sheer magnitude as to raise questions about whose will, if anyone's, drove these developments. What were people thinking as they pursued the grand revolutionary designs that led to unprecedented social reforms and rapid modernization but also to man-made catastrophes and genocide? What kinds of plans and responses could they have had? Fiction reveals some record of their changing and diverse material, social, and imaginative worlds. Given the extraordinary volume of activity, what kinds of moral reflection figure in the works of these five decades?

Examining human agency in works of the Mao era is crucial to understanding Chinese fiction from the People's Republic for at least five reasons. First, fictional works cast light on the fundamental tension between voluntarism and determinism in Maoist ideology. Mao's concern with human will, evident from his earliest writings, would remain a keynote in the Party's literary and ideological orthodoxy. Yet inasmuch as voluntarism was a cornerstone of Mao's thought, it had to coexist with beliefs about the iron law of historical development toward a resolution of class conflict. Second, upon examination, works of the Mao period reveal a complexity that has not been sufficiently addressed. Even stories that served as propaganda for Communist principles often contain conflicting voices and reservations.

Third, scrutinizing the narrative and discursive logics of voluntarism in Mao-era works sheds light on the struggles of writers in the immediate post-Mao era who sought to come to different terms with people's recent experiences, with the aftermath in their hearts, and with the changed, new world with which they were left. For all their limitations and possibilities, Mao-era works established norms for subject matter and narrative techniques against which many later writings reacted. Fourth, understanding Mao-era works helps to place in context the rejection of rational voluntarism that marks much of the roots-seeking, modernist, and avant-garde fiction written since the early 1980s. A final reason is to identify similarities and differences between portrayals of agency in Mao-era works and those in works of the 1990s that represent free agency within the very different context of market transition. Any consideration of the challenges and implications of depicting human agency beyond a morally neutral or empty obsession with negative freedom has to confront the manipulation of agency in the Mao-era works.

1. POLITICAL PRESCRIPTIONS

Mao Zedong staked his thought on his conviction that the collective will of the masses could transform the nation's material base.[1] For Mao, to change people's consciousness was primary, for doing so could release the energy of the revolution that would eventually lead to a Communist utopia. Mao's commitment to "permanent revolution" and to continuous and unending change was rooted in his glorification of the will, a collective will that he believed could enable individuals to realize themselves in community and in turn transform the objective world.

If positively affirming a great utopian conception is relatively easy in political speeches, the task is much harder in literature. It is no simple matter either to live or to represent human will as Mao wished it to be, and the stories and novels written in response to Mao's directives raise fundamental questions about the nature of moral choice in the context

1. This theory is evident at least from Mao's "Xin minzhu zhuyi lun" (1940). In adapting Marxist theory to China's conditions and needs, Mao wanted the revolution's power to rest with the rural peasants rather than with either urban industrial sectors tainted by China's recent semicolonial experience or Party commissars who might eventually challenge his power. Mao's position that the superstructure could change the base was not accepted by some of his opponents in the Party. These opponents, most of whom Mao would purge during the Cultural Revolution, followed Marx (or a vulgar Marxist interpretation) in believing that the Party leadership should serve as the vanguard for the revolutionary masses in changing the material conditions that would then lead to a transformation of the superstructure of culture and social institutions.

of political imperatives. What should be the role of autonomous decision vis-à-vis the Party line? What should individuals do when service to the revolution hurts their families? These questions are as fundamental to politics as to fiction, and it is no accident that Mao and his supporters concerned themselves with the control of literature. Nor is it surprising that fiction frequently offered answers more ambiguous than those commanded, for it is the province of fiction to present different voices in dialogue.

Mao explicitly laid out his policies for literature with his "Zai Yan'an wenyi zuotanhui shang de jianghua" 在延安文藝座談會上的講話 (Talks at the Yan'an Forum on Literature and Art; 1942).[2] In these talks, Mao declared that the primary function of literature and art was to serve as instruments of the proletarian revolution. Literature was to be a means of uniting and educating the people in the ideology of liberation and the work of attacking class enemies. No longer was literature to be written for intellectuals, but for peasants, workers, and soldiers. This new orthodoxy demanded that literature focus on society in its revolutionary development.

This instrumentalism had predictably repressive implications for authorial freedom. For the next three and a half decades, until Mao's death in 1976, literature would be more in the service of politics than at any other time in China's long literary history. As is well documented, Mao's "Talks" ushered in the reign of socialist realism, and a series of "rectification" campaigns (*zhengfeng yundong* 整風運動) silenced other tendencies, particularly critical ones.[3] In 1953, Zhou Yang 周揚 laid out further rules for literary production, basically reiterating the tenets

---

2. Presented in May 1942, these talks were first published a year and a half later in *Jiefang ribao* (Liberation daily), October 19, 1943. See McDougall, *Mao Zedong's "Talks."*

3. After Mao's talks, the Communists at Yan'an launched a first campaign of "rectification," condemning Ding Ling, Ai Qing, and others for critical attitudes. Procedures for intellectual self-reform (*ziwo gaizao* 自我改造) were developed in rectification campaigns of the 1940s. To justify the need to deprive reactionaries of the right to speak, Mao outlined his theory of democratic dictatorship in an address on June 30, 1949: "Why must things be done this way? The reason is quite clear to everyone. If things were not done this way, the revolution would fail, the people would suffer, the country would be conquered." See Mao, "On the People's Democratic Dictatorship," 4: 417. In June 1950, the Seventh Central Committee launched a major rectification campaign involving the study of Marxism through criticism and self-criticism, and, by 1951, Mao had developed the procedures for self-reform into intellectual thought reform (*sixiang gaizao* 思想改造). See Wakeman, *History and Will*, 33.

of socialist realism as developed in the USSR.[4] As noted in Chapter 4, Zhou Yang had introduced socialist realism back in 1933, but his 1953 formulation was an important landmark articulating the Party's explicit demand that writers follow its rules.[5] From this time on, and especially after the 1955 campaign against Hu Feng 胡風 (1902–1985) and his support of "truthful writing" and the "subjective," the Party's developing literary policy laid out increasingly hazardous minefields of taboos against the remnants of old thinking and bourgeois humanism. David Pollard has articulated a list of some of the taboos established by the early 1960s: (1) factuality, or the presentation of real people and real things in an unflattering light of naturalism or critical realism based on perception rather than on rationality derived from proper political education, (2) psychological analysis, (3) human flavor that might transcend class lines, (4) humanism, (5) romantic love that in any way overshadows class or social issues, (6) middle characters, and (7) spontaneity, that is, actions not grounded in a thorough political education in the Party's ideology.[6] Reading this list, it is easy to surmise the ways these taboos would work against sideshadowing the complexities of moral experience.

The presentation of voluntarism and the exercise of supposedly freely willed choice was nonetheless central to socialist realism and the "revolutionary romanticism" (*geming de langmanzhuyi* 革命的浪漫主義) prescribed in 1958. As the Party waged a series of campaigns to foster cultural and literary production in accordance with its doctrines, and dutiful writers wrote literature to follow the revolutionary line, part of these writers' task was to illustrate the kind of voluntarism Mao preached. Yet the representation of collective voluntarism usually involves depicting individuals, and so writers faced complex choices about their portrayals of the characters' deliberations and actions. Were these actions autonomous and freely willed, or were these examples of good citizens internalizing Mao's authority?

---

4. The term "socialist realism" (*sotsialisticheskу realizm*) was first used in the USSR by Ivan Gronsky, chairman of the Organizing Committee of the Union of Soviet Writers and editor of *Izvestya* (News). The Organizing Committee detailed the principles of the genre in 1932, and Andrey Zhdanov promulgated the concept at the all-USSR Congress of Writers in August 1934. It was at this conference that Zhdanov announced Stalin's idea that writers should be "engineers of human souls." See Luker, "Introduction," 18–19.

5. Zhou, "Wei chuangzao geng duo de youxiu de wenxue yishu zuopin er fendou."

6. See Pollard, "The Short Story," 100–102.

2. THE PROVINCE OF FICTION

If it seems incredible that Mao would attempt, by political fiat, to establish a single agenda for the cultural production of an entire vast nation, it seems equally incredible that scholars would believe this design could thoroughly succeed. Of course, panegyric characterizations produced a simulated euphoria that on a cursory reading may conceal the questions these works raise. As a result, it may be tempting to conclude that the heroes exemplify boundless devotion, unflinching courage, and, at least by the end, utter certainty about the correctness of their values. Whereas Lu Xun and other May Fourth writers portrayed characters awakening into a disorienting uncertainty and sense of alienation, this fiction depicts characters embracing a totalizing ideology, as both favorable studies and dismissals of these works often note. However, even if authors refrained from attributing doubt to their characters, sparing them the pangs of self-criticism, the best of these stories present implicit criticisms and misgivings.

Reading these stories more closely, one is struck by the different voices that speak within them.[7] Was the vision, as presented in the texts, ever in fact totalizing? Ostensibly, these works sought to construct a logic based on the inevitable transformation of history and society preached by Marxist–Leninist–Mao Zedong thought. Yet at the moment of representation this logic breaks down as many of these stories include at least the whispers of conflicting messages. In theory, the ultimate end of a Communist utopia overshadows moral questions about the means. But the fiction portrayed not the utopia but the path to it, the struggle with the means.

As depicted in fiction, this struggle was often embodied in moments of individual moral decision. Official policies aiming to make literature an instrument of social control and adjustment must allow individual freedom of choice, even as they posit a single possible outcome for that choice. Revolution becomes a straightforward moral choice in which the individual must choose against self-interest in favor of the collective future. For, as historian Fredrick Wakeman writes, for Mao, "mere personal responsibility" was "a form of dangerous self-indulgence."[8] But what about dilemmas in which contributing to the revolution means

7. For an example of a scholar of Soviet literature who also questions the feasibility of socialist realism, see Robin, *Socialist Realism.*

8. Wakeman, *History and Will*, 42.

choosing against a child or a parent? The ways in which works written under Party constraints present such choices merit more investigation than they have received.

One good example of a work that allows for alternative readings is Wang Yuanjian's 王願堅 (b. 1929) "Dangfei" 黨費 (Party membership dues; 1954), a story that first appeared in the official *Jiefangjun wenyi* 解放軍文藝 (Liberation army literature). In describing a peasant woman's selfless efforts to help the Red Army even when her actions endanger the welfare of her five-year-old daughter, the story is representative of the hagiographic accounts that define the leftist canon. This story is particularly powerful, however, because it shows a mother committing acts that most parents would find not only difficult but devastating to their own humanity.

The conflict between the woman's loyalty to the Party and her responsibility to her daughter is central to the story's structure both in the official reading and in the one to be presented here. If it were not, the story would hardly fulfill its didactic function as propaganda. The way the story sideshadows the mother's resolute decisions with the daughter's anguish and the narrator's initial disbelief may guide readers to identify with the narrator and follow him to an acceptance of a utilitarian morality whereby sacrifice to the revolution trumps other responsibilities. Yet the story's presentation of these other voices may also leave a reader haunted by misgivings concerning such a surrender of parental obligation.

The story is told by a young first-person narrator who is twice sent to visit a loyal Party member living in a village controlled by the Nationalists. In a briefing, the narrator is told that this woman, Huang Xin 黃新, has already sent her husband to join the Red Army and the Long March. During the first visit, because he knows Huang is alone with her young daughter, the narrator refuses to accept her two silver dollars when she offers them to pay her Party dues. Yet this refusal proves decisive, since Huang chooses to spend one of the dollars for salt to prepare preserved vegetables for the soldiers on the mountain. In so doing, she risks her own safety and endangers her daughter as well. That she understands these risks is clear in her skillful handling of events when the Nationalist police arrive looking for the narrator upon his second visit. She is ready with a scheme to conceal him, but it leads to her own arrest, an arrest she has obviously anticipated insofar as she also instructs him about which villager to contact in the future and asks him to take her daughter to the Party hideout in the mountains. Her choice enables the narrator to get away and deliver the vegetables, but it leaves her small daughter without either parent.

Hiding in the attic, the narrator struggles to decide whether he should try to save Huang until she tells her daughter, "Do as Mommy said" (49). At this point he realizes that "Mommy" stands for the Party and that he too must do as the Party would want. His realization is chilling for it explains Huang's own rationale in deserting her daughter. Such obedience to political imperatives is unsettling in that it ignores all competing claims, relationships, and responsibilities. Such a narrow pragmatic rationality is one of the reasons these stories of devotion and daring seem unrealistic and ultimately disheartening. As these characters choose to strive for a future collective good, often identified with the present good of the Party, they shirk incompatible responsibilities, relationships, and persons. Moreover, such altruism comes not only at one's own expense but also at the expense of others, including dependents who have neither say nor alternative support.

In reading a story such as "Party Membership Dues," one may think Huang inhuman in her readiness to disregard her daughter's feelings and welfare. Her refusal to give even a single bean to her hungry, skinny girl demonstrates the degree to which she has hardened herself to her daughter's needs. She rationalizes her insensitivity when she rebukes the narrator's suggestions that she feed her daughter by saying, "If only we have our Party, have our Red Army, there's no telling how many children can be saved" (48). Faced with a woman whose zeal for the abstract future has made her numb to the immediate needs of her own child, the reader may be more than reluctant to call her free. One begins to suspect that the entire construction of choice may be but an expedient illusion to facilitate authoritarian control.

Whether Wang Yuanjian intended the mother's choices to create dramatic tension is unclear, but several elements of the story reinforce the sense of conflict by pulling at the reader's heartstrings. First, although he feels instructed by her words and heroism, the initial reactions of the participant first-person narrator raise doubts about the morality of the woman's actions. Next, the story depicts the little girl's wails, mentions how the narrator has to calm her down, and ends with the Party captain wiping the tearstains from the girl's face. Perhaps Wang includes these details to drive home the reality of the woman's sacrifice without intending to call into question her ultimate decision, but the reader cannot but be struck by the mother's callousness toward her child.

One could counter that my supposed reader here is a Westerner and consider Pollard's prudent warning about "how difficult it is for the outsider to respond to these stories as their authors presumably hoped: wrong tradition (Daniel), wrong outlook (humanism)."[9] But such stories may have given pause to Chinese readers as well, and possibly even to their authors. For there is no reason that writers, even Party faithfuls, should not be as ambivalent and complex as other people and that their works should not reflect such ambivalence and complexity.

As much as the force of ideological conviction may astound, total certitude occurs only in the most insipid works. Any decent work of fiction, even one written to illustrate a set program, presents elements that transcend such a program. The wailing of an abandoned child must drown out, at least for a moment, the grand narrative about the necessity of waging revolution. When such a meta-narrative breaks down, it raises questions about the wisdom of subordinating other ties to the fulfillment of one's duty to the revolution. Hegemonic ideologies threaten to reign as total explanations, but their fictional representations tend to expose their fragility.

Some scholars commenting on Mao-era works would have us think that nothing was so dead as the critical spirit of the May Fourth period. But had it truly died? If it had, would these works be fiction at all? And would a critical spirit have been able to reemerge so quickly during the Hundred Flowers period (1956–1957) when Mao briefly encouraged criticism and intellectuals cautiously challenged the Party's monopoly on all aspects of life?[10] That Mao so quickly responded with the repressive Anti-Rightist Campaign (*Fan youpai douzheng* 反右派鬥爭; 1957–1959) and condemned the stories written during the Hundred Flowers period as "poisonous weeds" (*ducao* 毒草) testifies to the survival of that critical spirit.

9. Pollard, "The Short Story," 119.

10. The term "hundred flowers" comes from a speech Mao gave on May 2, 1956, in which he encouraged intellectuals to identify the regime's errors. For the literature, literary debates, and criticism of the Hundred Flowers movement, see Nieh, *Literature of the Hundred Flowers.*

3. THE MORAL WAGES OF SELF-SACRIFICE IN *SONG OF YOUTH*

As the political dangers of writing about the present increased, writers found what means they could to write meaningful novels, and the hazards they faced may partly account for the turn to historical novels such as the immensely popular *Qingchun zhi ge* 青春之歌 (Song of youth; 1958, second edition 1960), by the Hunan-born Yang Mo 楊沫 (1915–1995). Yang's novel was made into a popular movie in 1959 and sold 1,700,000 copies by March 1960. Positive initial reviews led to an intense debate in which other critics disapproved of the novel's focus on intellectuals at the expense of workers and peasants and what they claimed was the heroine's underdeveloped political transformation. These criticisms led Yang Mo to revise the novel, adding ten chapters to the second edition published in 1960. Seven of the new chapters describe the heroine's work in the countryside and thus substantially increase her contact with peasants and sharpen the portrayal of her developing class consciousness.

Song of Youth depicts the coming-of-age of the heroine Lin Daojing 林道靜 as she grows from a melancholy, dreamy youth into an ardent revolutionary engaged in underground work to build the Communist Party and resist the Nationalist government's capitulation in the face of the Japanese invasion in the early 1930s.[11] As Daojing gradually gives up her romanticism, humanism, and sense of superiority over peasants, she experiences a personal, intellectual, political, and moral transformation. Daojing's political conversion comes as a rational response to social injustice and national crisis, from less conscious emotional and psychological needs, and from a millenarian belief in history based on understandings of Marxist theory. As the novel shows the shaping of collective responsibility integral to any politics, its young revolutionaries explicitly privilege a consequentialist morality in which individuals become interchangeable instruments for revolutionary action. Yet the main characters' willingness to adopt this utilitarian view and to sacrifice their own and their loved ones' lives is sideshadowed by voices that reject using people as mere means.

---

11. Although her heroine's life and background bear similarities to the author's own, Yang Mo stresses that her heroine and other characters are mostly composites of many people and that Lu Jiachuan (to be discussed later) is an idealized character without a real-life model at all. See Wu Yang, "Yang Mo and Her Novel," 114.

3.1 Social Injustice and National Crisis

The first and arguably most persuasive force that shapes Daojing's existence is her childhood suffering. The novel begins with the story of Daojing's mother, Xiuni 秀妮, a poor tenant farmer. Abducted at the age of 21 to be a concubine to the landlord Lin Botang 林伯唐, Xiuni is taken to Beijing, where she gives birth to Daojing, but she is sent away when Daojing turns one. Years later, a servant tells Daojing of Lin's cruel treatment of her mother, including the way he gave her as a gift to a friend and then refused to open the compound gates when she returned to retrieve her daughter. Finding the gates closed, Xiuni circled the compound madly screaming, "Give me back my child! Give me back my child!"[12] Afraid of losing face, school chancellor and "philanthropist" Lin had Xiuni tied up and returned to her mountain village. Although it is unclear how the servant could know the next part of Xiuni's story, she tells Daojing that upon returning to her village Xiuni briefly recovered her composure in the hope of seeing her beloved grandfather, and then she committed suicide upon finding him gone. Learning of her mother's tragic end, Daojing is haunted by her mother's cries for the rest of the novel.

Left in Lin's household, Daojing develops into a melancholy, quiet, and introverted girl. She is well treated only until Lin's wife, Xu Fengying 徐鳳英, gives birth to her own son. Thereafter, the stepmother neglects, physically mistreats, and humiliates Daojing. Although Daojing enjoys a brief period of fulfillment while attending boarding school and developing her mind, imagination, and ideals, her education is cut short when Lin goes bankrupt and runs off with a concubine. The stepmother then schemes to restore her finances by marrying off Daojing to a wealthy Nationalist official, and Daojing runs away to avoid this arranged marriage.

While at a seaside village and then back in Beijing, Daojing begins to confront social injustice beyond her own family. In the third chapter, while observing foreigners and wealthy Chinese by the seashore, Daojing notices a woman feeding her dog a saucer of milk. Two pages later, she sees a poor, emaciated woman mending a fishing net and trying to breastfeed her crying infant. Daojing speaks with the woman and elicits the story of her plight, so she is all the more grieved when in the fol-

12. Yang, *Yang Mo wenji*, 1: 18. Subsequent references to the novel are given in parentheses, and all translations are my own unless otherwise noted.

lowing chapter she learns that the woman, despairing, has jumped into the sea. Her horror over her society's injustice is further compounded when her employer schemes to marry her to a local official as a second wife. Distraught, she tries to throw herself into the sea but is rescued by her employer's nephew, a young university student named Yu Yongze 余永澤.

Concern about the Japanese invasion combines with Daojing's concern about the peasants' poverty and the straightened circumstances of women. While working as a teacher at the seaside village, Daojing is startled by news of the September Eighteenth Incident, the Japanese invasion of Shenyang, and then of other cities in northeastern China. She learns of the invasion as refugees from the northeast arrive by train on September 24, and at this point she meets the young revolutionary Lu Jiachuan 盧嘉川. Lu tells Daojing about the Nationalist government's inaction and initiates her political awakening.

As Daojing faces the predatory nature of her society, her viewpoint develops a hard, cold, sober side. When she can no longer bear her employer's harassment and once she has saved enough money for the trip, she returns to Beijing. Yet despite her education and diligence she is unable to find work and feels she has "few options except" to live with Yu Yongze. From a romanticism born of reading novels, Daojing adopts a class analysis of her society that is particularly sensitive to the predicament of women.

The terrible contrast between the spoiled dog and the starving infant mentioned above marks the first of four crucial juxtapositions that draw attention to economic disparities and drive Daojing to embrace socialist theory. The second juxtaposition exposes Yongze's selfishness and forces Daojing to recognize the fundamental conflict in their values. After Daojing has already begun to suspect the incompatibility of their respective views, her suspicions are confirmed by Yongze's stinginess toward a desperate peasant who visits from Yongze's home village. When the peasant begs for money and perhaps for relief regarding the rent he owes Yongze's family, Yongze gives the peasant only one *yuan.* When Daojing gives the peasant ten more *yuan*, Yongze severely chastises her for squandering his money. Yet that very day Yongze has spent almost five *yuan* to host a fellow student whose father might help Yongze find a job after graduation.

The third juxtaposition occurs when the Party sends Daojing to work as a governess in the countryside and she observes the extremity of her employer's greed. When an old peasant named Wang takes wheat from the landlord's field to feed his starving grandchildren, the elderly landlord beats him for stealing. A fourth explicit contrast is made when Daojing first returns from the countryside and her friend Bai Liping 白莉苹 drags her to a ball at the Beijing hotel. Daojing is dazzled by the hall with its polished floor, velvet curtains, and decorative lanterns with tassels, as well as by the guests in high-heeled shoes, makeup, and jewels. But the splendor of the occasion makes her blood race as the image of the poor, old peasant Wang and his starving grandchildren in the countryside flashes in her mind (358–59).

As the novel shows the social and political processes by which a Marxist politics inspires collective passions to mobilize and direct the characters' investment, it also reveals the tension between class difference and equality that politics seeks to use toward productive ends. For example, when working in the countryside, Daojing recognizes an old tenant farmer whose family her landlord father drove to ruin. In coming to terms with the tenant farmer's intense resentment, Daojing begins to confront her own class background. Whereas she had previously hated her father and stepmother for the way they treated her mother, she now hates them on behalf of others: "She only now truly felt the flavor of class hatred" (306). She also begins to hate her own "contamination" by her class background growing up in a bourgeois family (306). Having perceived the tenant farmer's resentment, Daojing is amazed when he saves her by alerting her that the landlord has discovered her tie to the Communists. After he accompanies her on her escape, he replies to Daojing's query about his change of heart: "You are not Lin Botang's daughter. You're a daughter making revolution. How could I still hate you? It's the CCP that taught me not to hate you" (348–49).

3.2 Social Processes and Emotional Motivations

The novel's emphasis on class sets parameters that constrain the way in which Daojing can profile herself in the public sphere of political struggle. Yet it also suggests ways that the Party's political narrative enables her exercise of agency. Far from denying the interrelationship between these constraining and enabling aspects, the novel highlights their mutual interaction. Daojing's attraction to the Party stems from her mother's mistreatment, her own subordinate status as the daughter of a concubine, and from the lack of opportunities available to her as a woman. At the same time, her class background as the daughter of a landlord necessitates a long period of initiation and trials before she can become a trusted Party member.

Daojing's concern about social injustice makes her sympathetic to revolutionary ideals, but her attraction to the Party also stems from her intense yearning for community. Isolated at home in her housewife role, Daojing is particularly susceptible to political influence when, soon after her rude realization of Yongze's selfishness, she meets young revolutionaries and longs to join them. "A passion she had never felt before started to rise in her heart. She yearned to join together with these people and participate in talking within the group" (104).

The importance of socialization comes out in the great extent to which other individuals, and particularly the young male revolutionaries Lu Jiachuan and Jiang Hua 江華, script, guide, and motivate Daojing's personal and political development. The combination of her attraction to Lu Jiachuan and the idealism he inspires is underscored by one of the few instances of backshadowing in the novel: "Many years later, she could still clearly remember the title of the first book Lu Jiachuan gave her to read" (115). Although several women inspire her too, including Lin Hong 林紅, her cellmate in the Nationalists' prison, the peasant cadre who poses as Jiang Hua's aunt in the countryside 李姑母, and Big Sister Liu 劉大姐, with whom Daojing does liaison work after officially joining the Party, the male revolutionaries influence her most profoundly. The intensity of the magnetism Lu Jiachuan exerts on Daojing can be seen when she lovingly strokes the propaganda leaflets he has left in her house before his arrest. When Daojing bravely goes out in the evenings disguised as a streetwalker to post the leaflets around the city, it is in part her desire to feel connected to Jiachuan that fuels her courage. Daojing's eagerness to undergo socialization and the extent of her transformation is brought out when she tells her schoolmate friend Wang Xiaoyan 王曉燕, "I'm no longer the me I was a year ago" (202).

In describing Daojing's sense of connection when she is finally allowed to join the CCP officially, the novel further underscores the role of emotion and the need for belonging: "From today on, I will unconditionally give my whole life to the Party, to this greatest and most lofty enterprise in the world. . . ." (437). The narrator describes Daojing feeling as any Party member does upon joining the Party, knowing that "he is no longer a common person" and that: "His fate would be tightly bound together with the fate of millions of people. His fate would be sacrificed to the liberation and happiness of millions of people" (437). After this bombastic buildup, it is hard not to sense a hint of irony when reading of Daojing's initial disappointment when she is first assigned to do office work (*jiguan gongzuo* 機關工作; 441). But this work is part of her humbling initiation, and she soon graduates to underground organizing at Beijing University.

The paramount task of overcoming self-importance is brought out in the way Daojing and other characters describe her transformation. As Xiaoyan says, whereas before Daojing spoke of her own ideals, hopes, and suffering, after her time in prison she talks only about their common work and other people's troubles and invests all her warmhearted energy in the larger collective project (442). The broadening of her concerns beyond herself is again brought out explicitly when one of her fellow resistance leaders at Beijing University asks Daojing how she changed from a melancholy, aloof person into such a stalwart revolutionary. She answers that she still has many faults but focuses on how much more important the obstacles to the Party's progress are than her own frustrations (494). As such an assertion suggests, in political contexts the question of agency outweighs that of identity.

3.3 Siding with History

Even as her knowledge of social injustice and her yearning for community motivate Daojing to turn to revolutionary activism, her commitment is also rooted in her faith in her role in the inevitable flow of history. Believing that history's laws have been made intelligible and that revolutionary action can respond to those laws to guarantee a more equitable future, Daojing wants to be on the side of History. This confidence is expressed in the narrator's description of Daojing's revelations upon first reading Marxist-Leninist theory:

> From these books, she saw the future of the development of human society. From these books she saw the brilliant rays of truth and the road that she as an individual should take. From these books she understood the reasons for [Du Fu's poem] "Within vermilion gates wine and meat [are left to] reek / On the road are men's bones frozen to death." She understood why her mother had died. (115)

In this way, Daojing's courage is intimately connected to her faith in a kind of predestination. She acts not only out of outrage over the injustice of current social inequalities but also out of utter confidence that history will eventually destroy the landlord class. Daojing voices this faith against her half-brother's justification of their father's exploitation of their tenant farmers to pay for his son's upcoming wedding: "Unless a person acts for himself, Heaven will condemn and Earth destroy him," her brother says, invoking a proverb (227). Daojing responds by invoking the inevitable crushing of the landlord class: "You know, this class has no future. It is inevitably doomed to perish!" (227).

Several other of the novel's characters also explicitly invoke the notion of a determined historical justice. Belief in a cosmic justice even comes from some surprising quarters, as when Song Yubin 宋郁彬, the landlord's son whose children Daojing teaches during her second assignment in the countryside, comments on his father's treatment of his tenant farmers: "When things become extreme, they inevitably reverse [in the opposite direction]. My father's treatment of the peasants is much too harsh" (330).

Similarly, when Daojing's friend Wang Xiaoyan's father, Professor Wang Hongbin 王鴻賓, becomes sympathetic to the revolutionary Party, he invokes the power of greater forces to explain his rationale: "It looks as if it is the [inevitable] trend of great forces. The Nationalists are so corrupt that it's no surprise all the citizens are dissatisfied" (423). It is this conviction that leads Professor Wang to join the students in the December the Sixteenth demonstration at the end of the novel: "Now he recognized the direction of world currents and humanity's irresistible general trends. Communism would inevitably win the final victory in the whole world and the whole of humanity" (597).

3.4 Sacrificing the Personal for the Collective

In the novel's presentation of radical personal sacrifices, a consequentialist morality is first invoked by the young revolutionary Lu Jiachuan: "In evaluating a person's actions, including all his hard work and struggle, more important than looking at his motivation is looking at his results. See if he is pushing the current society forward or gilding and holding onto the corrupt society" (120). Such a consequentialist ethics contrasts sharply with the Confucian emphasis on following the correct way regardless of outcomes.

The view that individuals are interchangeable instruments for the great utopian goal of revolution is voiced by Wang Xiaoyan when she recalls and comments on the poem (by Bai Juyi 白居易) that Daojing recited to her earlier in the novel (202):

> "No prairie fire can burn it utterly; the spring wind blows it back to life again." It's true. I thought that since you'd been arrested and could no longer work, I had to take your place and carry on your work. If I were arrested as well, then there would be many, many others who would take my place. . . . The summer fire will never completely extinguish it. (427/429)[13]

Xiaoyan's father, Professor Wang, makes the case for subordinating the individual to the revolutionary project in even starker terms when he replies to Jun Cai 君才 (the alias of the traitor Dai Yu 戴愉): "What do I as an individual matter? According to the Marxist viewpoint, only the masses count as the true heroes, only they are the world's creators. One individual, one individual is too insignificant to mention" (568).

The subordination of personal and familial ties to Party devotion marks the transformation of several other characters as well. For one, the young Yu Shuxiu 俞淑秀 places the Party above her mother when she regrets parting with Daojing as they are released from prison in July 1935: "My mother is not the most dear. You and Sister Zheng Jin, it's you I'll never forget. Mommy nurtured my body. But it's you—the Party—who have given me a soul" (424). Daojing reassures her that whatever geography divides them, they will be inseparable as long as their wills are united (425).

Most of the revolutionaries share a hardheaded will to sacrifice their lives for the revolution. In chapter 7, when the young student revolutionaries are on a train to Nanjing to protest the Nationalist Party's inaction, Luo Dafang 羅大方 asserts their fearlessness by stating his willingness to repeat the losses suffered in the March the Eighteenth Incident when the warlord Duan Qirui's troops fired on students protesting against imperialism in Tiananmen Square: "Even if we have to sacrifice many people—as in the March the Eighteenth Incident—fresh blood is the best thing to awaken people's hearts" (57). Such lines give the reader pause about the crossroads of, and possible mutual influence between, literature and politics, for they might even support the accusation of critics, such as Liu

13. Where a second number appears, it refers to the translation by Nan Ying.

Zaifu 劉再復 and Lin Gang 林崗, who charge that revolutionary literature serves as "an apology for all the cruelty and bloodshed generated by this struggle."[14]

Daojing demonstrates her ability to subordinate and even to redirect her most intimate desires in her overly rational reaction to Jiang Hua's declaration of love and to the meager chances they have to be together. Wondering if she could love this comrade whom she has respected for so long when for many years it was Lu Jiachuan who occupied her heart, she decides that she can because he deserves her love. "But, she no longer hesitated. Truly, a Bolshevik comrade such as Jiang Hua was worth her loving deeply and ardently. What reason could she have to refuse this person who had deeply loved her for so long?" (559). Two nights after the September Ninth movement in 1935, Jiang Hua is wounded escaping from arrest. When he comes to visit Daojiing he regrets how little he has to give her, and she replies that she feels lucky to be able to share their sufferings and joys together. "I often think, that I can have today, that I can realize my ideal—to be a glorious Communist warrior. Who gave me all this? It's you—the Party. As long as our cause develops, as long as the Party benefits, what do our personal affairs count?" (585).

At the end of the novel, Daojing's subordination of her personal happiness to the larger goals of the revolution is so complete that she greets the possible murder of her lover with chilling equanimity. When Jiang Hua disappears just as shots are fired during the demonstration, Daojing worries that he has been wounded, but she quickly calms herself: "But in the fierce tension of struggle, everything personal appeared so insignificant and inconsiderable. Daojing's worry for Jiang Hua flashed in her heart and then passed. She immediately joined with the tens of thousands, even more excitedly shouting with the voice of the whole Chinese people, 'Down with Japanese Imperialism!'" (611). Daojing's ability to let go of her concern for her lover and submerge herself in the mass rally might represent a courageous stoicism, but it may also betray how little she cares for herself as anything but a tool of history's processes. Since Daojing cannot affect the laws of history or her own contingent position within the struggle, her own wishes count for little.

14. Liu Zaifu and Lin Gang, "Zhongguo xiandai xiaoshuo zhong de zhengzhi xiezuo moshi," 96–97, quoted and translated in Zhang, "The Power of Rewriting," 300.

3.5 Sideshadows

Whereas the revolutionaries share a willingness to make themselves tools for the revolution, other characters in the novel voice opposition to such a utilitarian morality. First, worrying that Daojing is merely following a collective mania, several of her friends challenge her belief that she is acting of her own free will in devoting herself to the revolution. For example, when Daojing and Yongze start to argue about participating in politics, a sideshadow is cast when Yongze offers Daojing a quiet life as he explains his reluctance to involve himself further in politics:

> Jing, I believe that we can't do anything about these matters. There's a government and a military; what purpose can we pale-faced students serve with our bare hands and empty fists? Anyone can shout empty slogans. You know that I participated in the Student Patriotic movement, but that's in the past. Now—now I think it's better to immerse one's head in studying. We've become a family, let's take a more secure road. (113)

Second, although she later converts to socialism, Daojing's friend Xiaoyan is at first not only impervious to Daojing's lectures but resents Daojing's refusal to respect her views as she respects Daojing's (369). Daojing's browbeating of her friend instills skepticism in the reader about the morality of proselytizing and the ethical risks of dogmatism. Third, the novel presents alternatives to self-sacrifice in its portrayal of characters that desert the revolutionary cause for their own personal happiness. For example, Daojing's friend Bai Liping's decision to forsake the revolutionary struggle to marry a man who can support her in comfort is presented as a tangible model for Daojing.

In placing the characters' limited moral agency within the context of changing conditions and their own shifting commitments, the novel recounts the social processes by which the characters arrive at their values and frames of reference. The presentation of multiple characters' political transformations defends against the implication that Daojing's radicalism might merely be an effect of personal desperation. Yet, whereas the novel presents marriage to a rich man as Daojing's only alternative to becoming a revolutionary, characters with more options also turn to the revolution. In these cases, the elements that lead to Daojing's transformation—concern about social injustice, the sense of national crisis, a need to belong, and a belief in historical determinism—also motivate and guide other characters' political awakenings. In one moving example of a character galvanized by her sense of social justice, observing the Nationalists' persecution of Daojing converts her friend Wang Xiaoyan, the pampered daughter of a professor, to the principles of the revolutionaries: "From that day I saw clearly the black darkness of this society and the vicious face of the Nationalist Party. The first time Hu Meng'an was coercing you [to marry him], I still thought that he was [just] an evil individual; but, that incident truly taught me. Your blood washed the light into my eyes" (427).

Passages such as this one represent the relief the characters feel when they surrender to the culture of solidarity promoted by the Party, but the novel hardly presents such awakenings as inevitable. As large a role as core revolutionary values such as self-sacrifice and activism play in this popular novel, the lengthy narrative also stages characters' hesitations, misunderstandings, and mistakes as they travel toward their ultimate adherence to the revolution. Though they do not prevail, these considerations and the sideshadows they cast create a dialogue that lends both depth and enduring tensions to the novel's endorsement of revolutionary solidarity. In this way, Yang's novel also points to a fundamental duality in Marxism between determinism and voluntarism. On the one hand, the novel depicts characters that come to believe in a logic of history leading inevitably to socialism. Yet, under the pressure of that very logic, the novel posits the equally certain emergence of a revolutionary proletarian consciousness, and it voices enduring humanist reservations about the use of individuals as means for political history making.

4. REVOLUTIONARY ROMANTICISM

In 1958, during the tension that led up to the Sino-Soviet split, Vice-Minister of Culture Zhou Yang, at Mao's behest, advocated that a literature of "revolutionary romanticism" replace the literature of "socialist realism."[15] The newer name is more apt, even for many of the works of the preceding decade, but the substitution of the word "romanticism" for "realism" seems particularly appropriate for the year in which Mao launched the

15. Many scholars date the split to the withdrawal of Soviet experts in the summer of 1960, but relations between the two countries were souring at least since Khrushchev's denunciation of Stalin in 1956. The Soviets did not consult the Chinese regarding this denunciation or regarding their shift to the international policy of peaceful coexistence.

disastrous Great Leap Forward (*Dayuejin* 大躍進; 1958–1960).[16] In a significant shift, works of the early 1960s diminished the presentation of conflict to give the impression that society's problems could be, as Mao Dun put it, "solved in a morning."[17]

Critics have disparaged these works as lacking psychological characterization, but some of the texts do convey a strong psychological component. More striking is how short on plot many of these stories seem. Gone is the suspense that marked some of the earlier Mao-era works, both because the plots have become overly conventional and because, simply put, not much happens. Otherwise the conventions largely follow those marking earlier fiction of the Mao period: Agricultural stories recount how the collective wins over a "holdout." Industrial stories tell how a common worker cleverly outperforms those with expertise. Military stories portray courage and will. Other stories show people sacrificing comfort to work for the collective good.

Hao Ran's 浩然 (b. 1932) "Xing hua yu" 杏花雨 (Apricot blossom rain; 1962), for example, depicts a young man's feelings and perceptions with considerable sensitivity, but the story's events hardly seem proportional to the emotional buildup. The skillful opening creates a strong sense of atmosphere as the boy loses his way in the cold rain as he leads a horse back to his village after a trip to a veterinary station. The story next recounts the warmth of the small house into which a young woman welcomes the boy out of the rain. Without explicit description, the story conveys the young man's sexual excitement at finding himself alone with the young woman. Up to this point, the story seems promising.

The story's pace picks up with the introduction of more formulaic elements, yet its sensitivity almost instantly wanes. The woman's father-in-law comes home and chastises the two for talking rather than taking care of the sick horse: "Which is more urgent? Somebody eating, or curing a sick animal?"[18] With the entry of this stock character, the stern (*yan* 嚴) father figure, the story begins to slacken, not only in terms of psychological sensitivity but also in terms of interest. After caring for the horse, the exhausted boy goes to rest in another room. When he hears the young woman's husband describe his plan to deliver wheat cakes to people stranded on the other side of a river, the young man jumps up and

16. For a carefully researched account of the calamity of the Great Leap Forward, see Becker, *Hungry Ghosts*.

17. Quoted in Mills, "Literature in Fetters," 291.

18. Hao Ran, "Xing hua yu," 143.

offers to help deliver the food, stressing that he is a fine swimmer. The story can be read as a tale of progress from the boy's shame over his desire for comfort to his climactic decision to forgo rest to deliver food to those stranded because of hard rains.

The problem with the presentation of rational choice in such stories is that the simplicity of the options makes it hard to take these decisions seriously. One finishes such stories asking, "Is that all?" Of course, apathy poses an abiding problem, particularly for those waging revolution. But what kind of decision-making training presents people with choices like the one in the story: You can either huddle in your bed not wishing to go out in the rain, or you can serve the collective good. One can only feel bewildered by this method of rousing people from their apathy, particularly in light of the brutality of some of the methods used in real life.

Consequently, stories of this period tend to be fragmentary. As much as they depict agency, the near-total lack of ambiguity makes free choice irrelevant. Only through posing more complex situations can fiction show people following their revolutionary free will despite their inclinations to reject such responsibilities. Works of revolutionary romanticism such as "Apricot Blossom Rain" paint a world where all choices reduce to a mere matter of balancing alternatives according to an accepted scale. They erase the need for people to determine on which values their choices will depend, or the possibility that they may be torn by conflicting values. If freedom means freedom from difficult choices, it must be asked if such a freedom is worth wanting.

5. VOICES OF DOUBT

Although the characters' limited choices make the stories of the early 1960s simplistic, they are not univocal in their endorsement of Party values. Li Tuo 李陀 and other critics have rightly decried the repressive, monological nature of *Mao wenti* 毛文體 (Mao discourse or Mao-speak) and examined its persistence in the post-Mao era.[19] Reckoning the ongoing power of this style should not lead us to oversimplify how this discourse operated in its heyday, however. Could such a discourse ever really contain all the voices of a novel or a story? When one reads works of socialist realism against the grain, against their stated intentions, it is hard to ignore the other messages that creep in once one is attentive to sideshadows.

19. Li, Zhang, and Wang, "Yuyan de fanpan," 79–80.

For example, Hao Ran's story "Caixia" 彩霞 (Bright Clouds; 1961) can be read as a panegyric of Li Caixia 李彩霞 (Bright Clouds Li), but the story also expresses Caixia's ambivalence about performing more than her share of work and her criticisms of the revolutionary cadres, from her husband, who is the team leader, to the peasants who are supposed to be leading the revolution. In extolling the way Caixia solves problems, the story also suggests that these problems would worsen without her and thus defies the dictate that literature show Party policies working as intended. For example, Caixia attempts to refuse the mending work her husband assigns her by exclaiming, "I'm all thumbs [at sewing]: I'm not going to take care of it."[20] The story then shows her husband tricking her into doing the work, suggesting that he does not respect her feelings. Driving the point home, Caixia brings out her sacrifices by complaining about the burden she bears and about the lack of recognition or positive reinforcement. The tale of Caixia's ability to make herself work when she would prefer to relax and play with her baby may demonstrate her devotion, but this message does not silence her ambivalence.

The story expresses its most serious criticism when Caixia scolds the peasant who comes asking her for advice about what to do in the team leader's absence. In her response, Caixia comments explicitly on the peasant's passivity and lack of initiative:

> What's the matter with you? You've got a good head and you think of the production team's interest. What's more, you've an eye that notices what should be done. The only trouble is you don't dare take the initiative and say what you think. That won't do. The production team belongs to all of us. The team leader can't be everywhere. When he's not home, we should all act like masters in our own house.[21]

Of course, the peasant's passivity can be interpreted as a pernicious effect of tradition, and such lines can be read as instructive of how reform should work. Yet they can also be read as showing that the revolution is not going as planned. It may be no accident that "Caixia" was written during the period of recovery when the Party had to call off some of its policies connected with the disastrous Great Leap Forward. Even this much criticism might have been hazardous in the ensuing period.

20. Hao Ran, "Caixia," 473. The translation here is my own.
21. Hao Ran, "Caixia," 474–75; trans. Tung and Chen, 70.

6. THE CULTURAL REVOLUTION AND THE HAZARDS OF MORAL DILEMMAS

The further tightening of regulations for fiction writing during the Socialist Reeducation Campaign (1963–1966) and the Cultural Revolution (1966–1976) posed new challenges for the representation of moral decision. Presenting conflicting voices that give rise to moral dilemmas became increasingly hazardous as the Party leadership became progressively more authoritarian, and its supervision of culture became ever more integral to its supervision of political, economic, and social life. Literature's subordination to Party command was consolidated by the Party's encouragement of amateur writers, collective authorship, and a kind of manufacture rather than creation of literature. Writers were reduced, in the words of Joseph S. M. Lau, to being mere "literary mechanics" supplying technique as the least important members of the "three in one team" (*sanjiehe* 三結合) where the other members supplied the more important parts, life from the peasants and thought from the cadres.[22] Such practices led one author to refer to his short story as "a thousand-man cake."[23]

During the Cultural Revolution, Mao Zedong's wife Jiang Qing 江青 and Yao Wenyuan 姚文元, a Shanghai journalist who would become the mouthpiece for the Gang of Four, further developed the concept of revolutionary romanticism into a set of strict precepts and condemned works that did not follow these precepts.[24] To control artistic writing, Jiang supervised the revision of five operas, two ballets, and one symphonic suite to serve as eight "model theatrical works" (*yangbanxi* 樣板戲).[25] These works set the parameters for writing, articulated in a handy formula by Minister of Culture Yu Huiyong 于會泳 in a 1968 article: Works should portray the "three prominences" (*san tuchu* 三突出), whereby positive characters would dominate, heroic characters would be even more prominent, and the main heroic characters most salient of all. Objective truth, middle characters, psychological portraits,

---

22. Lau, "The Wounded," 128. The notion of "three-in-one" collective authorship began in the army and was one sign of the military's involvement in culture under Lin Biao, the Minister of Defense. See Mills, "Literature in Fetters," 296, 298.

23. Mills, "Literature in Fetters," 298.

24. Among other works, Yao Wenyuan condemned *Song of Youth* in his collection *The New Pine Tree*. See Hsu, *The Chinese Literary Scene*, 140.

25. McDougall and Louie, *The Literature of China*, 346.

romantic themes, and human feelings transcending class lines were denounced as "bourgeois" or "naturalistic." From the ominous publication of Yao Wenyuan's attack on the writer Wu Han 吳晗, "Ping *Hai Rui baguan*" 評海瑞罷官 (Criticizing *Hai Rui Is Dismissed from Office*) in November 1965, and especially at the Forum on Work of Literature and Art in the Army in February 1966 and in the "Summary" of the forum published in September 1967, the Party attacked not only traditional Chinese literature, foreign literature, and much of the left-wing literature of the 1930s but even many works of the Communist period up to 1965. Although they did not explicitly attack socialist realism, critiques of major Soviet practitioners such as Mikhail Sholokhov made clear that revolutionary romanticism had surpassed its origins in socialist realism and that writers had to overcome the pitfalls of realism, such as showing the shortcomings of characters, or risk attack for following the "black line" that combined bourgeois, revisionist, and 1930s ideas about literature and art.[26]

Obviously, such dictates are no formula for showing complex decision making under difficult circumstances or the struggle citizens confront in deciding between their nobler and baser desires. Yet such conflicts provide much of the substance of literature, particularly of longer works, so it is not surprising that official novel writing practically ceased.[27] Not a single novel was officially published from 1966 until February 1972. From 1972 until 1976, 126 novels were published, a tiny number compared with the outpouring of works in the post-Mao period but not a small number compared with the yearly production of novels between 1949 and 1966.[28] These Cultural Revolution novels often focused on military affairs, agriculture, industry, barefoot doctors, and the reeducation of educated youth (*zhishi qingnian* 知識青年, or simply *zhiqing* 知青) through the rustication movement (1968–1975) that sent some twelve million young urban Chinese "up to the mountains and down to the villages" (*shangshan xiaxiang* 上山下鄉) to live in remote areas during the Cultural Revolution.[29] Rather than represent conflict, such

26. Yang Lan, *Chinese Fiction of the Cultural Revolution*, 20–22.

27. Novels posed the greatest political risks because of the longer publication process and the more enduring nature of the product. The shorter a fictional work, the greater its chances were of slipping past the censors despite ambiguous messages.

28. Yang Lan, *Chinese Fiction of the Cultural Revolution*, 4.

29. See Louie, *Between Fact and Fiction*, 91.

novels tended to represent the force of giving oneself over to a great epic struggle. As Leo Lee comments on the heroism of Gao Daquan 高大全 (Mr. Great-Perfect Tall) in Hao Ran's *Jinguang da dao* 金光大道 (The great golden road; 1972 and 1974): "The epic quality of his novel has likewise transformed the mimetic levels of 'realism' into the realm of romance and myth. . . . In Hao Jan's 'romantic' world, there can be only one journey—the pilgrimage along the road to socialism."[30]

At the same time, it became increasingly important to posit personal freedom and choice even as the Party rendered them illogical by dictating the correct outcome for those choices and by calling for collective responsibility and mutual surveillance to enforce them. For in order for literature to play its role in such socialization and control, it has to take seriously the manipulation of individuals' moral reasoning. As Edward Gunn explains, literature's staging of individual choice served a vital didactic function:

> Chinese Communist literature from the early 1960s until 1977 primarily portrayed the individual as a rational entity composed of a set of personal and social values. The individual was seen as a producer who applies these values in the workplace (be it school, factory, farm, etc.) to make a decision about a work-related (production-related) problem.
>
> The theories behind this literature presumed that by presenting such a model of the self as a decision-making producer, above or to the exclusion of any other feature of the self, literary works would in a rational as well as emotional fashion educate readers to behave according to the model presented.[31]

Within these hazardous strictures, to their authors' credit and much to subsequent critical oversight, many works adapted to the political restrictions in creative and courageous ways. Issues of agency and determinism take on new meanings in the best of these novels, novels such as Ke Fei's 克非 (b. 1930) *Chun chao liu* 春潮流 (Swift is the spring tide; 1974), Shen Rong's 諶容 (b. 1936) *Wannianqing* 萬年青 (Evergreen; 1975), and Li Ruqing's 李汝清 *Wan shan hong bian* 萬山紅遍 (Ten thousand red-bordered mountains; 1976). The next section analyzes Shen Rong's novel to suggest ways such novels recast questions of individual and collective agency as they balance values of activism with traditional values of caution, contemplation, and human-heartedness.

---

30. Leo Lee, "The Solitary Traveler," 305.

31. Gunn, "Perceptions of Self and Values," 308–9.

7. CONSENSUS BUILDING AND COLLECTIVE AGENCY IN *EVERGREEN*

Shen Rong's *Evergreen* offers a strong example of a Cultural Revolution novel presenting a dialogue between conflicting voices and sideshadows of competing courses of action. The novel depicts a prolonged struggle between a misguided work team led by a county secretary that promotes household output quotas (*baochan dao hu* 包產到戶) and local villagers led by the heroic Party secretary who insist on collective production. Between the steadfast main hero Jiang Chunwang 江春旺 and the capitalist-roader Huang Guang 黃光, the novel presents a broad spectrum of popular attitudes. Some of the characters, including most of the so-called "middle and poor peasants," demonstrate their passionate commitment to collective farming. Others, including most of the former landowners and "rich peasants," are alienated from the collective faith and embrace the new household system.

Despite the somewhat clear ideological lines and their correspondence with the characters' class and family backgrounds, the novel's sympathetic portrayal of the community's long process of consensus building allows for the presentation of a spectrum of attitudes concerning the appropriateness of collective or private incentives, orientations, and values. As neighboring communities face the disastrous consequences of the Great Leap Forward and some attain unprecedented harvests using the individual household system from 1962 through 1964, some loyal cadres and peasants take seriously the need to consider this other system. In particular, Jiang Hongyun 江鴻運 leads a small group of middle peasants to support the household output system on the argument that it best conforms to his view of human nature: "Ever since ancient times, people have had selfish hearts. They most cherish their own things, and they are most conscientious about their own land."[32] Moreover, the advocates of the individual household system are not unequivocally negative characters. For example, in personally going to the village to encourage implementation of the household output quota system, County Secretary Huang Guang demonstrates important revolutionary values. Namely, he shows both a willingness to work hard and a loyalty to the Party, since the impetus for privatization seems to be coming from the highest levels of the Party. By narrating certain chapters from their perspectives, the novel

32. Shen, *Wannianqing*, 117.

conveys a degree of sympathy and respect for the characters endorsing privatization.

Formal elements in the novel also create a dialogue between revolutionary destiny and human agency. On the one hand, the novel's title, *Evergreen*, which is also the name of the central commune depicted, foreshadows the resilience and endurance of People's communes. Yet the novel's representation of the villagers' struggles and ethical dilemmas is far from deterministic. Instead, its sideshadowing of different perspectives and shifting allegiances offers a picture of multiple branching alternatives much richer than can be gleaned from most historical writing on struggles with collectivization. Although official literary policy stated that heroes should be filled with revolutionary optimism and always able to distinguish the correct from the wrong line, the novel shows many peasants only gradually committing themselves fully to resistance against the "capitalist wind" of the individual household quota system. For example, the Youth League secretary Jin Zhu 金柱 first visits a neighboring village to investigate its implementation of the household quota system and then voices the Youth League's opposition based on their empirical conclusions: "None of us agrees with the household quota system. The household quota system is simply individual laboring. We saw very clearly [what it led to] in Jiao Village. The poor get poorer. The rich get richer. The majority of the people are poor. The minority are rich."[33] Against a deterministic trajectory, the novel also shows the defenders of collectivism meeting with numerous setbacks, as when Huang Guang dismisses Jiang Chunwang from his position as Party secretary. Jiang maintains faith that the socialist cause will triumph, but the novel hardly makes this outcome look inevitable.

In a significant departure from the Maoist value of swift efficiency, Jiang Chunwang puts kindness and the humane treatment of his opponents above the rapid defeat of the individual household output quota system. Though some of Jiang Chunwang's comrades see his consideration of his adversary Huang Guang as a weakness and his efforts to spare Huang from public humiliation as detrimental to their cause, his concern to ensure that the commune reach its decisions by ethical means wins the reader's sympathy. Although the novel champions decisive action, goal-oriented behavior, forward motion, and "taking fate into one's own hands," it does not present these values in the way that

33. Shen, *Wannianqing*, 121.

clearly contrasts with "the traditional tendency to wait and see, toward caution and contemplation," as Ai-li Chin characterizes most Mao-era short stories.[34]

Especially in a novel as long as the 565-page *Evergreen*, values of caution, contemplation, and human-heartedness compete with values of activism in a much more complex way than in many shorter works of the Mao era. On the one hand, *Evergreen* represents core values that recur in Mao-era fiction: (1) ideological correctness, (2) willingness to work hard, (3) activism, (4) honesty, trustworthiness, and sincerity, (5) speaking out, (6) affection and caring for others, and (7) a willingness to turn oneself and one's loved ones into means for revolution and socialist transformation.[35] Yet the presentation of these values leaves much room for a dialogue among competing motives, means, and commitments.

Furthermore, Shen's novel is rare in world literature in its presentation of collective agency and decision making. Rather than focusing on a handful of main characters, the novel demonstrates the importance of the entire community. Numerous narrative detours present a vast number of characters' family backgrounds, traumatic upbringings, political socialization, and moral awakenings. These detailed subplots weave complicated webs of contingencies that lead the characters to both individual commitments and collective solidarity. Building consensus does not depend simply on bringing together individuals' interrelated commitments. Instead, solidarity results from a complex interchange between individual reflections and collective developments. One example of the interaction of character and socialization can be seen in the description of the coming-of-age of the main hero, Jiang Chunwang. In deference to the Maoist theory of blood descent (*xuetonglun* 血統論), the novel recounts how Jiang Chunwang's father, Da Lao Jiang 大老江, also performed heroic deeds to free himself and his fellow captives from Japanese conscription and then to save a youth caught during their escape by turning himself in despite the certainty of having to pay with his life. Yet the novel devotes at least as much space to the education, inspiration, and guidance provided to Chunwang by Jiang Yutian 江雨天, a livestock farmer who has watched over Chunwang since the latter was orphaned at the age of eight.

---

34. Chin, "Value Themes in Short Stories," 302.

35. The seventh value is my addition to the six values identified in Chin, "Value Themes," 302.

In a novel such as *Evergreen*, even if the characters' individual moral decisions may be overdetermined, the drama of the community's struggle retains ethical and political significance. Given the presentation of competing voices in such novels, it is unfortunate that so many scholars, be they advocates or critics of socialist realism, have so overestimated the ability of such literature to harness and shape readers' responses. Gunn well expresses the difficulty of controlling the ethical import of fiction in stating his conclusions concerning a readers' questionnaire he circulated in 1978:

> That their personal values were not correlated with their perception of values in a literary work and that they further could not agree on which values in the works were the most important suggest a failure in the literature as a vehicle for the rational conveyance of values and a sense of the priority of values relative to each other in their given, hypothetical situations.[36]

What this discussion of Mao-era works makes clear is that Mao-era works were hardly univocal in their endorsement of Party values. Forasmuch as these works present pragmatic, revolutionary decision making, they also show the power of other affective and aesthetic dimensions that at least accompany and sometimes directly compete with such rationality. Even when rationality appears to be the central or dominant aspect motivating the characters, many of these works suggest the great extent to which such rationality may mask need, fear, suffering, desire, or other emotional undercurrents. Hence, these popular stories and novels may have furthered dominant socialist ideology, but they also voiced resistance to reducing human experience to political rationalities. Such fiction presents the demands and possibilities of freedom and agency that millenarian schemes can neither silence nor contain.

36. Gunn, "Perceptions of Self and Values," 310.

6

Historical Trauma and Humanism in Post-Mao Realism

禍福無門，爲人自找
Fortune and misfortune have no [definite] door but are sought by humans for ourselves.

—Chinese proverb

Questions about historical destiny, moral responsibility, and political, social, and economic freedom shape much of the fiction written in the early post-Mao era. No other period speaks as clearly of the complex, heavy burdens of witness and conscience borne by modern Chinese writers. In "scar literature" and subsequent new realist works, narrators and key characters often lament the limitations of individual understanding and influence yet ultimately champion the possibility of meaningful human agency. Inspired by translations of nineteenth-century European fiction, many of these writers turned to explicit humanist themes and positions.

These works mark a high point in the representation of moral responsibility in twentieth-century Chinese fiction. Whereas in the West, the humanism of the Renaissance was a reaction to ideas and attitudes of the Middle Ages, in post-Mao China, humanism represented a break with the Mao-era emphasis on collective forces and inevitable historical laws. Against Mao's utopian teleology and totalizing explanations based on historical or economic determinisms, these works sought to safeguard the inescapable responsibility of human beings. Against the Mao-era emphasis on class as the determination of human worth, many of these works support the possibility of human betterment through reason, mutual understanding, and respect for authentic accounts of the human condition. In contrast to political and theoretical interventions, fiction writers sought to reform the Party and their society not by authority or threat but through thoughtfulness and compassion.

To promote the fuller development of human capabilities, intellectuals of the early Deng era used arguments and rhetoric reminiscent of the May Fourth era. Bolstering these arguments with readings of both liberal Enlightenment philosophy and contemporary Western theory, they again questioned what they viewed as fatalistic notions inherited from traditional Chinese thought. Yet many of their arguments shared with Confucian traditions several humanist assumptions. In all its variety, the Confucian tradition had continually treated the secular world and the family as primary objects of interest, and much of the post-Mao fiction also sought to treat everyday human affairs and intimate relations as legitimate objects of love and concern.

Post-Mao fiction is characterized by its great emphasis on the interpersonal nature of moral experience and ethical selfhood. In this chapter, I thus focus on ways these works use sideshadowing to show that moral action's meaning or efficacy depends not only on the individual actor but also on those affected or addressed. To begin this consideration, I briefly discuss several historically significant works and movements of the early post-Mao era. If works of revolutionary romanticism had invoked hallowed myths to endorse a Maoist version of history, fiction of the post-Mao period often undermined these myths, particularly their underlying faith in collective voluntarism. Later called "new realism" (*xin xieshizhuyi* 新寫實主義) to distinguish the genre from the realism prescribed by the Party, this fiction of the late 1970s and early 1980s recalled the May Fourth tradition of critical realism.[1] I then examine two works by Dai Houying 戴厚英 (1938–1996). The first, Dai's novel *Ren a, ren* 人啊，人！ (Humanity, o humanity!; 1980), depicts several characters' intense search for historical meaning, interpersonal understanding, and redemption. The second, Dai's novella *Suolian, shi rouruan de* 瑣鏈，是柔軟的 (Soft is the chain; 1982), exemplifies the humanist project of focusing on individual self-determination in the face of superstition and oppressive social norms.

I. TRAUMA AND RESPONSIBILITY IN SCAR LITERATURE (1977–1980)

Stories presenting increasingly complex moral dilemmas quickly followed Mao's death and the fall of the Gang of Four in 1976. Even before the

1. This term is used by Li Yi in "Wenyi xinzuo zhong suo fanying de Zhongguo xianshi," 2–9.

Party's official relaxation of thought control,[2] several stories mourned the spiritual state of the Chinese people who had suffered during the Cultural Revolution. Although the epithet "scar literature" (*shanghen wenxue* 傷痕文學) drew attention to the victims' suffering, this fiction increasingly hinted at the characters' roles as victimizers as well.

Usually considered the first work of the genre later called scar literature, Liu Xinwu's 劉心武 (b. 1942) short story "Banzhuren" 班主任 (The schoolmaster; November 1977) preaches an optimistic and patriotic faith in the country while also venturing to analyze the current "impoverishment of spiritual life" (10).[3] In Liu's story, the devoted teacher Zhang Junshi 張俊石 chooses to help a youth whose delinquency he attributes to his upbringing during the Cultural Revolution. As Zhang negotiates the boy's acceptance into his class and confronts some of his pupils' resistance, he realizes that many of the exemplary youth have likewise been harmed by the imposed political orthodoxy. Most notably, Zhang concludes that narrow-mindedness and an inability to think independently have crippled well-intentioned Youth League Branch Secretary Xie Huimin 謝惠敏. Several programmatic and preachy passages mar the story as Zhang lectures the reader on the need to cure abscesses in the body politic and blames the Gang of Four for the youngsters' limitations. Yet the story also expresses Zhang's impassioned faith in his ability to influence his students' development, "guide them to fix their eyes on a wider world, and engender their interest in all the achievements of human civilization" (18).

Whereas many early stories drearily denounced the Gang of Four for the country's ills and thus avoid issues of personal responsibility, bolder

---

2. In the Third Plenary Session of the Eleventh Party Congress held in late 1978, the Central Committee of the Communist Party set objectives to liberate thought and promote democracy. At the Fourth Congress of the All-China Federation of Literature and Art Workers in 1979, Deng Xiaoping and Zhou Yang promised "the sole criterion for deciding the correctness of all work should be whether that work is helpful or harmful to the accomplishment of the Four Modernizations" (Duke, "Chinese Literature in the Post-Mao Era," 4). Also in 1979, a state publishing house, Renmin chubanshe, issued a collection of critical works from the Hundred Flowers period entitled *Fresh Flowers Blooming Once Again*, a publication that Hong Kong critic Lee Yee takes to be a significant event in the liberalization of Chinese literature. See Lee Yee, *The New Realism*, 7.

3. Page numbers refer to Liu Xinwu, "Banzhuren," and the translations are my own. W. J. F. Jenner calls the story's appearance in 1977 the "return to life of contemporary Chinese writing." See Jenner, "Is a Modern Chinese Literature Possible?" 222.

stories carefully broached people's guilt over their participation in the persecution of their loved ones. These works became known collectively as scar literature in reference to one of the most poignant stories of modern Chinese fiction, Lu Xinhua's 盧新華 (b. 1954) "Shanghen" 傷痕 (Scar; 1978). In Lu's story, the protagonist, Wang Xiaohua 王曉華, disowns her mother after the latter is branded a "renegade." Leaving her mother only a short note, the sixteen-year-old Xiaohua runs away from Shanghai to work in a village in Liaoning province as part of the rustication movement. The story opens nine years later as Xiaohua travels back to Shanghai hoping to see her now-rehabilitated but dying mother. In describing the return journey and her reflections on her life away from home, the story accentuates Xiaohua's loneliness and her pain upon watching a mother and daughter together on the train. These details and her mother's written statements that she does not blame Xiaohua but only worries that the wounds in her daughter's heart may be worse than her own physical wounds lead the reader to see Xiaohua as a victim.

The considerable extent to which Xiaohua perceives her actions as stemming from her own will, however, allows "Scar" to raise disconcerting questions about people's perceived autonomy. How did Xiaohua come to believe official accusations against her mother over her own experience? Moreover, how is it that she sees her resolution to repudiate their bond as the result of her own individual determination? Loath to identify with a terrible criminal, Xiaohua reasons, "Both internal and external voices told her that she had to criticize her own petit bourgeois thoughts and sentiments and make a thorough and clean break with her mother" (141).[4]

Xiaohua experiences her departure as though she were taking her life in her hands to pursue her own dreams and plans, when in fact she is following the Party's program for molding her plans and dreams. To be a good revolutionary cadre, she must break with her mother. When her mother sends care packages, she returns them unopened, unaware that she thus becomes the active instrument of the Party's persecution of her mother. The barriers Xiaohua has erected to deaden her love for her mother become apparent when she doubts the truth of her mother's letter describing her rehabilitation, serious illness, and concern that time to see her daughter may be short (145). Xiaohua then dreams that her mother admits that she is guilty after all and so delays going to see her. Only

4. Page numbers refer to Lu Xinhua, "Shanghen," and the translations are my own.

after she receives official notification of her mother's reinstatement does Xiaohua hurry home to find that her mother has already passed away.

The possibility that Xiaohua could have acted otherwise, at least in trusting her mother's letter and not delaying her return, is sideshadowed by her boyfriend's suggestion that she inquire about her mother's status after the fall of the Gang of Four in 1976 and by his own decision to visit Xiaohua's mother in her stead. Is there any sense in concluding that Xiaohua plays an active role in causing her own and her mother's distress? Does Xiaohua even feel any remorse? Her recuperative comment at the story's end suggests her control over her emotions, but such emotional management leads the reader to imagine the remorse left unexplored: "Mama, my dear Mama, don't worry. Your daughter will never forget who poked these scars into your heart and mine. I'll definitely devote all my strength to the Party's cause" (147). Xiaohua's faith in her nation's progress toward a just and affluent society may belie a deep sense of collective grievance brought out in other parts of the story.

As Lu Xinhua's story does, many of the most popular works in the scar genre center on the harrowing personal choices that so often attend political upheaval. The impossible dilemmas into which the Cultural Revolution forced many individuals is driven home in the title and final line of Chen Guokai's 陳國凱 (b. 1938) "Wo yinggai zenma ban?" 我應該怎麼辦？ (What should I do?; 1979). The protagonist, Zijun 子君, believing her husband to have been driven to suicide during the Cultural Revolution, survives the harrowing loss and remarries only to confront her first husband's startling return at the end of the story. Not only does he tell her of his terrible torture, proof of which is only too horribly recorded in the terrible scars and split lip of his haggard face, but he also tells her that he could not have lived through his ordeals were it not for his thoughts of her and their child. Overcome by emotion, Zijun throws herself into his outstretched arms, and precisely at that moment she hears her second husband's footsteps on the stairs. His reappearance leaves Zijun in a panic, and the story's ending is left open with the woman's dilemma.

2. CHARACTER DETERMINISM IN REFORM LITERATURE

Although focus on realistic detail and individual suffering undermined notions of collective fate, some post-Mao stories substituted character or psychological determinism as a structuring principle. The political utility of attributing behavior to character or a hierarchy of prior motives is revealed in works of "reform literature" (*gaige wenxue* 改革文學), another of the genres grouped under the term "new realism." This fiction often divides the world into two halves, those who are promoting reform and those obstructing it. In probing the darker side of the socialist experiment, many works present not conflicted individuals wrestling with difficult ethical decisions, but struggles between "good guys" and "bad guys."

This stark contrast usually implies some version of character determinism, as in the first piece of reform literature, Jiang Zilong's 蔣子龍 (b. 1941) short novella "Qiao changzhang shangren ji" 喬廠長上任記 (Manager Qiao assumes office; 1979) and its sequel, "Qiao changzhang houzhuan" 喬廠長後傳 (Sequel to the story of Manager Qiao; 1980).[5] When Manager Qiao Guangpu 喬光朴 takes control of a heavy-duty electrical-machinery plant, he holds an exam to identify incompetents and then relegates them to a service team performing janitorial and other minor duties in his effort to reenergize production. Although not as simple or one-dimensional as the revolutionary heroes of earlier works and even occasionally subject to momentary discouragement, especially in the sequel, Manager Qiao is at heart an exemplar in every way. One could argue that it is Qiao's long career and correct experience that have made him the man he is, but it is difficult to imagine that Qiao was not simply born excellent. Each of the other characters, conversely, is at least in some way deficient. Although his wife's nephew becomes a model worker despite his personal dislike for Qiao, there appears little hope for reforming most of the other characters. The reader's familiarity with this method of characterization reinforces its deterministic implications in Jiang's subsequent stories such as "Yige gongchang mishu de riji" 一個工場密書的日記 (Diary of a factory manager; 1980) and "Bainian" 拜年 (New year's wishes; 1982).[6]

5. Although first greeted by hostile critics, particularly in the *Tianjin ribao* (Tianjin daily news), the earlier story won first prize as the Outstanding Short Story of 1979. See Lee Yee, *The New Realism*, 7.

6. My analysis of character determinism in Jiang's work is supported by his description of his approach in his essay "'Qiao Guangchang shangren ji' de shenghuo zhang": "My duty is simply to let the pen point follow Qiao Guangpu. A character can carry out things completely according to his own will. I only remind myself not to obstruct him, not to let him do things that would not accord with his character" (16).

In representing the complex burdens of moral responsibility, the best works of reform literature explicitly challenge such character determinism. For example, the possibility for personal transformation and for the younger generation to overcome the failings of their parents is presented in Zhang Jie's 張潔 (b. 1937) full-length novel on the reform era, *Chenzhong de chibang* 沉重的翅膀 (Heavy wings; 1981). Winner of the 1981 Mao Dun prize, the novel confronts industrial modernization, corruption, and personal compromise through the interwoven stories of several families and other individuals. The novel's complicated picture of power struggles and economic hardship suggests the mitigating circumstances in which the older characters often suppress their humanity. But it also suggests the possibility of slow change for the better both within individuals and across generations. The most compelling conversion is that of the protagonist, Zheng Ziyun 鄭子云, a vice-minister of heavy industry whose daughter Yuanyuan 圓圓 insists on marrying her boyfriend despite her parents' prejudice against his class background. After she accuses them of hypocrisy and leaves their home, Zheng realizes how much he has compromised his integrity to keep up appearances. As he goes after Yuanyuan in the final chapter, he reflects on his abdication of responsibility: "To cast off fetters from the outside world is perhaps not so hard, but to cast off one's own fetters, to surmount obstacles of one's own thinking, [in this] people often fail" (352).[7] Yet Zheng refuses to be swayed from his devotion to reform, and he insists on his own positive development in an internal monologue he addresses to Yuanyuan: "You must allow and accept that I am also a caterpillar in the process of undergoing a painful metamorphosis. Perhaps I won't necessarily turn into a butterfly before I die" (354). Although the novel allows that selfishness and fear can lead people to obstruct reform, ultimately it offers hope that honest analysis and individual accountability will lead to positive transformation.

Whereas the optimistic agenda of reform literature sometimes produces a prosaic dreariness, the relentless specificity of its concerns also urges people not to become instruments of ultimate plans, but to remain concerned about the particulars in their lives, their selves, and their families. After the ravages of Mao's program of ultimate goals, it is hardly surprising that authors might develop a fear of abstraction. One response is

7. Page numbers refer to Zhang Jie, *Chenzhong de chibang*, and translations are my own.

to stake everything on specific incidents and thus reintroduce individual people making individual choices as agents of history.

3. LITERATURE OF REFLECTION

The optimistic "reform literature" suggests that honest analysis and individual responsibility will lead to political and social progress. Many of the works called "literature of reflection" (*fansi wenxue* 反思文學) echo that implication, but they more squarely face the treacherous legacies of political corruption and upheaval. Such works often present so well the injustice and ineluctability of the political system that they render more remote the possibility of meaningful resistance. At their most intrepid moments, such works may not only condemn particular events and individuals, but also question the ideological foundations of the current regime. Some of the most dramatic moments in these works occur when a character is caught between two conflicting sets of norms, such as humanist and socialist. Shen Rong's novella "Ren dao zhongnian" 人到中年 (Reaching middle age; 1980), for example, introduces a self-sacrificing ophthalmologist, a model revolutionary who can perform seventeen operations in a morning, but cramped quarters, exhaustion, and finally failing health reduce her to a woman debilitated by depression and spiritual malaise.

In contrast to the Mao-era works' concentration on the revolution's progress in its positive aspects, such post-Mao-era works exposed China's social and economic problems, as well as the corruption and bureaucratism of the political system. Some authors used parody, as did Gao Xiaosheng 高曉聲 (b. 1928) in "Li Shunda zao wu" 李順大造屋 (Li Shunda builds a house; 1979), a tragicomedy about a peasant's repeatedly frustrated attempts to save up to build his family a home.[8] Others set out to expose the corruption and opportunism of the bureaucracy through shocking portrayals of rape, as in Liu Ke's 劉克 "Feitian" 飛天 (Feitian; 1979), influence peddling, as in Xu Mingxu's 徐明旭 "Diaodong" 調動 (Transfer; 1979), or fraud. Such fiction expressed disillusionment, apathy, and the utter exhaustion of a people still reeling from the anguish of their immediate revolutionary past.

8. On the story's use of technique and irony to invert Party ideology, see Leo Lee, "The Politics of Technique."

The tension between the power of political movements or corrupt officials and the individual agency of ordinary people is very pronounced in these works. The narrators in these stories often blame the system rather than individuals, but the presentation of events usually leads the reader to consider the individuals' acts. As Joseph Lau comments on the political commissar's shameless rape of the young Feitian: "For, unless the incidence of rape is treated as a subject for moral contemplation, . . . it serves no purpose as a literary work other than to confirm man's bestiality."[9] Moreover, the focus of the story is on Feitian herself, her complicity with the commissar after he helps her obtain an abortion, her realization of her own self-deception, and her refusal of Hai Lizi's 海離子 love after she returns to the temple where she had fallen in love with him.

As with many works of literature of reflection, Liu Ke's story not only explores the inhumanity of the immediate revolutionary past but also looks back to the period of "seventeen years" between 1949 and the onset of the Cultural Revolution in 1966. The story begins in 1958 when severe famine leads to the death of Feitian's mother and Feitian arrives at the remote rural temple to honor her mother's wishes.

The repetition of three discourses relevant to human agency structure the story's presentation of and challenge to the characters' fatalism. First, when the young cultural worker Hai Lizi first meets Feitian, he realizes that her poor deceased mother, like his own, "could bear any suffering and tragic fate, never complaining of the suffering, [viewing] the entire fault as her own" (118).[10] After the rape, Feitian takes this ability to endure a tragic fate and suffering as her mother's legacy to her, and she likewise blames everything on herself (130). Having allowed Commissar Xie 謝政委 to support her for six months, she "of course did not blame him, [seeing] the entire fault as her own" (133). Second, the story plays on the name Feitian (Flying sky), which Hai Lizi gives her when she conceals her real name. When Feitian contemplates suicide after her rape, the narrator comments that Feitian naturally could not fly away but had to stay in the human world (129). This theme is repeated elsewhere in the story, as when Feitian says only that she wants to fly away when asked whether she still loves Hai Lizi. Third, in the first section when the old monk and Lizi warn Feitian that she will have to leave their idyllic life together, the old monk recites a line (from *Dream of the Red Chamber*) about how

9. Lau, "The Wounded and the Fatigued," 135.

10. Parenthetical page numbers refer to Liu Ke, "Feitian," and translations are my own.

all banquets must disperse (121). The young Feitian rejects the fatalism this attitude implies: "Doesn't whether [they] disperse depend on people?" (121). Yet, after her ordeals serving in the army, Feitian recalls and endorses the saying about banquets to emphasize that she can no longer marry Hai Lizi (134). This time it is Lizi who invokes Feitian's objection of three years earlier (135).

Early on, the story explores the characters' self-defeating fatalism, but after the overriding force of the Cultural Revolution diminishes its significance, the ruin of the characters' community turns out to be inevitable. When the rebel factions descend on the temple at the end of the story, their violent intervention makes mincemeat of the characters' plans. The rebel guards destroy the temple, put Hai Lizi in a cowshed, and then cart him away. Yet even at this point Feitian blames herself since Lizi's persecution is assured by the testimony of his wife, a woman Feitian encouraged him to marry. "It seemed that things utterly shouldn't be this way, yet they nonetheless were this way. Could she blame Hui Yueshu? No. The entire fault was her own!" (139). At the end of the story, Commissar Xie and a young woman, presumably his new prey, see Feitian on the streets of Shanghai looking like a disheveled madwoman. Thereafter Feitian is no longer seen on the streets, and the narrator considers several possible outcomes, none reassuring.

In stories such as "Feitian," the characters' helplessness may partially arise from their inability to accept what agency they could have, as when Feitian refuses to accept that the love she shares with Hai Lizi could survive the ordeal of her rape. The story's sideshadowing of this possibility is partly but not completely eclipsed by their final political persecution. Yet ultimately the characters' helplessness results not from failures of courage, but from coercion and exploitation at the hands of others and inexorable political violations of freedom.

4. *HUMANITY, O HUMANITY!*

Dai Houying was among the first writers to explicitly champion humanist values in confronting the legacy of the Anti-Rightist Campaign and the Cultural Revolution. Her most famous novel, *Humanity, O Humanity!*, employs multiple means of sideshadowing to explore the complicated nature of human responsibility. The second in her trilogy on the fate of intellectuals that began with *Shi ren zhi si* 詩人之死 (Death of a poet;

1978, published 1982) and ended with *Kongzhong de zuyin* 空中的足音 (Footsteps in the void; 1986), *Humanity* was particularly criticized for its defense of "bourgeois humanist" values and was banned during the 1983 campaign against spiritual pollution (*jingshen wuran* 精神污染) until 1986.[11] As is evident in a 1984 article condemning the novel and its afterword as "a 'manifesto' of 1980s bourgeois humanism," Party critics made *Humanity* a scapegoat for their indictment of humanism as inattentive to class, even calling it "a 'narcotic' that makes people unable to push history forward following the socialist direction with a clear head."[12]

Yet the novel's endorsement of humanist values is complemented by other voices that admit the difficulty of achieving those ideals. Set soon after the fall of the Gang of Four, *Humanity* confronts the deep scars left by repressive political movements and their consequences for interpersonal relations. Accordingly, the novel depicts individuals in the grips of harsh cynicism and opportunism. Yet it also champions the possibility for forgiveness, integrity, and idealism by depicting several characters' hard-won steps toward enhanced personal and interpersonal understanding. The novel pleads for individual responsibility even while demonstrating how meager the worldly rewards of moral integrity may appear.

Moreover, the novel departs radically from Mao-era fiction in presenting the socialist transformation not only as not inevitable but as radically contingent and vulnerable. Through its narrative structure, the novel stages an encounter between larger political movements and the small but crucial openings for individual human agency. In recounting the spiritual and intellectual development of the protagonist, He Jingfu 何荆夫, and the censorship controversy surrounding his book *Makesizhuyi yu rendaozhuyi* 馬克思主義與人道主義 (Marxism and humanism), the novel occasionally slips into overtly didactic passages. Scholars in North America have criticized this didacticism, and Leo Lee dismisses Dai as "suffer[ing] from a case of 'thesis comes first' (*zhuti xian xing* [主題先性])."[13] More sympathetic, Michael Duke nonetheless concludes that Dai "fails to integrate her humanistic message into an artistically

11. The banning of *Ren a, ren* was reported in *Zhongguo shibao* (China times, North American ed.), October 25, 1983. See Duke, "Chinese Marxist Humanism," 233, n. 2. For a summary of Chinese articles on the novel, see *China News Analysis*, n. 1231 (April 23, 1982), mentioned in Duke, "Chinese Marxist Humanism," 234, n. 3. For extended discussion of the Chinese debate over the novel, see Pruyn, *Humanism.*

12. Zhang Ren and Yang Zhijie, "Cong 'A, ren . . . . . .' dao 'Ren a, ren!'" 11.

13. Leo Lee, "The Politics of Technique," 187.

achieved form."[14] As mentioned, Party critics in China objected to the novel's inattention to class and its implication that "the fate of this book [He Jingfu's *Marxism and Humanism*] was directly linked to the fate of China."[15]

Yet this long, thoughtful novel goes far beyond any simple political agenda. *Humanity* tackles big questions: the role of human agency in history, the importance of storytelling for making sense of moral responsibility, and the possibility of repair or redemption. Some critics may argue that it does not entirely succeed, but the effort is profoundly instructive and the emotional tenor often heartrending. The characters may not all be well rounded, but their fractured lives provide clear reasons for their brokenness and the alienation that inhibits their mutual understanding as well as the reader's access to their inner lives. In this discussion, I analyze the novel's exploration of the role of individual decision vis-à-vis larger political processes, the characters' conceptions of history, the psychological and social work of storytelling, and the possibility for personal transformation and redemption. In interpreting the novel's treatment of history and the possibility of repair, I focus on how the use of sideshadowing allows the novel to retain ethical ideals of moral agency and responsibility yet show that such ideals may require new definitions.

4.1 Forces of Circumstance

First and foremost, *Humanity* testifies to the situated limits and partialities of any understanding. Through ten points of view, direct dialogue, and some stream-of-consciousness narration, the novel's characters recount their shared historical experiences from their distinct perspectives. Although the novel is rooted in history, the steam engine of chronology does not drive it. Instead, the narrative present is interspersed with dreams, regrets, and extended flashbacks to convey the sometimes non-linear nature of memory and historical understanding.

The predicament of a younger generation trying to understand their parents' lives based on fragments of available evidence comes out in the three chapters narrated by the protagonist Sun Yue's 孫悅 daughter Hanhan 憾憾. In one of the novel's most memorable scenes, Hanhan views her history in the severed pieces of a photograph of her family ten

14. Duke, "Chinese Marxist Humanism," 181.

15. Zhang and Yang, "Cong 'A ren . . . ,'" 10.

years earlier. Because Hanhan's mother ripped up the photograph after Hanhan's father divorced her during the Cultural Revolution, Hanhan sees herself as torn in two, one half with her father and one half with her mother. Vividly illustrating the emotional rending of a child of divorce, this image encapsulates the brokenness of the novel's other characters as well. For although several recover a sense of integrity, each character has been torn apart by external events, either the decisions of specific individuals or the consequences of larger political movements.

The novel's presentation of these traumatic events suggests the impossibility of separating personal from political factors. The consequences of political circumstance are underscored from the first chapter, narrated by Sun Yue's ex-husband, the editor Zhao Zhenhuan 趙振環. Waking from a nightmare after his forty-fourth birthday party, Zhao reflects on how his assignment to Guangzhou separated him from Sun Yue, how his concern over her persecution changed into resentment of her political ideals and activism, and the way "instinct gradually oppressed reason" (44) as he became involved with the pretty worker Feng Lanxiang 馮蘭香.[16] Sideshadowing the missed chance for a reconciliation with Sun Yue, Zhao also remembers "trying to recover his reason" but discovering Lanxiang's pregnancy and, in a later chapter, the pressure to marry her exerted by Wang Pangzi 王胖子, whom he later learns is her married lover. The power of political campaigns to script people's inner emotions is seen in even more stark terms by Lanxiang herself when she blames changing Party directives for what she perceives as Zhao's change of heart: "At that time workers enjoyed favor, so you had some esteem for me. Now you intellectuals have favor, so of course you now consider Sun Yue to be better than me" (43). In showing the power of social norms and political ideology to influence people's frames of reference, the novel emphasizes that these frames are contingent and yet still compelling to the characters.

On a deeper level, the novel underscores the pervasive effects of political repression and social humiliation by showing how helplessness over external circumstances can lead people to cruel acts of self-harm or to participation in the persecution of their loved ones. Only gradually does the novel reveal the details of Zhao's betrayal and Sun Yue's

16. Where only one page number appears, it refers to Dai, *Ren a, ren*, and the translation is my own. Where two page numbers appear, the second is to the translation by Frances Wood.

political persecution as a rightist and "concubine" of her supervisor, but it conveys the depth of her devastation in three particularly compelling moments. First, after Zhao deserts Sun Yue to marry Lanxiang and uses Sun's political misfortune to divorce her with no financial responsibility for their daughter Huanhuan 環環, Sun Yue renames the child Hanhan 憾憾 (Regret), a name that confuses Hanhan and brings taunts from her schoolmates. Second, when Zhao visits Sun in the narrative present, begs for sympathy, and warns that his intense guilt makes him want to hurt himself, Sun Yue vividly remembers how the combination of political persecution and Zhao's desertion drove her to bang her head against the wall and beat her shoulders purple (288). Third, the novel portrays the accidental legacy of a parent's emotional anguish on her child when Sun Yue slaps Hanhan after she has been rude to the teacher Xu Hengzhong 許恆忠. Hanhan cries out: "Go ahead and hit me. Just beat me to death. I stopped wanting to live a long time ago" (173). Horrified that a youth could express such utter despair, Sun Yue asks Hanhan who taught her this phrase, but it is clear that Hanhan has learned these feelings from her mother.

By showing characters becoming aware of such incremental and unintended developments, the novel soberly faces conceptions of history that challenge humanist assumptions about individuals' power vis-à-vis larger social and historical processes. To this end, several passages reveal the difficulty of shielding one's own psychic and emotional structures from overriding political effects. The extent to which political ideology can shape people's perceptions and understandings is driven home when Sun Yue considers Xu Hengzhong's participation in the Party's persecution of He Jingfu: "Is it always one's own brain that one carries on one's shoulders? Not necessarily. Yet everyone always says that he thinks independently for himself and has asked a 'why' regarding each instance" (160).

4.2 History and Historical Understanding

While *Humanity* takes seriously forces of circumstance, the novel also underscores the role of individual intention in conferring meaning on any historical account. Without ever denying the incontestable historical weight of the Anti-Rightist Campaign or the Cultural Revolution, the novel refuses to make history the master text to which fiction must aspire. Instead, the novel suggests a two-part process of historical understanding. If one task involves selecting and arranging evidence into coherent narratives of the past, a second stage lets people discriminate among these accounts and choose which resources to apply to the present. The epigraph to part I calls attention to the fragmented nature of collective history and the role of individual interpretation and response: "In every person's brain is stored a part of history, and it is active [*huodong* 活動] according to its own respective ways" (33).

As if respecting the plurality of worthwhile historical lessons, the novel allows the characters to express their distinct views of history. Some characters view history in terms of its inexorable effects on the present. Such helplessness plagues the younger generation most of all, as in Hanhan's confusion over the reasons behind the ripped photograph and her own renaming. Yet many of the adult characters too, at least initially, experience themselves primarily as victims of larger historical processes. When Xu Hengzhong comes to excuse his role in persecuting He Jingfu, Sun Yue refuses to "settle accounts" because, she claims, they are not qualified to bear responsibility for history (95).

Yet Sun Yue distinguishes between the intransigence of past events and the possibility of learning from and responding to history. History's lessons she sees differently, as something for which individuals do bear account. This conviction drives her to reexamine her own past decisions, move beyond helpless victimization, and assume responsibility for her present relationships and future projects. At the same time, perhaps because she has suffered the misery of having others' versions of history imposed upon her, Sun Yue remains vigilant to view history's lessons as utterly individual: "You have your lessons. I have my lessons. In this matter, no one can shelter anyone else and no one can stand in for anyone else" (95).

As the unequivocal voice for humanism, He Jingfu insists that it is people who make history, but he also admits the complexity of human history making. After Hanhan befriends him as a kind of surrogate father despite her mother's coldness toward him, He Jingfu tells her his convictions about history: "The term history is utterly abstract. But the various ingredients that compose history and push it forward, especially people, are concrete and complicated, multifarious and strange" (310). He Jingfu's appreciation of contingency rings true insofar as he has enjoyed even less agency over his early life than the other characters. In love with Sun Yue while they were university students, he met not only with rejection but also with humiliation when the authorities used his pursuit of her as a weapon against him. Condemned as a rightist, he is exiled from their city and spends twenty years wandering the country as a menial laborer. When he is finally allowed to return to C city, he hopes to reunite with Sun Yue but initially meets only coldness and rejection.

Human influence triumphs over contingency for He Jingfu, however, because he maintains faith in Marxist explanations that assume a determined historical justice: "History is like an introverted person; it doesn't easily reveal its true emotions. But a day will come when you'll see that history is fair" (78–79). He Jingfu's faith in the justness of history underpins his conviction that Marxism is the most radical form of humanism. Although the authorities distort the meaning of He Jingfu's concern that class struggle should combat exploitation and oppression yet not divide people and families, the younger generation eagerly embraces his thesis. His faith that human life can have meaning so draws the young people to him that when the University Party Committee meets to discuss the fate of his book, an old professor points out a contradiction between the claims of those seeking to blacklist him and the students' obvious devotion to him.

Against Sun Yue's more modest and He Jingfu's more ambitious commitments to human responsibility for larger social change, many of the novel's secondary characters view history as a dangerous and ultimately expendable preoccupation. When He Jingfu entreats Xu Hengzhong to take responsibility for history, Xu argues against taking a stand because such discussions have "more thorns than roses" (*hua shao ci duo* 花少刺多; 87). In comparison to the idealists, the equivocal people may appear to be the lucky ones. Yet it is the main characters that win the reader's sympathy and inspire the deeper reflections. For whereas the cynics justify their resignation as realism, the idealists reject a view of reality that lets past injustices strangle future possibilities.

4.3 Redemption and the Social Work of Stories

One path for survivors of trauma who refuse to let the past determine the future is to organize and transform their own stories to secure some measure of agency. In Dai's novel, the truth is seldom triumphant or even comforting, but its very ambiguity and painfulness let people revise accounts that trap them in resentment or regret. In a world where absolute truth is but one casualty of political oppression, many of the characters still manage to rebuild both individual and interpersonal understandings through growing regard for their own scruples and respect for one another's perspectives.

Thus, far from endorsing relativism, the novel privileges the healing yet fragile possibilities for sympathy and mutual understanding. Although the different vantage points and rationalizations often serve to highlight the seemingly unbridgeable distance between the characters, their efforts to communicate hold promise for redeeming the future. One's individual conscience may be primary, but to transcend the past also requires forgiveness and tolerance. Although all these values depend on respect for human agency, forgiveness places an especially high premium on the human role in interpreting history. For forgiveness acknowledges the past yet allows an individual to select among the burdens of that inheritance.

Most of the novel's characters stake their lives on the possibility of redemption. For them, if one must bear blame for one's past mistakes, then one must also be allowed to redeem what can be repaired in the present. Zhao Zhenhuan, He Jingfu, and Sun Yue's friend Li Yining 李宜寧 offer three compelling examples of such faith in redemption. Although each meets with disappointments in trying to win over Sun Yue, they free themselves from considerable anguish and become more effective in their relations with others.

Although Zhao Zhenhuan accepts the awful certainty that what has been done cannot be undone, he preserves his hope for redemption and thus saves himself from suicide. Over time Zhao takes less and less to have been inevitable, and his progress toward assuming responsibility constitutes one of the main themes of the novel. In broad terms, Zhao develops from an initial fatal cynicism, through a self-serving effort to expiate his guilt, to a final acceptance of the consequences of his actions that allows him to value the possibilities that remain.

Zhao expresses his initial fatalism when he wonders how someone so inferior as Lanxiang could have drawn him away from Sun Yue. At a loss for an explanation, he attributes what happened to the power of greater forces, "the doing of ghosts and spirits" (*gui shi shen chai* 鬼使神差; 145/86). After revealing his despair about their marriage, he also invokes fatalism to justify his proposal of a cruel "three-point treaty" with Lanxiang: "Given that fate has brought us together, we should muddle along" (146). Zhao's treaty requires that they avoid revealing their conflicts to others, not mention Sun Yue in front of their daughter Huanhuan, and be honest with but not interfere with each other. After Zhao translates his proposals into simpler language that Lanxiang can understand, she agrees but forbids Zhao to write to Sun Yue. Yet Zhao insists on his freedom to write to Sun Yue, and in taking this step he begins to assume responsibility for his past actions. In a part of his letter presented for the first time through Hanhan's eyes, Zhao explains his alliance with Lanxiang as the result not of fate, but of his adoption of a cynical attitude (*wan shi bu gong* 玩世不恭) whereby he juggled with his own emotions and character (174).

Over time Zhao comes to appreciate his unclaimed choices in the past, a process realized as the novel sideshadows his abandonment of Sun Yue with his memories of his missed opportunities to treat her with more dignity. He remembers, for example, how he lied to her about his relations with Lanxiang, how he ripped up but could never forget a poem she sent, and how he refused to see her when she visited after receiving his letter demanding a divorce. He also remembers how he dismissed her warning not to marry Lanxiang despite the restraint she showed in writing him a long diary-like letter rather than making a scene or pleading her case to his friends.

Zhao's moral progress may at first offer little consolation insofar as it is too late for him to repair either his terrible betrayal of Sun Yue or his second unhappy marriage. Yet he hangs his hopes on the possibility that his honest expressions of regret can lead to greater understanding. When he realizes that his regret has little influence on Sun Yue, he curbs his expectations and accepts his situation by focusing on what scope for agency remains. He articulates this understanding twice (with slight variation) in his interior monologue: "I've lost what I was meant to lose, and I've found what I was meant to find" (413 and 414). Although one might wonder what master plan justifies Zhao's notion of "meant to," this conception does allow him to relinquish unattainable wishes, respect Sun Yue's initial refusal to excuse what he has done, and, more important, establish a relationship with Hanhan. The line's first appearance, as the epigraph to the final chapter, reinforces the novel's emphasis on the possibility of acceptance (405).

It is also significant that others support Zhao's faith that things can be set right. When Zhao tells He Jingfu that he feels as if he's mortgaged his soul to the devil to avoid political misfortune, He Jingfu encourages him to redeem it. Despite the threat Zhao might pose to He Jingfu's own prospects with Sun Yue, He Jingfu respects her right to decide her own fate: "God had given me the right to love other people, but [he] hadn't given me the right to deprive other people of love. I knew that Hanhan loved me, and I felt that Sun Yue loved me. But they certainly hadn't vested me with the right to decide their fate for them" (274/190 modified).

Whereas He Jingfu's own shipwrecked love for Sun Yue suggests the tragic fact that one can never go back in time, he never accepts that the unidirectional nature of time should entail people's emotions developing in only one direction. He appreciates the possibility for change, which makes his generosity toward Zhao all the more heroic. In maintaining faith that a new story could be written even as he respects Sun Yue's reluctance, He Jingfu also accepts that the new story could be quite different from the one he himself might wish for.

Sun Yue offers the most serious challenge to the other main characters' optimism about the possibility of redemption. Although she dreams of being with He Jingfu, she sees their chance for love as irretrievable. "Jingfu, the Sun Yue of your memory is a Sun Yue you created out of love. She never existed. The Sun Yue in front of you also has her 'past.' But this 'past' has already died. What's dead can't be reborn" (153). This line might lead the reader to wonder whether emotions dead can never be reborn. Yet, as if to reinforce the separation between her present and former selves, Sun Yue's interior monologue maintains the switch from first- to third-person narration as she recounts the despair she felt when her idols were smashed and all that she saw and felt lost its color. Moreover, the novel formally enacts the degree to which Sun Yue has repressed her feelings by first offering little indication about her feelings for He Jingfu. Only in chapter 9 does Sun Yue reveal to the reader that she reciprocated He Jingfu's love. Here she explains that his intensity scared her, so to resist his seduction she publicly declared her love for and married Zhao. In an interior monologue addressed to Zhao, Sun Yue reflects on how she sacrificed her love for He Jingfu: "I closed my eyes to the seduction of all that happiness. I locked up my own heart. In order to be loyal to you, I betrayed my own heart. Everything I had, I handed over to you. Although I felt regret, I could gain consolation from devotion. But you repaid [my] devotion with abandonment" (152–53).

Sun Yue suffers from a wound that will not heal, but she is also impaired by her refusal to surrender a romanticized view of immaculate love. Since Sun Yue is unwilling to tarnish their respective fantasies by attempting to live a love that would forcibly be different, she holds present possibilities hostage to a kind of perfectionism: "Old He, love the illusion of Sun Yue that you created out of love. I'm not willing to destroy it with the truth" (154). These comments do more than reinforce Sun Yue's earlier reflections about the transience of life: "Flowers blossom and fall just once a year. People are young and old just once in a lifetime" (151). Beyond her worry that later occurrences can tarnish an earlier dream, her comments imply that, to be beautiful, things must exist only once and in only one way. In considering the way this view constrains her, the reader may well share He Jingfu's frustration with Sun Yue's pessimism. For whereas the fleeting and irreplaceable nature of life may be what lends an intense significance to experiences, the precariousness of our time as mortal beings need not lead us to make a museum of unfulfilled fantasies.

Yet is it fair to attribute such agency to Sun Yue in light of the traumatic circumstances of her life? Does Sun Yue's refusal to live her love for He Jingfu fail to acknowledge the freedom left after political repression or does it demonstrate the irremediable effects of such repression? If the novel were a simplistic endorsement of humanism, it would stop at the first interpretation. Yet other passages suggest that Sun Yue's refusal may result from a hardheaded realism about the harm wrought by failures of compassion. "Every time I recall that period of history, I feel that I owe you a debt. A debtor and a debtee can't love as equals" (279). If one takes seriously Sun Yue's grasp of her compromised position, her intransigence stems not from unwarranted determinism about the irreversibility of the past but from legitimate concern about the past's continuing effects in the present. The sad truth could be that even when devotion would entail heroism beyond most people's capacities, failures of devotion irreparably damage relationships. Yet He Jingfu might object that such a view implies that relationships have a life of their own that the individuals involved cannot alter.

The important difference between Sun Yue's and He Jingfu's views lies in their assumptions about the degree to which people are held hostage to the past. If Sun Yue's reasoning shows how stories can erect barriers to change as easily as constitute possibilities for action, the crucial factor may be whether a person structures her life story around a premature sense of closure or as a segment in an unfinished and open narrative. Much of Sun Yue's unhappiness stems from her assumption that her story has already reached its conclusion: "What's missed is missed. Don't try to repair things that can't be repaired" (161). Yet Sun Yue tempers her denial of present possibilities as her sense of responsibility to He Jingfu and Hanhan leads her to confront the ongoing effects of her resignation.

For Sun as for Zhao, perceiving present opportunities depends on developing greater appreciation for her range of choices in the past. This growing sense of agency occurs in several steps, and each one helps appease her anger and indignation as she comes to consider her own role in their collective unhappiness. First, in explaining that she does not want sympathy, pity, or charity, Sun Yue asserts her attachment to her own decisions:

> I chose each step I took. Although these choices didn't represent my own feelings or will, and sometimes were even against my will, yet in the end they reflect my understanding and attitude toward life. I'm not willing to erase my steps or let others help me cover up those steps. These steps made me suffer and feel ashamed, but precisely because of that I treasure them. . . . No, I couldn't live with him [Jingfu]. I couldn't. . . . (182)

Second, three quarters of the way through the novel, Sun Yue wonders if many of their hardships might have been avoided had she initially chosen He Jingfu. This sideshadow of another possible course of events leads her to question whether she has wronged Zhao as much as been his victim. Her change of heart is voiced in the novel's final chapter when Zhao reads a letter in which Sun takes responsibility for their tragedy:

> It was perfectly clear to me that I yearned to and should marry Jingfu, [and] yet I married you. [I did] because I wasn't willing to bear the accusation of being ungrateful or of serving one state in the morning and another in the evening. And once Jingfu became a "rightist," I was even more unwilling to add "political blemishes" to my history. (409)

The novel never equates Zhao's real betrayal with Sun's possible one, but it does indicate the costly wages of self-deception and compromise. As Sun Yue seeks to explain what she comes to see as her failure to follow her heart, she admits the difficulty of distinguishing self-respect from vanity (183). She remembers wanting to accept Jingfu's love but fearing social and political sanction. In the narrative present as well, her repeated fantasies about living with He Jingfu founder in her fear of others' misunderstanding and scorn or even of a "historical reckoning" (*lishi de qingsuan* 歷史的清算; 279).

He Jingfu accepts Sun Yue's decision not to allow their love, but he suffers it with a sense of tragedy. For all his faith in human initiative, at this point he feels that they have been duped by the dark manipulations of a god of fate (*mingyun zhi shen* 命運之神) and strange combinations of forces (*gui shi shen chai, yin chai yang cuo* 鬼使神差，陰差陽錯; 280/195). Yet even as he considers that it may be his fate to live alone (281), he harbors hope insofar as he views Sun Yue's regard for her own feelings as the solid basis of her surviving humanity. For He Jingfu, humanity means the possibility of change.

What distinguishes the characters that develop compared to the more static ones is their willingness to respect and support viewpoints that run counter to their own. Even when their views and motives may seem irreconcilable, these characters still take steps to establish a sense of shared community that can acknowledge their differences. By contrast, the futility of refusing to listen to others is shown in the negative examples of University Party Secretary Xi Liu 奚流, his subordinate You Ruoshui 游若水, and the well-meaning but increasingly irrelevant senior university professor who waxes poetic about the rectification campaigns regardless of the current subject of conversation.

4.4 Comfort and Ambiguity

If one aspect of agency involves influencing events, another aspect concerns how one accommodates setbacks. Sun Yue's life choices and her consequent restiveness are sideshadowed by the modest contentment of her friend Li Yining. In contrast to Sun Yue's obsession with how things might have been, Li Yining adopts a practical outlook, refusing to dwell on illusions and impossibilities. As she urges Sun Yue to regret only things that one had the possibility of achieving, Li Yining insists on a person's ability to alter her response to hardships and diminish the level of her spiritual demand:

> It's because I've learned to be content with a life without too much wind and waves, and without too much color or fragrance. . . . You think that my heart is a stone? I know that the sun shines on us, that the icy snow freezes people, that flowers are beautiful, and that birds can fly. But I can decrease to the absolutely lowest level the sensitivity of my emotional response to all these things. (53)

Li Yining's life story, presented in a long passage set off as such, is no less harrowing than Sun Yue's, yet it has taught her different lessons. Having lost her first boyfriend after learning that he was already married, she married a man who denounced her during the Cultural Revolution. After falling prey to a dark and debilitating view of human relations as a mere struggle to survive, Yining recovered hope because of the warmth offered her by the family of one of her students. She eventually marries the student's brother, eight years younger and far less educated than she. Yining defends her decision to lower her spiritual demands as tied to her commitment to repay her simple husband's kindness. She describes her everyday pleasures as she rationalizes buying a TV, washing machine, and a tape recorder so that their daughter can learn foreign languages: "Material needs one by one occupied my spirit and at last substituted for the spiritual. Desires are boundless, and each desire can become a goal to strive for, leaving no time to consider anything else" (191).

Somewhat ironically, Sun Yue associates her high ideals with a failure of will and a surrender of her fate to Heaven. Telling Yining that she can't follow her lesson (*xue bu liao ni* 學不了你), Sun Yue concludes that she must therefore trust Heaven and follow fate (*ting tian you ming* 聽天由命; 194). Yet when Sun Yue defines fate later in the novel, she uses the notion to criticize a kind of bad faith wherein people refuse their own freedom.

> The spirit of fate looks so strong, as if it can play with different types of people in the palm of its hand. How many exceptionally intelligent and powerfully influential people have suffered its teasing? How many people has this phenomenon sunk into despair, [making them] thereby negate themselves and negate humanity? But isn't the reason this situation arises precisely that we're short of self-awareness, self-respect, and self-confidence? Isn't it precisely because we've unconditionally relinquished everything of our own to fate to arrange? What if we recovered our self-awareness, self-respect, and self-confidence? What if we retrieved all the rights we've given up? Then we could decide fate (*zhuzai mingyun* 主宰命運)? (329)

In my reading, Sun Yue's questions challenge habits by which people deny their own agency, but the questions take on a more urgent historical meaning and more sensitive political implications if, as Duke has proposed, the "God of fate" can be read as a symbol for the Chinese Communist Party.[17] Either way, Sun Yue's hypotheses here hardly silence her earlier refusal to simplify her view of the multiple interrelated factors

17. Duke, "Chinese Marxist Humanism," 168.

influencing her destiny. Namely, when Yining tells her to forget the past and start over as if tearing up a failed knitting project, Sun Yue replies by stressing the complicated nature of human life: "To knit you pull just one yarn. Human life involves thousands of strands and loose ends" (192). With this line, the novel suggests an implicit theory of narrative concerning both fiction and larger life stories. Through its complex narrative arrangement, the novel presents a showcase of the social work the characters' stories perform. The author emphasizes the evolving nature of lived understanding in her afterword: "Artistic truth is not an imitation of lived truth, but an author's accurate reflection of the dynamism [*neng-dong* 能動] of lived truth" (422).

By emphasizing the interpersonal nature of understanding, the novel finally raises questions not only about the morality of political compromise, personal betrayals, and self-deception but also about the nature and efficacy of love. Even Sun Yue, who has closed her heart after all the pain she has endured, reopens her heart over the course of the novel. Sun Yue's despair has infected Hanhan, but the contagion is not chronic. The steps they take to heal their relationship and the steps Hanhan takes to heal her relationship with her father and establish a bond with He Jingfu suggest the possibility that Hanhan may transcend her mother's understandable distrust of life.

Finally, despite He Jingfu's faith in Marxism as the highest form of humanism, the novel as a whole contests the pretense that a utopian political theory can offer solutions to human ailments. Instead, the novel testifies to the need for the gradual cultivation of a community of free individuals whose humanity depends on responsibilities that are irremediably both individual and shared. Though my reading of *Humanity, O Humanity!* in terms of its use of sideshadowing reveals possibilities of human agency, it also shows agency to be a problem not solved. The novel presents stark dilemmas where the intersection of responsibilities of family, friends, colleagues, political party, class, and community remains a center of conflict not resolvable by individuals alone.

5. *SOFT IS THE CHAIN*

Written two years after *Humanity*, Dai Houying's novella *Soft Is the Chain* continues her exploration of the ongoing effects of political trauma. Yet political corruption mainly serves as background as the novella explicitly questions both fatalistic notions and dominant views of gender inherited from traditional Chinese thought to consider the possibilities for self-determination in the face of superstition and oppressive social norms.

The character *ming* 命 (fate) appears 32 times in Dai's short novella and is used to describe each turning point in the life of the protagonist, Wen Ruixia 文瑞霞.[18] The first major event of the text tells how Ruixia is widowed at the age of 28 when her husband kills himself after he is wrongly accused of theft. Left with a five-year-old daughter and an unborn child, Ruixia invokes fate (*ming* 命) as she tries to come to terms with her husband's death: "I think everything is a result of fate. Hongzhong ran into a calamitous star this year. There was simply no way to avoid it" (174). The word *ming* also appears twice when Ruixia tells her brother-in-law that she wants to ask the security bureau chief to apply the death penalty to the real thief to force him to repay her husband's death with his life, to "compensate [with his] life for her husband's life" (*gei ziji de zhangfu diming* 給自己的丈夫抵命; 173).

The wide use of *ming* in the novella suggests its special power in establishing frameworks of interpretation. Not only does the character *ming* occur thirteen times in the quoted speech or reported thoughts of Ruixia herself, it also appears seven times in the third-person narration and twelve times in the quoted speech, dreams, or reported thoughts of the novella's other characters. Significantly, in discussing Ruixia's desire to toady to the bureau chief who oversaw the penal harassment that led to her husband's suicide, the narrator judges that a more "cultured" person would have appealed more readily to the notion of fate: "If Wen Ruixia had a little more culture, she would have said: This bureau chief is intimately tied to my fate. At every juncture at which my fate changes, [I] always run into him" (168). Such judgments testify to the fact that Ruixia's acceptance of the notion of fate is hardly individual, but rather one instance of a larger social response to unpredictable, and particularly ruinous, events.

Showing how belief in fate scripts the characters' conceptions of love, marriage, and mothering even before Ruixia's husband's tragic suicide, the novella goes on to recount Ruixia's difficult childhood and to suggest that her gender is the real cause of her fate: "As soon as Ruixia was born, her father knit his brow. Why did she have to be a girl? And once three sisters followed in her footsteps, her father became even more convinced

18. The novella runs just 65 pages in Dai Houying's collection *Suolian, shi rouruan de*, 163–227. Page references follow in the text, and all translations are my own.

that she was a daughter with a 'hard fate' [*ming ying* 命硬]" (179). At the same time, although the young Ruixia herself despairs about having been born a girl, she also attempts to influence her fate by appealing to the "Hemp Stalk Maiden" (*Majie gunian* 麻秸姑娘), a female celestial supposedly concerned with the fate of young women. Ruixia does so by tying together seven stalks of hemp, standing them upright in the ashes in front of the stove, imploring the Hemp Stalk Maiden to let her marry into a good family, and kowtowing three times when the stalks do not topple over, a sign of the immortal's willingness to listen (180–81).

Ruixia's active attempt to direct the will of this deity suggests her faith that she has at least some chance to influence her betrothal. The fate in which she believes would appear not to be fixed once and for all but to be at least potentially sympathetic to human longings. The range of human influence, however, is limited to changing one's particular lot within the existing social framework and never permits changing the conventions of that framework.

In this way, the concept of fate functions as one distinctive axis within a larger web of rationalizations for the existing social order. In the novella, fate (*ming* or *mingyun*) circulates among less common but related concepts, most of which are also invoked to defend traditional marriage arrangements. For example, the word *yun* appears alone when the young Ruixia feels fortunate to have a good husband: "She felt that she had met with good luck [*hao yun* 好運]" (183). Other evidence of Ruixia's submission to received opinions is presented in her acceptance of common sayings, such as "A good horse doesn't fit two saddles, a good woman doesn't marry a second husband" (204) and "No matter how the society changes, a family is still a family, a clan is still a clan" (204), the last two clauses of which are repeated a second and third time later in the novella (218, 219).

Returning to Ruixia's life after her husband's death, the narrative explains the feudal injunction by which her rural society still abides: If Ruixia bears a son, she will remain in her husband's family; if she bears a daughter, she can leave (204). Then the whole family gathers to "see if it's a boy or girl, for that would determine Ruixia's fate" (205). When the baby turns out to be a boy, the women in the family all cry and howl, for they realize that the baby's birth condemns Ruixia never to remarry (206): "This little life of not even 5 *jin* would be her . . . dictator for several decades. That's what the family's crying told her. Could Ruixia remarry? No. No. The family's cries were a command (*jiu shi mingling* 就是命令). She was determined to obey" (207).

Through Ruixia's reflections on what would have happened had she remarried, sideshadowing functions in this novella to rationalize Ruixia's unhappiness. True to the unknown risks of any unexplored path, these reflections both hint at a lost dream of happiness sacrificed and portend the threat of an outcome worse than the one she has. As part of her compliance, Ruixia wears clothes like an older woman's, does not venture out of doors, keeps her gaze down, and speaks little (204). Despite her knowledge of the new marriage law that would allow her to remarry, she never does, and on her fiftieth birthday, her family throws a party to honor her virtue and chastity.[19] At this point she remembers Liu Si 劉四, a man who had helped her secure food for her children during the famine and who wanted to marry her. She tells herself that it was a good thing she refused to marry, since doing so would have made her a criminal (193):

> If she were to tell anyone that there had been this man, that there had been this period, would everyone still respect her as they did today? Would her brother- and sister-in-law still call her the Jin's family's meritorious official? O, humanity! This type of fate is simply your lot: you want to taste sweetness, first you have to eat your fill of bitterness. (199)

Regret does not haunt Ruixia until she realizes that times have changed, and she cannot use her chastity to win good jobs and marriages for her children. When she wants to force her daughter to marry an official's son, the rest of the family insists that the daughter should make her own choice (212). The pain of recognizing the meager rewards of her sacrifice is laid bare in Ruixia's refusal to buy eyeglasses:

> She felt that it would be better not to see anything clearly after all. If she could see clearly, she would have seen that that old man was Liu Si. Wouldn't recognizing him just make her feel regret? . . . If she had known earlier that today would be like this, she would have realized that it would have been better to take that step. She didn't take it; whom did she have to blame? (216)

Ruixia ostensibly blames herself, yet her bewilderment also stems from a sense that her community has changed the rules on her. In accepting that her family's definition of her fate was indeed her fate, and that by

---

19. Even the head of the women's association flatters her, saying that "If it were the old society, we could even give you a chastity plaque" (196).

refusing Liu Si, "Ruixia was still Ruixia" (208), she had assumed that these terms would remain stable and that she could justify her 22 years of chastity by marrying her children well (165). Beyond her disappointment, Ruixia is thus thoroughly disoriented, and she likens herself to fallen, dried, yellow leaves, without roots or branches (216). The world seems to stop at her feet, and on the last page of the novella her family judges that she has fallen into a "spiritual crisis" (*jingshen weiji* 精神危機; 227).

Dai's *Soft Is the Chain* underscores the protagonist's realization that her submission to rules she took to be fated has led to an empty virtue and unnecessary loneliness. Yet whether Ruixia should have abided by the feudal injunction not to remarry or defied it in a gesture of individual freedom guaranteed by the Communist marriage law, the terms of her choice were clearly very restricted. In particular, her brother-in-law twice tells her that he and his wife would not blame her if she did remarry, but that she would have to leave her young son with them because he belongs to their family (217, 218). By sacrificing her own happiness and accepting what she decides is her fate to stay with her deceased husband's family, Ruixia expects to share in their future decision making. Yet the influence she awaits is denied her when the rest of the family adapts their belief system to allow the next generation to choose their own marriage partners. Of course, Ruixia is also allowed to enjoy new modern liberties: Unlike other women, she is permitted to smoke and drink (227), but these habits offer little consolation when her "only wish was to talk with someone" (224).

In the course of the narrative, the discourse reflects the decline of socially sanctioned belief in fate. It is noteworthy that the character *ming*, so prevalent earlier, appears only once in the last twenty pages (almost the last third) of the novella, and only in Ruixia's reminiscence that her in-laws hung a "long-life locket" (*changmingsuo* 長命鎖) on her baby son's neck (218). With the attenuation of the force of fate in the narrative, Ruixia confronts questions of responsibility that in her own case cannot but be demoralizing. Still condemned to suffer the injustices of gender inequalities, the modern woman blames herself for her backwardness, without the solace and pity that fatalistic explanations might provide.

At the same time, the tragedy of this novella raises questions that side-shadow Ruixia's own perspective. Would Ruixia really wish to condemn her daughter to a fate like her own? Is she unreasonable to resent that changes in her community's mores leave her bereft both before and after? As she contemplates her bereavement, the novella's presentation of her competing longings poses a fundamental question of modern Chinese fiction: Is the chain of the title her own submission to a fate imposed by feudal ethics, is it a chain others impose upon her, or is it both? If these works of fiction can teach by example, the difficulty of distinguishing individual from larger social beliefs urge further exploration of how specific groups use and are used by invocations of fate.

6. PSYCHOLOGICAL REALISM

Whereas many of the post-Mao works reveal troubling challenges to humanist ideals, these works also mark a deep commitment to compassionate agency. As humanist works promote human dignity and a sense of sanity, they also encourage readers to take control of their lives. Even as the more sophisticated works underscore the contradictions and difficulties, they strive to make sense of the world and to make social life more habitable.

It is no accident that serious fiction turned introspective during this period. Turning inward was one way writers could cope with an incomprehensible and authoritarian external world. Contemporary debates about individualism, humanism, and alienation and widespread anxiety concerning the psychic trauma wrought by violent political movements encouraged authors to focus on subjective perception.

Accompanying the onset of economic reforms, the rise of psychological fiction around 1980 also registered a decisive break from the cultural paradigm of the Mao period and reaffirmed the value of particular individuals and their inner struggles. As Perry Link has emphasized, the Deng regime could afford to permit writers a significant degree of freedom insofar as allowing that their critical works established the Deng regime's distance from the excessive repression of the Mao period and the extreme points of Maoist ideology.[20] This growing pluralism also allowed for the rise of avant-garde works, discussed in the next chapter, that registered more radical stylistic departures, more defiant ideological challenges, and more skeptical engagements with dilemmas of agency and determinism.

20. Link, *The Uses of Literature*.

7

Defiance and Fatalism in Roots-Seeking and Avant-Garde Fiction

Whereas the scar literature and new realist works discussed in the last chapter evoke a cautious sense of agency necessary for their embrace of moral responsibility, such humanist commitments were called into question by the cultural determinism of much "search-for-roots" (*xungen* 尋根) fiction and the extreme indeterminacy of much avant-garde experimentalism. Frequently overlapping in terms of the style of individual works, these two roughly contemporaneous literary trends have been celebrated for reviving artistic dissidence, for expanding the range of themes and narrative techniques, and for questioning the authority of any narrative.[1] Given what was until recently a socialist literary system supported by the Communist Party and Party demands for literature promoting the Four Modernizations, Chinese avant-garde fiction has presented an important challenge to dominant realist paradigms and ideologies promoting rational, collective social transformation. In departing from the mainstream of realism, be it May Fourth critical realism, the socialist realism of the Mao era, or the new realism of the post-Mao period, these works register skepticism toward any claim merely to record the facts and, more important, toward the ideologies that motivate wishes to do so. Specifically, modernist techniques and depictions of confusion, violence, and depravity in this writing cast doubt on the theories of revolution and

1. For 1980s Chinese fiction's return to modernism's oppositional position, including its thematization of the problematic status of the writer's authority, see Tang Xiaobing, "Residual Modernism," 9–10. See also Wang Jing, *High Culture Fever*, and Zhang Xudong, *Chinese Modernism*.

modernization that dominated public discourse in China throughout the twentieth century.

This chapter addresses dual aspects of defiance and fatalism in avant-garde works, including search-for-roots works, in terms of their depictions of agency and reflection on moral experience.[2] I begin by examining these works' greater formal, thematic, and ideological range, their challenge to theories of progress, and the value of such skepticism. Do these works, rich in sideshadowing and other modernist techniques that promote an open sense of temporality, ultimately strengthen or weaken moral attention and moral perception? In so asking, this chapter contrasts a critical modernism still committed to ethical ideals with a postmodernism that disputes the Confucian or Enlightenment meta-narratives that found such ideals.

Lest my later comments suggest a mistrust of avant-garde fiction's ability to engage ethical dilemmas, I first discuss the potential ethical power of avant-garde fiction. Although close consideration of avant-garde works reveals an often deterministic denial of agency discussed in the second half of this chapter, I set out expecting to find new and compelling ethical interventions in avant-garde works. For in a cultural context previously marked by extreme conformity, different narrative modes gain importance for considerations of moral responsibility. Defying the rosy, over-mechanical, over-schematized vision of life in Mao-era culture may have required exploring the power of negation before alternative visions or values could emerge.

1. CREATIVE DEFIANCE

1.1 The Critique of Explanatory Theories of Progress

In conjunction with their formal experimentalism, these avant-garde works express a generation's sense of helplessness in a period of unparalleled change and insecurity. From the bizarre transformation of humans into worms in Zong Pu's 宗璞 (b. 1928) "Wo shi shei?" 我是誰？ (Who am I?; 1979) to Can Xue's 殘雪 (b. 1953) ultra-vivid images that refuse to cohere into sense and Ge Fei's 格非 (b. 1964) Kafkaesque tales

2. Here I follow Leo Lee in viewing *xungen* and experimental movements as "complementary aspects of the same phenomenon" rather than seeing them in a linear succession wherein experimental fiction would follow the roots-seeking trend around 1987. See Lee, "Afterword," 380.

of incomprehensible persecution, the power of these works lies not in their meaning but in their bewilderment. Whereas the revolutionary or the modernizer assumes that theories enable one to understand a situation, avant-garde writing often denies the possibility of valid theories and explanations. Instead of interpretation and elucidation, these works amplify the chaos, opacity, and indeterminacy of the social world.

The troubled representation of agency in these works reflects the confusion remaining after discourses of progress and liberation become suspect. In no uncertain terms, many search-for-roots and avant-garde works imply that facing degeneration is more truthful than singing the praises of progress. Macabre acts of extreme violence and perverse sexuality are presented as if they show life at its least phony, most real, and most mordant. Ugliness feels true, for these works embark from an assumption that beauty and harmony are a lie, linked to either (a) a Confucian or bourgeois vision of nature and society as fundamentally balanced and ordered or (b) a socialist or modernizer's vision of human history as fundamentally progressive.

It is understandable that skepticism toward reason and progress would gain currency at this historical moment. In 1980s China, distrust of these ideals can be explained in at least two ways: First, voluntarism was a tainted pillar of Maoist orthodoxy and its emphasis on ultimate goals. The manipulation of individuals during the Cultural Revolution engendered a mistrust of rational choice in other contexts as well. When people realize how often their experiences of individual choice are caused by external manipulation, they awaken to the multiple obstacles to self-determination, from political control to the determining forces of heredity, environment, culture, or history.

Second, as Chinese society proceeded to implement the Four Modernizations, many young writers questioned the wisdom of human domination over nature or human control of destiny. Writer and critic Li Tuo 李陀 voices such disaffection in questioning the inevitability of modernization: "Is Western-style . . . modernization . . . really an irresistible trend? Does humanity have an alternative?"[3] Similar to modernist aesthetic and militant Luddite reactions to the historical project of modernization in Europe, the reaction of some Chinese intellectuals was to begin questioning modernity's conflicting potential to promote liberty, democracy, and

3. Li Tuo, "1985," 70; trans. Wedell-Wedellsborg, 128.

freedom but simultaneously science, technology, and global capitalism, forces thought by some to threaten those noble ideals.

Weary of the heavy affirmations of texts promoting revolution, development, and modernization, avant-garde works publicize a skepticism and a disenchantment with the whole notion of faith. Whereas humanist works sometimes confront similar predicaments concerning what people can know and control, they still strive to make sense of the world and to further possibilities for shared understanding and community. Suggesting that notions of rationality may be part of the problem, avant-garde texts spotlight breakdowns of meaning to question its very feasibility and desirability. By conveying an emotional anarchy bred in the tumult of changing political and social structures, this writing embodies a global literary aesthetic of disillusion with positivist, materialistic culture and of protest against such culture. It also voices a disillusion born of a world where the prevailing frame of reference seemed to be authoritarian myth tied to the "ten years of catastrophe" so recently endured during the Cultural Revolution.

To their credit, these works reveal the price of rapid social transformation and remind us that ideological programs, no matter how authoritarian, necessarily provoke resistance. The more idealist the dream of revolution or modernization, the more nihilistic and hostile will be the aesthetic protest against it. The question is whether these avant-garde works continue to embrace progressive paradigms based on reason, progress, and freedom. Or has this fiction moved on to a postmodern rejection of meta-narratives of progress?

Linked to the critique of progressive theories, avant-garde fiction engages at least three strategies that can serve ethical commitments. First, this fiction contests utopian discourses that risk turning individuals into mere means for abstract ends. In terms of both thematic content and expressive techniques, avant-garde works voice a desire for freedom by opening up a territory in which individual action regains or loses meaning *apart from* any contribution to revolutionary struggle or modernization. Second, by surrendering the cognitive security of teleological, linear thinking, avant-garde fiction allows questions about how to live well or ill.

Third, avant-garde fiction forcefully treats the power of physical needs and irrational motivations that demands to be taken seriously for a viable ethics. This attention to the body, desire, and sexuality contributes to these works' implicit critique of rationality. Much perceptive scholarship has addressed the significance of corporal imagery and sensual metaphors in contemporary Chinese fiction, from Gang Yue's theorizing about hunger, eating, and orality in works such as Lu Wenfu's 陸文夫 (b. 1928) "Meishijia" 美食家 (The gourmet; 1983), A Cheng's 阿城 (Zhong Acheng; b. 1949) "Qi wang" 棋王 (Chess king; 1984), and Mo Yan's 莫言 (Guan Moye 管謨業; b. 1956) *Jiu guo* 酒國 (Liquorland; 1992) to what Ling Tun Ngai calls "the politics of sexuality" in works by Zhang Xianliang 張賢亮 (b. 1936), Mo Yan, and Wang Anyi 王安憶 (b. 1954).[4] To these scholars' insights, I would add that privileging the power of sexual passion or other carnal desires often results in a fatalism regarding the frailty of individual decision in the face of bodily instincts or the mystical forces fueling sexual attraction. The peril to individual agency is voiced by the narrator of Wang Anyi's novella "Jinxiugu zhi lian" 錦繡谷之戀 (Love in brocade valley; 1987) when she describes the heroine's sense of helplessness as she becomes attracted to a writer at a conference at the Lu mountain resort: "It was as if all this were predetermined several decades earlier, [as if it all] were coexistent with this scene and circumstances, [as if all] were karmic destiny [*suming* 宿命], [all] were nature. In any event, she couldn't escape it and she didn't intend to escape it."[5]

1.2 Formal Dissidence: Subjectivity and Radical Skepticism

The reappearance of "experimental fiction" (*shiyan xiaoshuo* 實驗小說) in the late 1970s and the outpouring of such works since the mid-1980s signal a powerful desire to assert a critical distance from the realist tradition associated with progressive politics.[6] The objection to realism stems from concerns that much realist fiction betrays life when it simplifies events to make them accessible. Realism depends on the ideal of empiricism, yet this ideal collapses if one takes seriously the notion that "reality" exists only once people construct narratives, always biased, about the world. Thus, detractors would argue that realist narratives construct

4. Gang Yue, *The Mouth that Begs*; and Ngai, *Politics of Sexuality*. See also Zhong Xueping, *Masculinity Besieged?*; and Lu Tongling, *Misogyny.*

5. Wang Anyi, "Jinxiugu zhi lian," 41; my translation.

6. "In short," writes Joseph S. M. Lau in characterizing the countertradition of avant-garde works, "it represents an unceremonious departure from the 'China-obsessed' realist legacy of modern Chinese writing." See Lau, "China Deconstructs," 26.

meanings by correspondence not to some authentic reality but to theoretical abstractions.

By disputing assumptions about what people can know and control that underlie theories of revolution or modernization, experiments with antirealist narrative structures and techniques challenge the heady unrealities of idealism. One way to acknowledge the incomprehensible nature of the external world is through the inward turn that characterizes literary modernism. The quest for psychological analysis over and above social or class relations may be a shrewd reaction to official ideologies privileging the social and the collective. As contemporary debates about individualism and alienation and widespread anxiety concerning the psychic trauma caused by violent and rapid changes in Chinese society encouraged authors to focus on subjective perception, translations of Western authors, including Franz Kakfa, William Faulkner, Virginia Woolf, Gabriel García Márquez, and Milan Kundera, reinforced interest in modernist narrative techniques, particularly stream-of-consciousness narration (*yishiliu* 意識流) and magical realism (*mohuan xianshi zhuyi* 魔幻現實主義). Spurred by the "methodology fever" (*fangfalun re* 方法論熱) and "cultural discussion" (*wenhua taolun* 文化討論) of the decade, avant-garde writers turned to such antirealist techniques to voice a profound skepticism.

Of course, modernist techniques, specifically stream-of-consciousness narration, multiple points of view, and multiple narrators, mark some post-Mao humanist works as well. Yet, since the multiple viewpoints in humanist works do not ultimately conflict in irresolvable ways, they offer revised concepts of selfhood and reason to allow for greater personal and interpersonal responsibility, as in Dai Houying's *Humanity, O Humanity!*, discussed in the last chapter, or in Zhao Zhenkai's 趙振開 (b. 1949) *Bodong* 波動 (Waves; 1979), the first post-Mao novel to employ extreme narrative fragmentation but one that circulated widely only in the mid-1980s.[7] More radical than humanist works, avant-garde works dispute the very notions of selfhood and reason as well as collective understandings of human agency that underlie grand narratives of revolution or modernization.

Avant-garde writing engages in self-criticism by making more conspicuous fiction's techniques and methods, replete with problems, uncertainties, and gimmicks. Self-reflexive disruptions and competing, incom-

---

7. For the circulation of *Waves*, see Williams, "A New Beginning," 76.

patible accounts of events challenge narrative and historical authority to amplify a sense of indeterminacy in many of these works, from Ma Yuan's 馬原 (b. 1953) radical avant-garde stories such as "Gangdisi de youhuo" 岡底斯的誘惑 (Spell of the Gangdise mountains; 1985), "Ximalaya guge" 西馬拉雅古歌 (Old Himalayan song; 1986), and "Youshen" 游神 (Vagrant spirit; 1987) to Su Tong's 蘇童 (b. 1963) early novellas of "family history" retrospectives.[8] In employing metafictional techniques that underscore fragmentation and confusion, these works may steer clear of the determinism that can accompany naturalistic realism. Instead, their use of contradictions and negations achieves a sideshadowing that encourages interpretive humility. For example, in the fifth chapter of "Old Himalayan song," Ma Yuan's narrator interrupts protagonist Nuobu's 諾布 story about his father's murder to accuse Nuobu of lying and offer his own interpretation, with Freudian overtones, suggesting an Oedipal hatred of the father. Then, in chapter 6, the protagonist continues his tale as before, and the story never suggests that one version might be more accurate than another. The reader is left more puzzled about the story's epistemological implications than about its plot or subject.

1.3 Art for Art's Sake

In the Chinese context, the defense of "art for art's sake" served as another strategy for disputing grand theories of revolution and modernization. If authors reject the ideals and utopian ends art might serve, they may substitute the pursuit of aesthetic excellence or experimentation as an end in itself. After so many decades of literature subordinated to politics, the avant-garde turn to "art for art's sake" may have been a first step out from under the burdens of witness and conscience so heavy in the humanist-realist tradition.

Some critics have been quick to praise the avant-garde writers' anti-ideological tendency and to interpret their renewed attention to technique as an "antidote to political ideology" and thus as a literary form of dissidence.[9] Yet the implications of these works need to be examined

8. As Tang Xiaobing has argued, Su Tong's use of history challenges dominant ideology by recognizing the impossibility of knowing the past. See Tang, "The Mirror of History," 210.

9. Leo Lee, "The Politics of Technique," 161. For an example from a PRC-based critic, see Chen Bingzhao's praise of Su Tong's anti-ideological tendency in "Xiang chengshi wenxue maijin."

carefully. The use of modernist techniques may suggest a desire to establish a self-sufficient logic somehow autonomous or removed from politics. But the artist is never removed from relations of power and privilege, and these works, too, convey an ideology. What values underlie aesthetic excellence? Pleasure, play? Should we assume, as Wang Jing does, that "the making of a subject without a core who narrates without a purpose was a highly subversive act"?[10]

The turn to "art for art's sake" also served a politics of generational self-positioning. Although modernist works from the late 1970s written by older writers such as Wang Meng 王蒙 (b. 1934) and Zong Pu should be considered forerunners, Ma Yuan's metafiction and Can Xue's nightmarish surrealism of the early 1980s are often cited as the first examples of the "avant-garde fiction" (*xianfeng xiaoshuo* 先鋒小說) movement. Determined to be different from their predecessors, these and other writers born in the 1950s and 1960s, such as Liu Suola 劉索拉 (b. 1955), Mo Yan, and Ye Zhaoyan 葉兆言 (b. 1957), turned to modernist techniques to assert their position as proud latecomers.[11] Moreover, although much metafiction explicitly casts doubt on the relation of authorial intention to the work that results, the foregrounding of the narrator in metafiction often nonetheless reaffirms the artist's role as an individual versus the collective "art of the people" promoted by Mao.[12]

By using techniques forbidden during the Mao era, fictional innovations also tacitly endorsed and offered evidence of the political invention of the "New Era" (*xin shiqi* 新時期; 1979–1989) by which the Deng regime sought to distance itself from Maoist ideology.[13] Whereas modernist fragmentation may have cast doubt on notions of rationality and progress crucial to the Deng regime's modernization discourse, it also demonstrated the greater pluralism possible under the Deng regime. The use of narrative techniques associated with Western or Japanese literature could also be viewed as a realization of Deng's open-door policy. Although for some search-for-roots writers constructing a new national image and cultural consciousness meant resisting the imitation of Euro-

10. Wang Jing, *China's Avant-garde Fiction*, 4.

11. For a discussion of 1980s avant-garde writers, see Y. H. Zhao, "The Rise of Metafiction."

12. Zhang Xudong makes a similar comment on Fifth Generation filmmakers; see Zhang, *Chinese Modernism*, 344–46.

13. This argument is suggested throughout Zhang Xudong's *Chinese Modernism*.

American models, a large number of their works also borrowed heavily from techniques of Western modernism.

1.4 Trauma and Memory

Perhaps even more significant than the critique of progress, formal experimentation, or the privileging of art above politics is the thematic decadence of much avant-garde fiction.[14] Filled with images of sickness, degeneracy, and sadism, including grotesque details of sexual perversion and torture, such works explore behaviors that lie beyond conventional experience. And whereas much decadence in Western literature celebrates hedonistic pleasure, these works focus on inflicting pain, as in Mo Yan's detailed description of a Chinese butcher ordered by Japanese soldiers to skin alive one of his fellow villagers in *Hong gaoliang jiazu* 紅高粱家族 (Red sorghum; 1987).

Such decadence bespeaks these works' avowal of a collective memory of trauma. In setting their characters' fates against the background of an unspecified context of violence—the intermediate past of the Japanese invasion, the struggle between the Nationalists and the Communists, or older historical upheavals—these authors begin, consciously or unconsciously, to discharge the trauma of the Cultural Revolution. For example, might readers not think of the slicing out of tongues during Cultural Revolution struggle sessions when the young emperor in Su Tong's *Wo de diwang shengya* 我的帝王生涯 (My life as an emperor; 1992) orders that the neglected concubines' tongues be cut out so that he will not have to hear them wail?[15] Of course, calculating authors' intentions or readers' responses is a risky enterprise, but such inferences are not implausible given the prolific production of graphic accounts of violence after so terrible a human cataclysm.

The need to discharge traumatic memories may in part explain why decadent, avant-garde works would gain prominence at this particular moment. For modernist and metafictional techniques were not new in 1980s China.[16] Their reemergence was allowed and at the same time cir-

---

14. For a longer discussion of decadence as a response to revolutionary literature in the Chinese context, see Knight, "Decadence and Revolution."

15. Su Tong, *Wo de diwang shengya*, 19.

16. For modernist fiction from the Republican period, see Sabin, "Lu Xun," and Kinkley, *The Odyssey*.

cumscribed by the partial political liberalization of the early Deng era.[17] Aware that the guardians of orthodoxy were hardly in full retreat, writers may have wagered that experimental writing that avoided topical references to recent or present politics represented a safer way to convey the essence of traumatic historical memory. Through imaginative transformation, these works could issue a forthright demand to face the violence while refraining from directly criticizing the regime. Indeed, it may not be incidental that surges in experimental fiction followed on the heels of the Party's "Anti-Spiritual Pollution" Campaign of fall 1983 through spring 1984 and the Campaign against Bourgeois Liberalization of 1987.

Behind these portrayals of cruelty and alienation, the cynicism and disaffection prominent in post-1985 fiction express a dissident denial of faith in the Party's ability to set things in order. Not content to expose deception, hypocrisy, or corruption as was done in many realist works, many of these authors present an overt, pathological evil of incomprehensible proportions. Such writing reacts against humanist realism in part by resisting subject matter and narrative techniques that reinforce the status quo. These writers may be using techniques of defamiliarization to penetrate the tissue of complacency or, as Wang Dewei 王德威 (David Wang) speculates, they may be employing a "mimesis of depravity" to reveal how normal the grotesque and insane have become in order to awaken their readers.[18]

Whereas these works sound a common note of terror, their grotesque sensationalism has a dulling effect. The high-wire technical virtuosity and garish accounts of violence may dazzle the reader, but the stories themselves are less memorable. Yu Hua's 余華 (b. 1960) grotesque early works provide stark examples, such as the senseless violence of his "Yijiubaliu nian" 一九八六年 (The year nineteen eighty-six; 1986), "Xianshi yi zhong" 現實一種 (One kind of reality; 1987), discussed at the end of this chapter, and "Nantao jieshu" 難逃劫數 (Fate is inescapable; 1988). In the last story, a bride disfigures her husband by pouring acid on his

17. Party leaders communicated their degree of tolerance in shifting terms, from Deng's "Anti-Spiritual Pollution" slogan put forth at the Second Plenum of the Twelfth Central Committee in October 1983 to the promise of "creative freedom" (*chuangzao ziyou* 創造自由) put forth at the Fourth National Congress of the Chinese Writers Association, held in Beijing from December 29, 1985, to January 5, 1986.

18. See Wang Dewei's discussion of "familiarization of the uncanny" and the "mimesis of depravity" in his "Shiji mo de Zhongwen xiaoshuo," 204–6, 219. See also David Wang, "Chinese Fiction for the Nineties," 243.

face on their wedding night, and he later kills her. Such fiction may well indicate a criticism of society, but it also evokes the violence of a sensibility at war with itself. As instinctual compulsions overpower rational reflection, the unremittingly bleak world of much of this fiction admits no justice or compassion.

As violence can bespeak an inability to articulate ideas verbally, the representation of violence may express a kind of moral aphasia afflicting this generation. Inflicting or enduring pain may also remedy an absence of feeling. Such a longing for feeling is voiced by the young narrator in Yu Hua's "Shiba sui chumen yuan xing" 十八歲出門旅行 (On the road at eighteen; 1986) as he lies down in the cab of a truck vandalized by the mob that beat him: "I smell leaking gas and think of the smell of blood that leaked out of me. . . . I think that even if the truck's been battered, its heart is still intact, still warm. I know that my heart's warm, too."[19]

It is hard not to come away from such stories struck by a callow and furious contempt for human life. As the narrator's mother tells him in Ge Fei's "Remembering Mr. Wu You," "Killing a man is the same as killing a chicken" (2/15), or, as his brother tells him, "Killing a man is a lot easier than killing a chicken" (2/16).[20] The reader's discomfort may be salutary, but it needs to demand more than a mere recognition of horror. How should one respond to such violence and nihilism? These questions become more pressing in later avant-garde works, such as Mo Yan's *Liquorland* or Su Tong's treatment of the Cultural Revolution in *Chengbei didai* 城北地帶 (North of the city; 1995). In the latter novel, accounts of serial rape and murder are so unrelenting that they may numb the reader to the brutality portrayed.

In appreciating the defiant power of avant-garde works, this account fills in a picture of literary history that would present avant-garde works as resulting in an elitist dead end. For whereas the readership for serious fiction fell dramatically during this "pluralist" (*duoyuan* 多元) stage and more popular, commercial forms gained increasing market share, both avant-garde fiction and China's broader cultural history might have developed differently. Moreover, it is not that avant-garde writers tried and failed to present moral agency and other issues of concern to a broad

19. Yu Hua, *Shiba sui chumen yuan xing*, 28–29; trans. Jones, *The Past and the Punishments*, 10.

20. The first page number refers to Ge Fei, "Zhuiyi." The second refers to Howard Goldblatt's translation.

readership. By rendering possibilities for moral agency highly problematic, these avant-garde experiments call for a fundamental reconsideration of ethical categories and conceptions. It is to take seriously the transformative potential of avant-garde themes and techniques that this section has laid out the movement's challenge to a progressive worldview, realist techniques, instrumental uses of literature, and the denial of trauma and irrational motives.

2. THE UPSHOT OF DETERMINISM

What happens when cultural dissent challenges the very possibility of reason and progress? Might rejecting the focus on how the world ought to be, common to discourses of revolution or modernization, not amount to resigning oneself to the world as it is? Whereas avant-garde works may have important critical and even political effects, serious questions must be asked about whether they empower or disable the capacity for constructive analysis and moral responsibility. Such questions divide along two lines: first, whether these works convey the possibility of individual or collective agency and, second, whether such agency has an ethical basis. Insofar as avant-garde works do acknowledge possibilities for self-determination, many dispute humanist assumptions that such agency could serve good rather than evil or selfishness. Thus, beneath their rupture of realist narrative codes, these works reflect a deep rupture in shared values and norms.

Underneath its bold defiance of realist techniques and grand narratives of revolution and modernization, much avant-garde writing conveys its own meta-narrative, namely, an antiprogressive and ultimately nihilistic rejection of ideals. Challenging faith in human agency, many works embody multiple forms of determinism, and their interconnections are important to keep in mind. At the same time, analyzing distinct forms of determinism helps bring to light their moral implications. For this reason, the following focuses on the denial of agency in the antirealist countermovements in terms of (1) a soft determinism rooted in culture and tradition, (2) a hard determinism emphasizing the power of nature, heredity, and the environment, (3) an historical determinism often marked by an apocalyptic vision, and (4) a radical indeterminacy that severely undermines possibilities for moral deliberation.

2.1 Cultural Determinism and Search-for-Roots Fiction

One way in which the avant-garde works undercut notions of reason and progress is by privileging the determining power of tradition, cultural conditioning, and, for some, even abstract notions of national essence (*guocui* 國粹). As writers and other intellectuals in the 1980s increasingly pursued various forms of "cultural reflection" (*wenhua fansi* 文化反思), the power of culture became an important thematic and organizing principle in literary works, especially after the explicit rise of the search-for-roots movement. Combining a desire to trace the development of contemporary mentalities back to China's cultural heritage with a desire to assert China's cultural specificity, writers such as A Cheng, Gu Hua 古華 (b. 1942), Jia Pingwa 賈平凹 (b. 1953), and Lin Jinlan 林斤瀾 (b. 1923) joined in a mission to "search for roots." This mission responded to fervent theoretical debates about cultural subjectivity, "cultural-psychological structure" (*wenhuaxinli jiegou* 文化心理結構), and "cultural sedimentation" (*wenhua jidian* 文化積淀), to use philosopher Li Zehou's 李澤厚 (b. 1930) terms, as writers explored China's cultural and aesthetic traditions to ground the possibility of an alternative Chinese modernity. Though earlier nature writing by regional writers and earlier theoretical statements presage the search-for-roots trend,[21] the movement coalesced through intense discussions at a forum on literature in Hangzhou in late 1984 and was explicitly championed by Han Shaogong 韓少功 (b. 1953) in his article "Wenxue de gen" 文學的根 (The roots of literature; 1985).[22] As if responding to Han's argument that literature must grow out of a country's soil, in 1985 the Hunan branch of the Chinese Writers' Association sent a group of young writers to search for roots in the west of the country. The search-for-roots trend also voiced a backlash against the May Fourth cultural "rupture" (*duanlie* 斷裂),[23] against imitations of Western literature, and against those who hoped to use Western theory to reorient Chinese culture.

21. Some literary historians trace the search-for-roots movement back to a 1982 speech by Wang Zengqi and comments made by Li Tuo in March 1984. See Kinkley, "Shen Congwen's Legacy," 98.

22. "Literature has roots, and these roots must be deeply planted in the soil of a people's traditional culture. If the roots are not deep, then it will be difficult for the leaves to flourish" (Han, "Wenxue de gen," 2).

23. The term "rupture" appears in Huang, Chen, and Qian, "Lun 'ershi shiji Zhongguo wenxue,'" 5.

Diversity within the search-for-roots group complicates considerations of how the members' works enabled or inhibited expressions of agency and moral responsibility. In broad terms, writers appealed to the roots-seeking project to serve two very distinct purposes, as Link has pointed out. The first looked hopefully to both Han and minority Chinese cultures as a corrective to the excesses of the socialist experiment. The second sought to uncover deep cultural roots responsible for the country's afflictions.[24] Either of these approaches could potentially empower the exercise of agency: understanding one's personal or cultural past can make one more conscious of the past's ongoing effects, positive or negative. Yet, whereas theoretical statements often heralded the empowering potential of the roots-seeking project, the fictional works more often express a sense of the powerlessness of human beings in the grip of larger cultural, natural, or instinctual forces.

On the optimistic side, by opposing the denigration of Chinese tradition in many May Fourth and Mao-era writings, the search-for-roots cause implied hope that China's own traditions could serve as a source of renewal. This vein of the movement was inspired by the lyricism and attention to regional culture in the writings of Wang Zengqi 汪曾祺 (b. 1920) and his teacher Shen Congwen 沈從文 (1902–1988).[25] Many of the most discussed search-for-roots works voice great confidence in the value of culture and education and thus allow for the possibility of human betterment. In A Cheng's "Chess King," for example, an elderly man draws on Daoist wisdom to mentor the protagonist in the way of chess playing and enables the latter to win a championship, simultaneously defeating nine opponents. Similarly, in A Cheng's "Haizi wang" 孩子王 (King of the children; 1985), an educated youth teaches country children to read and to write their own essays, and in "Shu wang" 樹王 (King of trees; 1985), Confucian wisdom helps villagers respect the value of harmony between nature and human beings (*tian ren he yi* 天人合一) as they confront the destruction of their forest and Mao's directive that man conquer nature (*ren sheng yu tian* 人勝於天).

Yet much roots-seeking fiction subverts this hope for cultural renaissance with accounts of disaffection and degeneration. Largely written by

24. Link, *The Uses of Literature*, 34.

25. For a careful analysis of the similarities and differences between Shen Congwen's fiction and the works of Gu Hua, Wang Zengqi, He Liwei, and Han Shaogong, see Kinkley, "Shen Congwen's Legacy."

"educated youth" (*zhiqing* 知青) who had been exiled to rural areas during the rustication movement, many search-for-roots works focus above all on these youths' sense of alienation both in the countryside and when, changed by their experiences, they return to the cities. In Zhang Chengzhi's 張承志 (b. 1948) "Lüye" 綠夜 (Green night; 1981), for example, the protagonist returns to Mongolia eight years after serving time as a sent-down youth. He returns to see a little girl he loved, but finds that she has grown coarse and that an immense distance now separates them. If the colorful, almost legendary evocation of the steppe shows the intensity of the protagonist's nostalgic memory and attachment to his fragile ideal, his longing to escape his dreary life in the city betrays underlying emotional needs that he appears disinclined to address.

Moreover, even as many roots-seeking writers extolled the value of traditional cultures in their theoretical works, much of their fiction focuses on negative elements, particularly irrational urges, "superstitions," myths, and violence. In this way, many search-for-roots works share with avant-garde fiction a plot, as Leo Lee puts it, that "seems only to lead to a clash of some primordial and irrational forces out of human control."[26] Other works stress rural poverty and the compromises that result when the power of instinct wins out over moral considerations. For example, in Zheng Yi's 鄭義 (b. 1947) *Yuan cun* 遠村 (Remote village; 1983), poverty leads so many women to flee the area that those who remain accept awkward arrangements of polyandry. The description of desperate rural living conditions in this novel and Zheng's *Lao jing* 老井 (Old well; 1985) are more likely to inspire horror than idealization.[27] If roots-seeking fiction stages a reluctant confrontation between (a) traditional cultures, especially the cultures of China's "minority peoples," and (b) the forces of modernization, the native roots hardly look safer than the menace of modernization.

Most significant, in driving home the deterministic influences of the past, roots-seeking works tend to reinforce fatalistic paradigms, be they cultural, environmental, or politico-historical. The ruinous effects of

26. Leo Lee, "Afterword," 379.

27. Many of China's Fifth Generation filmmakers brought search-for-roots themes and tensions to their films. As did the descriptions in Zheng Yi's novels, Chen Kaige's depiction of barren landscapes and material poverty in his films *Huang tudi* (Yellow earth; 1984) and *Haizi wang* (King of the children; 1987) shocked urban viewers and renewed concern about the fate of the nation. For a discussion of Fifth Generation cinema, see Zhang Xudong, *Chinese Modernism*.

inherited hostility are starkly portrayed by Li Hangyu 李杭育 (b. 1957) in "Renjian yi yu" 人間一隅 (A corner of the human world; 1983). Set in 1934 in the city of Tongxing 同興, literally "Common prosperity," the story depicts callous residents who drive away refugees whom they blame for the ceaseless rain and proliferation of crabs that serve as free food for the destitute arrivals. Describing how the villagers exterminate the crabs until they become so expensive that the refugees cannot afford them, the narrator comments on the long-range effects of his ancestors' actions:

> Many years later, every time today's youth hear the old people talk about that event from the past, . . . they complain over the way older generations lay evil karma for their children and grandchildren, confusedly exterminating the crabs wholesale even to the point of resembling people these days who take measures to exterminate the "four pests," to the point that crabs in Tongxing sold for three bucks a catty, making it so [the refugees] couldn't afford to eat them.[28]

In such works, the search-for-roots project reinforces a deep cultural determinism (*wenhua jueding lun* 文化決定論). The novelist Li Rui 李銳 (b. 1951), worrying about the apparent new choices in his own works, voices this danger: "It's still the same old cultural determinism, a kind of linear causal logic, a kind of either/or mode, a kind of longstanding philosophical certainty."[29] The risk that emphasis on culture over history may blind people to ways cultural practices change over time is echoed in a telling comment by Zheng Wanlong 鄭萬隆 (b. 1944): "Space is eternal, while time—yesterday and today, past and present, history and reality—merely coexists."[30] Moreover, despite authors' concern to be geographically specific, rather than painting concrete local or regional culture, their fiction generally paints a mythologized national culture often dependent on an overly abstract concept of "Chineseness."[31] By mystifying notions of an essential Chinese culture, the project may lead to a chauvinistic nationalism and a sense of superiority founded on excluding outsiders, including—paradoxically—the very cultural minorities that roots-seeking fiction seeks to represent.

---

28. Li Hangyu, "Renjian yi yu," 2004; my translation.

29. Quoted in Pan Kaixiong, "'Zijue' wei ta dailai le shenma?" 118.

30. Zheng Wanlong, "Xiandai xiaoshuo," 80; trans. Zhang Yingjin, *The City*, 265.

31. Louie, "The Short Stories of Ah Cheng: Daoism, Confucianism and Life," in *Between Fact and Fiction*, 76–90, esp. 86.

2.2 *The Hard Determinism of Nature, Heredity, and Environment*

In search-for-roots and avant-garde works, even more devastating to possibilities for moral agency than the power of culture is a hard determinism that emphasizes the power of nature, heredity, and environmental conditioning. Even before the rise of the explicit search-for-roots movement, regionalist writers such as the prolific Liu Shaotang 劉紹堂 (b. 1936) wrote stories and novels placing the power of nature over modern civilization and human will. Many of these works use long descriptions of the sea, mountains, desert, or steppe to project the characters' nostalgia (*huaijiu* 懷舊), their yearning (*huai* 懷) for a past (*jiu* 舊) world less dominated by concrete, skyscrapers, and political campaigns.

By indicating the all-encompassing power of nature and the wise serenity attainable by accepting nature's course, many of these stories implicitly downplay the need for action or struggle in the human world. In Deng Gang's 鄧剛 (b. 1954) "Mi ren de hai" 迷人的海 (Sea of seduction; 1983) and Zhang Wei's 張煒 "Yi tan qingshui" 一潭清水 (A pond of clear water; 1984), for example, discussing and exploring nature offers the characters the possibility of communication but little possibility for action. Similar resignation to nature's course emerges in Shi Tiesheng's 史鐵生 (b. 1951) philosophical treatment of infirmity, destiny, and repetition in "Ming ruo qinxian" 命若琴弦 (Life like a lute string; 1985). In Shi's story, the older of two wandering blind minstrels finally breaks his thousandth cord, the number his teacher had told him would suffice to activate the prescription to cure his blindness. To his great disappointment, the prescription turns out to be only a blank piece of paper. After a period of despair, he realizes that even if dreams are illusory, having a goal is indispensable, and he passes the prescription on to his own student.

Other works focus on the power of heredity in their preoccupation with physical or mental disabilities, a theme that also bespeaks the apocalyptic undertones of the search-for-roots movement. In Han Shaogong's "Ba Ba Ba" 爸爸爸 (Pa Pa Pa; 1985), for example, the autistic protagonist narrowly escapes becoming a human sacrifice and then oddly survives his community's mass suicide. In this and Han's surrealist "Nü Nü Nü" 女女女 (Woman, woman, woman; 1985), the overlap with the avant-garde works becomes apparent. The rhetoric of sickness in these works simultaneously celebrates altered states as a window to the unconscious and associates bodily contamination and infection with cultural disaster.

2.2.1 White Dog and the Swing. Given the preoccupation with heredity in the avant-garde works, it is not surprising that serious authors might also explore the possibility of overcoming genetic determinism. Mo Yan's "Bai gou qiuqianjia" 白狗鞦韆架 (White dog and the swing; 1985), for example, ends with the eugenicist possibility of producing better offspring as the narrator-protagonist considers whether to conceive a child with his old friend Nuan 暖. The decision is all the more harrowing for the story's account of the narrator's guilt over having caused a swing accident that poked out Nuan's right eye. After ten years away, he visits his old village to learn that Nuan's disfigurement condemned her to marry an abusive mute with whom she has had mute and retarded triplets. Although Nuan reassures him three times that everything is the work of fate (58, 59, 68), the protagonist feels horrified by the contrast between what has become of her and what might have been.[32]

Mo Yan underscores the unrealized possibilities of Nuan's life by including multiple sideshadows in the narrative. Recalling Nuan's beauty and musical talents, the narrator thinks, "If it were not for her disfigurement, she would surely have become an actress" (53). They discuss their bygone hopes from before the accident, and Nuan tells the narrator how she almost became involved with an army captain. Another sideshadow is cast when Nuan takes responsibility for not having answered the narrator's letters and asks if he would have married her had she asked him. "I would have. Of course I would have," he answers (69).

The story's keen presentation of the role of contingency culminates in its open ending. Here, Nuan pleads with the narrator to make love to her so that she might have a normal child: "It's the perfect time in my cycle. . . . I want a child who can talk. . . . If you agree, you'll save me. If you don't agree, you'll destroy me. There are a thousand reasons and ten thousand excuses. Please don't give me reasons and excuses" (69). Since only an ellipsis follows this quotation and Mo Yan does not divulge the narrator's decision, the reader is left wondering what the protagonist will do, and what he or she might do in the same situation. Despite the story's appeals to fate, the presentation of this moral decision allows for a measure of human influence.

32. Parenthetical page numbers refer to Mo Yan, "Bai gou." Translations are my own.

2.2.2 Rice: *Environmental determinism.* Combining the power of nature and environmental determinism, Su Tong explores the phenomenon of compulsive behavior in his first full-length novel, *Mi* 米 (Rice; 1991). *Rice* describes the alarming physical and psychological mutilations that afflict the protagonist Five Dragons 五龍 after a famine forces him to flee his village. From the opening passage, when Five Dragons arrives in the city chewing his last handful of uncooked rice, the theme of rice serves to highlight the complicated links between instinctual nature and behavior conditioned by one's environment. Five Dragons's obsession with rice and his abnormal digestive habits may be rooted in his rural understanding and heritage, but the corruption and abuse of the city aggravate his pathology.[33] By depicting the degeneration of Five Dragons's craving for rice from an instinctual hunger into a crippling sadistic neurosis, the story highlights the artificiality of an urban existence that separates people from nature.

The novel suggests the individual's defenselessness against the city's corrupting power by foreshadowing Five Dragons's degradation and illness in the elements of the garish surroundings he confronts upon arriving in the city, including the stench of excrement and rotten meat, cigarette advertisements, announcements for outpatient venereal disease clinics (6–7/2), and a stiff, bluish corpse lying in the street (7–8/3).[34] Five Dragons's flight from this corpse ends only with his demeaning initiation into city life at the hands of the bully Abao 阿保 and his gang. They accuse Five Dragons of being a thief, crush his hand as he reaches for a piece of salted pig's head, and force him to call them "Daddy" (*die* 爹) before allowing him to eat. Then the gang members pin him down, force open his mouth, and pour down five bottles of hard alcohol. After this symbolic rape, the bullies throw Five Dragons to the ground, leaving him sick and ashamed. The self-perpetuating nature of the cycle of evil emerges when Five Dragons, powerful and well-off later in the novel, restages the humiliating scene, this time acting as the perpetrator as he and his cronies abuse other newcomers.

On the one hand, Five Dragons's manipulation of rice epitomizes his struggle for self-determination in a world that repeatedly excludes him

33. For an analysis that draws on Raymond Williams's *The Country and the City* to discuss the urban-rural transition in the novel, see Visser, "Displacement."

34. Page numbers are given in parentheses. The first is to the 1991 Taipei edition; the second is to Howard Goldblatt's translation.

from moral frameworks and denies him the opportunity to define himself through work or meaningful relationships. An object he can control, rice offers Five Dragons a means to cultivate emotional detachment in enduring the anxiety of displacement: "The subtle fragrance of raw rice . . . was the only smell that brought warmth and affection into his life, especially so far from home" (21/14). His obsession with rice becomes all the more desperate when he is unable to control his first wife, Cloud Weave 織雲, and so decides that he prefers rice to women: "Rice must be the best sleeping potion in the world, he sensed, certainly more effective than a woman's body" (92–93/78). Eating uncooked rice thus comforts Five Dragons in moments of powerlessness, such as when Cloud Weave announces that the baby she is carrying may be another man's child (122/105–6).

Whereas in his early poverty eating uncooked rice offers a way to satisfy his hunger, once Five Dragons can earn the means to procure rice, his craving for it becomes a fetish. As his obsession turns into a sexual fetish, what stimulates him is not just sex or physical sensations but the power to impose his will on women and force them to participate in his obsession. Satisfied at first with sprinkling rice on his wife's body, Five Dragons soon initiates his habit of putting rice into his wife's vagina (123/107). After he grows rich through illicit commerce in rice, he frequents brothels, inserts rice into each prostitute's vagina (179/159), and forces the prostitutes to eat raw rice (218/194). Five Dragons's increasing eagerness to violate norms may suggest the erotic charge many associate with transgression, but his violations of women's bodies also attest to an urge for self-assertion through exercising force over others.

Yet the novel mocks Five Dragons's belief in his own agency by emphasizing his subjugation to his environment and social situation. Though he uses rice to avoid dependence on other people, an addictive obsession hardly offers a way to gain freedom. Five Dragons resents the rice-emporium family's control over his life, but he never questions his own compulsive behavior. Although he remains a teetotaler because drinking "puts you at the mercy of sober people" (98/83–84), he does not try to resist his own self-destructive fixations on rice, sadistic sex, and power. His passivity vis-à-vis his own desires is evident when he expresses apprehension about his wet dreams: "He envisioned his energy being sapped to the point where he would be unable to achieve his goals in life" (93/79). Similarly, although Five Dragons expresses confidence about exercising moderation in his pursuit of illicit sex (91–92/77), he is not immune to his environment, for it is venereal disease that finally kills him.

Although improvements in Five Dragons's material and social status initially reinforce his faith in his ability to control his destiny using rice and other material means, as his social position rises the novel deals him consequences that sorely undermine the possibility of self-determination. For example, in an attempt to shape his image and publicize his status, wealth, and power, Five Dragons exchanges his perfectly healthy teeth for a set of gold ones (181–82/160–61). With this decision, his hedonism and materialism leave him literally misshapen, and the vanity and futility of his strategy are driven home on the novel's last page when his angry son Kindling Boy 柴生 tears the golden teeth from his dead father's mouth (299/266). Nor is Five Dragons spared consciousness of his failure. As he deteriorates, he longs for the young man he once was, one with an agile, robust body and eyes full of hope (238/211–12). Even after his dissolute sex life leads to gonorrhea (219/195), his attempt to cure himself with rice vinegar (237/211) conveys his abiding but futile faith in rice and his overestimation of his own ability to influence his health and destiny.

By underscoring how the impersonal power of modern cities can crush individuals, the novel shows that Five Dragons's neurosis is not individual but part of a far-reaching phenomenon of social desperation. The discovery of a child's corpse, still bloated with the raw rice that killed him, in a sack delivered to Five Dragons's rice shop (130–31/114–15) offers the most obvious evidence of the endemic nature of Five Dragons's affliction. Moreover, the novel sets Five Dragons's obsession against a background in which almost all the characters are gripped by abnormal fixations: Proprietor Feng's visits to opium parlors; Sixth Master's sexual abuse of his concubines, evident from purple welts on Cloud Weave's breasts (39/31); Cloud Weave's eagerness to engage in illicit sex; Kindling Boy's gambling; and Jade Embrace's craving for retribution. On one level, the characters' surrender to these obsessions shows their desperate longing for autonomy in a world where individual pursuits have little meaning. In describing Cloud Weave's affair with Abao, for example, the narrator comments on how transgression can offer a sense of freedom: "Cloud Weave felt daringly rebellious, and loved it" (59/48).

The characters may enjoy the illusion that they exercise free will by choosing to engage in extreme behavior, yet the novel underscores the extent to which their environment determines both the nature and the outcome of those choices. The cruelest acts result from the characters' craving for revenge, and their inability to transcend their vengeance lends a mechanistic aspect to the novel's already strong fatalism. The linking of evil acts with the natural element rice further intensifies the aura of inevitability, as in the horrifying episode in which Rice Boy 米生, the eldest son of Five Dragons and Cloud Silk 綺雲, uses rice to suffocate his little sister in revenge for the beating he received after she squealed on him for selling the family gold in exchange for candy.

The antagonism between the characters has led critic Chen Xiaoming 陳曉明 to associate the book with a kind of Social Darwinist survival of the fittest.[35] The novel denies any belief in meaningful human evolution and instead makes decadence appear immanent in human nature and history. The moral depravity of this panorama seems all the more absolute because it is unreflective and because the characters enjoy no redeeming qualities, no expanded awareness, and no moral development. Not only are the malefactors impelled toward evil, but they lack any moral inhibitions or compunction. How can one understand the absence of any sense of guilt in Rice Boy and the other perpetrators of abuse? Perhaps they do not experience their cruelty as such because the notion of cruelty depends on an ethics, yet the characters have no ethics. This result is hardly surprising, suggests the novel, given the environment that shapes them.

2.3 Historical Determinism and the Sense of Apocalypse

Given China's recent historical upheavals, the temptation to see people as prisoners of history is understandable, and the historical determinism of many roots-seeking and avant-garde works should be viewed in this context. As discussed above, these works are defiant in their honest testimony, whether direct or symbolic, concerning the trauma and anguish of the recent revolutionary past. At the same time, the combination of focus on violence and persecution with the use of narrative techniques that undercut notions of reason and autonomy often conveys a deterministic resignation.

The nature of this determinism often turns out to be profoundly apocalyptic, though avant-garde works place their apocalyptic moment

35. Chen Xiaoming, "Zui hou de yishi," 140.

in different specified or unspecified epochs. For whereas the specter of violent revolution looms large in these works, their decadent tenor denies a revolutionary's or modernizer's hopes for social transformation. In place of such faith in progress, these works tend to portray morality devolving or careening eerily out of the control of any human community. As the narrator of Mo Yan's *Red Sorghum* says in comparing himself unfavorably to his courageous grandparents, "Surrounded by progress, I feel a nagging sense of our species' regression" (2/4).[36]

In emphasizing a unidirectional sequence, theories of decadence or apocalypse run some of the same risks as those of revolution. Whether one believes in a force of progress or a force of degeneration, belief in such a force can blind people to processes of decision making necessary for individual and collective moral agency. Focus on the natural world can exacerbate the tendency to reduce human choices and possibilities to mere epiphenomena of a larger plan or naturalistic pattern. Along these lines, in many roots-seeking and avant-garde works, detailed descriptions of the natural world imply a naturalism that risks falsely associating human history with the evolutionary order of natural laws. In *Red Sorghum*, the narrator suggests such a naturalistic viewpoint in extolling the sorghum plants: "They understood the ways of the heavens and the logic of the earth" (9/10).

The challenge of depicting simultaneous and *equally plausible* possibilities is particularly difficult when writers place their narratives within an historical framework, as in works depicting pre-1949 rural China, such as *Red Sorghum.* Although the characters never succumb to resignation, the novel conveys a strong apocalyptic tenor. The narrator alludes to several historical moments, including his granddad's rape of his grandma in 1926, his father's hiding underneath floorboards in 1957, the famine of 1960, and the narrative present of 1985. While Mo depicts the characters' unrelenting primal energies and bold defiance of conventional morality, he situates these accounts within a strong historical determinism concerning their helplessness against the brutal ravages of the Japanese invasion of their village in 1939.

Mo Yan's struggle to re-narrate Chinese experience without falling into readily available models is evident in his ambitious use of accretion and montage in *Red Sorghum.* First written as five separate novellas, the

36. In this and subsequent references, the first page number refers to the 1988 Taipei edition, and the second number refers to Goldblatt's translation.

five chapters of the novel narrate essentially the same story, with each successive chapter filling in the picture and progressing the chronology only slightly.[37] This repetition, combined with historical knowledge concerning the invasion and the way revenge (*baochou* 報仇) works in the novel, all seem to preclude a sense of an open world.[38] At the same time, the connections and disconnections within and among the five novellas offer a way to rethink the novel in terms of how the incompatible elements, precisely because unresolved, redeem contingency and challenge determinism. The point is not to piece the fragments together or celebrate them as some kind of postmodern pastiche but to ask what the dialogue among them is saying.

On the level of discourse, the novel poses a dialogue between fate and agency that is divided largely along gender lines. The male characters, including the narrator, tend to accept and reinforce firm notions of fatalism while the female characters voice hope for other possibilities subject to individual human actions. A fatalistic rhetoric is most evident when the narrator's grandfather first touches his grandmother's foot: "My grandfather . . . felt a strange premonition blazing inside him and illuminating the path his life would take" (56/45–46). The narrator reinforces this notion of a linear path, subject to certain contingencies but not to individual will: "I've always believed that marriages are made in heaven and that people fated to be together are connected by an invisible thread. The act of grasping Grandma's foot triggered a powerful drive in Yu Zhan'ao to forge a new life for himself, and constituted the turning point in his life—and the turning point in hers as well" (56/46). Far from offering an avenue and impetus for freedom, love, for Mo's male characters, reinforces the novel's determinism. The narrator talks about an "iron law of love" (*aiqing de gangtie guilü* 愛情的鋼鐵規律; 369) in the three generations of his family, and, upon seeing Grandma dead in the sorghum field, his grandfather realizes "the grievous punishment life had meted out to him" (233/182) for his long affair with the servant Passion.

---

37. The first chapter, "Hong gaoliang" (Red sorghum), was first published as a novella in *Renmin wenxue* 3 (1986): 4–36. The full novel, *Hong gaoliang jiazu*, appeared in 1987.

38. On *bao* in the novel, see Ngai, *Politics of Sexuality*, 182, 253, n. 87: "The concept of *bao* is double-edged. It can be reprisal (*baochou*) or requital of kindness with gratitude (*bao'en*)."

Whereas the narrator and his grandfather focus on instinct and fate, his grandmother, as she lies dying in the sorghum field, voices the possibility for individual decision:

> My Heaven . . . you gave me a lover, you gave me a son, . . . you gave me thirty years of life as robust as red sorghum. . . . Don't take it back now. Forgive me, let me go! Have I sinned? Would it have been right to share my pillow with a leper and produce a misshapen, putrid monster to contaminate this beautiful world? What is chastity then? What is the correct path? What is goodness? What is evil? You never told me, so I had to decide on my own. . . . It was my body, and I used it as I thought fitting. (91/72)

Somewhat paradoxically, Mo's works both allow and deny opportunities for moral agency. His works may be among the most memorable of contemporary fiction precisely because they depict characters that assume real choices in deciding their lives, from the grandfather's rape of the grandma in the sorghum field and his murder of her leper husband to her own taking over of the distillery after her husband's murder. Many critics have emphasized the powerful sense of a life force that emerges in Mo's fiction, or the power of sexuality that can be both liberating and destructive.[39] Yet one of Mo's most interesting themes is the question of whether responsibility for evil lies within individuals or in forces beyond their control, such as fate, instinct, or history. For all their underlying determinism, the complex narrative structure of his novels implies at least a vague consciousness of freedom of choice and an invitation to believe that humanity is not necessarily bound to uncontrollable forces.

Significantly, the novel's structural indeterminacy is greatly attenuated in Zhang Yimou's 張藝謀 (b. 1950) film version of the first two novellas of *Red Sorghum*. Zhang renders the story as a linear narrative that results in a much more deterministic presentation. The tighter narrative achieves a gripping story,[40] but it suggests a celebration of national strength and military will very much at odds with the novel's Faulkneresque attention to the confusion of battle and the irrational nature of physical desires.[41] By its relentless focus on the concrete details of the characters' perceptions and bodily experiences, the novel manages to suggest the past's unfulfilled and unrealized possibilities and to deny the

39. Ngai, *Politics of Sexuality*, 24, chap. 2.

40. *Red Sorghum* won the Golden Bear award for best film at the 1988 Berlin Film Festival.

41. On Faulkner's influence on Mo Yan, see Inge, "Mo Yan and William Faulkner."

inevitability of the apocalyptic (and already confirmed) expectations of the narrative. Mo's purpose in highlighting the powerful energies and unrealized possibilities of the past is open to interpretation, but Kong Haili suggests a pointed political purpose. Far from expressing nostalgia, Kong asserts, Mo's family chronicle "implies criticism of the present, a cynical attitude toward social conventions, and even toward Chinese society in a large sense."[42]

2.4 Radical Indeterminacy

In performing the breakdown of language and other social codes, the more extreme avant-garde works jeopardize not only historical meaning but also interpersonal communication and the very constitution of our selves. What could be taken as surrealism in Zong Pu's "Who Am I?," for example, turns out to be a searing account of a persecuted scientist's nervous breakdown when the trauma of her abuse during political struggle sessions leads her to take literally the cruel labels pinned on her, such as "cow ghost" (*niugui* 牛鬼) and "snake spirit" (*sheshen* 蛇神): "'Am I merely a poisonous worm? No! Then what am I in the end?' Weimi painstakingly searched her thoughts amidst the colossal uproar."[43]

Moreover, despite an increased focus on subjectivity, promoted by critic Liu Zaifu's 劉再復 influential arguments for its importance,[44] these works very often eschew the role of heightened individual consciousness in pursuing moral or political agency. Whereas Mao-era works produced characters that could be exemplary decision makers, many avant-garde works draw characters without such competence. In general, the greater the focus on interior monologue, subjective perception, and impressionism, the more disempowered the characters become. They reflect on the world and their relation to it but often conclude that they are too crippled by their recent experiences to act. In Wang Meng's "Zase" 雜色 (Motley; 1981), for example, the protagonist's compassionate, prolonged musings addressed to his old horse suggest his desperate efforts to comprehend his alienation and lessen his terrible loneliness through some kind of conversation, but his meager dealings with fellow humans show a painful inability to connect. In the search-for-roots story

42. Kong, "The Spirit of 'Native-Soil,'" 67.

43. Zong Pu, "Wo shi shei?" 7.

44. See Liu Zaifu's influential essay "Wenxue de zhutixing" (Subjectivity in literature).

"Guiqulai" 歸去來 (Homecoming; 1985), Han Shaogong describes a man who visits a mountain village unsure of whether he has been there before. When the villagers welcome him but mistake him for someone else and praise him for a murder he believes he did not commit, he gives up trying to assert his identity and begins to wonder if he might not be the man after all. This extreme portrait of alienation and lost identity ends enigmatically with a line decrying the prison of identity: "I'm exhausted, [yet] I'll never be able to escape this giant self. Mommy!"[45]

In presenting such radical detachment, many avant-garde works dispute a humanist voluntarism and voice a deep wariness of any positive claims of truth, virtue, or correct thinking. Yet in so doing they tend to present a freedom from a totalitarian past or oppressive social norms rather than a positive freedom to engage with others in constructive projects. As avant-garde writers increase the elements of sensation and shock and confront readers with dark depths of their characters' tortured psyches, these works may reassert human power, but they offer no framework of values that might motivate a meaningful exercise of agency. Such fiction may suggest that the claims of affection are too tenuous to make social life tolerable.

Much of this fiction is marked by a nightmarish quality that seems to preclude compassionate social agency. In Yu Hua's "Xianshi yi zhong" 現實一種 (One kind of reality; 1987), the young boy Pipi's accidental murder of his baby cousin leads his family to an orgy of mutual destruction: The baby's father, Shanfeng, kills Pipi and is in turn killed by Pipi's father, his brother Shangang. The police execute Shangang a month later, and Shanfeng's wife arranges to have his body donated to medicine. In a cruel twist of fate, much as he would have wished and as Shanfeng's wife would have hated, Shangang's transplanted testes ensure that he produces offspring after all.

Is it possible to discern what the characters regard as reasons for their actions in such a story? The extent to which they relinquish reason is expressed in Shanfeng's reflections as he agrees to let Shangang tie up his torso and legs:

> Shanfeng became confused. It seemed to him as if his son's death had indeed been an entirely different matter, that it had had nothing to do with Pipi's death. And Pipi, he remembered now, had been killed when he kicked him into the air. But why did he do that? This was another thing he couldn't figure out at the

45. Han Shaogong, "Guiqulai," 37; my translation.

moment. He didn't want to think about it anymore; it would only make him feel dizzier. (220/48)[46]

Reading such lines, one finds no genuine evil in these characters, only an awesome lack of reason and humane agency.

3. THIRTEEN STEPS

The risk that radical indeterminacy, a refusal of linear temporality, and magical realism will undercut possibilities for agency forcefully emerges in Mo Yan's modernist novel *Shisan bu* 十三步 (Thirteen steps; 1989). A portrait of the disorienting landscape of changing values in contemporary urban China, the novel begins when a high school physics teacher, Fang Fugui 方富貴, collapses from overwork and exhaustion. First taken for dead, Fang revives, much to the displeasure of those who want to make his death a cause célèbre to improve teachers' conditions. Then the Beautiful World (*meili shijie* 美麗世界) mortuary's cosmetologist Li Yuchan 李玉蟬 convinces him to let her reconstruct his face to look like that of Zhang Hongqiu 張紅球, Li's husband and Fang's fellow physics teacher. This way Fang can take over Zhang's teaching duties so that Zhang can go out to make money. The proliferation of stories that ensues makes *Thirteen Steps* an absorbing showcase for the workings of sideshadowing.

The many embedded stories haunting the novel's characters reinforce the sense of an already written universe and suggest a universe of multiple branching alternatives. "Time's order is arranged by the novelist" (76), the narrator writes, and Mo freely intermingles past, present, and future in the novel.[47] This bold defiance of linear temporal order combines with an emphasis on direct perception and random associations to emphasize the frail and limited understanding of any given person, be it the characters, the "narrator" trapped in a cage, or the collective "we," apparently including the readers, to which the narration frequently refers. The length and detail of the novel's digressions further underscore the apparent power of chance and contingency over all but the implied author's controlling intelligence. In the end, the novel's radical indeterminacy

46. The first number refers to Yu Hua's *Shiba sui*. The second refers to Jeanne Tai's translation.

47. Parenthetical page numbers refer to the Taipei edition, and all translations are my own.

leaves the characters with little control, as is clear when the implied author addresses Fang's wife, Tu Xiaoying 屠小英, and describes her helplessness to resist the unfinished narration of the story: "You sense that you won't have the strength to resist the story's logic, the conclusion is already arranged. Your destiny is in the hands of the man in the cage" (203).

Numerous shifts between first-, third-, and even second-person narrative also undercut any notion of autonomy and make it difficult to pinpoint a center of power in this novel. "Why are the characters who appear in this book so sensitive to odors and so indifferent to the logic of language? We thrust these troubles onto the narrator with his head dirtied with chalk dust" (184). The novel offers a partial answer in a parenthetical statement that addresses the power of odors: "(Odors usually arouse desires)" (199). Yet the second part of the question, concerning discursive logic, only gains in urgency with the proliferation of voices that narrate the novel in addition to the narrator trapped in his cage.

A work as fragmented as *Thirteen Steps* suggests that sideshadowing's attention to multiplicity does not guarantee a sense of agency but may intensify a sense of cruel contingency or even reconfirm one's old fatalism. On the one hand, Mo's inclusion of alternative endings underscores multiple possibilities. For example, Tu Xiaoying meets with an unclear number of possible ends in the novel. First, the municipal Party committee elects her a representative for her model achievements. Second, the factory director discovers Xiaoying and a gigolo making love in a workshop. Third, the police arrest her for counterfeiting money. Fourth, she marries the wealthy secretary of the municipal discipline committee and becomes pregnant with his child. Fifth, she drowns herself in the beautiful river. Sixth, confused and disheveled, Xiaoying runs back and forth between city hall and the mortuary to look for her husband until someone places her in the municipal mental hospital. Seventh, Xiaoying sacrifices her life saving public property in a fire. In some cases, these ends may well be sequential, though the relationship among them is unclear. Yet the last three or four endings conflict with one another, though Xiaoying might have married the high official and then met with one of the other three ends. Indeed, the "husband" for whom she searches in her penultimate end could be either the high official or the "deceased" Fang Fugui.

Moreover, the characters' utter failure to achieve their goals shows how a world may appear even *more* fixed because an author shows alternative possibilities and then has his narrator deny that human actors can have any influence on their realization:

> Life plans are most often thrown completely into disarray by unexpected events. Such situations in which unexpected events demolish our plans and lead to changes in our history and destiny occur every day, every hour, every instant in every person, every household, and every country. Marxists explain such phenomena as contingency and necessity. Non-Marxists explain such phenomena as destiny and God's will. (75)

Additionally, in presenting the force of necessity or destiny in this disorienting world, the novel makes a claim to typicality and prophecy: "We suspect this may be a trap on the part of the narrator. Does a chalk eater deserve trust? He says, I told you, even if all this did not really happen, these things nonetheless absolutely could have happened and inevitably will happen" (320).[48]

Assertions of an unknowable but rigid inevitability could render the characters of Mo's novels helpless. Such a statement in a novel about cloning might also be a warning about new biotechnologies and their moral and social consequences. At the very least, it invites the reader not to dismiss the novel's moral implications as she might its magical realist trappings. At the same time, it may be that Mo's narrator warns his readers in order to suggest that such unhappy social arrangements are inevitable only if society remains on its present course. It may be because Mo wants to understand human existence without recourse to any fatalistic telos or deterministic paradigm that he leaves his endings fragmented, frustrating any expectation of epiphany or metaphysical consolation. To end his text neatly would mean realizing the kind of single, unique meaning or historical teleology that his novels seem to reject. Indeed, in the epilogue (not included in the translation) to *Red Sorghum* and subsequent interviews, Mo has suggested that he did not consider the saga finished and deliberately included many hidden brushstrokes (*fubi* 伏筆) foreshadowing threads he planned to pick up in later "sequels."[49]

48. In Chinese, "chalk eater" is an epithet for someone in the teaching profession.

49. Reports differ about Mo Yan's project of sequels. Some claim that he planned two more novels and an additional collection of novellas to make the Red Sorghum family saga total 1,000,000 words. See Ngai, *Politics of Sexuality*, 174–75, 252, n. 81.

In roots-seeking and avant-garde works, agency is at best highly problematic. These works reveal a systematic intrigue of choice yet deny characters the ability to act in ways understandable as ethical agency. If life is inevitably a product of forces greater than individuals and their intentions, schemes, and life plans, agency may be little more than gesture, illusory and ineffective. Individuals may be presented as choosing, but they choose erroneously and in vain, acting as independent variables only when complicit in their own demise.

What is the logical consequence of the nihilism of many avant-garde works? What does it mean when characters believe they have no choice but to contribute to brutality in the world? Surely, it does not prove brutality is irremediable, but it does suggest a crisis of values that could oppose cruel behavior. In giving the world over to the forces of culture, nature, destiny, or history, these works do not encourage hope for human capacities to develop compassion. I hope they do not foreshadow or pave the way for growing social anomie and passivity in the face of increasing economic and social inequalities.

8

Self-Ownership and Capitalist Values in 1990s Chinese Fiction

With China's economic reforms of the 1980s and 1990s, fictional depictions of moral agency and determinism have turned increasingly to stories of individual initiative and self-determination. These depictions introduce both heightened expectations for individual freedom and new forms of determinism concerning the development of Chinese society and the roles of its citizens. Much cultural discourse now implies that China's market reform and growing participation in global commerce prove the inevitability of evolution toward free market capitalism. At the same time, the development toward equality, community, and human self-realization that many Marxists once held to be inevitable looks highly uncertain in the absence of an organized working class and in the face of ecological limitations preventing the material abundance Marx predicted. As China makes its transition from Party dominance over economic planning and industry to a still undefined mix of socialism and capitalism, its citizens must renegotiate norms and values. As what looks inevitable and what looks uncertain change so dramatically, do these shifts enhance or jeopardize commitments to moral responsibility?

In treating dilemmas of agency and determinism within new and unstable frameworks of market exchange, Chinese fiction offers new perspectives on the relationship between Enlightenment values and capitalism. To what extent do fictional works of the 1990s continue to voice commitments to values, principles, and programs capable of promoting equality, community, and human welfare? How does one reconcile such

Enlightenment values with their complicity with exploitative economic structures and social practices?

The stakes behind such questions rise inasmuch as representations of capitalism and capitalist values dominate many recent works. The ascendancy of capitalism is especially evident in the works of the "latecomers" (*wanshengdai* 晚生代), for the most part writers born in the 1960s, such as Diao Dou 刁斗, He Dun 何頓, Han Dong 韓東, Qiu Huadong 邱華棟, Shu Ping 述平, Zhang Min 張旻, and Zhu Wen 朱文.[1] Critic Chen Xiaoming 陳曉明 argues that these writers' works have replaced pursuits of modernist and Enlightenment projects with depictions of the pursuit of profit, commodity fetishism, and consumerism.[2] If these works represent and sometimes even explicitly promote practices that enable capitalist exploitation, to what extent do they also present values that might contest free market capitalist fundamentalism? In a decade of vast shifts in economic, moral, and gendered power relations, what do these works suggest about the relative currency of capitalist or socialist ideology? Do they render heroic the individual pursuit of wealth and the predatory nature of market society? Or do they bespeak yearnings that oppose the growing hegemony of consumer capitalism?

Certainly, recent Chinese fiction both reinforces and challenges new regimes of commodification and consumption. Yet some of this fiction also betrays a troubled but enduring relationship to Confucian or Enlightenment ideals of social responsibility and progress toward justice and human dignity. In this chapter, I briefly define what I mean by capitalist and Enlightenment values and then examine the stakes involved in distinguishing between Enlightenment ideals and more specific capitalist values through analyses of Yu Hua's *Xu Sanguan mai xue ji* 許三觀賣血記 (Xu Sanguan the blood seller; 1995) and Zhou Weihui's 周衛慧 (b. 1973) *Shanghai baobei* 上海寶貝 (Shanghai baby; 1999). In examining these works' treatment of self-ownership, class, gender, ethics, and political disenchantment, I posit the perseverance of Confucian and Enlightenment values of responsibility that contest the determinism of free market capitalist fundamentalism.

1. For discussion of and examples of works by these writers, see the articles and stories in *Mingbao yuekan* (Mingbao monthly), August 1997.
2. See Chen Xiaoming, "Xianfengpai zhi hou," 33.

1. CAPITALIST AND ENLIGHTENMENT VALUES

In beginning this inquiry, one confronts two very different problems. The first is to disentangle modernity, capitalism, and Enlightenment from one another conceptually, in terms of life-enhancing and life-negating values. The second is to situate these values within the contexts of different histories, West and East. Of course, no one can disentangle these concepts and their histories all at once. Yet one can address particular aspects in specific contexts, and for this reason Chinese fiction can play a valuable role in redeeming the Enlightenment project's commitment to human welfare. Before turning to the context of 1990s Chinese fiction, here I briefly distinguish capitalist from Enlightenment values in more general terms.

One definition of capitalism identifies an economic system characterized by open competition in a putatively "free" market, in which private or corporate entities own the means of production and distribution and employ wage laborers, and development corresponds to increasing accumulation and reinvestment of profits. Fiction, however, generally represents capitalism not in a strict economic sense but in terms of its cultural, and specifically moral, ramifications. How does contemporary Chinese fiction picture China's economic transformation and its effects on social norms? What values does this fiction associate with the development of capitalism?

Capitalist values and practices include the opportunity for entrepreneurship, the desire for wealth, the sanctioning of acquisition and accumulation, and resultant regimes of consumerism and commodification. An increasingly capitalist system also demands adjustments to rapid change, the ability to update and remold oneself or one's enterprises to profit from a changing environment, and the subordination of other goals to the maximization of economic profit.[3] Greater disparities between rich and poor also lead to the rise of a leisure class and the development of values that regard material labor as unworthy and predatory exploitation as excusable.[4] Risk taking, gambling, outsmarting others, and hardnosed "pragmatism" all connote hallowed capitalist values.

---

3. Geographer David Harvey refers to the restructuring of the global economy since the late 1970s as the regime of "flexible accumulation" to emphasize corporations' greater geographical mobility and flexibility in employment arrangements, markets, products, and consumption practices. See Harvey, *The Condition of Postmodernity*.

4. See Thorstein Veblen (1857–1929), *The Theory of the Leisure Class*.

A capitalist framework can promote rights of self-ownership and opportunities for self-realization, but it also introduces deterministic assumptions concerning human nature. Whereas the need to engineer souls suited for a socialist society theoretically allowed for human change even as actual practices compromised and crushed the humanity of so many, free market capitalism assumes human nature to be fundamentally rational and self-seeking, determined by and in turn determining a brutal economy of competition. Rational choice theory accounts for the values which actors seek to maximize in utilitarian terms, and market theory seldom considers that specific cultures produce these utilitarian terms. Examining Chinese fiction both introduces other terms and draws attention to the contingent and arbitrary nature of this dominant utilitarian calculus.

To continue the discussion begun in Chapter 1, the Enlightenment refers to a philosophical movement of eighteenth-century Europe and America whose advocates sought to use rationalism, empiricism, or a synthesis of the two (Kant's case) to critically examine previously accepted doctrines and institutions. Although the diversity and conflicts among thinkers associated with the Enlightenment hardly gave rise to a single coherent movement, certain common themes and values can be identified. First, there is the high estimation of individual reason and secularism. Rather than rely on religious or other traditional belief systems, Enlightenment projects encouraged individuals to investigate the world using reason, analysis, and empirical methods. The quarrel of *les modernes* against *les anciens* did not wholly reject tradition, but it subjected traditional beliefs, especially church doctrine, superstitions, and myth, to scrutiny and skepticism that undermined their authority in favor of a this-worldly conception of human responsibility.

Second, Enlightenment projects were based on faith in progress and the idea that human beings can use reason and empiricism to improve their environment and enrich their daily lives. Whereas many thinkers criticize the costs of material progress, especially connected economic, political, and social injustices and the ravages visited on the environment, the pursuit of progress has also led to more (though not unambiguously) humane treatment of criminals and the mentally ill. Along these lines, the Enlightenment's most important legacy is the commitment to freedom and values such as autonomy, equality, justice, and human dignity. The pursuit of such values underlies further commitments to specific political systems, particularly representative democracy, a system that depends on the notion of "one person, one vote" and thus promotes the formation of individual subjects and citizens.

Repressed during the Cultural Revolution, explicit appeals to Enlightenment notions were made again during the 1980s, particularly by social scientists reading both Western Enlightenment philosophy and contemporary Western cultural theory. Enlightenment concepts were also central to what Zhang Xudong rightly names the Deng regime's "political invention" of the New Era by which the regime sought to distance itself from Maoist ideology and gain legitimacy by advancing a rational, progressive, and economically secure world.[5] During the "Great Cultural Discussion" (1985–1989), intellectuals implicitly supported this political invention through their dual commitments to integrate China into the global economy and rebuild a national culture attentive to local traditions. Seeking to rethink Marxism and socialist humanism in terms of both traditional Confucian culture and Western theory, these intellectuals pursued what some refer to as a renewed "second enlightenment" project. "Most important," writes Zhang, "the enlightenment project, the leitmotif of modern Chinese intellectual history, was once again activated in a critical reexamination of the past."[6]

In a careful study of changing Chinese appeals to modernity, Xu Ben has highlighted ways that 1980s intellectual discussions and official policies invoked Enlightenment notions to promote programs of gradual modernization and reform that departed significantly from the May Fourth emphasis on modernity as radical revolution and fundamental change.[7] Moreover, even within this gradualist approach, Party officials focused more narrowly on economic and technological development, whereas intellectuals sought to advance human capabilities and democratic institutions. The Tiananmen massacre, explains Xu, caused another deep rupture in intellectual commitments insofar as it darkened prospects for democracy and bolstered arguments for postmodern rejections of such Enlightenment notions. Xu warns, however, that the "Post-ist" theorists' view, that the trauma of 1989 discredited the radicalism of 1980s sociocultural criticism, often implicitly endorses neoconservative and neo-authoritarian positions that support the status quo: "Not only

5. Zhang Xudong, *Chinese Modernism*, 9.

6. Zhang Xudong, *Chinese Modernism*, 46.

7. Xu Ben, *Disenchanted Democracy*, 90–91.

is the combined force of a Leninist party-state and a rampant market economy too powerful to allow for effective intellectual opposition or resistance, the reality is too full of incongruities to allow for imagining focused social change and for creating critical initiatives to appeal to the public."[8]

Like earlier scholarship emphasizing the conceptual differences and difficulties of translating these terms and values,[9] Xu's insights remind us of the limitations of theoretical discourses that treat abstractions as if they had concrete, material significance. It is also important to remember that, in the Western context as well, "the Enlightenment," especially as a noun, is a term more often used in retrospect and was certainly never the name of a unified system of belief. Contested even among their promoters, Enlightenment ideals have been regularly subjected to criticism and pessimism. As discussed in Chapter 1, skepticism regarding the Enlightenment and its ideals broadened further as the industrial revolution, urban centralization, the theories of Marx and Freud, and the World Wars exacerbated anxieties about the direction of human endeavors. In *Dialektik der Aufklärung* (1944), one of the most influential criticisms of the Enlightenment, Max Horkheimer and Theodor Adorno argue that many philosophical concepts originated "in the marketplace" to legitimate conditions of domination, and that Enlightenment reason tends to hide modes of abstraction and instrumental rationality that further domination and repression.[10] Specifically, by reducing everything to quantities that could be subject to an omnipotent exchange principle, market rationality disregards qualitative differences that would resist such abstraction if moral criteria were allowed purchase.

Although critics of the Enlightenment hold that capitalist and Enlightenment values are largely inseparable, defenders argue against conflating the two. The study of literature can contribute to this debate insofar as much modern fiction, representing concrete means by which economic power is deployed, stages circumstances of capitalist economic systems that suggest their distance from Enlightenment values. In this way, Yu Hua's and Weihui's novels offer narratives of historically situated predicaments that can help differentiate Enlightenment values of freedom, autonomy, and the importance of not treating people as mere

8. Xu Ben, "Contesting Memory," 169.

9. Lydia Liu, *Translingual Practice*, 10–20, esp. 17.

10. See Horkheimer and Adorno, *Dialectic of Enlightenment*, 21–22.

means from the more limited and specifically capitalist value of self-ownership.

In selecting and interpreting these works, I do not presume to unearth or pin down the sources of ambivalence toward capitalist values. Though I explore the novels' internal structures, metaphors, sideshadows, and ambiguities, as well as their relation to the context of sociopolitical and economic changes, I do not claim that the texts themselves amount to particular ideological stances. Such a claim would require speculations about the authors' intentions and the control these intentions might exercise on their products that would disregard the multiple voices that characterize most fictional works. Instead, I probe the works' ambivalence toward capitalist values, sometimes explicit and sometimes implicit, to demonstrate that such analyses of Chinese fiction can enhance more abstract philosophical discussions of modernity's precarious contradictions.

2. 1990s CHINESE FICTION

If my argument holds about the ambivalence toward market transition, how does recent Chinese fiction show capitalist values as delivering only the material promises of modernity (and perhaps only to the few) while failing to deliver the other promises of modernity, those of social, moral, or legal progress? I explore such questions to argue for an ongoing commitment to values of justice, dignity, equality, and rationality in a body of fiction that largely spurns this legacy. Presenting this argument to Western readers is especially important in light of the high proportion of works selected for translation that are anti-Enlightenment and anti-humanist.[11]

Looking to 1990s fiction for some comment on how Chinese citizens have responded to economic restructuring, one might first ask which

---

11. In a recent essay, Howard Goldblatt acknowledges his own immense influence on the selection of Chinese literature available to readers of English: "I have been involved in the production of two dozen or more translations of modern and contemporary Chinese fiction, and while the results of those endeavors can in no way reflect all the literary twists and turns in post-Mao China, they fairly represent my own tastes in literature, some of the strictures in which I work, and, most important, the essence of Chinese novels and short stories to which English-language readers have been exposed." See Goldblatt, "Border Crossings," 337.

practices and behaviors writers treat in their works. How does this fiction depict the social consequences of increasing market liberalization? What does it suggest about the types of men and women that Chinese society now selects and shapes?

In addition to a large number of stories about characters becoming small business owners and the social consequences of market liberalization, the 1980s and 1990s brought an increase in literature glorifying deviant behavior. Called "China noir" or "post-utopian" (*houwutuobang* 後烏托邦) by some critics, these works extol a taste for new heights of wickedness and dissolution.[12] For one, a new gangster genre named "hooligan fiction" (*liumang xiaoshuo* 流氓小說) showed the more disaffected of the children of China's economic boom world becoming mafia-like entrepreneurs engaged in prostitution, extortion, and other organized criminal activity. This genre was made famous by Wang Shuo's 王朔 (b. 1958) novels, such as *Wanzhu* 頑主 (Masters of mischief; 1987), *Wan de jiushi xintiao* 玩得就是心跳 (Playing for thrills; 1988), and "Yi dian zhengjing mei you" 一點正經沒有 (Not an ounce of seriousness; 1989), and his 1991 television series *Bianjibu de gushi* 遍輯部的故事 (Stories from the editorial board).[13]

Human agency may be individually meaningful in these works, but it seldom proves very socially meaningful. For many of these writers have fallen into a disoriented and angry limbo, and whereas works such as Wang Shuo's may represent a "strain of Taoist anarchism,"[14] they mostly glorify a relativistic culture. Similar to much avant-garde fiction, this popular fiction depicts embittered young people who have given up trying to change their society. Since the characters respond to the world cynically and pragmatically, willing to do anything in their self-interest, one suspects that these writers may regard rebellion as an end in itself. The unqualified nature of Wang's cynicism is well described by critic Yan Jingming 閻晶明:

> The "operators" of his [Wang Shuo's] pen despise all that is noble; for them [nobility] is nothing but a cloak of hypocrisy. They don't believe in anything, because for them beliefs are nothing more than lies concocted for people. . . . They are in outright rebellion against the social order and moral standards, for

12. Zhang Yiwu, "Lun 'houwutuobang' huayu."
13. See Barmé, "Wang Shuo and *Liumang* ('Hooligan') Culture."
14. Lau, "China Deconstructs," 30.

they think that order and morality are but smokescreens masking the scene of a vile and ridiculous farce.[15]

Filled with a postmodern allure of pleasure and play, these works bespeak a desire for freedom from a totalitarian past and oppressive social norms, but do they bespeak desire for agency to engage in meaningful projects?

Numerous portrayals of fiscal corruption have also appeared, some specifically targeting joint ventures with foreigners, as in Liu Heng's 劉恆 (b. 1954) *Canghe bairi meng* 蒼河白日夢 (Daydream on the Cang river; 1993).[16] Other works treat gluttony, adultery, and legal corruption as in Mo Yan's *Liquorland*, sexual excess as in Jia Pingwa's *Feidu* 廢都 (The abandoned capital; 1992), serial rape as in Su Tong's *North of the City*, or drug addiction and sadomasochism as in Weihui's banned *Shanghai Baby*, discussed at the end of this chapter. Do such works glorify or problematize the organization of sexuality in fetishized modes that can be used to mobilize consumer spending?

A second set of questions asks how writers thematize these practices and behaviors. How do they bring home the impact of destabilizing social and economic changes? To what extent do they reproduce or challenge Western conceptions of capitalist modes of life? Do their works support the views of leftists in China who see contemporary evils as the fruit of capitalism or the views of reformers who blame corrupt systems and dispositions inherited from the Mao era or earlier?[17] In stories of the brave new capitalist world, do the newly recognizable characters behave as victims, observers, and consumers or perform as agents and entrepreneurs? Does greater availability of consumer goods bring freedom or slavery? What standards do such narratives pose for evaluating behavior and social practices? Simply making standards explicit can sometimes produce comedy, or tragicomedy, as in Yu Hua's novel to be examined below.

Finally, what do these texts suggest has been lost? In addition to subtle but recurrent references to nostalgia for the natural environment, these

15. Yan Jingming, trans. Barmé, quoted in Lau, "China Deconstructs," 30.

16. For an analysis comparing negative visions of market reforms in Jiang Zilong's "Shoushen ji" (Records from a trial; 1989) and Liu Heng's novel *Daydream on the Cang River* with more optimistic portrayals in Jia Pingwa's stories, see Pirazzoli, "The Free-Market Economy."

17. This question was suggested by Edward Friedman, letter, September 6, 2000.

works prominently record the loss of political idealism about ultimate goals. At the same time, the maturation of political disenchantment seems to lead to a reassertion of specific commitments to family or other individuals. This renewed emphasis on fulfilling one's commitments underlies the following analyses of works by Yu Hua and Weihui.

3. SELF-OWNERSHIP AND MORAL OBLIGATION IN YU HUA'S *BLOOD SELLER*

Yu Hua's novel *Blood Seller* offers a strong case of the ambivalence toward capitalist values that I find in a significant portion of 1990s Chinese fiction. Beginning with *Huozhe* 活著 (To live; 1992), Yu's novels express a strong humanistic tendency that makes them profoundly different not only from his own earlier nihilistic stories discussed in the last chapter but also from the works by Wang Shuo or the "latecomers" mentioned above. Turning away from his early phantasmagoric, avant-garde experiments with the boundaries between the real and the unreal, Yu constructs *To Live* and *Blood Seller* within a realist mode that operates by arousing sympathy for human suffering and reflection about suffering's causes and possible human responses. Yet, whereas some critics see literature's turning away from avant-garde experimentalism toward humanism as a result of its cooptation by mass culture, I view novels such as Yu's as profoundly critical.

3.1 To Live

To Live offers the protagonist Fugui's 福貴 frank account of desperate rural conditions and the arbitrary and murderous political programs that seem to dictate each succeeding eventuality. As Fugui develops from an inveterate gambler and philanderer into a caring husband and father, everyone and everything he holds dear is nonetheless taken away from him. Although the novel also exposes the brutality of Party officials and Red Guards blindly obedient to commands from the center, Fugui blames himself for reforming too slowly to spare his family the grief he causes them, and it is with a self-deprecating tone that he recounts his moral transformation, including harrowing accounts of how he tried to sell his daughter and how he terrorized his son. The novel ends with the death of Fugui's last remaining relative, his young grandson Kugen

苦根. Yet, even when a residual life force and the memory of his loved ones offer the only justifications to go on living, Fugui is not driven to despair but carries on with resignation.

Like *To Live*, *Blood Seller* underscores the characters' resilience, but it also presents a much greater impression of self-determination. This presentation has to be scrutinized to bring out the novel's critical potential, in part because the later novel employs a very different narrative approach. In *To Live*, the main story is framed by Fugui's encounter with the young, wandering, first-person narrator from the city, an arrangement that results in a more conspicuous presentation of the storytelling. The entire first chapter forms the front frame, and short back frames end each of the successive chapters. Structurally, these frames help manage the leaps in time within the fast-paced narrative. By providing convenient stopping points, they also function like the wedge in traditional Chinese *huaben* 話本 tales. The uninvolved narrator also mediates the reader's transition in and out of the story. Finally, the humor of these sections increases the affective distance of the narration and offers respite from the intense pathos of Fugui's parsimonious chronological narration of the main story. Finally, the many peripeteia make it difficult to pinpoint a climax in *To Live*, whereas *Blood Seller* follows a more straightforward climactic progression. A combination of omniscient third-person narration and direct dialogue reinforces the later novel's illusion of objectivity and artlessness, and the characters embody ideas and social processes so seamlessly that nothing theoretical is left exposed. Yet the novel raises philosophical questions no less urgent for their naturalistic portrayal.

3.2 Self-Ownership and Autonomy in Xu Sanguan the Blood Seller

In Yu Hua's *Xu Sanguan the Blood Seller* (literally "Record of Xu Sanguan selling blood"), the protagonist's repeated sale of his blood symbolizes the importance of self-ownership, where self-ownership refers to the full sovereignty over oneself and possession of full rights respecting one's body and abilities. In a soul-searching examination of the relationships among self-ownership, freedom, and equality, British philosopher G. A. Cohen (b. 1941) confronts the central place of self-ownership in both Marxist and libertarian thought in order to bolster the Marxist challenge to libertarianism.[18] This section draws on Cohen's discussion of self-ownership to explore Yu's representation of one family's response to China's political, economic, and social transitions. Through interpreting Yu's novel, I argue with Cohen that analyzing the uses of self-ownership diminishes its attractiveness as a primary value in favor of values less complicit with capitalist principles.

Cohen attaches great importance to self-ownership because it grounds commitments to liberty, including the Marxist condemnation of exploitation, while at the same time threatening equality insofar as it supports libertarian objections to programs of distributive justice. According to Cohen, libertarians rely on the thesis that self-ownership should guarantee "the right not to (be forced to) supply products or service to anyone" (215) to legitimate a laissez-faire economy that permits differences of talent to produce income disparities, in part by making "not helping" morally distinct from "harming":

> It is useful to remind ourselves, here, why self-ownership excludes a duty to help (save where not helping also counts as harming). If I own myself, I own my parts and powers, which are the wherewithal for helping others. Since it is in general true of ownership that I need not devote what I own to another's benefit, it is true of self-ownership that I need not devote myself to anyone else's benefit, and I therefore have no duty to help others. And harming induced by market competition qualifies as acceptable in light of the concept of self-ownership.[19]

Whereas Cohen respects the logical coherence of the concept of self-ownership, he raises objections to some of the moral and political implications of the libertarian principle of maximal self-ownership and seeks to reduce its appeal by distinguishing it from "not being a slave, possessing autonomy, and not being used merely as a means" (230). Drawing on Cohen's work for my discussion of Yu's novel, I first focus on ways that the notion of self-ownership provides the social, economic, and moral foundations for selfhood and autonomy in the novel. Second, I bring out some of the limits and failures of this notion when it is taken as a universal category. Third, I make explicit how capitalist self-ownership falls short of a meaningful sense of Enlightenment autonomy.

---

18. Cohen, *Self-Ownership, Freedom, and Equality.*

19. Cohen, *Self-Ownership*, 228. On this logic, libertarians accept taxes to finance police protection of property while rejecting redistributive income taxation on the basis that it violates full self-ownership of one's earnings.

3.2.1 Social, economic, and moral selfhood. The social function of blood selling is established when Xu Sanguan's grandfather conveys to Sanguan that only a man who has sold blood can call his body sturdy (*jieshi* 結實), and when Sanguan's two friends Genlong 根龍 and Ah Fang 阿方 first teach him how to sell his blood through an initiation process that includes rituals such as gorging himself with water beforehand and eating pork liver afterward. Selling blood thus functions as a means to male identity formation and for establishing solidarity with others. The invocation of the term "identity formation" here underscores the belief common among social psychologists and sociologists that the self and its motives are not static but rather intimately connected to and constructed by social contexts and processes of socialization.[20] Underscoring the importance of social interaction for interpreting one's place in the world, the social dimension reemerges toward the end of the novel when Sanguan teaches the two Lai brothers the art of selling blood, and again when Sanguan is over sixty and suffers a crisis of identity because a blood taker will no longer buy his blood. These episodes show that Sanguan's blood selling is not only a heart-wrenching struggle for survival but also a struggle for identity, belonging, status, uniqueness, and coherence. These compelling personal motivations make all the more poignant the paradigmatic way blood selling recruits Sanguan into a capitalist system based on private ownership.

In addition to social benefits, Sanguan's blood selling provides him economic power and moral autonomy insofar as it proves and exploits his self-ownership. Since selling blood constitutes a voluntary exchange within a libertarian system, by engaging in this commerce Sanguan possesses, as a moral and legal right, the franchise to dispose over himself and his body as a slaveholder could utilize a slave.[21] Due to its broad intuitive appeal, self-ownership appears as a plausible foundation for moral agency.

On the economic level, self-ownership seems to allow Sanguan a considerable degree of self-determination. He first sells his blood to found a family, specifically by buying material goods so that Xu Yulan 許玉蘭 will marry him. On their first date, Sanguan even counts on his fingers how much money he has spent before asking Yulan when she will marry

20. See, for example, Tyler, Kramer, and John, *The Psychology of the Social Self.*

21. This formulation follows the definition of self-ownership offered by Cohen, *Self-Ownership*, 68.

him. The humor of this passage is undercut when Yulan protests about the coercive nature of Sanguan's assumption that she should be indebted to him: "I thought that I was eating for free. You didn't say that once I'd eaten your treats I'd have to marry you" (64).[22] Yet, a month later when pressured by her father, Yulan agrees to marry Sanguan provided he meet her material demands. Sanguan sells his blood a second time for property when he uses the proceeds to redeem his family's household goods after their confiscation by the father of a boy mangled by their son Yile 一樂, a son who turns out to have been fathered by another man. The need to compensate the hospitalized boy's family here also recalls the limits of self-ownership, in that people may act on their desires only to the extent that they do not violate the rights of others. Sanguan's third blood sale reinforces this notion when he spends some of the money on gifts for a woman he has just seduced on her sickbed. Though his plan backfires when the gifts alert her husband to the "rape," Sanguan is able to assuage his wife's anger over the adultery by surrendering the remaining cash for her to buy new clothes.

After his family has eaten nothing but gruel for 57 days during the Great Leap Forward, Sanguan sells his blood a fourth time to buy them a proper meal. During the Cultural Revolution, he sells his blood a fifth time to give money to his two sent-down sons so they can eat better and buy their team leaders gifts that might facilitate earlier transfers back to the city. Less than one month later, he sells his blood a sixth time for connections, exchanging economic for social capital, when he uses the money to entertain his son Erle's 二樂 team leader. Finally and within just a couple more weeks, Sanguan sells his blood a series of at least five more times to raise money to pay Yile's medical bills once Yile has been sent to a Shanghai hospital for aggravated hepatitis.

3.2.2 Advantages and liabilities of self-ownership. Insofar as Sanguan's sale of his blood heralds the appeal of the free exchange of goods, Yu's novel can be interpreted as reinforcing positive possibilities of a market system for the realization of human agency. Through highlighting the ability to sell oneself and one's labor power at the most optimum times, the novel demonstrates the ability of the protagonist to make and act on his own

22. Page numbers refer to the 1997 Taipei edition. All translations are my own. For an expert translation of Yu's novel published since the completion of this chapter, see Yu, *Chronicle of a Blood Merchant.*

choices and to control his own life. This presentation of individual agency supports a libertarian theory of self-ownership that underlies much of the logic of present market reforms toward a capitalist economic system that treats labor power as a commodity and depends on the production of commodities for market exchange (rather than for direct consumption). "The libertarian principle of self-ownership," writes Cohen, "says that each person enjoys, over herself and her powers, full and exclusive rights of control and use, and therefore owes no service or product to anyone else that she has not contracted to supply."[23] Such a principle may appeal since it appears to defend autonomous decision making, but it assumes an ideal of autonomy that fails to take into account structural and social factors such as the costs of health care in the event of self-harm.

At the same time, the novel also exposes contingent factors influencing self-ownership, and this attention to differences indicates ways in which the category is not a universal one. For one, in several instances, connections and bribes are necessary before the blood taker will accept Sanguan's blood. For another, with or without consent, self-ownership rights may be alienated or transferred, as in marriage. For example, in describing Yulan's lack of freedom in deciding her betrothal, the novel shows the way gender often thwarts idealized notions about self-ownership that might purport to make it a foundation for equality. The gender imbalance is made clear first when Yulan's other suitor, He Xiaoyong 何小勇, forces her to have sex with him, and again years later when Sanguan learns of the rape and focuses only on the act's violation of his legal ownership of his wife: "But Xu Yulan was a woman Sanguan had spent money to marry and bring home" (97). His illiberal, self-centered reaction to Yulan's assault recalls an insightful point made by Wang Dewei in his introduction to the novel: To Sanguan, the foundation of his marriage is based on the sacrifice of virgin blood.[24] Yet since under his interrogation Yulan tells Sanguan that it was he with whom she slept first (79), the novel casts a sideshadow that leaves ambiguous whether the grievousness of the sexual betrayal here derives from the loss of the hymen blood that determines Yulan's value in this sexual economy or from the act of adultery that led to the birth of Yile.

Despite these qualifications regarding the serious liabilities of an overly idealist notion of self-ownership, the numerous ways Sanguan uses

---

23. Cohen, *Self-Ownership*, 12.

24. See Wang Dewei, "Shanghen jijing, baoli qiguan," 27.

blood selling to found and care for his family recall the importance of this Enlightenment notion for personal accountability in fulfilling one's commitments. At the same time, since Sanguan repeatedly subordinates and exploits his self-ownership to meet his obligations to his family, a question arises as to whether the novel makes self-ownership a normative value of independent importance, or whether its importance derives from its connection to other moral values. Even as Sanguan acts within an unpredictable social framework marked by conflicts over sexual access to women, children's violence, and state political domination, his moral orientation derives from an emphasis—perhaps a Confucian emphasis—on fulfilling one's roles in the family.

In addition to loyalty to family, the novel introduces other distinct standards of moral and social responsibility. For one, in a characteristic Enlightenment move, the novel satirizes superstition at the same moment that it presents a case for forgiveness and the value of human life. Specifically, when He Xiaoyong is hit by a truck and lies in a coma in the hospital, a fortune-teller advises He's wife that the only way to save him is to have his son climb atop He's roof and scream for his father to return. Since He has only the illegitimate son fathered when he raped Yulan, Yulan convinces Sanguan that they should help, and Sanguan talks to Yile: "Yile, in the past He Xiaoyong wronged us. That's in the past. We shouldn't still bear a grudge. Now that He Xiaoyong's very life is at risk, what's important is to save his life. Whatever you say, He Xiaoyong is also a person. When a human life is at stake, then one should save it. Besides, he's your blood father" (191).

3.2.3 Self-ownership as short of autonomy. In showing the characters' ethical transformations as they embrace moral standards, in this case humanist ones, such passages suggest the priority of the values of survival and self-sacrifice for the good of others over the ideal of self-ownership. In describing at length Yile's suffering as he sits on the roof, the novel makes clear that the adults' concern to save He's life leads them to disregard Yile's reluctance and force him to participate in their superstitious ritual. Yet, even as they violate Yile's self-ownership by stranding him on the roof, he exercises autonomy by refusing to do their bidding until Sanguan is brought in to coax him. A sideshadow is cast by the possibility that Sanguan might not participate in coercing Yile to this extent, but he extends himself further yet by promising to be Yile's blood father (*qindie* 親爹) if

Yile calls out to He's spirit. Sanguan performs his vow by cutting his own face and threatening, with blood running down his cheek, to take a knife to anyone who again dares to say that Yile is not his own son.

In another example of personal transformation, Sanguan goes from bearing his wife great hostility for her affair with He Xiaoyong to risking social ridicule in order to provide for her: During the Cultural Revolution, when Red Guards force Yulan to stand on a street holding a sign saying "Prostitute Xu Yulan" (*Jinü Xu Yulan* 妓女許玉蘭), Sanguan brings her food and water. Moreover, when compelled to conduct a home struggle session against Yulan in which Yile says he hates his mother and loves Sanguan, Sanguan confesses his own infidelity so that their sons will judge her less harshly: "I'm just like your mom; we've both committed mortal errors. You shouldn't hate her" (217).

Because Sanguan admits his transgression to convey to his sons that people are both fallible and capable of forgiveness and moral development, his integrity reinforces the positive aspect of self-ownership. Yet in such instances the personal sphere in which he acts raises further questions about what grounds the underlying metaphor of self-ownership. In the economic sphere, is it not possible that this metaphor likens the self to a thing in a way that undermines those very qualities that distinguish humans as moral agents, namely, the possibility of fulfilling one's projects and commitments to others? Cohen has a phrase that points out the situated nature of any claims of self-ownership: "For market competition harms losers, and market competition is the social soul of self-ownership" (227). Yet it might be worthwhile to redefine the "social soul of self-ownership" as lying in one's relationships and responsibilities to others more generally, a redefinition that could reveal more starkly the antagonism between the pursuit of wealth in market competition and human self-realization in community. Perhaps it would be better to defend the notion of a self not in terms of ownership but in terms of capacities that can be realized and expanded within given social contexts and communities.[25] In this light, the novel also models the rich Confucian conceptions of selfhood as fulfilled through roles and obligations within a web of relations that cultivate human nature.[26]

25. This formulation was inspired by economist Amartya Sen's definition of development as a process of expanding the capabilities that people enjoy. See Sen, *Development as Freedom*.

26. For example, see Tu Wei-ming, *Confucian Thought*.

In the novel's culminating example of ethical transformation, Sanguan transcends the grudge he bears Yile for his paternity from another man by acknowledging their mutual affection earned from years of fulfilling their roles as father and son. As if to deflate an irrational fixation on blood relations and to suggest that voluntary alliances are at least as powerful, the novel shows Sanguan resolving to sell his own blood at a possibly lethal rate to save the life of his illegitimate son.

Sanguan's risky selling of his own blood points out the liabilities of an exclusive focus on rights of self-ownership. While the novel posits certain Enlightenment rights and values within a basic normative framework, it also challenges the Kantian moral imperative not to treat persons as means only. Whereas Kant's principle allows for the instrumental use of people on the condition that they are also treated as ends, it seems clear that Sanguan treats himself as a mere means, a fact made painfully clear by the question of whether the blood takers will allow him to sell his blood so often as to endanger his life. Sanguan's insistence on his prerogative to sell his blood is grounded in the notion that self-ownership rights should withstand paternalistic intervention. The logic behind Sanguan's assertion of his right to sell his blood is, moreover, mirrored by his protest against having to pay for his own blood transfusion. After he collapses during his third blood donation along his route to Shanghai, the hospital gives him a blood transfusion that costs him the equivalent of selling his blood twice. "Buying and selling have to be just," Sanguan protests. "When I sold my blood to them, they knew, but when they sold blood to me, I didn't know at all" (265). Sanguan's indignation reveals the conflict between individual rights of self-ownership and protective medical benevolence, analogous to political conflicts between "laissez-faire" liberalism dedicated to individual liberty and "welfare-state" or "egalitarian" liberalism that assigns the state a strong protective role in promoting social betterment.

The depiction of Sanguan's near self-destruction also suggests the extent to which the enterprising man of affairs, presumably sober, hard-headed, and practical, turns out to be utopian and monomaniacal. When the blood taker at Songlin sends Sanguan away because he looks sickly, and Sanguan purposely gets a sunburn that disguises his ill health and convinces the blood taker to buy his blood, is he ingenious or horribly reckless? As Sanguan gambles with his life, he wins inasmuch as he lives. But he benefits from a kind of moral luck. What if he had died along the way and never reached Shanghai with the money? Since moral standards cannot depend on moral luck, this highly plausible sideshadow raises a crucial question: Does such self-ownership secure autonomy? The answer would have to be no, since most commitments to autonomy aim at a more robust notion. The exercise of autonomy may never escape contingencies, but it would be hoped that its calculus would not depend fundamentally on arbitrary chance.

Furthermore, how much autonomy is possible in the face of the standardizing imperative of the market? In his desperate efforts to turn his own body into cash, Sanguan epitomizes one aspect of the Enlightenment mind-set. Forced to participate in a modern market economy, he has a very instrumental rationality that sustains his pursuit of his objectives. Yet Sanguan is hardly sovereign. To provide for his family's basic survival he must maltreat his body, and he cannot set his price. Such self-exploitation is seldom detached from larger economic structures, a fact made clear by Sanguan's dependence on medical institutions, their biotechnologies, and their gatekeepers. By making his own blood an external object for sale, Sanguan suffers objectification, alienation, and self-estrangement of the kind Marx described as constituting the alienation of labor. "First, the fact that labour is external to the worker, i.e., it does not belong to his essential being; that in his work, therefore, he does not affirm himself but denies himself, . . . does not develop freely his physical and mental energy but mortifies his body and ruins his mind."[27] Marx's generalization is embodied in Yu Hua's direct, unsentimental way of dispatching the details of Sanguan's ill health during his frantic blood selling: "The Xu Sanguan of this time was pale and thin, his four limbs without strength, his head dizzy and swollen. Blurry eyed, with a persistent ringing in his ears, his bones were aching and sore to the point that taking steps made his legs feel as if they were floating" (262).

Sanguan's repeated sales of his blood may exercise his self-ownership, but the practice is but a pale shadow of autonomy given that the social, economic, and political conditions under which he lives hardly allow him acceptable options.[28] If *To Live* exposed the corruption and brutality of medical institutions under Communism, *Blood Seller* shows the dark side

27. Marx, "Economic and Philosophic Manuscripts of 1844," 74.

28. "A person is autonomous only if he has a variety of acceptable options available to him to choose from, and his life became as it is through his choice of some of these options" (Raz, *The Morality of Freedom*, 204, quoted in Cohen, *Self-Ownership*, 238).

of medical care in a market economy: "My son's in a Shanghai hospital. . . . I have to raise enough money to deliver to him. If [we] don't have money, the doctors won't give my son injections and medicine" (278). In such a predicament, the right to exploit the possession of one's body seems like a hollow compensation.

Of course, this objection to a narrow focus on self-ownership reveals a paradox in connected appeals to broader ideals of autonomy. Namely, it may be that individuals could enjoy meaningful moral "autonomy" only under social conditions ensuring basic human welfare such that a father would never have to risk his own health to pay for his son's medical treatment. Yet the provision of such public benefits would require the state's appropriation of its citizens' labor power and wealth in a way that, according to libertarians, would violate their economic autonomy. Given this dilemma, the proponents of free market capitalism rationalize the absence of safety nets by presuming the primacy of self-ownership and consent in the economic realm and by sponsoring cultural products and discourses that bolster the impression of moral autonomy. It is on account of such mystifications that Marxist critics often disapprove of humanistic, "bourgeois" literature, but such works can also reveal the contradictions implicit in many capitalist values and the usefulness of complementing individualistic interpretations with social ones.

As described above, the main ways that Sanguan does exercise autonomy lie in his personal ethical choices to forgive Yulan and save Yile in their times of need. Yet what happens when Sanguan no longer faces dire opportunities for altruism? The extent to which Sanguan sees his very identity as based on his ability to be a subject with economic capacities and to provide for his family comes out in the last chapter. Now over sixty, Sanguan's lifeworld is much improved. Whereas the Cultural Revolution violated his wife's self-ownership by condemning her to struggle sessions and long days on her feet as an object of public humiliation, and whereas it violated Yile's and Erle's self-ownership by sending them down to the countryside, Sanguan's sons are now back, married with kids, and Sanguan and his wife have enough money. They live amid new clothing stores and other signs of economic prosperity. Yet Sanguan feels nostalgia about selling blood and craves pork liver, so he decides to sell his blood for the first time in eleven years. "Today he would sell his blood for himself. It would be the first time he sold it for himself. . . . Today he's selling blood only in order to eat pork liver and drink millet wine" (286). Yet to

Sanguan's dismay the young, new blood drawer refuses to take his blood because of his advanced age. Upon realizing that no one would want his blood, Sanguan walks around town in circles, crying. He worries, sadly: what if his family needed money?

Luckily, Yulan can afford to take Sanguan for the meal he wants, and the novel's happy ending might reinforce assumptions that a market society will create greater productivity and prosperity. Yet the novel also expresses concerns about changing values and their transmission. For example, what have Sanguan's sons, Yile, Erle, and Sanle, learned from their father about the pursuit of solidarity, health, or dignity? The reader has to wonder when they urge him not to cry in the street primarily out of their concern to preserve appearances: "Dad, don't cry. If you want to cry, go cry at home. Don't make a spectacle of yourself here" (290).

Far from feeling self-congratulatory for his record of self-reliance and risk taking, at the end of the novel Sanguan appears to be culturally disenfranchised. Wang Dewei has argued that at least when Sanguan sells his blood he exercises a greater degree of self-determination than is allowed the characters of Yu Hua's earlier novel *To Live*. In *To Live*, the Communist society that functions in the name of the people increasingly resembles a vampire after the protagonist's son dies in the process of donating blood and his daughter dies in childbirth because of incompetent medical care.[29] But how much choice do the characters in Sanguan's market world have? What mores or institutions might safeguard against the destruction of moral values and social solidarity in the utilitarian pursuit of economic means?

Furthermore, is it clear that the reader should interpret Sanguan's self-mastery as a sign of possibilities for the reform of Chinese society at large? To be sure, as China's citizens sustain an unparalleled pace of change, the capitalist market will continue to exercise social influence. An enterprising risk taker willing to sacrifice his life's blood for his family, Sanguan's farming of his own body also reminds us that the post-Mao de-collectivization of agriculture and the return to peasant family economies are partly to credit for the tremendous rise in China's gross domestic product. Perhaps no system works as peasant family agriculture does to encourage self-exploitation and generate wealth.

China's experience reminds us that capitalism is not a monolithic institution but a set of situated practices. As sociologist Richard Titmuss

29. Wang Dewei, "Shanghen jijing," 26.

writes in a comparative study of the U.S. commercial and British voluntary systems for collecting human blood, "If dollars or pounds exchange for blood then it may be morally acceptable for a myriad of other human activities and relationships also to exchange for dollars or pounds."[30] The issues of self-ownership, autonomy, and selfhood raised in Yu Hua's novel bear on concerns about the propriety of commodifying aspects of human personhood all the more pertinent in light of developments in medical technologies and trade laws that have led to increasing market exchanges in human organs, genetic material, and reproductive services.[31]

Despite making a hero of a self-exploiting peasant, Yu's novel may not promote free market capitalism over welfare state capitalism or even market socialism as much as raise questions about whether the supposed laws of markets really harmonize diverse interests. Can human welfare be calculated in terms of economics? Capitalist self-ownership is not the same as autonomy, and values must be judged according to moral as well as economic criteria.

4. SELF-OWNERSHIP AND CULTURAL CITIZENSHIP IN WEIHUI'S *SHANGHAI BABY*

Self-ownership can also serve as a guiding metaphor to explore questions of freedom and responsibility in Weihui's banned novel, *Shanghai Baby*. Written by the provocative young Shanghai-based writer Weihui,[32] the novel offers a telling account of young Chinese urban residents as they struggle for sovereignty over their values, decisions, bodies, and abilities in the face of headlong economic and social changes that could overpower such sovereignty. Chronicling a little over a year in the life of CoCo, a 25-year-old Shanghai novelist, the novel revolves around CoCo's emotionally fraught betrayal of her impotent lover Tiantian 天天, her sadomasochistic affair with a married German businessman, and her composition of a novel that appears to be *Shanghai Baby* since she at one point reads aloud verbatim from an earlier passage (14, 39–40).[33] In the rest of this chapter, I suggest that the novel reinforces both liberal

30. Titmuss, *The Gift Relationship*, 198.

31. For a thoughtful critique by a legal scholar of universal commodification, see Radin, *Contested Commodities*.

32. Although now widely identified as a Shanghai writer, Weihui herself is originally from Ningbo. She prefers to drop her surname, Zhou, and use only her given name.

33. Page numbers within the text refer to Weihui, *Shanghai baobei*.

and Confucian values as the characters reinvest in personal projects and intimate, particularistic relations in response to market transitions that compromise earlier expectations of collective solidarity.

More broadly, the novel shows a changing ethical landscape within which understandings of what it is to be a responsible citizen, friend, or lover are linked to evolving discourses and new frames of reference. As forces for liberation the novel celebrates cosmopolitan choice, cultural empowerment, and lifestyle control, but the novel's trajectory also foregrounds the fragility of interpersonal commitments within a changing social order. Beginning with a discussion of positive conceptions of cosmopolitanism and cultural citizenship (section 4.1), I highlight possible advantages and pitfalls of cultural identity and cultural rights (4.2). I then explore how class privileges (4.3) and gender roles (4.4) complicate the significance of these ideals and the possibility of their realization. Finally, I consider whether the novel offers new social opportunities (4.5).

4.1 Cosmopolitanism and Cultural Citizenship

Weihui's novel attends in detail to local practices and also presents several cosmopolitan conceptions of cultural citizenship, from Stoic and Epicurean traditions to Kant's cosmopolitanism of philosophical modernity, to more nihilistic, decadent, and postmodern varieties. The concept of cultural citizenship undermines an assumed connection between collective membership and the nation-state in a way that can distinguish life-enhancing values of belonging, participation, and access from the potentially destructive and exclusionary ramifications of nationalism. Cultural citizenship both underscores the role of cultural rights, privileges, and obligations in enabling political change and draws attention to the opportunities participation in culture offers citizens to take responsibility for evolving social, economic, and ethical values.

Greater cosmopolitan awareness furthers cultural citizenship insofar as it can help national citizens claim rights that they may argue are prior to and independent of particular legal systems. Cosmopolitanism also broadens the range of opportunities for self-transformation for, as Anthony Appiah writes, "the freedom to create oneself—the freedom that liberalism celebrates—requires a range of socially transmitted options from which to invent what we have come to call our identities."[34]

34. Appiah, "Cosmopolitan Patriots," 625.

The novel's emphasis on media and other cultural practices to posit meaningfulness, critique practices of domination, and establish communities with respect for difference suggests a conception of cultural citizenship that sociologist Nick Stevenson views as a key tool for confronting transnational capitalism.[35] In this way, enhanced cosmopolitan cultural citizenship offers important possibilities for resisting hegemonic market forces as well as for transcending one's inherited moral shortcomings and entrenched biases.

Despite the empowering potential of a broadening cultural citizenship, in *Shanghai Baby* protagonist CoCo's pursuit of a cosmopolitan lifestyle leads her to suffer several affronts to her national, sexual, and ethical dignity. First and foremost, CoCo's affair with transnational businessman Mark endangers her national loyalty as well as her partnership with Tiantian. Along these lines, John Crespi analyzes CoCo's love triangle in terms of national allegory. In this reading, the impotent Tiantian functions as a symbol for the Chinese nation, whereas Mark "begs to be read as an ultra-potent, ultra-rational, and fundamentally amoral embodiment of invasive yet oh-so irresistible overseas capital."[36]

Extending Crespi's astute analysis, one can probe further the notion of adultery as more than sexual betrayal. As Laura Kipnis writes: "Adultery has become the favored metonym for all broken promises, intimate and national. . . . It's about the fear that adultery *puts things at risk*; from the organization of daily life to the very moral fabric of the nation."[37] Yet what does it mean when a tale of adultery can be read as a threat to the social contract? It has to say something about the particular historical moment. With the widespread economic restructuring mandated for China's entry into the World Trade Organization, and with the Chinese state reducing or eliminating many economic safety nets and thereby retreating from earlier promises of collective solidarity, is it surprising that a citizen's loyalty might waver?

Since cultural citizenship pertains to participation in cultural institutions, the popularity and censorship of Weihui's novel rekindle thorny questions concerning rights of self-ownership, freedom of expression, and citizens' obligations to civil society. These issues of reception cast a shadow on the possibilities for self-invention and cultural citizenship that

35. Stevenson, "Globalization," 42.
36. Crespi, "*Shanghai Babe* and the Impasse," 6.
37. Kipnis, "Adultery," 294.

emerge in the novel itself, and they make more urgent questions about the role of Weihui's intricate Web site, and the Internet more broadly, in demanding access to cultural citizenship.[38] First issued in September 1999, the novel had sold at least 80,000 copies and was in its seventh printing by March 2000. That month Chengdu's rival tabloids published front-page photographs of Weihui wearing a revealing sheer blouse and misquoted, she claims, her comment about allowing readers to see "the breasts of the Shanghai Babe."[39] The incident led to complaints by Party officials, state media denunciations of Weihui as "decadent, debauched and a slave of foreign culture," and a ban on her novel.[40] The ban only increased the novel's popularity, and its commercial success testifies to its importance as one cultural lens on the political, aesthetic, or moral sensibilities of young Shanghai citizens at the turn of the century.

4.2 Cultural Identity and Cultural Rights

Inquiry into how Weihui's culturally accomplished protagonist forms her identity reveals several axes of inclusion and exclusion that define cultural identity and cultural citizenship in the novel. As CoCo's frame of reference expands, and she revels in free mobility and circulation, what values does she sanction? One answer is that, in celebrating her access to elite culture, CoCo accords a specific place to national, ethnic, and civic cultural distinctions.

Since CoCo explicitly juxtaposes her precarious individual life, "as insignificant as an ant," against Shanghai's seemingly invincible prosperity, "rooted in the foundation of material civilization" (14), the awe the city inspires seems to inflame CoCo's intense craving for personal distinction.[41] For the city of Shanghai is much more than background in Weihui's novel. Instead, the treatment of setting suggests the importance of CoCo's relationship to her urban environment. At several points, CoCo describes the sounds and sights of Shanghai, with its unique mix of new municipal engineering projects and scattered historical remains that "adorn the city's conscience" (159).

Moreover, by titling her novel *Shanghai baobei*, literally "Shanghai darling," Weihui reifies the idea of a Shanghai culture and the concept

38. See http://goldnets.myrice.com/wh/.

39. Pomfret, "The New Censorship," A16.

40. Smith, "Sex, Lust, Drugs."

41. Unless otherwise noted, all translations are my own.

of a Shanghai native. Her protagonist may not share all the beliefs and values she posits as common to Chinese or Shanghai culture, but CoCo is aware of them, takes seriously their persistent influence, and thereby contributes to their perpetuation. Her guilt over her affair, for example, shows that she is not amoral or unaware of morality. Similarly, when she warns Tiantian to protect his valuables at the train station because of the migrant workers (*waidi mingong* 外地民工; 87) there, she tacitly implies a solidarity among city dwellers who commonly believe their security is threatened by outsiders.

Making CoCo's allegiances explicit suggests the tenacity of a sense of shared destiny, tradition, and memory among Shanghai and Chinese citizens faced with globalization. If globalizing processes bring greater mobility and higher expectations for political, civil, social, and cultural rights, they also bring threats of increased exploitation and disenfranchisement. The novel suggests these new forms of exploitation in its sympathetic portrayals of a hapless door-to-door vacuum cleaner salesman (52–53) and a novice taxi driver who can't find his way (71). CoCo voices a sense of collective disenfranchisement after the wife of an American bank executive orders her and her friends to leave a lawn where they're picnicking. The affront to their national dignity is only worsened by the wife's complaint that they are disrupting the peace and quiet for which the couple pays US$ 25,000 a month. Angry and bewildered, CoCo and her friends reflect on their position as Chinese citizens:

> On the way [back], we brought up the story of the sign in the former French concession. The sign said "No Chinese or dogs allowed." Yet now various big transnational companies' financial magnates and tycoons were staging a comeback. Such forceful economic momentum would undoubtedly bring [a sense of] psychological superiority and cultural hegemony. So this new breed for the first time keenly experienced a sense of national self-respect. (84)

Despite this claim to national self-respect (*minzu zizunxin* 民族自尊心), the novel seldom articulates esteem for the Chinese nation or its products. Whereas CoCo continuously conveys high regard for Western cultural products and influences, the few references to Chinese traditions or Chinese-made goods seem to offer small, perhaps tongue-in-cheek, consolation to national pride. CoCo's father, for example, feels proud that on his recommendation some of the visiting European scholars in his department have begun smoking Chinese "Imperial Crown" cigars

(125–26). The irony here lies partly in the fact that tobacco is native to tropical America but even more in the fact that it is foreign endorsement that confers value.

The comfort that self-categorization can offer in confronting threats to national dignity is suggested by CoCo's intense investment in her personal identity, in whatever it is that makes CoCo CoCo, and which purportedly endures as she changes. Yet what loss of self accompanies CoCo's invention of her hip, cosmopolitan identity? Does she overcome her need for affirmation from the dominant culture? Does breaking taboos against masturbation, homoeroticism, or sexual availability offer more than a negative freedom from repressive cultural norms?

From the opening of the novel, Coco describes how experiences of her deviation from the norm have sensitized her to her own stigmatization. For one, she recounts how, after the publication of her earlier collection of fiction, entitled *Hudie de jianjiao* 蝴蝶的尖叫 (Shriek of the butterfly), "rumors spread like wildfire that I was a bisexual with violent tendencies" and men sent pornographic pictures and letters to her (67). Over the course of the novel, CoCo assigns increasing meaning to her distinguishing differences as she stabilizes her identity as a writer.

> As soon as he [Tiantian] brought up my novel, . . . I knew that I would return to Shanghai and continue writing. Tiantian liked me that way. It was also clear to me that I could only be that way. Otherwise I would lose a lot of people's love, including my own. Only by writing could I differentiate myself from the common and bothersome people, make myself different from the masses. (110)

CoCo's investment in her own distinction, an investment she enacts in her willed practice of writing, draws attention to the way a marginality one chooses, as CoCo chooses hers, differs from a marginality to which one is subjected. This point relates to the distinction made in Chapter 7 between a decadence of resignation stemming from fatalism and a creative decadence amounting to a gesture of defiance or freedom. Although the speaker in the afterword expresses resignation, within the novel CoCo insists on her transgressive, defiant role. Fundamentally, CoCo's license to break taboos and invent her hip persona depends on class distinctions that must be continuously cast anew within a changing economic and social environment.

4.3 Cultural Capital, Class Privilege, and Market Capitalism

By sideshadowing multiple "could-have-been-otherwise" contingencies in the lives of her mostly privileged characters, Weihui accords a decisive role to self-determination. This presentation of agency subverts Communist ideology by rejecting a deterministic paradigm based on an individual's class position. For example, whereas CoCo and her more conventional cousin Zhusha begin with more or less equivalent social status, they reach quite different positions. The individual differences that intervene to change their circumstances cannot be explained away in terms of class. Character determinism is a possible explanation, but the characters' wills also seem to exert real power. Even if some of CoCo's and her friends' decisions strike the reader as self-destructive or wanton, they are decisions made by the characters themselves in efforts to determine their own lives.

Yet, although class position is no longer the determinant of one's future in accordance with socialist ideology, class privilege appears to be a requirement for freedom of choice in the world of the novel. Well-meaning celebrations of cosmopolitanism often neglect this intimate connection between cultural citizenship and class privilege, particularly within market systems that require exchanges of different types of capital (economic, political, social, symbolic, and cultural) for their legitimacy and perpetuation. The role of class distinction cannot but dominate in a novel harnessing so many cultural references, historical and contemporary, elite and popular, political and erotic. Moreover, in detailing her semi-autobiographical protagonist's self-conscious positioning as a popular writer, Weihui reinforces an ideology of charisma that obscures the role of social and economic class in the formation of tastes and preferences. Comparing her coming literary achievement to the success of Bill Gates and Gong Li, CoCo presents herself as a member of an international metropolitan elite. Whether citizenship adheres to city, nation, or a cosmopolitan aesthetic, its realization seems to depend on unacknowledged class privilege.

Here it is important to address the specific cultural citizenship upon which both the author's and her protagonist's commercial and literary successes depend. Like Weihui herself, CoCo is a graduate of the Chinese department of Shanghai's distinguished Fudan University. CoCo's father is a university professor who talks to her about Sartre, telling her that she has to bear all the possible consequences of her actions (231). CoCo's class status is evident also in her visits to a psychoanalyst, her parents' hourly maid (*zhongdiangong* 鐘點工), and her descriptions of her "yuppie" cousin who frequents an upscale women's health club. CoCo has also learned English, though she relies on Mark's translating help when his journalist friend interviews her, and the characters throw around trendy English words such as "party animal" (39), "Groupie" (106), "House," and "Trip-Hop" (71). Weihui includes Chinese translations for many of these terms, but either version functions as a marker of cultural distinction.

Numerous references to foreign writers and musicians also indicate how the acquisition of cultural capital confers status. Each of the novel's 32 chapters begins with one or more epigraphs from Western thinkers, writers, musicians, and philosophers. From writers Marguerite Duras and Henry Miller to songwriters Joni Mitchell and Tori Amos, these cultural references support and script CoCo's construction of her counternormative identity, but they do so within a dominant political economy that often associates things Western with modernity, advancement, and power. CoCo also refers to Vivaldi's "Four Seasons," the artists Modigliani, Matisse, and Salvador Dalí, and other markers of elite culture such as knowledge of mixed drinks (73).

CoCo's consumption of these symbolic commodities demonstrates market capitalism's promotion of both a culture of immediate pleasure and an elite culture based on practices of deferred gratification that increase class inequalities. The number of specific brand names mentioned in the novel could qualify it as "Kmart realism," described by one scholar as "a fiction of brand names and contemporary cultural references, work that achieves texture without substance and that invokes an array of material practices it fails to investigate or challenge."[42] The importance CoCo attributes to fluency in elite cultural codes is made plain in her requirements for her lovers: "I can't see myself talking love with a man who can't recite ten proverbs, five philosophical allusions, and three musicians" (32). As these cultural references mark and perhaps seek to legitimate her class privilege, CoCo's access to and fluency in both high culture and popular culture of the West depend on material conditions connected to the modern market economy.

42. Clark, "Contemporary Short Fiction," 150.

What does it mean when people associate citizenship more with access to consumer goods than with civil and cultural rights? Several scenes in *Shanghai Baby* reflect the central role of shopping in the protagonist's management of her emotions as well as the consumer society's promotion of immediate gratification: "Like other young women, whenever I was in a bad mood, I would roam around this street, wickedly buying without cease. I'd buy a big pile of pretty, weightless things to take home. Most of these clothes I'd wear only once or twice" (88).

Yet CoCo also voices Enlightenment commitments to caring for the least well off. She shows this sense of perspective on the troubles of the rich and famous when she grows impatient with the famous bisexual makeup artist Flying Apple 飛苹果. To his complaints that his girlfriends are jealous of his boyfriends, she responds: "Our country still has eight hundred million peasants worrying about how to eke out a modest living. You are already a remarkably fortunate person" (108). CoCo seems here to condemn excessive narcissism that might crowd out concerns about increasing disparities.

At the same time, the novel's celebration of aesthetic connoisseurship leads to attitudes many readers might find morally dubious. A tense moment occurs at a party, for example, when an overseas student from Sarajevo verbally attacks a young American in anger over the U.S. bombing of Yugoslavia. CoCo's guests, mostly beautiful fashion models, glance over watchfully but reserve any judgment: "From a moral justice point of view they supported the Kosovar, but from an aesthetic point of view they sympathized with [the guy who] resembled Leonardo DiCaprio, Johnson" (223).

Is it possible to separate cultural citizenship from its economic and political dimensions? Might glorifying the pleasures of the market not foster greater consumption, hedonism, and political complacency? Romanticizing serial consumption, CoCo asserts her prerogative to live a throwaway lifestyle when Tiantian tells her to quit her job: "To quit a job, leave a partner, throw something away, these behaviors of abandon were almost instinctual for a woman like me, as easy as turning over one's hand. To drift from one goal to another [was a way] of exerting myself to the utmost and preserving the life force" (21–22).

Whereas CoCo classifies her character as belonging to a seemingly set category of capricious, impulsive, and vibrant women, the novel leaves unclear just what motivates CoCo. Her rejection of certain moral values (such as honesty) may stem more from a desire to escape her loneliness than from a pursuit of pleasure. For it is far from clear whether her affair with Mark brings her much happiness. CoCo reveals her desperation to escape her loneliness when she buys a plane ticket on the spur of the moment to go to Beijing to see some casual friends for Christmas (105). She doesn't mention the expense involved in this exercise in free mobility, yet later she alludes to money troubles as one reason why she gives her father socks for his 53rd birthday (126).

In contrast to her pursuit of individual distinction, in two passages CoCo describes her writing as an "extinguishing of self" (132) and a way of "discovering my true existence [and] overcoming the terror of loneliness, poverty, death, and all the other terrible things that can happen" (166). CoCo's use of the term *niepan* 涅槃, nirvana (132), echoes notions of Buddhist detachment, though it might also be read as an Epicurean quest for freedom from pain and emotional disturbance.

4.4 Free to Be a Cosmo Girl: Gender and Cultural Citizenship

Would CoCo even have a story to tell were it not for her affair with Mark? This question calls attention to the degree to which Weihui's novel reproduces traditional narratives of gendered experience. Although CoCo rejects her parents' expectations, she hardly eludes the legacy of sex roles and stereotypes. Her internalized misogyny might even play a key role in allowing her to rationalize her deception of Tiantian: "Women are all born liars," CoCo asserts, "especially when they are circulating among several men" (62). Moreover, graphic accounts of her sadomasochistic affair with Mark may glamorize the tyranny of neo-imperialism and gender oppression as much as make readers wary.

> He didn't show a shred of pity; he didn't stop for a moment. The pain suddenly turned into indulgence. . . . I imagined him wearing a Nazi uniform, imagined what the boots and leather coat would be like. Those two blue Germanic eyes would have a certain callousness and bestiality. This sort of imagining effectively fueled my bodily excitement. (61)

Do CoCo's sexual experiences feed her liberation or her oppression? CoCo considers herself more fortunate than most women, "because, according to statistics, this or that problem marks the sex life of about 70 percent of Chinese women, and 10 percent of women have never had an orgasm in their lives" (68). Yet to explain her submission to Mark she also describes a "masochistic joy" (*shou nue de kuaile* 受虐的快樂) that renders her mind "useless" (*bu ding yong* 不頂用; 59). The worst affront to CoCo's sense of sexual dignity occurs when Mark takes her to have sex in a filthy bathroom in a dance club. Such passages may seem tawdry, yet CoCo is trying to say something serious about the power of sexual attraction and the inadequacy of discourses that underestimate its importance. When she comes to understand that she's fallen in love with her "sex partner," CoCo remarks somewhat derisively that "feminist arguments have never been able to demolish this kind of sexual hypnotism" (238). Yet, since she believes that Mark will never leave his wife, CoCo feels powerless to influence the future of their relationship. Thus, in order to defend herself against her deepening attachment, she distances herself by stealing money from Mark's wallet and then later his wedding ring from his finger while he sleeps during their final night together.

It is also significant that CoCo uses commercial media representations not only as a script for her engagement in consumer rituals of self-presentation but also as a moral compass for her actions. When she spends an afternoon with Mark and his unsuspecting wife, Eva, she likens the dynamics to representations in popular culture. As if market capitalism depends on such degradations, the novel highlights CoCo's tireless pursuit of style, glamour, and savoir-faire: "I love that sense of self-love in penciling my eyebrows and applying lipstick and blusher. For this I would be willing to be a woman again in my next life" (94).

As CoCo excels at the intensive labor of synthesizing femininity, she might be seen as freely inventing a persona. Individual choices about embodying femininity take on particular significance after the suppression of signs of femininity and eroticism during the Mao era.[43] Yet at one point CoCo herself becomes painfully self-conscious about her complicity with her objectification as a sex object: After reveling in the attention she receives while wearing her red bikini, she shudders as "feminism raises its head," and she wonders on what grounds she wants to look like "a mindless Barbie doll" (172).

43. Evans, "Marketing Femininity," 229.

4.5 New Social Opportunities?

In reproducing gender roles that make her morally uneasy, does CoCo implicitly hold out hope for better alternatives? When she deceives Tiantian despite his request that she not lie to him (77), how does this deception fit into the modern self that CoCo is trying to perform? If feelings of unique worth grow through fulfilling responsibilities to others, what values organize CoCo's obligations and focus? First, she commits more and more to her project of writing for a public readership and increasingly grasps the advantages pursuing such a project offers over a focus on her bodily beauty. "I thought paradise wouldn't be any better," she writes of a reclusive period she devotes to writing. "To be carefree and at ease, without scruples, without men to pay attention to your hairstyle and clothing" (166). Toward the end of the novel, CoCo asserts the value of creative projects for conferring meaning on one's life when she urges Tiantian to pursue his painting more seriously: "It's not an issue of whether or not you become famous, but rather it provides a firm support to give to your own heart, a reason to live happily to the end of your life" (206).

Second, CoCo deepens her expressions of filial piety, culminating in her week's stay at her parents' apartment after her mother breaks a leg (chap. 27) and then her return to live with them after Tiantian's funeral. CoCo also expresses respect for her parents' traditional family values in recounting their refusal to accept rent from her cousin Zhusha: "Our own kin! What kind of people would we be to be so money-grubbing? Even in a market economy one must respect family ties and uphold certain principles, right?" (125/126).[44]

Third, until she is overcome by her desire to be with Mark during his final days in Shanghai, CoCo sustains a sense of mutual responsibility vis-à-vis Tiantian. She articulates this sense of responsibility when she reproaches him for asking her how she would respond to his death:

> Don't talk to me about life and death, love and hatred, the self, the essential self, all those words that can drive a person mad. We live together, don't we? . . . If you have ideas about my life these days, tell me the specifics. . . . I'll change. . . . Just stop talking in such terrifying terms. . . . Such talk is too irresponsible. (162)

---

44. Here the first page number refers to the original and the second to Humes's translation.

Yet, despite having received a letter from Tiantian in which he tells her that she is his only reason to go on living (177), without an alibi CoCo disappears to engage in a multiday sexual rendezvous with Mark before his transfer back to Germany. They make love until she bleeds, and, watching herself dress, she feels "like a toy doll that's been excessively raped" (239). Already plagued by a mixture of self-disgust and self-pity, CoCo is gripped by practical fear when she arrives home to find Tiantian gone to their friend Madonna's and unwilling to talk to her.

Tiantian returns to CoCo, but his brokenness results in a relapse that leads to a fatal overdose. The tragedy of his death hardly chastens CoCo, but it casts quite a pall on the novel's celebration of sexual freedom and transgression. Of course, some may read *Shanghai Baby* as presenting adultery as metaphor for the desire or even need to seek personal happiness. Along these lines, Laura Kipnis has proposed considering adultery as "a form of social articulation, a way of organizing grievances about existing conditions into a collectively imagined form, and one which offers a vehicle for optimism about other, better possibilities" (294). Yet, given Tiantian's senseless premature death, other readers may finish Weihui's novel disenchanted with transgression and ready to reembrace the security of monogamy.

At the same time, the novel's sideshadowing of CoCo's intensely conflicted feelings about her liaisons also reveals the extent to which sexual identities can inform broader self-conceptions, especially as the landscape of possible sexualities becomes more varied and the rules shift regarding sexual behavior and attendant moral obligations. Although the portrayal of heterosexual love ultimately reinforces conventional prudence, honesty, and monogamous commitment, the novel contests heterosexism in its sympathetic inclusion of gay, lesbian, and bisexual characters. In making these groups visible, the novel challenges the history of repression they have suffered. Some of CoCo's friends and their acquaintances pursue rather extreme forms of self-invention, such as the Internet correspondent of her friend Spider, a reformed computer hacker who now works in software development, Internet installation, and computer sales. When CoCo asks Spider about his Internet girlfriend, he tells her that Mei'er "is a girl on the net, but a man in life" and wants to get a sex change (89–90).

By representing a wide range of sexual practices, penchants, and identities and sideshadowing multiple possibilities for CoCo's own sexual expression, the novel points both to the role of choice and to the power of norms and ambivalence. In particular, some of CoCo's comments point toward normalizing homosocial attraction. Challenging the simple division of straight and gay, she acknowledges her own sensual enjoyment of women at several points. "The feeling of having one's face stroked by a pair of fair [i.e., woman's] hands may be several times nicer than a man's solicitude," she says of her visit to a beauty shop for a facial (116). More revealing, CoCo gives the following explanation for her exit from the bathroom where Madonna wants CoCo to admire her naked body: "The way she was touching herself made it hard for a person to bear; any person would have a reaction, regardless of whether it were a man or a woman" (118). She also mentions the bed sharing among female roommates she had known at Fudan University, and one night she lets Madonna sleep cuddled up against her: "I was able to sense her warmth, her breath, her sorrow, and her dreams. . . . Her body had an absorbing sex appeal (as a woman, I could experience this all the more clearly)" (122). Toward the end of the novel, CoCo passes from inclination to act when she French kisses and is mildly fondled by a lesbian German film director. Yet the fact that their parting is located on a public street and is policed by Mark secures safe limits to her crossing the "ambiguous border" (*aimei de jiexian* 曖昧的界限; 210).

For all its celebration of expanding possibilities for the exercise of individual choice and agency, at several moments Weihui's novel also voices a kind of fatalism, but the narrator generally invokes this fatalism in cultivating compassion for the moral weaknesses of others. For example, when CoCo considers the "lethal connection" (*zhiming de guanxi* 致命的關係) between the ambiguous causes of Tiantian's father's death and Tiantian's fate, she refuses to judge the dark secrets in Tiantian's mother's past. Instead, she appeals to the Buddhist notion of an eternally revolving wheel of transmigration: "Everything is completely bound together. There is a cause and inevitably there is an effect, just like the eternal revolving of [the Buddhist] law's wheel in the natural world" (191).

By staging the way the characters face up to Tiantian's death, Weihui may want nothing less than to contribute to an ethic of the human person, in part by posing fundamental questions about the value of life. In the novel's last chapter, CoCo sends e-mails to Mark and her lesbian

German friend, Shamir, to tell them about Tiantian's fatal overdose, yet she writes that her heart feels calm because her novel is almost finished. Although CoCo views the novel as "the best present to give Tiantian and that period of [my] life" (261), the reader is left bewildered by her equanimity. If CoCo is trying to give a sense and perhaps even a beauty to Tiantian's death, why does she think the answer lies in making fame her raison d'être (1)? One possibility is that through writing CoCo seeks to transcend the insignificance of isolated selfhood through testifying to the importance of others.

In closing, CoCo recounts her offer to escort home Tiantian's bereaved grandmother to stop her from harassing Tiantian's mother, whom the grandmother blames for Tiantian's demise. When the grandmother asks CoCo who she is, her inquiry prompts the intense self-questioning that closes the novel: "Indeed. Who am I? Who am I?" (264). In the two-page afterword, a speaker that seems to be the voice of the author offers an answer in terms of Weihui's relation to her first-person narrator-protagonist:

> This novel can be called a semi-autobiographical book. I tried to hide myself well in the words and lines, but I discovered that it's difficult. I had no way to betray my simple life philosophy, no way to conceal that kind of shudder rising from the soles of one's feet, that painful fervor. Even though much of the time I passively accept all that fate bestows on me, I'm such a fatalistic, contradictory, and inscrutable young woman. (265)

Does Weihui's novel promise new ways of perceiving our selves and our social opportunities? In living her life as an ongoing experiment and in the process compromising Tiantian's trust, does CoCo explore moral agency in a meaningful way? Or is Crespi correct in reading the novel as foreclosing possibilities and leading to what he calls "an impasse of postmodern self-promotion"?[45] Crespi's critique is a serious one, yet I would argue that the novel also presents enough sideshadows to set up a dialogue between what CoCo did and what she might have done. Rereading the epigraphs and intertextual references, the reader is left to consider the gap between what CoCo took from all her cultural resources and what she might have taken. The novel also offers the possibility of moral growth from where CoCo is on the last page to where she might be in her next narrative, especially since she calls the novel "both a memorial and a beginning" (266).

---

45. Crespi, "*Shanghai Babe* and the Impasse," 5.

Similar to Xu Sanguan's harvesting of his blood, CoCo's exploitation of her beauty and sexuality may violate the Kantian moral imperative not to treat humanity (in one's own person or in another) as a means only. A cynical reader might accuse CoCo of using her body and even her relationships as means to gather enough marketable life experience to write a popular novel. A cynical critic might accuse Weihui of using her identity as a Shanghai cosmopolitan and as one of China's contemporary "glamour girl writers" (*meinü zuojia* 美女作家) to market her semi-autobiographical novel. Yet, to be fair, one needs to be sensitive about one's own cultural citizenship and privilege. Regardless of the pressures and circumstances that led Weihui to write her novel as she did, one can acknowledge her courage in portraying the contradictions of CoCo's troubled pursuit of agency.

EPILOGUE

The Heart of Time

> We hoped; we waited for the day
> The state would wither clean away,
> Expecting the Millennium
> That theory promised us would come:
> It didn't.
>
> —W. H. Auden, *New Year Letter* (1940)

AN ETHICAL APPROACH TO CHINESE FICTION

This book argues that concepts of agency and determinism offer a key to interpreting modern Chinese fiction. Since a culture's literature speaks in terms it makes essential, interpretive lenses extend the range and depth of appreciation across cultures. I hope that this framework thus helps bring these novels and stories to life for Western readers, for the works I present demonstrate a deep commitment to moral agency in the face of pervasive deterministic discourses. If some writers, such as the avant-garde ones discussed in Chapter 7, leave human feelings suspended before seemingly inevitable situations that admit slim possibilities for moral deliberation, others continue to explore issues of freedom and responsibility in ways that have much to teach us. Treatments of time and agency in Chinese fiction open up dimensions of moral agency in relation to narrative and encourage reflections on human freedom, ethics, purposes, and understandings.

One of this book's aims has been to include Chinese fiction in considerations of modernity and what its legacy is to become. Throughout I have sought to distinguish philosophical projects of modernity, material projects of economic and industrial modernization, and aesthetic, critical reactions named "modernism." Yet even more than may be the case for many other national literatures, Chinese stories and novels depend on their dialogue with the historical contexts that framed their creation. Viewing this interrelationship as a passageway rather than an obstacle, I hope I have shown how Chinese fiction continues to embody a Confucian emphasis on the unity of polity and culture and illuminate Jean-Paul Sartre's 1948 definition of literature as engaged.[1]

Specifically, this book explores how Chinese fiction challenges the habits of bad faith by which some of the characters tend to underestimate their agency and deny their potential, individually or collectively, to transcend conditions they confront. In highlighting the use of sideshadowing that creates a sense of time open to human agency, I suggest the extent to which Chinese fiction retains the spirit of the Confucian or Sartrean project. For the odyssey of Socialist revisionism is still very much under way in China, and Chinese citizens have considerable agency to direct that process. Whereas some conclude that the source of harm may be the long-revered Marxist paradigm itself, others question all paradigms, all programs. Yet radical skepticism toward paradigms may create a vacuum in commitments that would ground meaningful notions of agency. As Western thinkers grapple with modernity, a split has occurred between defenders of liberal notions of moral agency and critics of the project of modernity who seek to go beyond the understandings of that project. Suspicious that a "post-modern" orientation may give little purchase to moral agency or assessments of values, I side with those who want to heal the pathologies of modernity while promoting its ethical ideals.[2]

I believe that modern Chinese fiction offers unique resources for redeeming the commitment to human welfare voiced by Confucian and Enlightenment thinkers. For, as discussed most in Chapter 8, this fiction explores Enlightenment notions of agency while engaging and extending Confucian values, recasting liberal commitments in less individualistic ways. Confucian values, though contested, repressed, and distorted in the twentieth century, offer important perspectives for curbing some of the excesses of overly individualistic or teleological perspectives on agency.

In this way, twentieth-century Chinese fiction holds great significance for readers committed to the moral validity of literature and to the task of restoring a sense of the worth of human life. In the absence of an open political forum, literature assumes greater importance as a means of addressing and influencing social, political, and economic change. Using a broader set of ethical approaches to deal with moral questions,

---

1. Sartre, *Qu'est-ce que la littérature?*

2. Habermas, "Modernity Versus Postmodernity," 9.

twentieth-century Chinese fiction comes to terms with modernity in ways rare in contemporary Western literature. One cannot take twentieth-century Chinese literature lightly. Nor can one turn away from it lightly.

This book invites readers to turn toward Chinese fiction. Without presuming to offer a comprehensive or systematic description, I analyze major works to underscore the complexity and social significance of Chinese fiction's treatments of moral agency. Considerations of moral agency illuminate both well-known works and less discussed works, such as the late-Qing novels and Mao-era fiction. A chronological presentation was in order because I sometimes read the conventional canon of modern Chinese literature against the grain. Rather than finding increasingly bold challenges to fatalistic paradigms in more experimental works, I suggest that such works sometimes saw a retrenchment of fatalism, resignation, or relativism. Conversely, some works of humanist realism offer unique interventions that critique overly individualistic conceptions of agency and suggest ways that moral responsibilities are irremediably both individual and shared.

Chinese fiction stages a dialogue that could not be played out in the realm of political ideas. Twentieth-century political and intellectual discourse in China, often polarized at extremes of dogmatism or relativism, sometimes showed little tolerance for such dialogue. Fiction is by its nature a dialogue, as the chapter on Mao-era fiction argues is the case even under the most stringent strictures. In politics, a single-minded drive in the name of utopian ends easily sows the seeds of totalitarianism. Serious fiction abides neither utopia nor totalitarianism.

Since an authoritarian government's ability to quell dissent may be grounded in marginalizing meaningful notions of agency, attention to the framing of moral agency allows Chinese fiction its full role in disputing dominant ideology and offering alternatives. To appreciate the dimensions of agency in Chinese fiction, it may be necessary to consider a given work as part of the larger dialogues it addresses. In Chinese fiction, the ethical is seldom divorced from political analysis and action. This may be why it is difficult to publish a translated Chinese story in a high-circulation U.S. magazine. Standing alone, a Chinese story may not speak to a reader unfamiliar with its context. Although one must be cautious about deciding political effects of texts, I present one account of those larger dialogues.

SEEING DETERMINISM DIFFERENTLY

Investigating the dialectic of agency and determinism in Chinese fiction led me to see moral agency differently. Starting from a perception of the dominance of various determinisms, I asked why the tension between agency and determinism has been such a persistent theme in modern Chinese fiction. Whereas my approach was guided by interlocking concerns for philosophical problems of moral agency and ethical and epistemological issues of storytelling, closely reading twentieth-century Chinese fiction shifted my focus to an appreciation of a situated ethics that acknowledges the weight of the given while still demanding moral action. This focus led me to a deeper understanding of the Confucian emphasis on context and of the importance of cross-cultural inquiry into narrative's role in ethical reasoning.

Closely reading Chinese fiction posed new questions about the meaning of moral agency. I became more sensitive to contradictions inherent in my initial idealization of the dialectic of freedom and determinism. At the start, I might have asked whether moral agency belonged to the individual or to a society, that is, whether agency would be better viewed as individual or collective. The stories and novels taught me to question such an opposition between the social and the personal. Perhaps moral agency is worked out in relationships, by people whose very humanity depends on both their subjection to what is given and their volitional response in an open process of relating to others. If so, what might this perspective teach readers uncomfortable with fictional worlds that preclude the strong sense of choice Western readers tend to expect?

If fiction offers hope that the past does not preempt the future and that human communities have agency in creating our conditions, the most instructive texts are those that put agency to the test. As stated in the Introduction, one reason to read fiction is for its demonstration that history, economics, character, upbringing, and other material and social forces, despite their pervasive and undeniable power, do not thwart the possibility for meaningful human intervention. In depicting human agency as profoundly bound by and at the same time potentially influencing both the structures of its surroundings and the processes of its articulation, Chinese fiction allows for a more fully dialogic understanding of agency.

Above all, human-heartedness depends on the possibility of an ethics attentive to the openness of the future. The heart of time gives people a modicum of freedom and affirms the life instinct to engage the world in ways that make a difference. Concerned about ways that storytelling affects ideas about time and moral agency, I have considered links between narrative and ethical norms. Viewing ethical decision as interwoven with conceptions of time and inferences of causality that depend on narrative helps one to appreciate presentations of agency within different fictional genres and the avenues they offer to discern agency in new ways.

In this light, Chinese fiction offers different grounds upon which to define notions of power, ethics, progress, and agency. On what grounds would a contemporary Confucian judge another culture as civilized?[3] A Confucian might answer that a culture would be civilized when unable to bear the suffering of others. Is an ethical individual one who maximizes conscious choice and rational action, or might it be one who responds to her circumstances with the most human-heartedness?

The hope that fiction is politically effective becomes more urgent at times when hope diminishes regarding other paths of collective social transformation. Although fictional works are products of the social world, the multiple voices within them and the interpretations they inspire can transcend and even transform habits of understanding that create the boundaries and possibilities of that world. It is difficult to see other than through the lenses of our conditioning, but it is not impossible. For one quality that fiction can restore in us is the agency to dream.

3. This question was posed to the audience by John Berthrong of Boston University at the conference "Confucian Humanism in the Contemporary World," American Academy of Arts and Sciences, Cambridge, Mass., February 28, 2002.

Reference Matter

Bibliography

A Cheng 阿城. "Haizi wang" 孩子王 [King of the children]. *Renmin wenxue* 人民文學 305 (1985.2). Rpt., *Xiaoshuo yuekan* (1985.5): 2–14.

———. "Qi wang" 棋王 [The chess king]. *Shanghai wenxue* 上海文學 82 (1984.7): 15–35.

———. "Shu wang" 樹王 [King of the trees]. *Zhongguo zuojia* 中國作家 (1985.1). Rpt., *Xiaoshuo xuankan* (1985.3, supplement): 3–22.

A Ying 阿英 (Qian Xingcun 錢杏邨). *Wan Qing xiaoshuo shi* 晚清小說史 [A history of late Qing fiction]. (1937) Shanghai: Zuojia chubanshe, 1958.

Althusser, Louis. *Lenin and Philosophy and Other Essays.* Trans. Ben Brewster. New York: Monthly Review Press, 1971.

Anderson, Marston. *The Limits of Realism: Chinese Fiction in the Revolutionary Period.* Berkeley: University of California Press, 1990.

Appiah, Kwame Anthony. "Cosmopolitan Patriots." *Critical Inquiry* 23 (Spring 1997): 617–39.

Arendt, Hannah. *On Violence.* New York: Harcourt Brace Jovanovich, 1972.

Ayer, A. J. "Freedom and Necessity." *Polemic* 5 (1946). Rpt., Watson, ed., *Free Will* (q.v.), 15–23.

Ba Jin 巴金. *Miewang* 滅亡 [Destruction]. Shanghai: Kaiming shudian, 1929.

Bady, Paul. "*Le pousse-pousse* de Lao She." *La critique* 6 (1975): 599–614.

Balibar, Etienne. "Citizen Subject." Trans. James B. Swenson, Jr. In Cadava Edwards et al., eds., *Who Comes After the Subject?* New York: Routledge, 1991, 33–55.

Ball, Terence. "Power." In Robert E. Goodin and Philip Petlit, eds., *A Companion to Contemporary Political Philosophy.* Oxford and Cambridge, Mass.: Blackwell, 1993, 548–57.

Barmé, Geremie. "Wang Shuo and *Liumang* ('Hooligan') Culture." *Australian Journal of Chinese Affairs* 28 (July 1992): 23–64.

Becker, Jasper. *Hungry Ghosts: Mao's Secret Famine.* New York: The Free Press, Simon and Schuster, 1996.

Beijing shifan daxue Zhongwenxi xiandai wenxue jiaoxue gaige xiaozu 北京師範大學中文系現代文學教學改革小組, ed. *Zhongguo xiandai wenxueshi cankao ziliao* 中國現代文學史參考資料 [Reference materials on modern Chinese literary history]. 3 vols. Beijing: Gaodeng jiaoyu chubanshe, 1959.

Béja, Jean-Philippe. "Le poids des rites" [The weight of rites]. *La quinzaine littéraire* 596 (1–15 mars 1992): 13.

Bernstein, Michael André. *Foregone Conclusions: Against Apocalyptic History.* Berkeley: University of California Press, 1994.

Birch, Cyril, ed. *Anthology of Chinese Literature.* 2 vols. New York: Grove Press, 1965–72.

———. "Change and Continuity in Chinese Fiction." In Goldman, ed., *Modern Chinese Literature in the May Fourth Era* (q.v.), 385–404.

Cai Yuanfeng 蔡元豐. "Mi de Minian: Jieshao Su Tong de diyibu changpian" 米的迷念：介紹蘇童的第一部長篇 [The allure of rice: An introduction to Su Tong's first novel]. *Xin bao* 新報 (*Hong Kong Economic Journal*) 12, July 11, 1993.

Cai Yuanpei 蔡元培 (Cai Jiemin 蔡孑民). "Yi meiyu dai zongjiao shuo" 以美育代宗教說 [On the replacement of religion with aesthetic education]. *Xin qingnian* 3.6 (August 1917).

Calinescu, Matei. *Five Faces of Modernity: Modernism, Avant-Garde, Decadence, Kitsch, Postmodernism.* Durham, N.C.: Duke University Press, 1987.

Chen Bingzhao 陳炳釗. "Xiang chengshi wenxue maijin" 向城市文學邁進 [Striding forward toward urban literature]. *Xin bao* 12, July 11, 1993.

Chen Duxiu 陳獨秀. "Aiguo yu zijuexin" 愛國與自覺心 [Patriotism and self-consciousness]. *Jiayin zazhi* 甲寅雜誌 [The tiger] 1.4 (April 1915): 1–6.

———. "Dong xi minzu genben sixiang zhi chayi" 東西民族根本思想之差異 [The fundamental distinction in the thinking of Eastern and Western peoples]. *Qingnian zazhi* 青年雜誌 [Youth magazine] 1.4 (December 1915): 283–87.

———. "Jinggao qingnian" 警告青年 [Call to youth]. *Qingnian zazhi* 1.1 (September 1915): 1–6.

———. "Wenxue geming lun" 文學革命論 [On literary revolution]. *Xin qingnian* 新青年 2.6 (February 1917): 1–4. Trans. Timothy Wong. In Denton, ed., *Modern Chinese Literary Thought* (q.v.), 140–45.

———. "Wuren zuihou zhi juewu" 吾人最後之覺悟 [Our ultimate awakening]. *Qingnian zazhi* 1.6 (Feburary 1916): 1–4.

———. "Yijiuyiliu nian" 一九一六年 [The year 1916]. *Qingnian zazhi* 1.5 (January 1916): 1–4.

Chen Guokai 陳國凱. "Wo yinggai zenma ban?" 我應該怎麼辦？ [What should I do?]. *Zuopin* 作品 (1979.2): 37–50. Trans. Kenneth Jarrett. "What Should I do?" In Link, ed., *Stubborn Weeds* (q.v.), 73–96.

Chen Pingyuan 陳平原. *Zhongguo xiaoshuo xushu moshi de zhuanbian* 中國小說敘述模式的轉變 [Changes in narrative forms in Chinese fiction]. Shanghai: Shanghai renmin chubanshe, 1988.

Chen Pu 陳普. "Guanyu 'xungen' yu wenxue chuangzuo zhong de wenhua wenti" 關於'尋根'與文學創作中的文化問題 [On the "search for roots" and the cultural problems in creative literary works]. In Wei Shi 韋實, ed., *Xinshinian wenyi lilun taolun gaiguan* 新十年文藝理論討論概觀 [Perspectives on theoretical issues in literature and art in the new decade, 1976–1987]. Guilin: Lijiang chubanshe, 1988, 334–59.

Chen Xiaoming 陳曉明. "Fankang weiji: Lun 'xin xieshi'" 反抗危機：論 "新寫實" [Against crisis: Review of the new realism], *Wenxue pinglun* 文學評論 [Literary review] (1993.2): 88–100.

———. "Xianfengpai zhi hou, wanshengdai de jueqi yu weiji" 先鋒派之後，晚生代的崛起與危機 [After the avant-gardists, the latecomers' rise and crisis]. *Mingbao yuekan* 明報月刊 [Mingbao monthly] (August 1997): 33–39.

———. "Zui hou de yishi: 'Xianfengpai' de lishi ji qi pinggu" 最後的儀式： "先鋒派" 的歷史及其評估 [The last ritual: History of the "avant-garde" and its appraisal]. *Wenxue pinglun* 文學評論 (1991.5): 128–41.

Cheng, Ching-mao. "The Impact of Japanese Literary Trends on Modern Chinese Writers." In Goldman, ed., *Modern Chinese Literature in the May Fourth Era* (q.v.), 63–88.

Cheng Fangwu 成仿吾. "Cong wenxue geming dao geming wenxue" 從文學革命到革命文學 [From literary revolution to revolutionary literature]. *Chuangzao yuekan* 創造月刊 1.9 (Feb. 1, 1928). Rpt., Shanghai wenyi chubanshe, ed. *Zhongguo xin wenxue daxi, 1927–1937: Wenxue lilun ji* (q.v.), 2: 34–40.

Chin, Ai-li. "Value Themes in Short Stories, 1976–1977." In Goodwin C. Chu and Francis L. K. Hsu, eds., *Moving a Mountain: Cultural Change in China.* Honolulu: University Press of Hawai'i, 1979, 280–304.

Chong, Woei Lien. "Mankind and Nature in Chinese Thought: Li Zehou on the Roots of Maoist Voluntarism." *China Information* 11.2/3 (1996/1997): 138–75.

Chow, Rey. "Rereading Mandarin Ducks and Butterflies: A Response to the 'Postmodern' Condition." *Cultural Critique* 5 (winter 1986/1987): 69–93.

Chow, Tse-tsung. "The Anti-Confucian Movement in Early Republican China." In Arthur F. Wright, ed., *The Confucian Persuasion.* Stanford, Calif.: Stanford University Press, 1960, 288–312.

———. *The May Fourth Movement: Intellectual Revolution in Modern China.* Stanford, Calif.: Stanford University Press, 1960.

Clark, Miriam Marty. "Contemporary Short Fiction and the Postmodern Condition." *Studies in Short Fiction* 32.2 (1995): 147–59.

Cohen, G. A. *Self-Ownership, Freedom, and Equality.* Cambridge: Cambridge University Press, 1995.

Cong Weixi 從維熙. "Daqiang xia de hong yulan" 大牆下的紅玉蘭 [Red magnolias beneath the wall]. *Shouhuo* 收穫 [Harvest] 16 (1979.2): 5–38.

Crespi, John A. "*Shanghai Babe* and the Impasse of Post-modern Self-promotion." Talk presented at the Association of Asian Studies Annual Meeting, Chicago, March 22, 2001.

Cuddon, J. A. *A Dictionary of Literary Terms.* London: Penguin, 1979.

Curien, Anne, ed. *Anthologie de nouvelles chinoises contemporaines.* Paris: Gallimard, 1994.

Dai Houying 戴厚英. *Kongzhong de zuyin* 空中的足音 [Footsteps in the void]. Guangzhou: Huacheng chubanshe, 1986.

———. *Ren a, ren* 人啊，人！[Humanity, o humanity!] (1980). Rpt., Taipei: Xidai shuban youxian gongsi, 1987. Trans. Frances Wood. *Stones on the Wall.* New York: St. Martin's Press, 1985.

———. *Shi ren zhi si* 詩人之死 [Death of a poet] (1978). Fuzhou: Fujian renmin chubanshe, 1982.

———. *Suolian, shi rouruan de: Dai Houying zhongduanpian xiaoshuoxuan* 瑣鏈，是柔軟的：戴厚英中短篇小說選 [Soft is the chain: Selections from Dai Houying's short- and medium-length fiction]. Guangzhou: Huacheng chubanshe, 1982.

de Bary, Wm. Theodore. "Neo-Confucian Cultivation and the Seventeenth Century 'Enlightenment.'" In de Bary and the Conference on Seventeenth-Century Chinese Thought, eds., *The Unfolding of Neo-Confucianism.* New York: Columbia University Press, 1975, 141–216.

Dennett, Daniel. *Elbow Room: The Varieties of Free Will Worth Wanting.* Cambridge, Mass.: The MIT Press, 1984.

Denton, Kirk A., ed. "General Introduction." In Denton, ed., *Modern Chinese Literary Thought* (q.v.), 1–61.

———. *Modern Chinese Literary Thought: Writings on Literature 1893–1945.* Stanford, Calif.: Stanford University Press, 1996.

Dihle, Albrecht. *The Theory of Will in Classical Antiquity.* Berkeley: University of California Press, 1982.

Dirlik, Arif. *The Origins of Chinese Communism.* New York: Oxford University Press, 1989.

Dissanayake, Wimal, ed. *Narratives of Agency: Self-Making in China, India and Japan.* Minneapolis: University of Minnesota Press, 1996.

Dolezelová-Velingerová, Milena, ed. *The Chinese Novel at the Turn of the Century.* Toronto: University of Toronto Press, 1980.

———. "Lu Xun's "Medicine.'" In Goldman, ed., *Modern Chinese Literature in the May Fourth Era* (q.v.), 221–31.

———. "Narrative Modes in Late Qing Novels." In Dolezelová-Velingerová, ed., *The Chinese Novel* (q.v.), 57–75.

———. "The Origins of Modern Chinese Literature." In Goldman, ed., *Modern Chinese Literature in the May Fourth Era* (q.v.), 17–35.

———. "Typology of Plot Structures in Late Qing Novels." In Dolezelová-Velingerová, ed., *The Chinese Novel* (q.v.), 38–56.

Du Yaquan 杜亞泉. "Geren zhi gaige" 個人之改格 [Reforming the individual]. *Dongfang zazhi* 東方雜誌 [Eastern miscellany] 10.12 (June 1914): 1–4.

Duke, Michael S. "Chinese Literature in the Post-Mao Era: The Return of 'Critical Realism.'" In Michael S. Duke, ed., *Contemporary Chinese Literature: An Anthology of Post-Mao Fiction and Poetry.* Armonk, N.Y.: M.E. Sharpe, 1985, 3–6.

———. "Chinese Marxist Humanism: Dai Houying's Novel *Ren a, ren!*" In Michael S. Duke, ed., *Blooming and Contending: Chinese Literature in the Post-Mao Era.* Bloomington: Indiana University Press, 1985, 150–81.

Eco, Umberto. *The Limits of Interpretation.* Bloomington: Indiana University Press, 1990.

Egan, Michael. "Characterization in *Sea of Woe.*" In Dolezelová-Velingerová, ed., *The Chinese Novel* (q.v.), 165–75.

Elvin, Mark. "The Magic of Moral Power: Hao Ran, *The Children of the Western Sands.*" In Mark Elvin, *Changing Stories in the Chinese World.* Stanford, Calif.: Stanford University Press, 1997, 149–77.

Evans, Harriet. "Marketing Femininity: Images of the Modern Chinese Woman." In Timothy Weston and Lionel Jensen, eds., *China beyond the Headlines.* Lanham, Md.: Rowman and Littlefield, 2000, 217–44.

Feng Youlan 馮友蘭. "Bogesen de zhexue fangfa" 柏格森的哲學方法 [Bergson's philosophical method]. *Xin chao* 新潮 3.1 (September 1921): 13–24.

Fitzgerald, John. *Awakening China: Politics, Culture and Class in the Nationalist Revolution.* Stanford, Calif.: Stanford University Press, 1996.

Fong, Gilbert. "Time in *Nine Murders*: Western Influence and Domestic Tradition." In Dolezelová-Velingerová, ed., *The Chinese Novel* (q.v.), 116–28.

Foot, Philippa. "Free Will as Involving Determinism." *Philosophical Review* (1957): 439–50.

Foucault, Michel. *Discipline and Punish: The Birth of the Prison.* Trans. Alan Sheridan. New York: Vintage, 1979.

Frankfurt, Harry G. "Freedom of the Will and the Concept of the Person." *Journal of Philosophy* 68.1 (January 1971): 5–20. Rpt., Watson, ed., *Free Will* (q.v.), 81–95.

Fu Sinian 傅斯年. "Rensheng wenti faduan" 人生問題發端 [Making a start on the problem of human life] *Xin chao* 1.1 (January 1919): 5–17.

——— (pseud. Meng Zhen 孟真). "Zhongguo wenyi jie zhi binggen" 中國文藝界之病根 [The source of disease in China's literary circles]. *Xin chao* 1.2 (February 1919): 343–44.

Fung, You-lan (Feng Youlan 馮友蘭). *A Short History of Chinese Philosophy.* Ed. Derk Bodde. New York: Macmillan, 1948.

Gadamer, Hans Georg. *Wahrheit und Methode.* Tübinger: Mohr, 1960.

Gálik, Marián. *The Genesis of Modern Chinese Literary Criticism.* London: Curzon Press, 1980.

Gao Xiaosheng 高曉聲. "Lu Shunda zao wu" 李順大造屋 [Li Shunda builds a house]. *Yu hua* 雨花 (1979.7). Rpt., Tang Dacheng, ed. *Zhongguo xin wenyi daxi: 1976–1982 duanpian xiaoshuo ji* (q.v.), 1: 420–31.

Gao Yihan 高一涵. "Yijiuyiqi nian sixiang zhi geming" 一九一七年思想之革命 [The thought revolution of 1917]. *Xin qingnian* 2.5 (January 1917).

———. "Zizhi yu ziyou" 自治與自由 [Autonomy and freedom]. *Xin qingnian* 1.5 (1916): 381–84.

Gao Yuan 高元. "Fei mimi zhuyi" 非秘密主義 [Anti-secretism]. *Xin chao* 1:4 (April 1919): 667–72.

Ge Fei 格非 (Liu Yong 劉勇). "Mizhou" 迷舟 [Lost boat]. *Shouhuo* 68 (1987.6): 96–106.

———. "Zhuiyi Wuyou xiansheng" 追憶烏攸先生 [Remembering Mr. Wu You] (1986). Rpt., Ge Fei. *Mizhou.* Beijing: Zuojia chubanshe, 1989, 1–10. Trans. Howard Goldblatt. "Remembering Mr. Wuyou." In Wang, ed., *China's Avant-Garde Fiction* (q.v.), 15–22.

Geming wenxue lunzheng ziliao xuanbian 革命文學論爭資料選編 [Selection of materials on the revolutionary literature debate]. 2 vols. Beijing: Renmin wenxue chubanshe, 1981.

Giddens, Anthony. *The Consequences of Modernity.* Stanford, Calif.: Stanford University Press, 1990.

———. *The Constitution of Society.* Berkeley and Los Angeles: University of California Press, 1984.

Goldblatt, Howard. "Border Crossings: Chinese Writing, in Their World and Ours." In Timothy Weston and Lionel Jensen, eds., *China beyond the Headlines.* Lanham, Md., and Boulder, Colo.: Rowman and Littlefield, 2000, 327–46.

Goldman, Merle, ed. *Modern Chinese Literature in the May Fourth Era.* Cambridge, Mass.: Harvard University Press, 1977.

Gu Jiegang 顧頡剛. "Duiyu jiu jiating de ganxiang" 對於舊家庭的感想 [Reflections on the old family system], *Xin chao* 1.2 (February 1919): 161–63.

Guang Sheng 光升. "Zhongguo guominxing ji qi ruodian" 中國國民性及其弱點 [Chinese national character and its weaknesses]. *Xin qingnian* 2.6 (1917): 495–505.

Gunn, Edward M., Jr. "Perceptions of Self and Values in Recent Chinese Literature." In Hegel and Hessney, eds., *Expressions of Self in Chinese Literature* (q.v.), 308–41.

———. *Rewriting Chinese: Style and Innovation in Twentieth-Century Chinese Prose.* Stanford, Calif.: Stanford University Press, 1991.

Guo Moruo 郭沫若. *Ganlan* 橄欖 [Olives]. Shanghai: Chuangzaoshe chubanbu, 1926.

———. *Luo ye* 落葉 [Fallen leaf] (1926). Shanghai: Guanghua shuju, 1934.

———. *Wo de younian* 我的幼年 [Years of my youth]. (1929). Rpt., *Wo de tongnian* 我的童年 [My childhood years]. Hong Kong: Wenxue chubanshe, 1956.

Gutman, Huck. "Rousseau's *Confessions*: A Technology of the Self." In Luther H. Martin, Huck Gutman, and Patricia H. Hutton, eds., *Technologies of the Self: A Seminar with Michel Foucault.* Amherst: University of Massachusetts Press, 1988, 99–120.

Habermas, Jürgen. "Modernity Versus Postmodernity." Trans. Seyla Benhabib. *New German Critique* 22 (winter 1981): 3–15.

———. *The Philosophical Discourse of Modernity: Twelve Lectures.* Trans. Frederick Lawrence. Cambridge, Mass.: The MIT Press, 1987. Trans. of *Der philosophische Diskurs der Moderne: Zwölf Vorlesungen.* Frankfurt: Suhrkamp, 1985.

Han Shaogong 韓少功. "Ba Ba Ba" 爸爸爸 [Pa Pa Pa]. *Renmin wenxue* 309 (1985.6): 83–102.

———. "Guiqulai" 歸去來 [Homecoming]. *Shanghai wenxue* 93 (1985.6): 30–37.

———. "Nü Nü Nü" 女女女 [Woman, woman, woman]. *Renmin wenxue* (1986). Rpt., Han Shaogong, *Ba Ba Ba.* Changchun: Shidai wenyi chubanshe, 2001, 42–90.

———. "Wenxue de gen" 文學的根 [The roots of literature]. *Zuojia* 作家 [The writer] (1985.4): 2–5.

Hanan, Patrick, trans. *The Sea of Regret: Two Turn-of-the-Century Romantic Novels.* Honolulu: University of Hawai'i Press, 1995.

———. "The Technique of Lu Hsün's Fiction." *Harvard Journal of Asiatic Studies* 34 (1974): 53–96.

Handwerk, Gary J. *Irony and Ethics in Narrative: From Schlegel to Lacan.* New Haven, Conn.: Yale University Press, 1985.

Hao, Chang. *Chinese Intellectuals in Crisis: Search for Order and Meaning, 1890–1911.* Berkeley: University of California Press, 1987.

Hao Ran 浩然. *Bright Clouds.* Trans. Tung Chen-sheng and Chen Yu-hsien. Beijing: Foreign Language Press, 1974.

———. "Caixia" 彩霞 [Bright clouds]. *Renmin wenxue* (1962.2): 49–54. Rpt., Li Guowen, ed., *Zhongguo dangdai wenxue zuopin jingxuan* (q.v.), 468–79. Trans. Tung Chen-Sheng and Chen Yu-Hsien. In Hao Ran, *Bright Clouds* (q.v.), 61–76.

———. "Xing hua yu" 杏花雨 [Apricot blossom rain] (1962). Rpt., *Xing hua yu.* Shanghai: Zuojia chubanshe, 1964, 136–51.

Harrington, Mona. *Care and Equality.* New York: Knopf, 1999.

Harvey, David. *The Condition of Postmodernity: An Enquiry into the Origins of Cultural Change.* Cambridge, Mass.: Basil Blackwell, 1990.

Hauser, Arnold. *The Social History of Art.* 4 vols. New York: Knopf, 1951.

Hegel, Robert. *The Novel in Seventeenth-Century China.* New York: Columbia University Press, 1981.

Hegel, Robert, and Richard Hessney, eds. *Expressions of Self in Chinese Literature.* New York: Columbia University Press, 1985.

Hegel, W. G. F. *Faith and Knowledge.* Trans. Walter Cerf and H. S. Harris. Albany: State University of New York Press, 1977.

Heidegger, Martin. "Der Europäische Nihilismus" [European nihilism]. In *Nietzsche,* vol. 2. Pfullingen: Günther Neske, 1961.

Holoch, Donald. "A Novel of Setting: *The Bureaucrats.*" In Dolezelová-Velingerová, ed., *The Chinese Novel* (q.v.), 129–49.

Holquist, Michael. *Dialogism: Bakhtin and His World.* London: Routledge, 1990.

Hong Lingfei 洪靈非. *Liuwang* 流亡 [Exile]. Shanghai: Xiandai shuju, 1928.

Horkheimer, Max, and Theodor Adorno. *Dialektik der Aufklärung* [Dialectic of Enlightenment] (1944). Frankfurt: S. Fischer, 1969. Trans. John Cumming. *Dialectic of Enlightenment.* New York: Herder and Herder, 1972.

Hsia, C. T. *A History of Modern Chinese Fiction, 1917–1957,* 2nd ed. New Haven, Conn.: Yale University Press, 1971.

———. "Obsession with China: The Moral Burden of Modern Chinese Fiction." In Hsia, *A History of Modern Chinese Fiction* (q.v.), 533–36.

Hsu, Kai-yu. *The Chinese Literary Scene: A Writer's Visit to the People's Republic.* New York: Vintage, 1975.

Hu Shi 胡適. "Buxiu" 不朽 [Immortality]. *Xin qingnian* 6.2 (1919): 113–22.

———. "Wenxue gailiang chuyi" 文學改良芻議 [Suggestions for a reform of literature]. *Xin qingnian* 2.5 (January 1917): 1–11. Trans. Kirk Denton. In Denton, ed., *Modern Chinese Literary Thought* (q.v.), 123–39.

Hu Yepin 胡也頻. *Guangming zai women de mianqian* 光明在我們的面前 [The light is before us]. Shanghai: Chunqiu shudian, 1930.

Huang Ziping 黃子平, Chen Pingyuan 陳平原, and Qian Liqun 錢理群. "Lun 'Ershi shiji Zhongguo wenxue'" 論'二十世紀中國文學.' *Wenxue pinglun* (1985.5): 3–13.

Huters, Theodore. "Blossoms in the Snow: Lu Xun and the Dilemma of Modern Chinese Literature." *Modern China* 10.1 (January 1984): 49–77.

———. "From Writing to Literature: The Development of Late-Qing Theories of Prose." *Harvard Journal of Asiatic Studies* 47.1 (June 1987): 51–96.

———. "Ideologies of Realism in Modern China: The Hard Imperatives of Imported Theory." In Liu and Tang, eds., *Politics, Ideology, and Literary Discourse in Modern China* (q.v.), 147–73.

———. "A New Way of Writing: The Possibilities for Literature in Late Qing China, 1895–1908." *Modern China* 14.3 (1988): 243–76.

Huyssens, Andreas. "Mapping the Postmodern." *New German Critique* 33 (fall 1984): 5–52.

Inge, M. Thomas. "Mo Yan and William Faulkner: Influences and Confluences." *The Faulkner Journal* 6.1 (fall 1990): 15–24.

James, William. *Pragmatism: A New Name for Some Old Ways of Thinking.* New York: Longmans, Green and Co., 1931.

Jameson, Fredric. "Third-World Literature in the Era of Multinational Capitalism." *Social Text: Theory, Culture, Ideology* 15 (1986): 65–88.

Jenner, W. J. F. "Is a Modern Chinese Literature Possible?" In Wolfgang Kubin and Rudolph G. Wagner, eds., *Essays in Modern Chinese Literature and Literary Criticism.* Bochum, Germany: Brockmeyer, 1982, 192–230.

Jia Pingwa 賈平凹. *Feidu* 廢都 [The abandoned capital]. Beijing: Beijing chubanshe, 1993.

Jiang Zilong 蔣子龍. "Qiao changzhang houzhuan" 喬廠長後傳 [Sequel to the story of Manager Qiao]. *Renmin wenxue* 245 (1980.2). Rpt., Li Yi, ed. *Zhongguo xin xieshi zhuyi wenyi zuopinxuan* (q.v.), 269–87.

———. "Qiao changzhang shangren ji" 喬廠長上任記 [Manager Qiao assumes office]. *Renmin wenxue* 238 (1979.7): 3–26. Rpt., Tang Dacheng, ed. *Zhongguo xin wenyi daxi: 1976–1982 duanpian xiaoshuo ji* (q.v.), 1: 394–419.

———. "'Qiao changzhang shangren ji' de shenghuo zhang" '喬廠長上任記'的生活帳 [A life account of 'Manager Qiao assumes office']. *Shiyue* 十月 [October] 6 (1979.4): 13–17.

Kahn, Charles H. "Discovering the Will: From Aristotle to Augustine." In John M. Dillon and A. A. Long, eds., *The Question of "Eclecticism": Studies in Later Greek Philosophy.* Berkeley and Los Angeles: University of California Press, 1988, 234–59.

Ke Fei 克非. *Chun chao liu* 春潮流 [Swift is the spring tide]. 2 vols. Shanghai: Shanghai renmin chubanshe, 1974.

Kenny, Anthony. *Aristotle's Theory of the Will.* New Haven, Conn.: Yale University Press, 1979.

Kinkley, Jeffrey C., ed. *After Mao: Chinese Literature and Society, 1978–1981.* Cambridge, Mass.: Harvard University Press, 1985.

———. "The New Chinese Literature: The Mainland and Beyond." *CHOICE: Current Reviews of Academic Books* 31.8 (April 1994): 1249–65.

———. *The Odyssey of Shen Congwen.* Stanford, Calif.: Stanford University Press, 1987.

———. "Shen Congwen's Legacy in Literature of the 1980s." In Widmer and Wang, eds., *From May Fourth to June Fourth* (q.v.), 71–106.

Kipnis, Laura. "Adultery." *Critical Inquiry* 24 (winter 1998): 289–327.

Kittay, Eva Feder. *Love's Labor: Essays on Women, Equality, and Dependency.* New York: Routledge, 1999.

Knight, Deirdre Sabina. "Agency Beyond Subjectivity: The Unredeemed Project of May Fourth Fiction." *Journal of Modern Literature in Chinese* 1.2 (1998): 1–36.

———. "Capitalist and Enlightenment Values in 1990s Chinese Fiction: The Case of Yu Hua's *Blood Seller.*" *Textual Practice* 16.3 (winter 2002): 547–68.

———. "Decadence, Revolution and Self-Determination in Su Tong's Fiction." *Modern Chinese Literature* 10 (1998): 91–111.

———. "Gendered Fate." In Lupke, ed., *The Magnitude of Ming* (q.v.), 272–90.

———. Review of *The Other Shore: Plays by Gao Xingjian* (trans. Gilbert Fong Hong Kong: The Chinese University Press, 1999). *Journal of Asian Studies* 61.1 (2002): 216–18.

———. "Scar Literature and the Memory of Trauma." *The Columbia Companion to Modern East Asian Literature.* Ed. Joshua Mostow. New York: Columbia University Press, 2003, 527–32.

———. "Shanghai Cosmopolitan: Class, Gender and Cultural Citizenship in Weihui's Fiction." *Journal of Contemporary China* 12.37 (November 2003): 639–53.

Kong, Haili. "The Spirit of 'Native-Soil' in the Fictional World of Duanmu Hongliang and Mo Yan." *China Information* 11.4 (1997): 58–67.

LaCapra, Dominick. *History and Criticism.* Ithaca, N.Y., and London: Cornell University Press, 1985.

Lao She 老舍. "Yue'yar" 月牙兒 [Moon crescent]. In *Yinghaiji* 櫻海集 [Cherries and the sea]. Shanghai: Renjian shuwu, 1935. Rpt., Shu Ji 舒濟, ed. *Lao She* 老舍. Hong Kong: Sanlian shudian, 1988, 107–32.

Laplace, Pierre Simon. *Théorie analytique des probabilities.* Paris: V Courceir, 1820. Trans. F. W. Truscott and F. L. Emory. *A Philosophical Essay on Probabilities.* New York: Dover, 1951.

Larson, Wendy, and Richard Kraus. "China's Writers, the Nobel Prize and the International Politics of Literature." *Australian Journal of Chinese Affairs* 21 (January 1989): 143–60.

Lau, D. C, trans. *Mencius.* 2 vols. Hong Kong: The Chinese University Press, 1984.

Lau, Joseph S. M. (Liu Shaoming). "China Deconstructs: The Emergence of Counter-Traditions in Recent Chinese Writing." *The Stockholm Journal of East Asian Studies* 5 (1994): 25–35.

———. "The Wounded and the Fatigued: Reflections on Post-1976 Chinese Fiction." *Journal of Oriental Studies* 20 (1982): 128–42.

Lau, Joseph S. M., and Howard Goldblatt, eds. *The Columbia Anthology of Modern Chinese Literature.* New York: Columbia University Press, 1995.

Lee, Leo Ou-fan (Li Oufan). "Afterword: Reflections on Change and Continuity in Modern Chinese Fiction." In Widmer and Wang, eds., *From May Fourth to June Fourth* (q.v.), 361–83.

———. "Genesis of a Writer: Notes on Lu Xun's Eduational Experience, 1881–1909." In Goldman, ed., *Modern Chinese Literature in the May Fourth Era* (q.v.), 161–88.

———. "The Politics of Technique: Perspectives of Literary Dissidence in Contemporary Chinese Fiction." In Kinkley, ed., *After Mao* (q.v.), 159–90.

———. *The Romantic Generation of Modern Chinese Writers.* Cambridge, Mass.: Harvard University Press, 1973.

———. "In Search of Modernity: Some Reflections on a New Mode of Consciousness in Twentieth-Century Chinese History and Literature." In Paul Cohen and Merle Goldman, eds., *Ideas Across Cultures: Essays on Chinese Thought in Honor of Benjamin I. Schwartz.* Cambridge, Mass.: Harvard University Press, 1990, 109–35.

———. "The Solitary Traveler: Images of Self in Modern Chinese Fiction." In Hegel and Hessney, eds., *Expressions of Self in Chinese Literature* (q.v.), 282–307.

Lee, Yee (Li Yi), ed. *The New Realism: Writings from China after the Cultural Revolution.* New York: Hippocrene, 1983.

Lemon, Lee T., and Marion J. Reis, eds. *Russian Formalist Criticism: Four Essays.* Lincoln: University of Nebraska Press, 1965.

Leys, Simon, trans. *The Analects of Confucius.* New York: W. W. Norton, 1997.

Li Boyuan 李伯元. *Guanchang xianxing ji* 官場現形記 [Record of the operations of official circles] (1901–1906). Nanchang: Jiangxi renmin chubanshe, 1989.

Li Dazhao 李大釗. *Li Dazhao xuanji* 李大釗選集 [Selected writings of Li Dazhao]. Beijing: Renmin chubanshe, 1959.

———. "Qingchun" 青春 [Spring]. *Xin qingnian* 2.1 (September 1, 1916): 1–12.

Li Guowen 李國文, ed. *Zhongguo dangdai wenxue zuopin jingxuan (1949-1999): Duanpian xiaoshuo juan* 中國當代文學作品精選 (1949–1999)。短篇小說卷 [Choice selections of contemporary Chinese Literature 1949–1999: Short Stories]. 2 vols. Beijing: Beijing shiyue wenyi chubanshe, 1999.

Li Hangyu 李杭育. "Renjian yi yu" 人間一隅 [A corner of the human world] (1983). Rpt., Zheng Shusen, ed. *Xiandai Zhongguo xiaoshuo xuan* (q.v.), 5: 1999–2018.

Li Jieren 李劼人. *Baofengyu qian* 暴風雨前 [Before the storm] (1936). 2nd ed. 1955. Rpt., Hong Kong: Guang jiao jing chubanshe, 1977.

———. *Dabo* 大波 [Great wave] (1937). 2nd ed. 1956. 4 vols. Rpt., Beijing: Zuojia chubanshe, 1963.

———. *Sishui weilan* 死水微瀾 [Ripples on dead water] (1936). 2nd ed. 1955. Rpt., Hong Kong: Guang jiao jing chubanshe, 1977.

Li Oufan 李歐梵 (Leo Ou-fan Lee). "Zhongguo xiandai xiaoshuo de xianquzhe" 中過現代小說的先驅者 [The forerunners of modern Chinese fiction]. In Li Oufan, ed., *Xinganjuepai xiaoshuo xuan* 新感覺派小說選 [Selections of fiction of the new sensibilities school]. Taipei: Yunchen wenhua shiye gufen youxian gongsi, 1988, 1–16.

Li Ruqing 黎汝清. *Wan shan hong bian* 萬山紅遍 [Ten thousand red-bordered mountains]. 2 vols. Beijing: Renmin wenxue chubanshe, 1976.

Li Tuo 李陀. "1985." *Jintian* 今天 [Today] 3/4 (1991): 59–73. Trans. Anne Wedell-Wedellsborg. In Henry Zhao and John Cayley, eds., *Under-Sky Underground: Chinese Writing Today*. London: Wellsweep, 1994, 115–30.

Li Tuo, Zhang Ling 張陵, and Wang Bin 王斌. "Yuyan de fanpan: Jinliangnian xiaoshuo xianxiang" "語言"的反叛—近兩年小說現象 [The revolt of language: Fictional phenomena of the last two years]. *Wenyi yanjiu* 文藝研究 (1989.2): 75–80.

Li Yi 李怡 (Lee Yee). "Wenyi xinzuo zhong suo fanying de Zhongguo xianshi: Daixu" 文藝新作中所反映的中國現實：代序 [Chinese reality as reflected in recent literary works: By way of introduction]. In Li yi, ed., *Zhongguo xin xieshi zhuyi wenyi zuopinxuan* (q.v.), 2–9.

———. *Zhongguo xin xieshi zhuyi wenyi zuopinxuan* 中國新寫實主義文藝作品選 [Selected works of Chinese new realist literature]. Hong Kong: Qishi niandai zazhishe, 1980.

Li Yizhi 李亦氏. "Rensheng weiyi zhi mudi" 人生唯一之目的 [The sole purpose of life]. *Qingnian zazhi* 1.2 (October 1915): 125–32.

Liang Qichao 梁啓超. "Lun xiaoshuo yu qunzhi zhi guanxi" 論小說與群治之關係 [On the relationship between fiction and the government of the people]. *Xin xiaoshuo* (1902). Rpt., Xu Zhongyu, ed. *Zhongguo jindai wenxue daxi* (q.v.), 302–3. Trans. Gek Nai Cheng. In Denton, ed., *Modern Chinese Literary Thought* (q.v.), 74–81.

———. "Yi yin zhengzhi xiaoshuo xu" 譯印政治小說序 [Forward to the publication of political novels in translation]. *Qing yi bao* 清議報 1 (December 1898). Rpt., Xu Zhongyu, ed. *Zhongguo jindai wenxue daxi* (q.v.), 303–8. Trans. Gek Nai Cheng. In Denton, ed., *Modern Chinese Literary Thought* (q.v.), 71–73.

Lin Shu 林紓. "*Kuairou yusheng shu* qianbian xu" 塊肉余生述前邊序 [Preface to part 1 of *David Copperfield*]. In *Kuai rou yusheng shu* 塊肉余生述. Shanghai: Shangwu, 1908. Trans. Yenna Wu. In Denton, ed., *Modern Chinese Literary Thought* (q.v.), 84–86.

Link, E. Perry, Jr. *Mandarin Ducks and Butterflies: Popular Fiction in Early Twentieth-Century Chinese Cities.* Berkeley: University of California Press, 1981.

———, ed. *Stubborn Weeds: Popular and Controversial Chinese Literature after the Cultural Revolution.* Bloomington: Indiana University Press, 1983.

———. *The Uses of Literature: Life in the Socialist Chinese Literary System.* Princeton, N.J.: Princeton University Press, 2000.

Liu E 劉鶚. *Laocan youji* 老殘遊記 [The travels of Lao Ts'an]. Hong Kong: Guangxin chubanshe, n.d.

———. *The Travels of Lao Ts'an.* Trans. Harold Shadick. New York: Columbia University Press, 1990.

Liu Heng 劉恆. *Canghe bairi meng* 蒼河白日夢 [Daydream on the Cang river]. Beijing: Zhojia chubanshe, 1993.

Liu, James J. Y. *The Chinese Knight-Errant.* Chicago: University of Chicago Press, 1967.

———. *Chinese Theories of Literature.* Chicago: University of Chicago Press, 1975.

Liu Kang and Xiaobing Tang, eds. *Politics, Ideology, and Literary Discourse in Modern China: Theoretical Interventions and Cultural Critique.* Durham, N.C.: Duke University Press, 1993.

Liu Ke 劉克. "Feitian" 飛天 [Feitian]. *Shiyue* 5 (1979.3): 116–39.

Liu, Lydia H. *Translingual Practice: Literature, National Culture, and Translated Modernity—China, 1900–1937.* Stanford, Calif.: Stanford University Press, 1995.

Liu Shaoming 劉紹明 (Joseph S. M. Lau) and Huang Weiliang 黃維樑, eds. *Zhongguo xiandai zhong duanpian xiaoshuo xuan* 中國現代中短篇小說選 [Selections of modern Chinese novellas and short stories]. 2 vols. Hong Kong: Youlian chubanshe, 1984.

Liu Xinwu 劉心武. "Banzhuren" 班主任 [Schoolmaster]. *Renmin wenxue* 219 (1977.11): 16–29. Rpt., Tang Dacheng, ed., *Zhongguo xin wenyi daxi: 1976–1982 duanpian xiaoshuo ji* (q.v.), 1: 4–18.

Liu Zaifu 劉再復. "Wenxue de zhutixing" 文學的主體性 [Literature's subjectivity]. *Wenxue pinglun* (1985.6): 11–26 and (1986.1): 3–19. Rpt., Liu Zaifu. *Liu Zaifu ji* 劉再復集 [Works of Liu Zaifu]. Harbin: Heilongjiang jiaoyu chubanshe, 1988, 72–125.

———. "Zhongguo chuantong wenhua dui ren de sheji" 中國傳統文化對人的設計 [Traditional Chinese culture's designs on humanity]. In Liu Zaifu and Lin Gang 林崗. *Chuantong yu Zhongguoren* 傳統與中國人 [Tradition and the Chinese]. Hong Kong: Sanlian shudian, 1988, 375–92.

Liu Zaifu and Lin Gang 林崗. "Zhongguo xiandai xiaoshuo zhong de zhengzhishi xiezuo moshi: Cong 'Chun can' dao 'Taiyang zhao zai sang gan shang'" 中國現代小說的政治式寫作—從'春蠶'到'太陽照在桑乾上'. [The political mode of writing in modern Chinese fiction: From *Spring silkworms* to *The sun shines over the Sanggan river*]. In Tang Xiaobing, ed., *Zai jiedu* (q.v.), 90–107.

Louie, Kam. *Between Fact and Fiction: Essays on Post-Mao Chinese Literature and Society.* Broadway, NSW, Australia: Wild Peony, 1989.

Lovell, Julia. "Gao Xingjian, the Nobel Prize, and Chinese Intellectuals: Notes on the Aftermath of the Nobel Prize 2000." *Modern Chinese Literature and Culture* 14.2 (fall 2002): 1–50.

Lu, Tonglin. *Misogyny, Cultural Nihilism, and Oppositional Politics: Contemporary Chinese Experimental Fiction.* Stanford, Calif.: Stanford University Press, 1995.

Lu Wenfu 陸文夫. "Meishijia" 美食家 [The gourmet]. *Shouhuo* 39 (1983.1): 4–45.

Lu Xinhua 盧新華. "Shanghen" 傷痕 [Scar]. *Wenhui bao,* August 11, 1978. Rpt., Tang Dacheng, ed. *Zhongguo xin wenyi daxi: 1976–1982 duanpian xiaoshuo ji* (q.v.), 1: 140–47.

Lu Xun 魯訊 (Zhou Shuren 周樹人). *A Brief History of Chinese Fiction* (1959). Trans. Yang Hsien-yi and Gladys Yang. Rpt., Beijing: Foreign Language Press, 1982.

———. *Lu Xun quanji* 魯訊全集 [Collected works of Lu Xun]. 20 vols. Beijing: Renmin wenxue chubanshe, 1973.

———. "On the Power of Mara Poetry." Trans. Shu-ying Tsau and Donald Holoch. In Denton, ed., *Modern Chinese Literary Thought* (q.v.), 96–109.

———. *Selected Stories of Lu Hsun* (1960). Trans. Yang Hsien-yi and Gladys Yang. New York: W. W. Norton, 1977.

———. *Zhongguo xiaoshuo shi lue* 中國小說史論 [A brief history of Chinese fiction]. Beijing: Beijing shuju, 1923–25.

Luker, Nicolas, ed. "Introduction." In Nicolas Luker, ed., *From Furmanov to Shokolov: An Anthology of Classics of Socialist Realism.* Ann Arbor, Mich.: Ardis, 1988, 11–38.

Luo He 羅禾. "Wan Qing xiaoshuo zhuanji" 晚清小說專輯 [Special dossier on late Qing fiction]. *Lianhe wenxue* 聯合文學 [UNITAS: a literary monthly] 1.6 (1985): 10–18.

Luo Jialun 羅家倫 (pseud. Yi 毅). "Wusi yundong de jingshen" 五四運動的精神 [The spirit of the May Fourth movement]. *Meizhou pinglun* 每週評論 23 (May 26, 1919): 1.

Lupke, Christopher, *The Magnitude of Ming: Essays on Command, Allotment, Life and Fate in Chinese Culture.* Honolulu: University of Hawai'i Press, 2004.

Lyell, William, trans. *Lu Xun: Diary of a Madman and Other Stories.* Honolulu: University of Hawai'i Press, 1990.

Ma Yuan 馬原. "Gangdisi de youhuo" 岡底斯的誘惑 [Spell of the Gangtise mountains]. *Shanghai wenxue* 89 (1985.2): 47–65.

———. "Ximalaya guge" 西馬拉雅古歌 [Old Himalayan song] (1986). Rpt., *Ma Yuan wenji* 馬原文集. Vol. 3. *Ai wu* 愛物. Beijing: Zuojia chubanshe, 1997, 86–102. Trans. Chantal Chen-Andro. "Vieille chanson himalayenne." In Curien, ed., *Anthologie* (q.v.), 211–30.

———. "Youshen" 游神 [Vagrant spirit]. *Shanghai wenxue* 112 (1987.1): 4–12.

MacIntyre, Alasdair. *After Virtue.* 2nd ed. Notre Dame, Ind.: University of Notre Dame Press, 1984.

Mao Dun 茅盾 (Shen Yanbing 沈雁冰). "Chuncan" 春蠶 [Spring silkworms]. *Xiandai* 現代 [Les contemporains] 2.1 (November 1932). Rpt., *Mao Dun quanji* (q.v.), 8: 312–37.

———. *Hong* 虹 [Rainbow] (1929), *Mao Dun quanji* (q.v.), 2: 1–271.

———. *Lu* 路 [Road] (1931), *Mao Dun quanji* (q.v.), 2: 275–380.

———. *Mao Dun quanji* 茅盾全集 [Complete works of Mao Dun]. 33 vols. Beijing: Renmin wenxue chubanshe, 1984–85.

———. *Shi* 蝕 [Eclipse] (1927–1928), *Mao Dun quanji* (q.v.), 1: 3–430.

———. "Ziranzhuyi yu Zhongguo xiandai xiaoshuo" 自然主義與中國現代小說 [Naturalism and modern Chinese fiction] (1922). Rpt., *Mao Dun quanji* (q.v.), 18: 225–26.

Mao Zedong 毛澤東. "On the People's Democratic Dictatorship." In Mao, *Selected Works* (q.v.), 4: 411–24.

———. *Selected Works of Mao Tse-tung.* 5 vols. Beijing: Foreign Language Press, 1975.

———. "Xin minzhuzhuyi lun" 新民主主義論 [On new democracy]. *Zhongguo wenhua* 中國文化 1 (February 15, 1940). Trans. *Selected Works of Mao Tse-tung* (q.v.), 2: 339–84.

———. "Zai Yan'an wenyi zuotanhui shang de jianghua" 在延安文藝座談會上的講話 [Talks at the Yan'an Forum on Literature and Art]. (1942). *Jiefang ribao* 解放日報 October 19, 1943. Trans. McDougall, *Mao Zedong's "Talks at the Yan'an Conference"* (q.v.).

Martin, Helmut, and Jeffrey Kinkley, eds. *Modern Chinese Writers: Self-Portrayals.* Armonk, N.Y.: M.E. Sharpe, 1992.

Marx, Karl. "Economic and Philosophic Manuscripts of 1844." In Robert C. Tucker, ed., *The Marx-Engels Reader*, 2nd ed. New York: W. W. Norton, 1978, 66–125.

———. *The Eighteenth Brumaire of Louis Bonaparte* (1852). Rpt., New York: International Publishers, 1975.

McDougall, Bonnie S. *The Introduction of Western Literary Theories into Modern China, 1919–1925.* Tokyo: Center for East Asian Cultural Studies, 1971.

———. *Mao Zedong's "Talks at the Yan'an Conference on Literature and Art": A Translation of the 1943 Text with Commentary.* Ann Arbor: University of Michigan Center for Chinese Studies, 1980.

McDougall, Bonnie S., and Kam Louie. *The Literature of China in the Twentieth Century.* New York: Columbia University Press, 1997.

Meisner, Maurice. *Li Dazhao and the Origins of Chinese Marxism.* Cambridge, Mass.: Harvard University Press, 1967.

Metzger, Thomas. *Escape from Predicament: Neo-Confucianism and China's Evolving Political Culture.* New York: Columbia University Press, 1977.

Mills, Harriet C. "Literature in Fetters." In Ross Terrill, ed., *The China Difference.* New York: Harper and Row, 1979, 285–304.

———. "Lu Xun: Literature and Revolution—From Mara to Marx." In Goldman, ed., *Modern Chinese Literature in the May Fourth Era* (q.v.), 189–220.

Mo Yan 莫言 (Guan Moye 管謨業). "Bai gou qiuqianjia" 白夠鞦韆架 [White dog and the swing] (1985). Rpt., Mo Yan. *Jinfa ying'er* 金髮嬰兒 [The golden-haired baby]. Wuhan: Changjiang wenyi chubanshe, 1993, 50–69.

———. *Hong gaoliang jiazu* 紅高粱家族 [Red sorghum family]. Beijing: Jiafangjun wenyi, 1987. Rpt., Taipei: Hongfan shudian, 1988. Trans. Howard Goldblatt. *Red Sorghum: A Novel of China.* New York: Viking, 1993.

———. *Jiu guo* 酒國 [Liquorland]. Taipei: Hongfan shudian, 1992.

———. *Shisan bu* 十三步 [Thirteen steps]. Taipei: Hongfan shudian, 1990.

———. *Tiantang suantai zhi ge* 天堂蒜臺之歌 [The garlic ballads]. Taipei: Hongfan shudian, 1989.

Morson, Gary Saul. *Narrative and Freedom: The Shadows of Time.* New Haven, Conn.: Yale University Press, 1994.

Nan Fan 南帆. "Zai xushi: Xianfeng xiaoshuo de jingdi" 再敘事：先鋒小說的境地 [Re-narrate: The condition of avant-garde fiction]. *Wenxue pinglun* (1993.3): 21–32.

Ng, Mau-sang. *The Russian Hero in Modern Chinese Fiction.* Hong Kong: The Chinese University Press; Albany: State University of New York Press, 1988.

Ngai, Ling Tun. *Politics of Sexuality: The Fiction of Zhang Xianliang, Mo Yan and Wang Anyi.* Ann Arbor, Mich.: UMI, 1994.

Nieh, Hualing, ed. *Literature of the Hundred Flowers.* 2 vols. New York: Columbia University Press, 1981.

Nozick, Robert. *Anarchy, State, and Utopia.* New York: Basic Books, 1974.

Nussbaum, Martha C. "The Future of Feminist Liberalism." *Proceedings and Addresses of the American Philosophical Association* 74.2 (November 2000): 47–79.

———. *Women and Human Development: The Capabilities Approach.* Cambridge: Cambridge University Press, 2000.

Onega, Susana, and José Angel García, eds. *Narratology: An Introduction.* London: Longman, 1996.

Owen, Stephen. *An Anthology of Chinese Literature: Beginnings to 1911.* New York and London: Norton, 1996.

Pan Kaixiong 潘凱雄. "'Zijue' wei ta dailai le shenma?—Du Li Rui jinzuo" "自覺"爲他帶來了甚麼？讀李鋭近作 [What has "self-consciousness" brought him? Reading Li Rui's recent works]. *Wenxue pinglun* (1994.1): 118–21.

Pickowicz, Paul. "Qu Qiubai's Critique of the May Fourth Generation: Early Chinese Marxist Literary Criticism." In Goldman, ed., *Modern Chinese Literature in the May Fourth Era* (q.v.), 351–84.

Pirazzoli, Melinda. "The Free-Market Economy and Contemporary Chinese Literature." *World Literature Today* 70.2 (Spring 1996): 301–10.

Plaks, Andrew. *The Four Masterworks of the Ming Novel: Ssu ta ch'i-shu.* Princeton, N.J.: Princeton University Press, 1987.

———. "Terminology and Central Concepts." In David L. Rolston, ed., *How to Read the Chinese Novel.* Princeton, N.J.: Princeton University Press, 1990, 73–123.

Pollard, David E. "The Short Story in the Cultural Revolution." *China Quarterly* 73 (March 1978): 99–121.

Pomfret, John. "The New Censorship in China: Anatomy of a Book-Banning." *The Boston Sunday Globe* (2 July 2000): A16.

Price, Donald. *Russia and the Roots of Chinese Revolution.* Cambridge, Mass.: Harvard University Press, 1974.

Průšek, Jaroslav. "Introduction to *Studies in Modern Chinese Literature.*" Originally published in German in *Studien zur modernen Chinesischen Literatur.* Berlin: Akademie-Verlag, 1964. Rpt., *The Lyrical and the Epic* (q.v.), 29–73.

———. *The Lyrical and the Epic: Studies of Modern Chinese Literature.* Ed. Leo Ou-fan Lee. Bloomington: Indiana University Press, 1980.

———. "Subjectivism and Individualism in Modern Chinese Literature." *Archiv Orientální* 25 (1957): 261–83. Rpt., *The Lyrical and the Epic* (q.v.), 1–28.

Pruyn, Carolyn S. *Humanism in Modern Chinese Literature: The Case of Dai Houying.* Bochum, Germany: Brockmeyer, 1988.

Qian Xingcun 錢杏邨. "Siqu le de A Q shidai" 死去了的阿Q時代 [The bygone age of Ah Q]. *Taiyang yuekan* 太陽月刊 [Sun society monthly] (March 1928). Trans. Paul Foster and Sherry Mou. In Denton, ed., *Modern Chinese Literary Thought* (q.v.), 276–88.

———. "Zhongguo xinxing wenxue zhong de jige juti de wenti" 中國新興文學中的幾個具體問題 [Several concrete problems concerning China's new literature], *Tuohuangzhe* 1.1 (10 January 1930): 341–82. Rpt., *Geming wenxue lunzheng ziliao xuanbian* (q.v.), 2: 915–46.

Qu Qiubai 瞿秋白 (pseud. Song Yang 宋陽). "Dazhong wenyi de wenti" 大眾文藝的問題 [On the problem of mass literature and art]. *Wenxue yuebao* 1.5 (10 June 1932). Rpt., Shanghai wenyi chubanshe, ed. *Zhongguo xin wenxue daxi, 1927–1937: Wenxue lilun ji* (q.v.), 2: 347–55.

Radin, Margaret Jane. *Contested Commodities.* Cambridge, Mass.: Harvard University Press, 1996.

Raz, Joseph. *The Morality of Freedom.* Oxford: Oxford University Press, 1986.

Robin, Regine. *Socialist Realism: The Impossible Aesthetic.* Trans. Catherine Porter. Stanford, Calif.: Stanford University Press, 1992.

Robinet, Isabelle. *Taoism: Growth of a Religion.* Trans. Phyllis Brooks. Stanford, Calif.: Stanford University Press, 1997.

Rolston, David L., ed. *Traditional Chinese Fiction and Fiction Commentary: Reading and Writing Between the Lines.* Stanford, Calif.: Stanford University Press, 1997.

Rou Shi 柔石. *Eryue* 二月 [February]. Shanghai: Chunchao shuju, 1929.

———. "Wei nuli de muqin" 爲奴隸的母親 [Slave mother] (1930). In Liu Shaoming and Huang Weiliang, eds., *Zhongguo xiandia zhong duanpian xiaoshuo xuan* (q.v.), 1: 285–306.

Sabin, Margery. "Lu Xun: Individual Talent and Revolution." *Raritan* 9.1 (Summer 1989): 41–67.

Sangren, P. Steven. "Dialectics of Alienation." *Man* 26 (1991): 67–86.

Santangelo, Paolo. "Destiny and Retribution in Late Imperial China." *East and West* 42.2–4 (December 1992): 377–442.

Sartre, Jean-Paul. *L'être et le néant* [Being and nothingness]. Paris: Gallimard, 1943.

———. *L'existentialisme est un humanisme* [Existentialism is a humanism]. Paris: Nagel, 1946.

———. *Qu'est-ce que la littérature?* [What is literature?]. Paris: Gallimard, 1948.

Schram, Stuart. *The Political Thought of Mao Tse-tung.* New York: Frederick A. Praeger, 1972.

Schwarcz, Vera. *The Chinese Enlightenment: Intellectuals and the Legacy of the May Fourth Movement of 1919.* Berkeley: University of California Press, 1986.

Schwartz, Benjamin. *In Search of Wealth and Power: Yen Fu and the West.* Cambridge, Mass.: Harvard University Press, 1964.

Sen, Amartya. *Development as Freedom.* New York: Knopf, 1999.

Shanghai wenyi chubanshe 上海文藝出版社, ed. *Zhongguo xin wenxue daxi, 1927–1937* 中國新文學大系，1927–1937 [Anthology of Modern Chinese Literature, 1927–1937]. 20 vols. Vol. 2. *Wenxue lilun ji* 文學理論集 [Literary criticism, part 2]. Shanghai: Shanghai wenyi chubanshe, 1987.

Shen Rong 諶容. "Jianqu shisui" 減去十歲 [Ten years deducted]. *Renmin wenxue* 317 (1986.2): 7–18.

———. "Ren dao zhongnian" 人到中年 [At middle age]. *Shouhuo* 21 (1980.1): 52–92.

———. *Wannianqing* 萬年青 [Evergreen]. Beijing: Renmin wenxue chubanshe, 1975.

Shi Tiesheng 史鐵生. "Ming ruo qinxian" 命若琴弦 [Life like a lute string]. *Xiandai ren* 現代人 (1985.2). Rpt., Li Guowen, ed. *Zhongguo dangdai wenxue zuopin jingxuan* (q.v.), 1: 878–900.

Shklovsky, Viktor. "Iskusstvo kak priëm" (1917). Trans. Lee Lemon and Marion Reis. "Art as Technique." In Lee T. Lemon and Marion J. Reis, eds., *Russian Formalist Criticism: Four Essays.* Lincoln: University of Nebraska Press, 1965, 3–24.

Skinner, B. F. *Beyond Freedom and Dignity.* New York: Knopf, 1972.

Smith, Craig G. "Sex, Lust, Drugs: Her Novel's Too Much for China." *The New York Times.* May 11, 2000.

Sohlman, Ragnar. *The Legacy of Arthur Nobel: The Story Behind the Nobel Prizes.* London: The Bodley Head, 1983.

Stevenson, Nick. "Globalization, National Cultures and Cultural Citizenship." *The Sociological Quarterly* 38.1 (Winter 1997): 41–66.

Su Tong 蘇童. *Chengbei didai* 城北地帶 [North of the city]. Taipei: Maitian chuban gongsi, 1995.

———. *Mi* 米 [Rice]. *Zhongshan* (1991.3): 4–94. Rpt., Taipei: Yuanliu chuban gongsi, 1991. Trans. Howard Goldblatt. *Rice.* New York: William Morrow, 1995.

———. *Wo de diwang shengya* 我的帝王生涯 [My life as an emperor]. 1992. Rpt., Hong Kong: Tiandi tushu youxian gongsi, 1993.

Sun, Lung-Kee. "Chinese Intellectuals' Notion of 'Epoch' (*Shidai*) in the Post-May Fourth Era." *Chinese Studies in History* 20.2 (Winter 1986–1987): 44–74.

T'ang, Chün-yi. "The T'ien Ming [Heavenly Ordinance] in Pre-Ch'in China." *Philosophy East and West* 11.4 (January 1962): 195–218.

Tang Dacheng 唐達成, ed. *Zhongguo xin wenyi daxi: 1976–1982 duanpian xiaoshuo ji* 中國新文藝大系：1976–1982 短篇小說集 [Compendium to China's new literature: 1976–1982 collected short stories]. 2 vols. Beijing: Zhongguo wenlian chuban gongsi, 1986.

Tang, Xiaobing 唐小兵. *Chinese Modern: The Heroic and the Quotidian.* Durham, N.C.: Duke University Press, 2000.

———. "The Mirror of History and History as Spectacle: Reflections on Hsiao Yeh and Su T'ung." *Modern Chinese Literature* 6 (1992): 203–20.

———. "Residual Modernism: Narratives of the Self in Contemporary Chinese Fiction." *Modern Chinese Literature* 7 (1993): 7–30.

———, ed. *Zai jiedu: Dazhong wenyi yu yishi xingtai* 再解讀：大眾文藝與意識形態 [Reinterpretation: Mass culture and ideology]. Oxford and Hong Kong: Oxford University Press, 1993.

Tilly, Charles. "The Trouble with Stories." In Bernice Pescosolido and Ronald Aminzade, eds., *The Social Worlds of Higher Education: Handbook for Teaching in a New Century.* Thousand Oaks, Calif.: Pine Forge Press, 1999, 256–70.

Titmuss, Richard M. *The Gift Relationship: From Human Blood to Social Policy.* New York: Pantheon, 1971.

Tsau, Shu-ying. "The Rise of 'New Fiction.'" In Dolezelová-Velingerová, ed., *The Chinese Novel* (q.v.), 18–37.

Tu, Wei-ming. *Confucian Thought: Selfhood as Creative Transformation.* Albany: State University of New York Press, 1985.

Tyler, Tom R., Roderick M. Kramer, and Oliver P. John, eds. *The Psychology of the Social Self.* Mahwah, N.J.: Lawrence Erlbaum Associates, 1999.

Veblen, Thorstein. *The Theory of the Leisure Class: An Economic Study in the Evolution of Institutions.* New York: The Macmillan Company, 1899.

Visser, Robin. "Displacement of the Urban-Rural Confrontation in Su Tong's Fiction." *Modern Chinese Literature* 9 (1995): 113–38.

Voelke, André-Jean. *L'idée de volonté dans le stoicisme.* Paris: Presses universitaires de France, 1973.

Wakeman, Frederic, Jr. *History and Will: Philosophical Perspectives of Mao Tse-tung's Thought.* Berkeley: University of California Press, 1973.

Wang Anyi 王安憶. "Jinxiugu zhi lian" 錦繡谷之戀 [Brocade valley] (1987). Rpt., Wang Anyi. *Xiaocheng zhi lian* 小城之戀 [Love in a small town]. Ed. Bo Yang 柏楊. Taipei: Linbai chubanshe, 1988, 17–102.

———. "Miandui ziji" 面對自己 [Facing oneself]. Shanghai, August 25, 1986. Essay from the conference volume of the International Conference on Contemporary Chinese Literature. Jinshan, Shanghai, November 1986. Trans.

Ellen Lai-shan Yeung. "Needed: A Spirit of Courageous Self-Examination." In Martin and Kinkley, eds. *Modern Chinese Writers* (q.v.), 125–26.

Wang, David Der-wei. "Chinese Fiction for the Nineties." In Wang and Tai, eds., *Running Wild* (q.v.), 238–58.

———. *Fin-de-Siècle Splendor: Repressed Modernities of Late Qing Fiction, 1849–1911.* Stanford, Calif.: Stanford University Press, 1997.

Wang Dewei 王德威 (David Der-wei Wang). "Shanghen jijing, baoli qiguan: Yu Hua de xiaoshuo" 傷痕即景，暴力奇觀—余華的小說 [Glimpses of scars, wonders of violence: Yu Hua's fiction]. In Yu, *Xu Sanguan mai xue ji* (q.v.), 7–31.

———. "Shiji mo de Zhongwen xiaoshuo: Yuyan si ze" 世紀末的中國小說: 預言四則 [Fin de siècle Chinese fiction: Four predictions]. In Wang, *Xiaoshuo Zhongguo* (q.v.), 201–25.

———. *Xiaoshuo Zhongguo: Wan Qing dao dangdai de Zhongwen xiaoshuo* 小說中國：晚清到當代的中國小說 [Fiction, China: Chinese fiction from the late Qing to contemporary times]. Taipei: Maitian chuban gongsi, 1993.

Wang, David Der-wei, and Jeanne Tai, eds. *Running Wild: New Chinese Writers.* New York: Columbia University Press, 1994.

Wang, Jing, ed. *China's Avant-Garde Fiction: An Anthology.* Durham, N.C.: Duke University Press, 1998.

———. *High Culture Fever: Politics, Aesthetics, and Ideology in Deng's China.* Berkeley: University of California Press, 1996.

Wang Luyan 王魯彥. "Lima" 李媽 [Lima, or Servant Li]. In *Luyan xuanji* 魯彥選集 [The selected works of Wang Luyan]. Shanghai: Wanxiang shuwu, 1936, 117–42.

———. "Wuding xia" 屋頂下 [Under the roof]. *Wenxue* 文學 1.4 (October 1, 1933). Rpt., *Luyan xuanji* 魯彥選集 (q.v.), 68–98.

Wang Meng 王蒙. "Zase" 雜色 [Motley]. In *Wangmeng ji* 王蒙集 [Selected works of Wang Meng]. Fuzhou: Haixia wenyi chubanshe, 1981, 140–88.

Wang Shuo 王朔. *Please Don't Call Me Human.* Trans. Howard Goldblatt. New York: Hyperion East, 2000.

———. *Wan de jiushi xintiao* 玩得就是心跳 [Playing for thrills] (1988). In Wang, *Qianwan bie ba wo dang ren* 千萬別把我當人 [Please don't call me human]. Beijing: Renmin Zhongguo chubanshe, 1992, 147–95. Trans. Howard Goldblatt, *Playing for Thrills.* New York: William Morrow, 1997.

———. *Wanzhu* 頑主 [Masters of mischief]. *Shouhuo* 68 (1987.6): 24–52.

———. "Yi dian zhengjing mei you" 一點正經沒有 [Not an ounce of seriousness] (1989). In *Wang Shuo wenji* 王朔文集. Vol 4. Beijing: Huayi chubanshe, 1992, 66–154.

Wang Tongzhao 王統照. *Chunyu zhi ye* 春雨之夜 [Night of spring rain] (1924). Shanghai: Shangwu yinshuguan, 1937.

———. *Yi ye* 一葉 [A leaf]. Shanghai: Shangwu yinshuguan, 1922.

Wang Xiaolian 王孝廉 et al., eds. *Wan Qing xiaoshuo daxi* 晚清小說大系 [Com-pendium of late Qing fiction]. Taipei: Guangya chuban gongsi, 1984.

Wang Yuanjian 王願堅. "Dangfei" 黨費 [Party membership dues]. *Jiefangjun wenyi* 解放軍文藝 [Liberation army literature] 40 (1954.12): 44–49.

Watson, Gary, ed. *Free Will.* Oxford Readings in Philosophy. Oxford: Oxford University Press, 1982.

Weihui 衛慧. *Shanghai baobei* 上海寶貝 [Shanghai baby]. Shenyang wenyi: Chunfeng, 1999. Trans. Bruce Humes. *Shanghai Baby.* New York: Simon and Schuster, 2001.

"Wenxue yanjiu hui jianzhang" 文學研究會簡章 [Statement of principles of the Literary Research Association]. *Xiaoshuo yuebao* 12.1 (January 1921).

Widmer, Ellen, and David Der-wei Wang, eds. *From May Fourth to June Fourth: Fiction and Film in Twentieth-Century China.* Cambridge, Mass.: Harvard University Press, 1993.

Williams, Philip. "A New Beginning for the Modernist Chinese Novel: Zhao Zhenkai's *Bodong.*" *Modern Chinese Literature* 5.1 (1989): 73–89.

Williams, Raymond. *The Country and the City.* London: Chatto and Windus, 1973.

Wong, Wang-chi. *Politics and Literature in Shanghai: The Chinese League of Left-Wing Writers, 1930–1936.* Manchester and New York: Manchester University Press, 1991.

Wu Jianren 吳趼人(Wu Woyao 吳沃堯). *Ershinian mudu zhi guai xianzhuang* 二十年目睹之怪現狀 [The strange situation witnessed over the last twenty years] (1903–1909). Nanchang: Jiangxi renmin chubanshe, 1988.

Wu, Yang. "Yang Mo and Her Novel *The Song of Youth.*" *Chinese Literature* 9 (September 1962): 111–16.

Xiao Jun 蕭軍 (Tian Jun 田軍). *Bayue de xiangcun* 八月的鄉村 [Village in August]. (1935). Shanghai: Zuojia shuwu, 1947.

"Xin chao fakan zhiqu shu" 新潮發刊志趣書 [Aims of the publication of *New Tide*]. *Xin chao* 1:1 (January 1919): 1–3.

Xiong Yuezhi 熊月之. *Xixue dongjian yu wan Qing shehui* 西學東漸與晚清社會 [The dissemination of Western learning and late Qing society]. Shanghai: Shanghai renmin chubanshe, 1994.

Xu, Ben. "Contesting Memory for Intellectual Self-Positioning: The 1990s New Cultural Conservatism in China." *Modern Chinese Literature and Culture* 11.1 (Spring 1999): 157–92.

———. *Disenchanted Democracy: Chinese Cultural Criticism after 1989.* Ann Arbor: University of Michigan Press, 1999.

Xu Dishan 許地山. *Zhui wang laozhu* 綴網勞蛛 [The vain labor of the spider]. Shanghai: Shangwu yinshuguan, 1925.

Xu Mingxu 徐明旭. "Diaodong" 調動 [Transfer]. *Qingming* 清明 2 (1979.10): 58–95.

Xu Zhongyu 徐中玉, ed. *Zhongguo jindai wenxue daxi* 中國近代文學大系 [A treasury of modern Chinese literature]. *Wenxue lilun ji er* 文學理論集二 [Essays on literary theory, vol. 2]. Shanghai: Shanghai shudian, 1995.

Yang, Lan. *Chinese Fiction of the Cultural Revolution.* Hong Kong: Hong Kong University Press, 1998.

Yang Mo 楊沫. *Song of Youth.* Trans. Nan Ying. 3rd ed. Beijing: Foreign Language Press, 1978.

———. *Yang Mo wenji* 楊沫文集 [Collected works of Yang Mo]. Vol. 1. *Qingchun zhi ge* 青春之歌 [Song of youth]. Beijing: Shiyue wenyi chubanshe, 1992.

Yang, Xianyi. "On 'The Travels of Lao Can.'" *Chinese Literature* (December 1982): 79–83.

Ye Shaojun 葉紹鈞 (Ye Shengtao 葉聖陶). *Gemo* 隔膜 [Barriers]. Shanghai: Shangwu yinshuguan, 1922.

———. *Ni Huanzhi* 倪煥之 [Ni Huanzhi] (1928). Shanghai: Kaiming shudian, 1929.

Yi Baisha 易白沙. "Kongzi pingyi" 孔子評議 [A critique of Confucius]. *Xin qingnian* 1.6; 2.1 (February 1916; September 1916).

Yu Dafu 郁達夫. "Bodian" 薄奠 [A humble sacrifice] (1924). In *Hanhui ji* 寒灰集 [Cold ashes]. Shanghai: Chuangzaoshe chubanshe, 1927. Rpt., *Yu Dafu wenji* (q.v.), 1: 288–99.

———. "Chenlun" 沉淪 [Sinking] (1921). Rpt., Yu Dafu. *Yu Dafu xuanji* 郁達夫選集 [Selected works of Yu Dafu]. Hong Kong: Wenxue chubanshe, 1957, 2–41.

———. *Miyang* 迷羊 [Lost sheep] (1928). Rpt., Shanghai: Beixin shuju, 1930.

———. "Sinking." Trans. J. S. Lau and C. T. Hsia. In Lau and Goldblatt, eds., *Columbia Anthology* (q.v.), 44–69.

———. *Ta shi yige ruo nuzi* 她是一個弱女子 [She is a weak woman]. Shanghai: Fufeng shuju, 1932. Rpt., *Yu Dafu quanji* 郁達夫全集. 12 vols. Vol. 2. Hangzhou: Zhejiang wenxue chubanshe, 1992, 279–375.

———. "Wenxue gaishuo" 文學概說 [General comments on literature]. In *Yu Dafu wenji* (q.v.), 5: 65–100.

———. "Wenxue shang de jieji douzheng" 文學上的階級鬥爭 [Class struggle in literature]. *Chuangzao zhoubao* 創造週報 4, May 27, 1923. Trans. Haili Kong and Howard Goldblatt. In Denton, ed., *Modern Chinese Literary Thought* (q.v.), 263–68.

———. *Yu Dafu wenji* 郁達夫文集. 12 vols. Guangzhou: Huacheng chubanshe, 1982.

Yu Hua 余華. *Chronicle of a Blood Merchant.* Trans. Andrew F. Jones. New York: Pantheon, 2003.

———. *Huozhe* 活著 [To live]. *Shouhuo* (1992). Rpt., Yu Hua. *Huozhe*. Hong Kong: Boyi chuban jituan, 1994.

———. "Nantao jieshu" 難逃劫數 [Fate is inescapable]. *Shouhuo* 74 (1988.6): 64–82.

———. *The Past and the Punishments.* Trans. Andrew F. Jones. Honolulu: University of Hawai'i Press, 1996.

———. *Shiba sui chu men yuanxing* 十八歲出門遠行 [On the road at eighteen]. Taipei: Yuanliu chuban gongsi, 1990.

———. "Shiba sui chumen yuan xing" 十八歲出門旅行 [On the road at eighteen]. *Beijing wenxue* 北京文學 (1987.1). Rpt., Yu Hua. *Shiba sui chu men yuanxing* (q.v.), 17–29. Trans. Jones. *The Past and the Punishments* (q.v.), 3–11.

———. "Xianshi yi zhong" 現實一種 [One kind of reality]. *Beijing wenxue* (1988.1). Rpt., Yu Hua. *Shiba sui chu men yuanxing* (q.v.), 181–248. Trans. Jeanne Tai. In Wang and Tai, eds. *Running Wild* (q.v.), 21–68.

———. *Xu Sanguan mai xue ji* 許三觀賣血記. 1996. Rpt., Taipei: Maitian chuban gongsi, 1997.

———. "Yijiubaliu nian" 一九八六年 [1986]. *Shouhuo* 68 (1987.6): 62–95. Rpt., Yu Hua, *Shiba sui chu men yuanxing* (q.v.), 43–101.

Yu Peilin 余培林, ed. *Laozi duben* 老子讀本 [Laozi reader]. 11th ed. Taipei: Sanmin shuju, 1995.

Yu Pingbo 俞平伯. "Shehui shang duiyu xin shi de gezhong xinli guan" 社會上對於新詩的各種心理觀 [Various psychological views about new poetry prevalent in society]. *Xin chao* 2:1 (October 1919): 163–71.

Yue, Gang. *The Mouth that Begs: Hunger, Cannibalism, and the Politics of Eating in Modern China.* Durham, N.C.: Duke University Press, 1999.

Yue Hengjun 樂蘅軍. *Yizhi yu mingyun: Zhongguo gudian xiaoshuo shijieguan zonglun* 意志與命運—中國古典小說世界觀綜論 [Will and fate: A comprehensive discussion of the worldview of classical Chinese fiction]. Taipei: Da'an chubanshe, 1992.

Zeng Pu 曾樸. *Nie hai hua* 孽海花 [Flower in a sinful sea]. Shanghai: Shanghai guji chubanshe, 1980.

———. "Tseng P'u: A Flower in a Sinful Sea." Trans. Rafe de Crespigny and Liu Ts'un-yan. In Liu Ts'un-yan and John Minford, eds., *Chinese Middlebrow Fiction: From the Ch'ing and Early Republican Eras.* Hong Kong: The Chinese University Press, 1984, 137–98.

Zhang Chengzhi 張承志. "Lüye" 綠夜 [Green night] (1981). Trans. Isabelle Bijon. "La nuit verte." In Curien, ed., *Anthologie* (q.v.), 93–111.

Zhang Jie 張潔. *Chenzhong de chibang* 沉重的翅膀 [Heavy wings]. Beijing: Renmin wenxue chubanshe, 1981. Rpt., Nanchang: Baihuazhou wenyi chubanshe, 1998.

Zhang Ren 張韌 and Yang Zhijie 楊志杰. "Cong 'A, ren. . . . . .' dao 'Ren a, ren!'—ping jin ji nian wenxue chuangzuo zhong de ren xing, rendaozhuyi wenti" 從 '啊，人。。。。。。' 到 '人啊，人!' 一評近幾年文學作中的人性，人道主義問題 [From 'Ah, humanity" to "Humanity, o humanity"—critiquing problems of human nature and humanism in literary creation of the last few years]. *Wenxue pinglun* (1984.2): 3–12.

Zhang Wei 張煒. "Yi tan qingshui" 一潭清水 [A pond of clear water]. *Renmin wenxue* 298 (1984.7): 56–63.

Zhang, Xudong. *Chinese Modernism in the Era of Reforms: Cultural Fever, Avant-Garde Fiction, and the New Chinese Cinema.* Durham, N.C., and London: Duke University Press, 1997.

———. "The Power of Rewriting: Postrevolutionary Discourse on Chinese Socialist Realism." In Thomas Lahusen and Evgeny Dobrenko, eds., *Socialist Realism without Shores.* Durham, N.C.: Duke University Press, 1997, 282–309.

Zhang, Yingjin. *The City in Modern Chinese Literature and Film: Configurations of Space, Time and Gender.* Stanford, Calif.: Stanford University Press, 1996.

Zhang Yiwu 張頤武. "Lun 'houwutuobang' huayu: Jiushi niandai Zhongguo wenxue de yizhong quxiang" 論 '後烏托邦' 話語：九十年代中國文學的一種趨向 [On the post-utopian discourse: A tendency of Chinese literature of the 1990s]. *Wenyi lilun* 文藝理論 [Literary and artistic theory] 66 (1993): 181–87.

Zhang Ziping 張資平. *Chongjiqi huashi* 沖積期化石 [Fossils in alluvial deposits]. Shanghai: Chuangzhaoshe, 1922.

Zhao, Henry Y. H. *The Uneasy Narrator: Chinese Fiction from the Traditional to the Modern.* Oxford: Oxford University Press, 1995.

Zhao, Y. H. "The Rise of Metafiction in China." *Bulletin of the School of Oriental and African Studies* 55.1 (1992): 90–99.

Zhao Zhenkai 趙振開. *Bodong* 波動 [Waves]. *Jintian* 4 (June 1979): 31–71; 5 (August 1979): 1–13 and 29–48; and 6 (October 1979): 21–56.

Zheng Shusen 鄭樹森, ed. *Xiandai Zhongguo xiaoshuo xuan* 現代中國小說選. 5 vols. Taipei: Hongfan, 1989.

Zheng Wanlong 鄭萬隆. "Xiandai xiaoshuo zhong de lishi yishi" 現代小說中的歷史意識 [Historical consciousness in modern fiction]. *Xiao shuo chao* 小說潮 (1985.7): 79–80.

———. "Wo de gen" 我的根 [My roots]. *Shanghai wenxue* 92 (1985.5): 44–46.

Zheng Yi 鄭義. *Lao jing* 老井 [Old well]. *Dang dai* 當代 (1985.2): 4–73. Rpt., Zheng Yi. *Lao jing.* 3rd ed. Taipei: Haifeng chubanshe, 1989.

———. *Yuan cun* 遠村 [Remote village]. *Dang dai* 當代 (1983.4): 87–122. Rpt., Zheng Yi. *Yuan cun*. Taibei: Haifeng chubanshe, 1990, 25–161.

Zhong, Xueping. *Masculinity Besieged? Issues of Modernity and Male Subjectivity in Chinese Literature of the Late Twentieth Century.* Durham, N.C.: Duke University Press, 2000.

Zhou Yang 周揚. "Guanyu 'shehuizhuyi de xianshizhuyi yu geming de langmanzhuyi'" 關於 '社會主義的現實主義與革命的浪漫主義' [Concerning socialist realism and revolutionary romanticism]. *Xiandai* 1.4 (November 1933). Rpt., Zhou Yang. *Zhou Yang ji* 周揚集 [Collected works of Zhou Yang]. Ed. Zhongguo shehui kexueyuan keyan ju zuzhi. Beijing: Zhongguo shehui kexue chubanshe, 2000, 1–14.

———. "Wei chuangzao geng duo de youxiu de wenxue yishu zuopin er fendou" 爲搶造更多得優秀的文學藝術作品而奮鬥 [Fight to create even more outstanding works of literature and art] (1953). Rpt., Beijing shifan daxue, *Zhongguo xiandai wenxue shi cankao ziliao* (q.v.), 3: 71–95.

Zhou Zuoren 周作人. "Ren de wenxue" 人的文學 [Humane literature]. *Xin qingnian* 5. 6 (December 1918): 575–84.

———. *Zhongguo xin wenxue de yuanliu* 中國新文學的源流 [The origins of modern Chinese literature]. Beijing: Beiping renwen shudian, 1932.

Zong Pu 宗璞 (Feng Zongpu 馮宗璞). "Wo shi shei?" 我是誰？ [Who am I?]. *Changchun* 長春 (1979.12): 4–7.

Index

Harvard East Asian Monographs
(* out-of-print)

*1. Liang Fang-chung, *The Single-Whip Method of Taxation in China*
*2. Harold C. Hinton, *The Grain Tribute System of China, 1845–1911*
3. Ellsworth C. Carlson, *The Kaiping Mines, 1877–1912*
*4. Chao Kuo-chün, *Agrarian Policies of Mainland China: A Documentary Study, 1949–1956*
*5. Edgar Snow, *Random Notes on Red China, 1936–1945*
*6. Edwin George Beal, Jr., *The Origin of Likin, 1835–1864*
7. Chao Kuo-chün, *Economic Planning and Organization in Mainland China: A Documentary Study, 1949–1957*
*8. John K. Fairbank, *Ching Documents: An Introductory Syllabus*
*9. Helen Yin and Yi-chang Yin, *Economic Statistics of Mainland China, 1949–1957*
10. Wolfgang Franke, *The Reform and Abolition of the Traditional Chinese Examination System*
11. Albert Feuerwerker and S. Cheng, *Chinese Communist Studies of Modern Chinese History*
12. C. John Stanley, *Late Ching Finance: Hu Kuang-yung as an Innovator*
13. S. M. Meng, *The Tsungli Yamen: Its Organization and Functions*
*14. Ssu-yü Teng, *Historiography of the Taiping Rebellion*
15. Chun-Jo Liu, *Controversies in Modern Chinese Intellectual History: An Analytic Bibliography of Periodical Articles, Mainly of the May Fourth and Post–May Fourth Era*
*16. Edward J. M. Rhoads, *The Chinese Red Army, 1927–1963: An Annotated Bibliography*
*17. Andrew J. Nathan, *A History of the China International Famine Relief Commission*
*18. Frank H. H. King (ed.) and Prescott Clarke, *A Research Guide to China-Coast Newspapers, 1822–1911*
*19. Ellis Joffe, *Party and Army: Professionalism and Political Control in the Chinese Officer Corps, 1949–1964*

*20. Toshio G. Tsukahira, *Feudal Control in Tokugawa Japan: The Sankin Kōtai System*

*21. Kwang-Ching Liu, ed., *American Missionaries in China: Papers from Harvard Seminars*

*22. George Moseley, *A Sino-Soviet Cultural Frontier: The Ili Kazakh Autonomous Chou*

23. Carl F. Nathan, *Plague Prevention and Politics in Manchuria, 1910–1931*

*24. Adrian Arthur Bennett, *John Fryer: The Introduction of Western Science and Technology into Nineteenth-Century China*

*25. Donald J. Friedman, *The Road from Isolation: The Campaign of the American Committee for Non-Participation in Japanese Aggression, 1938–1941*

*26. Edward LeFevour, *Western Enterprise in Late Ching China: A Selective Survey of Jardine, Matheson and Company's Operations, 1842–1895*

27. Charles Neuhauser, *Third World Politics: China and the Afro-Asian People's Solidarity Organization, 1957–1967*

*28. Kungtu C. Sun, assisted by Ralph W. Huenemann, *The Economic Development of Manchuria in the First Half of the Twentieth Century*

*29. Shahid Javed Burki, *A Study of Chinese Communes, 1965*

30. John Carter Vincent, *The Extraterritorial System in China: Final Phase*

31. Madeleine Chi, *China Diplomacy, 1914–1918*

*32. Clifton Jackson Phillips, *Protestant America and the Pagan World: The First Half Century of the American Board of Commissioners for Foreign Missions, 1810–1860*

*33. James Pusey, *Wu Han: Attacking the Present Through the Past*

*34. Ying-wan Cheng, *Postal Communication in China and Its Modernization, 1860–1896*

35. Tuvia Blumenthal, *Saving in Postwar Japan*

36. Peter Frost, *The Bakumatsu Currency Crisis*

37. Stephen C. Lockwood, *Augustine Heard and Company, 1858–1862*

38. Robert R. Campbell, *James Duncan Campbell: A Memoir by His Son*

39. Jerome Alan Cohen, ed., *The Dynamics of China's Foreign Relations*

40. V. V. Vishnyakova-Akimova, *Two Years in Revolutionary China, 1925–1927*, tr. Steven L. Levine

41. Meron Medzini, *French Policy in Japan During the Closing Years of the Tokugawa Regime*

42. Ezra Vogel, Margie Sargent, Vivienne B. Shue, Thomas Jay Mathews, and Deborah S. Davis, *The Cultural Revolution in the Provinces*

43. Sidney A. Forsythe, *An American Missionary Community in China, 1895–1905*

*44. Benjamin I. Schwartz, ed., *Reflections on the May Fourth Movement: A Symposium*
*45. Ching Young Choe, *The Rule of the Taewŏngun, 1864–1873: Restoration in Yi Korea*
46. W. P. J. Hall, *A Bibliographical Guide to Japanese Research on the Chinese Economy, 1958–1970*
47. Jack J. Gerson, *Horatio Nelson Lay and Sino-British Relations, 1854–1864*
48. Paul Richard Bohr, *Famine and the Missionary: Timothy Richard as Relief Administrator and Advocate of National Reform*
49. Endymion Wilkinson, *The History of Imperial China: A Research Guide*
50. Britten Dean, *China and Great Britain: The Diplomacy of Commercial Relations, 1860–1864*
51. Ellsworth C. Carlson, *The Foochow Missionaries, 1847–1880*
52. Yeh-chien Wang, *An Estimate of the Land-Tax Collection in China, 1753 and 1908*
53. Richard M. Pfeffer, *Understanding Business Contracts in China, 1949–1963*
*54. Han-sheng Chuan and Richard Kraus, *Mid-Ching Rice Markets and Trade: An Essay in Price History*
55. Ranbir Vohra, *Lao She and the Chinese Revolution*
56. Liang-lin Hsiao, *China's Foreign Trade Statistics, 1864–1949*
*57. Lee-hsia Hsu Ting, *Government Control of the Press in Modern China, 1900–1949*
*58. Edward W. Wagner, *The Literati Purges: Political Conflict in Early Yi Korea*
*59. Joungwon A. Kim, *Divided Korea: The Politics of Development, 1945–1972*
60. Noriko Kamachi, John K. Fairbank, and Chūzō Ichiko, *Japanese Studies of Modern China Since 1953: A Bibliographical Guide to Historical and Social-Science Research on the Nineteenth and Twentieth Centuries, Supplementary Volume for 1953–1969*
61. Donald A. Gibbs and Yun-chen Li, *A Bibliography of Studies and Translations of Modern Chinese Literature, 1918–1942*
62. Robert H. Silin, *Leadership and Values: The Organization of Large-Scale Taiwanese Enterprises*
63. David Pong, *A Critical Guide to the Kwangtung Provincial Archives Deposited at the Public Record Office of London*
*64. Fred W. Drake, *China Charts the World: Hsu Chi-yü and His Geography of 1848*
*65. William A. Brown and Urgrunge Onon, translators and annotators, *History of the Mongolian People's Republic*
66. Edward L. Farmer, *Early Ming Government: The Evolution of Dual Capitals*
*67. Ralph C. Croizier, *Koxinga and Chinese Nationalism: History, Myth, and the Hero*

*68. William J. Tyler, tr., *The Psychological World of Natsume Sōseki*, by Doi Takeo

69. Eric Widmer, *The Russian Ecclesiastical Mission in Peking During the Eighteenth Century*

*70. Charlton M. Lewis, *Prologue to the Chinese Revolution: The Transformation of Ideas and Institutions in Hunan Province, 1891–1907*

71. Preston Torbert, *The Ching Imperial Household Department: A Study of Its Organization and Principal Functions, 1662–1796*

72. Paul A. Cohen and John E. Schrecker, eds., *Reform in Nineteenth-Century China*

73. Jon Sigurdson, *Rural Industrialism in China*

74. Kang Chao, *The Development of Cotton Textile Production in China*

75. Valentin Rabe, *The Home Base of American China Missions, 1880–1920*

*76. Sarasin Viraphol, *Tribute and Profit: Sino-Siamese Trade, 1652–1853*

77. Ch'i-ch'ing Hsiao, *The Military Establishment of the Yuan Dynasty*

78. Meishi Tsai, *Contemporary Chinese Novels and Short Stories, 1949–1974: An Annotated Bibliography*

*79. Wellington K. K. Chan, *Merchants, Mandarins and Modern Enterprise in Late Ching China*

80. Endymion Wilkinson, *Landlord and Labor in Late Imperial China: Case Studies from Shandong by Jing Su and Luo Lun*

*81. Barry Keenan, *The Dewey Experiment in China: Educational Reform and Political Power in the Early Republic*

*82. George A. Hayden, *Crime and Punishment in Medieval Chinese Drama: Three Judge Pao Plays*

*83. Sang-Chul Suh, *Growth and Structural Changes in the Korean Economy, 1910–1940*

84. J. W. Dower, *Empire and Aftermath: Yoshida Shigeru and the Japanese Experience, 1878–1954*

85. Martin Collcutt, *Five Mountains: The Rinzai Zen Monastic Institution in Medieval Japan*

86. Kwang Suk Kim and Michael Roemer, *Growth and Structural Transformation*

87. Anne O. Krueger, *The Developmental Role of the Foreign Sector and Aid*

*88. Edwin S. Mills and Byung-Nak Song, *Urbanization and Urban Problems*

89. Sung Hwan Ban, Pal Yong Moon, and Dwight H. Perkins, *Rural Development*

*90. Noel F. McGinn, Donald R. Snodgrass, Yung Bong Kim, Shin-Bok Kim, and Quee-Young Kim, *Education and Development in Korea*

91.* Leroy P. Jones and Il SaKong, *Government, Business, and Entrepreneurship in Economic Development: The Korean Case*

92. Edward S. Mason, Dwight H. Perkins, Kwang Suk Kim, David C. Cole, Mahn Je Kim, et al., *The Economic and Social Modernization of the Republic of Korea*

93. Robert Repetto, Tai Hwan Kwon, Son-Ung Kim, Dae Young Kim, John E. Sloboda, and Peter J. Donaldson, *Economic Development, Population Policy, and Demographic Transition in the Republic of Korea*

94. Parks M. Coble, Jr., *The Shanghai Capitalists and the Nationalist Government, 1927–1937*

95. Noriko Kamachi, *Reform in China: Huang Tsun-hsien and the Japanese Model*

96. Richard Wich, *Sino-Soviet Crisis Politics: A Study of Political Change and Communication*

97. Lillian M. Li, *China's Silk Trade: Traditional Industry in the Modern World, 1842–1937*

98. R. David Arkush, *Fei Xiaotong and Sociology in Revolutionary China*

99.* Kenneth Alan Grossberg, *Japan's Renaissance: The Politics of the Muromachi Bakufu*

100. James Reeve Pusey, *China and Charles Darwin*

101. Hoyt Cleveland Tillman, *Utilitarian Confucianism: Chen Liang's Challenge to Chu Hsi*

102. Thomas A. Stanley, *Ōsugi Sakae, Anarchist in Taishō Japan: The Creativity of the Ego*

103. Jonathan K. Ocko, *Bureaucratic Reform in Provincial China: Ting Jih-ch'ang in Restoration Kiangsu, 1867–1870*

104. James Reed, *The Missionary Mind and American East Asia Policy, 1911–1915*

105. Neil L. Waters, *Japan's Local Pragmatists: The Transition from Bakumatsu to Meiji in the Kawasaki Region*

106. David C. Cole and Yung Chul Park, *Financial Development in Korea, 1945–1978*

107. Roy Bahl, Chuk Kyo Kim, and Chong Kee Park, *Public Finances During the Korean Modernization Process*

108. William D. Wray, *Mitsubishi and the N.Y.K, 1870–1914: Business Strategy in the Japanese Shipping Industry*

109. Ralph William Huenemann, *The Dragon and the Iron Horse: The Economics of Railroads in China, 1876–1937*

110.* Benjamin A. Elman, *From Philosophy to Philology: Intellectual and Social Aspects of Change in Late Imperial China*

111. Jane Kate Leonard, *Wei Yüan and China's Rediscovery of the Maritime World*

112. Luke S. K. Kwong, *A Mosaic of the Hundred Days:. Personalities, Politics, and Ideas of 1898*

113.* John E. Wills, Jr., *Embassies and Illusions: Dutch and Portuguese Envoys to K'ang-hsi, 1666–1687*

114. Joshua A. Fogel, *Politics and Sinology: The Case of Naitō Konan (1866–1934)*

115.* Jeffrey C. Kinkley, ed., *After Mao: Chinese Literature and Society, 1978–1981*

116. C. Andrew Gerstle, *Circles of Fantasy: Convention in the Plays of Chikamatsu*

117. Andrew Gordon, *The Evolution of Labor Relations in Japan: Heavy Industry, 1853–1955*

118.* Daniel K. Gardner, *Chu Hsi and the "Ta Hsueh": Neo-Confucian Reflection on the Confucian Canon*

119. Christine Guth Kanda, *Shinzō: Hachiman Imagery and Its Development*

120.* Robert Borgen, *Sugawara no Michizane and the Early Heian Court*

121. Chang-tai Hung, *Going to the People: Chinese Intellectual and Folk Literature, 1918–1937*

122.* Michael A. Cusumano, *The Japanese Automobile Industry: Technology and Management at Nissan and Toyota*

123. Richard von Glahn, *The Country of Streams and Grottoes: Expansion, Settlement, and the Civilizing of the Sichuan Frontier in Song Times*

124. Steven D. Carter, *The Road to Komatsubara: A Classical Reading of the Renga Hyakuin*

125. Katherine F. Bruner, John K. Fairbank, and Richard T. Smith, *Entering China's Service: Robert Hart's Journals, 1854–1863*

126. Bob Tadashi Wakabayashi, *Anti-Foreignism and Western Learning in Early-Modern Japan: The "New Theses" of 1825*

127. Atsuko Hirai, *Individualism and Socialism: The Life and Thought of Kawai Eijirō (1891–1944)*

128. Ellen Widmer, *The Margins of Utopia: "Shui-hu hou-chuan" and the Literature of Ming Loyalism*

129. R. Kent Guy, *The Emperor's Four Treasuries: Scholars and the State in the Late Chien-lung Era*

130. Peter C. Perdue, *Exhausting the Earth: State and Peasant in Hunan, 1500–1850*

131. Susan Chan Egan, *A Latterday Confucian: Reminiscences of William Hung (1893–1980)*

132. James T. C. Liu, *China Turning Inward: Intellectual-Political Changes in the Early Twelfth Century*

133.* Paul A. Cohen, *Between Tradition and Modernity: Wang T'ao and Reform in Late Ching China*

134. Kate Wildman Nakai, *Shogunal Politics: Arai Hakuseki and the Premises of Tokugawa Rule*
135.* Parks M. Coble, *Facing Japan: Chinese Politics and Japanese Imperialism, 1931–1937*
136. Jon L. Saari, *Legacies of Childhood: Growing Up Chinese in a Time of Crisis, 1890–1920*
137. Susan Downing Videen, *Tales of Heichū*
138. Heinz Morioka and Miyoko Sasaki, *Rakugo: The Popular Narrative Art of Japan*
139. Joshua A. Fogel, *Nakae Ushikichi in China: The Mourning of Spirit*
140. Alexander Barton Woodside, *Vietnam and the Chinese Model.: A Comparative Study of Vietnamese and Chinese Government in the First Half of the Nineteenth Century*
141.* George Elison, *Deus Destroyed: The Image of Christianity in Early Modern Japan*
142. William D. Wray, ed., *Managing Industrial Enterprise: Cases from Japan's Prewar Experience*
143.* T'ung-tsu Ch'ü, *Local Government in China Under the Ching*
144. Marie Anchordoguy, *Computers, Inc.: Japan's Challenge to IBM*
145. Barbara Molony, *Technology and Investment: The Prewar Japanese Chemical Industry*
146. Mary Elizabeth Berry, *Hideyoshi*
147. Laura E. Hein, *Fueling Growth: The Energy Revolution and Economic Policy in Postwar Japan*
148. Wen-hsin Yeh, *The Alienated Academy: Culture and Politics in Republican China, 1919–1937*
149. Dru C. Gladney, *Muslim Chinese: Ethnic Nationalism in the People's Republic*
150. Merle Goldman and Paul A. Cohen, eds., *Ideas Across Cultures: Essays on Chinese Thought in Honor of Benjamin L Schwartz*
151. James M. Polachek, *The Inner Opium War*
152. Gail Lee Bernstein, *Japanese Marxist: A Portrait of Kawakami Hajime, 1879–1946*
153.* Lloyd E. Eastman, *The Abortive Revolution: China Under Nationalist Rule, 1927–1937*
154. Mark Mason, *American Multinationals and Japan: The Political Economy of Japanese Capital Controls, 1899–1980*
155. Richard J. Smith, John K. Fairbank, and Katherine F. Bruner, *Robert Hart and China's Early Modernization: His Journals, 1863–1866*
156. George J. Tanabe, Jr., *Myōe the Dreamkeeper: Fantasy and Knowledge in Kamakura Buddhism*

157. William Wayne Farris, *Heavenly Warriors: The Evolution of Japan's Military, 500–1300*
158. Yu-ming Shaw, *An American Missionary in China: John Leighton Stuart and Chinese-American Relations*
159. James B. Palais, *Politics and Policy in Traditional Korea*
160.* Douglas Reynolds, *China, 1898–1912: The Xinzheng Revolution and Japan*
161. Roger R. Thompson, *China's Local Councils in the Age of Constitutional Reform, 1898–1911*
162. William Johnston, *The Modern Epidemic: History of Tuberculosis in Japan*
163. Constantine Nomikos Vaporis, *Breaking Barriers: Travel and the State in Early Modern Japan*
164. Irmela Hijiya-Kirschnereit, *Rituals of Self-Revelation: Shishōsetsu as Literary Genre and Socio-Cultural Phenomenon*
165. James C. Baxter, *The Meiji Unification Through the Lens of Ishikawa Prefecture*
166. Thomas R. H. Havens, *Architects of Affluence: The Tsutsumi Family and the Seibu-Saison Enterprises in Twentieth-Century Japan*
167. Anthony Hood Chambers, *The Secret Window: Ideal Worlds in Tanizaki's Fiction*
168. Steven J. Ericson, *The Sound of the Whistle: Railroads and the State in Meiji Japan*
169. Andrew Edmund Goble, *Kenmu: Go-Daigo's Revolution*
170. Denise Potrzeba Lett, *In Pursuit of Status: The Making of South Korea's "New" Urban Middle Class*
171. Mimi Hall Yiengpruksawan, *Hiraizumi: Buddhist Art and Regional Politics in Twelfth-Century Japan*
172. Charles Shirō Inouye, *The Similitude of Blossoms: A Critical Biography of Izumi Kyōka (1873–1939), Japanese Novelist and Playwright*
173. Aviad E. Raz, *Riding the Black Ship: Japan and Tokyo Disneyland*
174. Deborah J. Milly, *Poverty, Equality, and Growth: The Politics of Economic Need in Postwar Japan*
175. See Heng Teow, *Japan's Cultural Policy Toward China, 1918–1931: A Comparative Perspective*
176. Michael A. Fuller, *An Introduction to Literary Chinese*
177. Frederick R. Dickinson, *War and National Reinvention: Japan in the Great War, 1914–1919*
178. John Solt, *Shredding the Tapestry of Meaning: The Poetry and Poetics of Kitasono Katue (1902–1978)*
179. Edward Pratt, *Japan's Protoindustrial Elite: The Economic Foundations of the Gōnō*
180. Atsuko Sakaki, *Recontextualizing Texts: Narrative Performance in Modern Japanese Fiction*

181. Soon-Won Park, *Colonial Industrialization and Labor in Korea: The Onoda Cement Factory*
182. JaHyun Kim Haboush and Martina Deuchler, *Culture and the State in Late Chosŏn Korea*
183. John W. Chaffee, *Branches of Heaven: A History of the Imperial Clan of Sung China*
184. Gi-Wook Shin and Michael Robinson, eds., *Colonial Modernity in Korea*
185. Nam-lin Hur, *Prayer and Play in Late Tokugawa Japan: Asakusa Sensōji and Edo Society*
186. Kristin Stapleton, *Civilizing Chengdu: Chinese Urban Reform, 1895–1937*
187. Hyung Il Pai, *Constructing "Korean" Origins: A Critical Review of Archaeology, Historiography, and Racial Myth in Korean State-Formation Theories*
188. Brian D. Ruppert, *Jewel in the Ashes: Buddha Relics and Power in Early Medieval Japan*
189. Susan Daruvala, *Zhou Zuoren and an Alternative Chinese Response to Modernity*
190.* James Z. Lee, *The Political Economy of a Frontier: Southwest China, 1250–1850*
191. Kerry Smith, *A Time of Crisis: Japan, the Great Depression, and Rural Revitalization*
192. Michael Lewis, *Becoming Apart: National Power and Local Politics in Toyama, 1868–1945*
193. William C. Kirby, Man-houng Lin, James Chin Shih, and David A. Pietz, eds., *State and Economy in Republican China: A Handbook for Scholars*
194. Timothy S. George, *Minamata: Pollution and the Struggle for Democracy in Postwar Japan*
195. Billy K. L. So, *Prosperity, Region, and Institutions in Maritime China: The South Fukien Pattern, 946–1368*
196. Yoshihisa Tak Matsusaka, *The Making of Japanese Manchuria, 1904–1932*
197. Maram Epstein, *Competing Discourses: Orthodoxy, Authenticity, and Engendered Meanings in Late Imperial Chinese Fiction*
198. Curtis J. Milhaupt, J. Mark Ramseyer, and Michael K. Young, eds. and comps., *Japanese Law in Context: Readings in Society, the Economy, and Politics*
199. Haruo Iguchi, *Unfinished Business: Ayukawa Yoshisuke and U.S.-Japan Relations, 1937–1952*
200. Scott Pearce, Audrey Spiro, and Patricia Ebrey, *Culture and Power in the Reconstitution of the Chinese Realm, 200–600*
201. Terry Kawashima, *Writing Margins: The Textual Construction of Gender in Heian and Kamakura Japan*

202. Martin W. Huang, *Desire and Fictional Narrative in Late Imperial China*
203. Robert S. Ross and Jiang Changbin, eds., *Re-examining the Cold War: U.S.-China Diplomacy, 1954–1973*
204. Guanhua Wang, *In Search of Justice: The 1905–1906 Chinese Anti-American Boycott*
205. David Schaberg, *A Patterned Past: Form and Thought in Early Chinese Historiography*
206. Christine Yano, *Tears of Longing: Nostalgia and the Nation in Japanese Popular Song*
207. Milena Doleželová-Velingerová and Oldřich Král, with Graham Sanders, eds., *The Appropriation of Cultural Capital: China's May Fourth Project*
208. Robert N. Huey, *The Making of 'Shinkokinshū'*
209. Lee Butler, *Emperor and Aristocracy in Japan, 1467–1680: Resilience and Renewal*
210. Suzanne Ogden, *Inklings of Democracy in China*
211. Kenneth J. Ruoff, *The People's Emperor: Democracy and the Japanese Monarchy, 1945–1995*
212. Haun Saussy, *Great Walls of Discourse and Other Adventures in Cultural China*
213. Aviad E. Raz, *Emotions at Work: Normative Control, Organizations, and Culture in Japan and America*
214. Rebecca E. Karl and Peter Zarrow, eds., *Rethinking the 1898 Reform Period: Political and Cultural Change in Late Qing China*
215. Kevin O'Rourke, *The Book of Korean Shijo*
216. Ezra F. Vogel, ed., *The Golden Age of the U.S.-China-Japan Triangle, 1972–1989*
217. Thomas A. Wilson, ed., *On Sacred Grounds: Culture, Society, Politics, and the Formation of the Cult of Confucius*
218. Donald S. Sutton, *Steps of Perfection: Exorcistic Performers and Chinese Religion in Twentieth-Century Taiwan*
219. Daqing Yang, *Technology of Empire: Telecommunications and Japanese Expansionism, 1895–1945*
220. Qianshen Bai, *Fu Shan's World: The Transformation of Chinese Calligraphy in the Seventeenth Century*
221. Paul Jakov Smith and Richard von Glahn, eds., *The Song-Yuan-Ming Transition in Chinese History*
222. Rania Huntington, *Alien Kind: Foxes and Late Imperial Chinese Narrative*
223. Jordan Sand, *House and Home in Modern Japan: Architecture, Domestic Space, and Bourgeois Culture, 1880–1930*
224. Karl Gerth, *China Made: Consumer Culture and the Creation of the Nation*

225. Xiaoshan Yang, *Metamorphosis of the Private Sphere: Gardens and Objects in Tang-Song Poetry*
226. Barbara Mittler, *A Newspaper for China? Power, Identity, and Change in Shanghai's News Media, 1872–1912*
227. Joyce A. Madancy, *The Troublesome Legacy of Commissioner Lin: The Opium Trade and Opium Suppression in Fujian Province, 1820s to 1920s*
228. John Makeham, *Transmitters and Creators: Chinese Commentators and Commentaries on the Analects*
229. Elisabeth Köll, *From Cotton Mill to Business Empire: The Emergence of Regional Enterprises in Modern China*
230. Emma Teng, *Taiwan's Imagined Geography: Chinese Colonial Travel Writing and Pictures, 1683–1895*
231. Wilt Idema and Beata Grant, *The Red Brush: Writing Women of Imperial China*
232. Eric C. Rath, *The Ethos of Noh: Actors and Their Art*
233. Elizabeth Remick, *Building Local States: China During the Republican and Post–Mao Eras*
234. Lynn Struve, ed., *The Qing Formation in World-Historical Time*
235. D. Max Moerman, *Localizing Paradise: Kumano Pilgrimage and the Religious Landscape of Premodern Japan*
236. Antonia Finnane, *Speaking of Yangzhou: A Chinese City, 1550–1850*
237. Brian Platt, *Burning and Building: Schooling and State Formation in Japan, 1750–1890*
238. Gail Bernstein, Andrew Gordon, and Kate Wildman Nakai, eds., *Public Spheres, Private Lives in Modern Japan, 1600–1950: Essays in Honor of Albert Craig*
239. Wu Hung and Katherine R. Tsiang, *Body and Face in Chinese Visual Culture*
240. Stephen Dodd, *Writing Home: Representations of the Native Place in Modern Japanese Literature*
241. David Anthony Bello, *Opium and the Limits of Empire: Drug Prohibition in the Chinese Interior, 1729–1850*
242. Hosea Hirata, *Discourses of Seduction: History, Evil, Desire, and Modern Japanese Literature*
243. Kyung Moon Hwang, *Beyond Birth: Social Status in the Emergence of Modern Korea*
244. Brian R. Dott, *Identity Reflections: Pilgrimages to Mount Tai in Late Imperial China*
245. Mark McNally, *Proving the Way: Conflict and Practice in the History of Japanese Nativism*

246. Yongping Wu, *A Political Explanation of Economic Growth: State Survival, Bureaucratic Politics, and Private Enterprises in the Making of Taiwan's Economy, 1950–1985*
247. Kyu Hyun Kim, *The Age of Visions and Arguments: Parliamentarianism and the National Public Sphere in Early Meiji Japan*
248. Zvi Ben-Dor Benite, *The Dao of Muhammad: A Cultural History of Muslims in Late Imperial China*
249. David Der-wei Wang and Shang Wei, eds., *Dynastic Crisis and Cultural Innovation: From the Late Ming to the Late Qing and Beyond*
250. Wilt L. Idema, Wai-yee Li, and Ellen Widmer, eds., *Trauma and Transcendence in Early Qing Literature*
251. Barbara Molony and Kathleen Uno, eds., *Gendering Modern Japanese History*
252. Hiroshi Aoyagi, *Islands of Eight Million Smiles: Idol Performance and Symbolic Production in Contemporary Japan*
253. Wai-yee Li, *The Readability of the Past in Early Chinese Historiography*
254. William C. Kirby, Robert S. Ross, and Gong Li, eds., *Normalization of U.S.-China Relations: An International History*
255. Ellen Gardner Nakamura, *Practical Pursuits: Takano Chōei, Takahashi Keisaku, and Western Medicine in Nineteenth-Century Japan*
256. Jonathan W. Best, *A History of the Early Korean Kingdom of Paekche, together with an annotated translation of* The Paekche Annals *of the* Samguk sagi
257. Liang Pan, *The United Nations in Japan's Foreign and Security Policymaking, 1945–1992: National Security, Party Politics, and International Status*
258. Richard Belsky, *Localities at the Center: Native Place, Space, and Power in Late Imperial Beijing*
259. Zwia Lipkin, *"Useless to the State": "Social Problems" and Social Engineering in Nationalist Nanjing, 1927–1937*
260. William O. Gardner, *Advertising Tower: Japanese Modernism and Modernity in the 1920s*
261. Stephen Owen, *The Making of Early Chinese Classical Poetry*
262. Martin J. Powers, *Pattern and Person: Ornament, Society, and Self in Classical China*
263. Anna M. Shields, *Crafting a Collection: The Cultural Contexts and Poetic Practice of the* Huajian ji 花間集 *(Collection from Among the Flowers)*
264. Stephen Owen, *The Late Tang: Chinese Poetry of the Mid-Ninth Century (827–860)*
265. Sara L. Friedman, *Intimate Politics: Marriage, the Market, and State Power in Southeastern China*
266. Patricia Buckley Ebrey and Maggie Bickford, *Emperor Huizong and Late Northern Song China: The Politics of Culture and the Culture of Politics*

267. Sophie Volpp, *Worldly Stage: Theatricality in Seventeenth-Century China*
268. Ellen Widmer, *The Beauty and the Book: Women and Fiction in Nineteenth-Century China*
269. Steven B. Miles, *The Sea of Learning: Mobility and Identity in Nineteenth-Century Guangzhou*
270. Lin Man-houng, *China Upside Down: Currency, Society, and Ideologies, 1808–1856*
271. Ronald Egan, *The Problem of Beauty: Aesthetic Thought and Pursuits in Northern Song Dynasty China*
272. Mark Halperin, *Out of the Cloister: Literati Perspectives on Buddhism in Sung China, 960–1279*
273. Helen Dunstan, *State or Merchant? Political Economy and Political Process in 1740s China*
274. Sabina Knight, *The Heart of Time: Moral Agency in Twentieth-Century Chinese Fiction*